# Building Communities
# of Compassion

# Building Communities *of* Compassion

## Mennonite Mutual Aid in Theory and Practice

**Edited by Willard M. Swartley and Donald B. Kraybill**

Foreword by J. Winfield Fretz

*A Pandora Press U.S. Book*

**Herald Press**

*Scottdale, Pennsylvania*
*Waterloo, Ontario*

**Library of Congress Cataloging-in-Publication Data**
Building communities of compassion : Mennonite mutual aid in theory and
practice / edited by Willard M. Swartley and Donald B. Kraybill.
    p. cm.
    "A Pandora Press U.S. book"
    Includes bibliographical references.
    ISBN 0-8361-9094-7 (alk. paper)
    1. Mennonites—Charities. 2. Mennonites—Doctrines.
I. Swartley, Willard M., 1936- . II. Kraybill, Donald B.
BX8128.W4B85  1998
289.7—dc21                                                                 98-16375
                                                                                  CIP

All Bible quotations are used by permission, all rights reserved, and unless
otherwise indicated are from the *New Revised Standard Version Bible*, copyright © 1989, by the Division of Christian Education of the National Council
of the Churches of Christ in the USA. NIV, *The Holy Bible, New International
Version*, copyright © 1973, 1978, 1984 International Bible Society, Zondervan
Bible Publishers; RSV, *The Revised Standard Version of the Bible*, copyrighted
1946, 1952, © 1971, 1973 by the Division of Christian Education of the National Council of the Churches of Christ in the U.S.A.

The diagrams on pages 25 and 26 of this book are used with the permission of the Editrice Pontifico Istituto, and are taken from George Panikulam,
*Koinonia in the New Testament: A Dynamic Expression of the Christian Life*,
copyright © 1979, Biblical Institute Press, Rome, pp. 7, 39.

BUILDING COMMUNITIES OF COMPASSION
Copyright © 1998 by Herald Press, Scottdale, Pa. 15683
    Published simultaneously in Canada by Herald Press,
    Waterloo, Ont. N2L 6H7. All rights reserved
Library of Congress Catalog Number: 98-16375
International Standard Book Number: 0-8361-9094-7
Printed in the United States of America
Book design by Michael A. King and Nöel R. King, Pandora Press U.S., in
consultation with Jim Butti, Herald Press
Cover design by Jim Butti

07 06 05 04 03 02 01 00 99 98 10 9 8 7 6 5 4 3 2 1

*To J. Winfield Fretz*
*Tireless champion of mutual aid*

# Abbreviations

**AMC**     Archives of the Mennonite Church (Goshen, Ind.)

**ANRW**    *Aufstieg und Niedergang der römischen Welt*, ed. H. Temporini and W. Haase

**CMP**     Church Member Profile

**Fond**    Archive term: records of an individual, family, or corporate body

**GC**      General Conference Mennonite Church

**JPS**      Jewish Publication Society

**JSNTSS**  Journal of the Study of the New Testament supplement series

**MC**      Mennonite Church

**MCC**     Mennonite Central Committee

**MDS**     Mennonite Disaster Service

**MMA**    Mennonite Mutual Aid

**MAO**    Mennonite Archives of Ontario

**PA**      Particular Archive

**TA**      Täuferakten

**STAZ**    Staatsarchiv Zurich

# Contents

*Foreword by J. Winfield Fretz* • 9
*Acknowledgments* • 11
*Introduction* • 13

**PART ONE: BIBLICAL FOUNDATIONS**
Chapter  1  Mutual Aid Based in Jesus and Early Christianity
        by Willard M. Swartley • 21

Chapter  2  Nehemiah: An Old Testament Model
        by Wilma Ann Bailey • 40

**PART TWO: THEOLOGICAL AND ETHICAL
        PERSPECTIVES**
Chapter  3  Mutual Aid as "Practice"
        by Joseph J. Kotva, Jr. • 57

Chapter  4  Mutual Aid: Harbinger of the Kingdom?
        by Cornelius A. Buller • 80

**PART THREE: HISTORICAL CASE STUDIES**
Chapter  5  Mutual Aid Among the Augsburg Anabaptists,
        1526-1528
        by Jeni Hiett Umble • 103

Chapter  6  Mutual Aid Among the Swiss Brethren, 1550-1750
        by John D. Roth • 119

Chapter 7 Mutual Aid Among Dutch Waterlander
Mennonites, 1605-1668
by Mary S. Sprunger • 144

**PART FOUR: ORGANIZATIONAL CASE STUDIES**
Chapter 8 Changing Patterns of Mutual Aid in Ontario,
1864-1994
by E. Reginald Good • 171

Chapter 9 My Brother's Keeper: The Origins of Mennonite
Mutual Aid
by Albert N. Keim • 192

Chapter 10 Fifty-Year Partners: Mennonite Mutual Aid and the
Church
by Steven M. Nolt • 213

**PART FIVE: CONTEMPORARY ISSUES AND PRACTICE**
Chapter 11 Mutual Aid and the "New Voluntarism"
by Conrad L. Kanagy • 247

Chapter 12 Mennonite Mutual Aid: A Margin of Difference?
by Keith Graber Miller • 264

Chapter 13 The Changing Face of Corporate Care
by Donald B. Kraybill • 293

*Epilogue: A Vision for the Future, by Howard L. Brenneman • 306*
*Select Bibliography of Mennonite Mutual Aid • 309*
*Contributors • 317*
*About Herald Press, Pandora Press, and Pandora Press U.S. • 319*

# Foreword

Mennonites and other Christians who value the Christian teaching on sharing material resources will welcome publication of these essays, which focus on biblical, Anabaptist, Mennonite, historical, sociological, and contemporary economic aspects of mutual aid. Willard Swartley and Donald Kraybill, veteran scholars, directed the Mutual Aid study project and co-hosted the "Building Communities of Compassion" conference in 1996 when these papers were first presented. They respectively provide the essays "Mutual Aid Based in Jesus and Early Christianity" and "The Changing Face of Mutual Aid" as bookends to this stimulating material.

Howard Brenneman, president of Mennonite Mutual Aid, closed the conference with an informative and challenging address on "A Vision for the Future of Mutual Aid." This address was especially significant because Brenneman's vision of mutual aid stands in fresh contrast to that of many Mennonite corporate executives (which Brenneman also was earlier) in profit-making business. In these few years of his presidency, MMA has already demonstrated the validity of a mutual aid philosophy generating practical and ethical ways of successfully providing churchwide health coverage.

To my knowledge, the conference was the first to encourage academic people—through stipends provided by MMA—to research, write, and present scholarly papers on subjects of their own choosing related to mutual aid. Presenters at the conference explored aspects of mutual aid related to their own interests and fields of study. The conference was a stimulus to their own scholarly areas of pursuit and an inspiration to others interested in mutual aid philosophy and practice.

A historical note is appropriate to set this project in the context of earlier efforts to understand and promote mutual aid in the Mennonite church. In 1955 Mennonite Central Committee invited all known local and regional Mennonite mutual aid societies to a meeting to form a single fraternal organization slated to find ways of working together. As a result of that meeting, the Association of Mennonite Aid Societies, which immediately adapted the acronym, AMAS, was created. Twenty-one societies made up the new organization.

At its 1958 annual meeting at Smithville, Ohio, AMAS drafted and approved a significant statement that could be considered its constitution. The document included the following items:
- a definition of mutual aid,
- a set of guiding principles,
- a summary of lessons from history, and
- goals and concerns for mutual aid in local congregations and the larger church.

In 1970 AMAS published *The Compassionate Community*, a 573-page paperback of devotional addresses given at its annual meetings 1958-1970. The book was distributed primarily among AMAS members. It has been timely after nearly thirty years to convene another conference on mutual aid and publish these essays. It is heartening to see mutual aid revived and expanded as a virtue to be honored and promoted in our individual and collective lives.

—*J. Winfield Fretz,*
*President Emeritus and*
*Emeritus Professor of Sociology*
*Conrad Grebel College*

# Acknowledgments

In the spirit of our topic, this effort was a collaborative project that benefited from mutual assistance in many ways. We enjoyed a collegial relationship with Mennonite Mutual Aid (MMA), which initiated the project as one of many efforts to celebrate its golden anniversary as a churchwide agency, 1945-1995. We owe special thanks to Howard Brenneman and Vyron Schmidt, as well as to Dean Preheim-Bartel, who generously assisted our research at every turn. To the many other staff members of MMA who contributed in many ways to the project, we also offer sincere thanks.

The project began with a call for research proposals. Nearly two dozen scholars responded. After sifting through their proposals, we invited ten persons to participate. We as project directors also prepared chapters. In addition, near the end of the project we invited Keith Graber Miller to contribute a paper originally prepared for another setting.

The research team met in June 1995 for a two-day orientation at the Associated Mennonite Biblical Seminary (AMBS), Elkhart, Indiana. This briefing provided a good opportunity to establish a common conceptual focus and to learn of each other's projects. The bulk of the research was conducted in the summer and fall of 1995. The scholars gathered again at AMBS, January 26-28, 1996, to report their findings at a public conference titled "Building Communities of Compassion." This gathering provided a forum for the researchers to report their preliminary findings and to test them in a public setting. The chapters were then refined and edited for this volume.

We have many debts of gratitude. To all the members of the team of researchers, we offer thanks for their hard work, cooperation, and goodwill. In addition we are grateful for financial subsidy provided by Mennonite Mutual Aid and generous support from the Institute of Mennonite Studies and the Young Center of Elizabethtown (Pa.) College. Our colleagues, Brenda Spiker, Gretchen Wenger, and Ruth Liechty, provided kind help, clerical assistance, and editorial support. Ruth, in addition, worked hard on final manuscript preparation. As director of IMS, Ross Bender administered the project in cooperation with the editors. We are grateful for the publisher's editorial contributions and the readiness of editor Michael A. King to publish this volume as a first in the new Herald Press/Pandora Press U.S. relationship.

Finally, we are thankful to have this opportunity to collaborate for the first time. Through this experience we celebrate a thirty-year friendship kindled in the classrooms of Eastern Mennonite College in 1966. In every way this has been a mutually satisfying project which we hope makes at least a modest contribution to building communities of care and compassion in our churches and around the world.

*—Willard M. Swartley*
*Elkhart, Indiana*
*Donald B. Kraybill*
*Elizabethtown, Pennsylvania*

# Introduction

A n Amish farmer recently described mutual aid in this manner.
"In the spring when I am plowing on the higher slopes of my
farm, I can see six other church members plowing with their teams. I
know that if I got sick or something, all six of those teams would be
here plowing my field."[1] For this Amishman, the meaning of mutual
aid is clear, but for Mennonites coping with the complexities of modern
life, the definition has blurred.

From their origins in the sixteenth-century Anabaptist movement,
Mennonites have been committed to provide material aid to the needy
in their ranks. Membership in Mennonite circles has historically carried
responsibilities to assist others in the household of faith struggling with
material misfortune of one sort or another.

Mennonite mutual aid is a reciprocal responsibility, based on
biblical teaching, to provide material aid to other church members who
face special economic and physical hardships. Such help involves giving labor, services, goods, gifts, and payments in both spontaneous and
organized forms at local and churchwide levels. This definition of mutual aid has three key components: *membership, material needs and resources*, and *reciprocity*.

Christians typically live in overlapping circles of social responsibility: family, church, community, society. Mutual aid is directed
toward fellow church members. Thus it differs from other forms of
benevolence—charity, service, and neighborliness—which address
general human need regardless of membership and without expectations of reciprocity. The service ministries of such agencies as Men-

13

nonite Disaster Service and the Mennonite Central Committee are not technically mutual aid. Even service to Christians of other denominations does not strictly fit the definition.[2]

Mutual aid is thus not unlimited obligation, as some have suggested; rather, it limits itself to the denominational family. Focusing on meeting material needs within the church is somewhat restrictive yet offers clarity of purpose and understanding. Human need proliferates around the world, and the gospel of Christ calls Christians to compassion. However, the Christian response of love to such need is service and charity, not mutual aid.

Mutual aid seeks to meet the special *material* and *physical* needs that arise among church members. They obviously have many needs—emotional, social, spiritual—which can be addressed through interpersonal support and care in the context of the church. Prayer and support groups, counseling, and visiting do offer mutual support to believers but do not typically involve material aid. Although some of these needs may intertwine with material misfortune, the church's role in addressing them falls outside our understanding of mutual aid. Furthermore, although mutual aid is an expression of care in the midst of material hardship, its primary aim is not to create an egalitarian society or to promote a communal sharing of goods.

Finally, mutual aid involves reciprocity—a willingness to give and receive. Mutual aid is *mutual* aid. In this sense it involves both *expectations* and *obligations*. The healthy farmer plowing his field anticipates that other church members will help plow the fields if he becomes ill. But he also carries an obligation to help when misfortune strikes a neighbor. The mutuality of mutual aid also distinguishes it from charity and service, which carry no obligation to reciprocate. Mennonite mutual aid does not pretend to promote a society of equals, offer help for social and psychological problems, nor serve the vast pockets of human need around the world. Mennonite mutual aid provides a cushion of support by church members for those among them who have experienced material hardships.

Many Christian groups have long practiced various forms of mutual aid. Those that immigrated to the United States often established mutual aid societies in the nineteenth and early twentieth centuries. Material care in the church is not unique to Mennonites. Nevertheless, mutual aid in its many forms has been an enduring trademark of Mennonite communities. Why have Mennonites shown such persistent interest in mutual aid? A blend of theological and socioeconomic factors have helped foster such Mennonite commitments to mutual care.

Mennonite theological understandings stem from the Anabaptist movement of sixteenth-century Europe. The Anabaptist view of the church provided theological underpinnings for mutual aid. The church was conceived as a visible body of Christ mirroring the kingdom of heaven. It was made up of adults who had voluntarily decided to follow Christ in daily life. They were thus aware of the obligations of membership. The church was seen as a new redemptive society where the love and corporate care of members were simply assumed to be a norm of redeemed behavior. Members were members one of another and called to share their spiritual and material burdens. The Anabaptist understanding of discipleship accented the importance of obedience to Christ in all dimensions of life. An emphasis on stewardship emphasized the fact that material goods were ultimately owned by God and under the temporary care of members of the community.

Another factor that fostered mutual aid was Anabaptist insistence on separation of church and state. The ultimate authority for the life and conduct of the church was grounded in Scripture, the commands of Christ, and the practice of the early church. The theological chasm between church and state encouraged the descendants of Anabaptists in later years to stress the importance of relying on the church rather than the state for the care of its members. Old Order Mennonite and Amish groups continue this tradition of political independence by refusing to participate in social security and other programs of government subsidy, including some for agriculture.

The primacy, centrality, and visibility the Anabaptists gave to the church made mutual aid a natural consequence. The Hutterites, one of several branches of the Anabaptist movement, argued that an Anabaptist understanding of the church requires a community of goods where all members share material resources on an equal footing. Seeking to recover the spirit and practice of the apostolic church recorded in Acts 2 and 4, the Hutterites formed a communal society.

James Stayer has recently argued that community of goods was a typical practice in the households of other early Anabaptist groups as well. Stayer (1991:9) suggests that by the 1540s many of the Anabaptist communities were practicing an "economics of mutual aid." They expected members of the church to share one another's material burdens in the spirit of Christian love.

Rresponding to charges that the Anabaptists held property in common, Menno Simons (1956:558) said,

> We do not teach and practice community of goods. But we teach
> and maintain by the word of the Lord that all truly believing Chris-

tians are members of one body and are baptized by one spirit into one body (1 Cor. 12:13); they are partakers of one bread (1 Cor. 10:18), they have one Lord and one God (Eph. 4:5-6).

It is only "Christian and reasonable," Menno argued, that

All those . . . called into one body and love in Christ Jesus, are prepared by such love to serve their neighbors, not only with money and goods, but also after the example of their Lord and head, Jesus Christ, in an evangelical manner with life and blood.

The essays in this volume provide windows—analytical and narrative portholes—which offer glimpses into the myriad expressions of mutual aid. These essays are not comprehensive; a full and systematic history of mutual aid remains to be written. We have invited scholars to write on five key aspects of mutual aid: (1) biblical foundations, (2) theological and ethical underpinnings, (3) selected historical case studies, (4) the emergence of formal organizations, and (5) contemporary issues faced by the church. The select bibliography brings together key sources and offers a bibliographic map for others who want to explore the topic.

These essays were chosen to highlight pivotal moments and issues in the saga of mutual aid. Our efforts represent the first scholarly effort to tell the story of Mennonite mutual aid in a single volume. We hope this book will stir the imagination of others who will someday provide a fuller account of the legacy of mutual aid. And we hope our efforts will also prod faithful Christians of every stripe to build communities of care where members bear each other's burdens.

## Notes

1. This paraphrased, edited quote comes from an Amish farmer in Ohio.

2. This definition differs with Redekop's (1989:436-438) argument that mutual aid is unlimited obligation. Such a definition stretches the concept so broadly that it effectively erases meaningful distinctions between mutual aid and notions of charity and service. Fretz's (1947:9) somewhat vague definition describes mutual aid as, "Christian love in action. . . . using the resources God has given us for his glory and the good of ourselves and our fellowmen. It is a way of limiting selfish desires for the good of the larger group or the community of which we are members." The larger group or community for Fretz could refer to the civic community or even the nation. In another place Fretz (1947:8) is more explicit: "The purpose of mutual aid is to help needy church people to help themselves rather than to give them direct relief."

Kreider (1972) adopts the definition given at the All Mennonite Conference on Christian Mutual Aid at Smithville, Ohio in 1964. The statement endorsed by the conference described mutual aid as the use of the resources of the church, "to serve the mutual needs of its individual members and to contribute to the more effective equipment of the Christian community for its mission in the world" ("Statement" 1964). Building on the Smithville statement, Kreider (p. 21) proposes two functions of mutual aid: (1) assistance within the church; (2) the extension of the Christian mission to the world. Although the discussions of mutual aid in the *Mennonite Encyclopedia* (vols. III and V) do not formally define mutual aid, all the illustrations in these articles depict care within the church—Mennonites helping Mennonites with material needs.

## References

Fretz, J. Winfield
  1947   *Christian Mutual Aid: A Handbook of Brotherhood Economics*. Akron, Pa.: Mennonite Central Committee.

Hernley, H. Ralph, Ed.
  1970   *The Compassionate Community*. Scottdale, Pa.: Association of Mennonite Aid Societies.

Kreider, Carl
  1972   *Care One For Another: Mutual Aid in the Congregation*. Scottdale, Pa.: Mennonite Publishing House.

Menno Simons ·
  1956   *The Complete Writings of Menno Simons*. Trans. Leonard Verduin, ed. J. C. Wenger. Scottdale, Pa.: Herald Press.

Redekop, Calvin
  1989   "Mutual Aid: Unlimited Obligation," *Gospel Herald* (June 13): 436-38.

"Statement on Christian Mutual Aid"
  1964   Smithville, Ohio, June 4-6. In *The Compassionate Community*, ed. H. Ralph Hernley (1970): 569-573.

Stayer, James M.
  1991   *The German Peasant's War and Anabaptist Community of Goods*. Montreal: McGill-Queen's University Press.

# Part One
# Biblical Foundations

# A Note on the Mennonite Church (Old and MC)

Often in telling the story of Mennonite mutual aid, writers in this book aim to distinguish between the various denominational groups and bodies involved. Particularly as the story enters the twentieth century and the founding of Mennonite Mutual Aid, Inc. (MMA), writers distinguish between other bodies of Mennonites and that branch variously called—during the eras of which the writers tell—the (Old) Mennonite Church or, by the 1970s, simply, the Mennonite Church (MC).

Because MMA was founded and run primarily by and for (Old) or MC Mennonites until recent decades, references in the MMA story which do not distinguish between groups will generally be to these Mennonites.

It may be helpful to readers to know that the General Conference Mennonites emerged as distinct from the (Old) Mennonites in the 1800s. Then in the 1990s the two groups voted to merge, and in 1997 the unified body was designated the Mennonite Church by the vote of both groups.

To complicate matters, prior to reorganization in the 1970s, the (Old) Mennonite Church included a structure called the "General Conference," which, except for the strange coincidence of names, had nothing to do with the General Conference Mennonite Church.

# 1

# Mutual Aid Based in Jesus and Early Christianity

## Willard M. Swartley

This essay explores the theological foundations of mutual aid in the New Testament and among Christians in the second and third centuries. Willard M. Swartley suggests that the theme of loving one's neighbor as oneself was the cornerstone of mutual aid in Jesus' teaching. In the early church, *koinonia* motivated the practice of mutual aid. Swartley then traces the teaching of early church leaders on mutual aid and explores practices and problems of the growing church in the second to fourth centuries. He concludes with seven observations about the practice of mutual aid.

## New Testament Foundations

In his social world study of early Christianity, John Gager (1976:140) identifies as the key to the movement's survival, growth, and success "a single, overriding internal factor," namely,

> the radical sense of Christian community—open to all, insistent on absolute loyalty, and concerned for every aspect of the believer's life. From the very beginning, the one distinctive gift of Christianity was this sense of community.

Assessing the nature of this experience of community, William Walsh and John Langan (1977:112) rightly assert that an essential part of this sense of community depended on the willingness of Christians to aid those in need and on the teachings of the Christian church with regard to the right use of material goods.

Community and mutual aid: these were the twin pillars of early Christian life and the key to its survival and growth. Is such a statement accurate? Certainly the Holy Spirit must be honored in this assessment as well as the living, reigning Jesus Christ. But the social expression of this Christ-Spirit reality was a community of love engaging in mutual aid.

The two prominent New Testament models of practicing mutual aid are those of "having goods in common" (Acts 2 and 4) and Paul's collection of money for the poor in Jerusalem. While these are hardly prescriptive models for how mutual aid *must* be done, since they differ from each other, they do provide normative characteristics for Christian practice of mutual aid today. Both are anchored in the experience of koinonia, which had its origins in Jesus and his ministry.[1] Hence we turn first to Jesus' life and teachings, then later to New Testament practices of mutual aid.

When looking to Scripture for models of mutual aid, one must decide on criteria for what to include or exclude. Are all acts of compassion, like Jesus' healings, included? Or must material goods be involved, so that the feeding of the 5,000 counts, even if Jesus' healings don't? Is almsgiving mutual aid? To maintain some precision, I define mutual aid as caring assistance in a community context in which some bond of relationship exists. Some sense of reciprocity is usually present but certainly not the obligation to keep record of payback, or pressure to do something immediately in return. Further, material, physical, and spiritual elements may be part of the exchange. If some bond of relationship is not present, the compassionate act is charity or almsgiving, a broader category than mutual aid.

## Jesus

Jesus' teaching to "love your neighbor as yourself" is the moral foundation for mutual aid. This injunction has its foundation in the Old Testament (Lev. 19:18) but comes to center stage in Jesus' teaching and ministry.[2] Jesus gives this command in the context of answering the question, "What must I do to inherit eternal life?" Since the questioner is rich, Jesus' answer links "loving the neighbor" with giving to the poor and gaining eternal life.[3]

In another story the love command is also linked to gaining eternal life (Luke 10:25), illustrated by the action of the Good Samaritan (10:29-37). Here the "enemy" risks himself to help the wounded and share his resources for the nursing care. The command to love the neighbor appears also in Romans 13:8-10; Galatians 5:14; and James 2:8. The oft-quoted golden text for mutual aid practice, "Bear one another's burdens," is itself grounded in this same neighbor-love command: "In this way you will fulfill the law of Christ" (Gal.6:2). Sharing wealth and possessions with the needy is thus foundational to the gospel. Indeed, Jesus' proclamation of the kingdom of God contextualized Jubilee practice— bringing blessing to the poor and woe to the rich (Batey; Karris; Pilgrim; Ringe; Sloan; Stegemann; Swartley 1994:76-80; Yoder: 21-75).

In Jesus' ministry we see several samples of true mutual aid. The most striking is that of the women who supported Jesus and his itinerant band of disciples "out of their means" (Luke 8:1-3). These women apparently had significant resources or access to them. One, Joanna, wife of Herod's steward Chuza, certainly had access to resources. Reciprocally, these women were also recipients of Jesus' healing and spiritual care. They were included in the new community of Jesus' disciples. It appears that the early band of disciples shared freely with each other on a daily basis. Through the mention in John's gospel of Judas' intent to betray Jesus, we learn that Jesus and his disciples had a common purse (12:6).

Social world studies of Jesus refer to "local sympathizers" who, in village after village, provided housing and food for Jesus and his itinerant band. Mary and Martha, together with Lazarus, exemplify this type of hospitality in Bethany. But likely some Galilean families functioned in a similar way (Luke 10:1-9). Since Jesus spent much of his public ministry around Capernaum, local supporters there also must have provided lodging and food.

The encounter between Jesus and Zacchaeus (Luke 19:1-10) exemplifies mutual aid. Jesus announces that he is going to have dinner with Zacchaeus. Jesus receives a meal, but Zacchaeus receives much more. Jesus' first gift is his self-invitation to table fellowship. This signals his acceptance of Zacchaeus; through this gesture he extends the new kingdom community to Zacchaeus. Zacchaeus is so grateful for this gift that he offers to pay back fourfold if he defrauded anyone in his tax business. Then comes Jesus' second gift: salvation to the house of Zacchaeus (v. 9). Zacchaeus both gives and receives. Since Jesus identifies himself with the poor, cheated, and oppressed, he too receives and gives.

The women who anointed Jesus' feet and head with oil, pouring out love to and receiving from Jesus forgiveness and affirmation, also exemplify genuine acts of mutual care for one another. The women who went to the tomb to anoint Jesus' body after his burial completed a mutual aid relationship. They were helped by Jesus, included into his disciple band, and now they care for him.

This kind of mutual care for each other was clearly empowered by Jesus' teachings on money and warnings against wealth. Jesus called his followers to share freely of their resources and to trust God for daily provisions ("Give us today our daily bread"). He taught them not to lay up treasures on earth. In guiding the rich young ruler to eternal life, Jesus extended the commandments to include selling possessions and giving to the poor (Mark 10:17-22). Almsgiving in itself is not mutual aid (see Matt. 6:2-4), but like mutual aid it is grounded in the non-possessive attitude toward money and material goods.

## Koinonia in the New Testament

The dominant motivation for mutual aid as practiced in Acts and the Pauline churches is *koinonia*, translated as fellowship, partaking or sharing, communion, or partnership (González 1990:83). This term occurs in the key texts where early Christians practice material aid: Acts 2:42 (*koina* in v. 44 and 4:32); 2 Corinthians 8–9 (toward the beginning and end, 8:4 and 9:13, evidently as an inclusion motif); Romans 15:26-27; Philippians 4:15-16. Community of goods in Acts 2 and 4 was not a commitment to voluntary detachment and poverty, but rather to "the ideal of a charity which cannot tolerate need among one's own" (Dupont: 95). Partnership in material resources is specified as ministry (*diakonia*, used in Rom. 15:31; 2 Cor. 8:4; 9:1, 12, 13 in relation to the collection). This indicates the importance placed on the "collection" in relation to the gospel itself. Mutual aid is not an add-on to the gospel any more or less than is peacemaking. It lies at the essential core of the gospel and is a chief characteristic of koinonia, the sharing of and in the gospel.

Strikingly, the same term, koinonia, is used to speak of and expound the believer's relationship to Christ, the Spirit, even to God.[4] *Participation in* (koinonia) is the fundamental mode of understanding Christian experience. As 2 Peter 1:3-6 indicates, this finds its consummation in our partaking of divine nature. But this is possible only because Jesus Christ first partook of human nature and suffered with us, bearing the limitations and finitude of human flesh and historical existence.

This point is clear in Hebrews 2:14: "Since likewise the children share flesh and blood, he himself likewise shared the same things." In this verse a form of koinonia (*kekoioneken*) occurs in the first line. Another word similar in meaning, *metesken*, appears in the second line. Both are partaking or sharing terms. In short, Jesus Christ partook of and shared in humanity so that we might partake of and share in the divine. Jesus' example is the ultimate dimension of New Testament koinonia theology.

When the Corinthians need instruction on partaking rightly of the Lord's Supper (1 Cor. 10:16ff.), again the language of koinonia-sharing-partaking occurs to show the indissoluble connection between the Spirit-bestowed, God-given koinonia and this meal that commemorates Christ's death. In the koinonia bond we also understand our own sufferings as participation (koinonia) in Christ's sufferings and glory.[5]

Material aid to one another flows in this all-embracing koinonia gospel-event. The Indian writer, George Panikulam, who inspired me in these insights, shows in diagram form how mutual aid is one part of the larger gospel koinonia experience.

See below (Panikulam 1979:7, with adaptation):

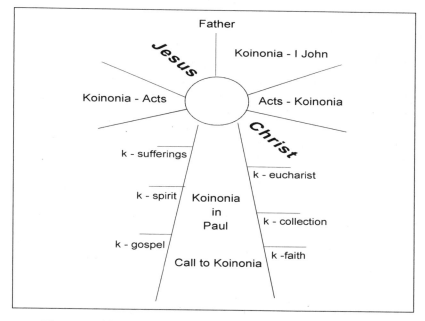

The textual basis for this view that mutual aid is grounded in New Testament koinonia theology arises from Paul's extended discussion of the collection from the Gentile churches for the brothers and sisters in Jerusalem (2 Cor. 8–9; Rom. 15:25-31). The single richest text for mutual aid is 2 Corinthians 8–9. The term koinonia is used strategically in 8:4 in relation to partaking-sharing in the service-ministry (diakonia). And in 9:13 the generosity of sharing (koinonias) is noted. But, in addition, this emphasis is under the umbrella of the larger gospel reality that God's grace prompts and enfolds all sharing-koinonia experience and action.

The term for grace, *charis*, is used ten times in these two chapters. Its first use marks action and initiative from God to us in Jesus Christ.

"We want you to know, brothers and sisters, about the grace of God." At the other end of the appeal is the return of grace, thanksgiving to God: "Thanks (grace) be to God for his indescribable gift" (9:15). The eight uses in between point out the horizontal movement of the grace. In these eight *pointing out* uses of charis we have a persuasive basis for mutual aid, with seven strands of rationale:

(1) It is an expression of God's grace (8:1ff.).
(2) It proves the genuineness of one's love (8:8, 24).
(3) It expresses the fruit of the Spirit (8:7-8).
(4) It follows the example of Jesus Christ, who, "though he was rich became poor" (8:9).
(5) It works toward equality (8:13-15).
(6) It is to be done generously (8:2) and cheerfully (9:7), with assurance that the Lord will multiply the giver's resources (9:8-10).
(7) It is a ministry that meets the needs of other saints (9:12-13).

Indeed, numerous levels of practical theology and persuasion are at work in the biblical texts to provide motivation or moral reason for believers to participate in this koinonia mandate and practice.

So the text begins with grace pointing down, from God to us humans, then pointing out from humans to humans, and then pointing up to God in a response of thanksgiving. Thus the grace/charis triangle is completed. Panikulam summarizes the point in this adapted chart (p. 39):

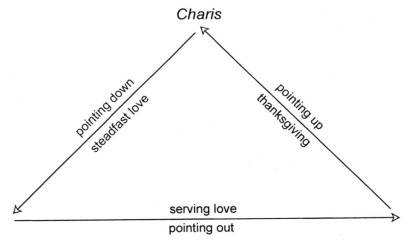

The sharing of material means is but one movement in this *charis* participation-partaking-sharing matrix of Christian salvation, life, and hope. The force of this chart is lost if we unhook its emphases from the larger Pauline insistence that charis and koinonia, as well as diakonia, describe the entire Christian experience.

Early in Acts, God pours out the Holy Spirit on believers, and they then participate in and partake of a common life of Spirit renewal. They share their goods because they have shared of the same Spirit.[6] Participation and partaking occur again, in a different form of sharing, in Acts 6 and 11. But the theological base is the same: "They devoted themselves to the koinonia" means that "this sharing of goods was an outward expression of their sharing in divine things: this community of material possessions stemmed from the *koinonia* of Christ" (Davies 1958:28).

This koinonia act of sharing money is an expression of Christ's own self-giving on our behalf (2 Cor. 8:9). As Davies puts it, "This is the very essence of the Gospel, and it is enshrined in the everyday process of mutual aid whereby self-giving to the brethren [*sic*] is giving to Christ who gave Himself for us" (p. 33). After narrating the history of events that led the early apostles to extend to Paul the right hand of fellowship-koinonia, thus embracing Gentiles into the faith-fellowship or koinonia, Jouette Bassler (1991:96) uses the following words to describe koinonia:

> The Gentiles would demonstrate through their willing participation in the gift their sense of solidarity with the Jewish Christians, and the latter would in turn reaffirm by their acceptance of the gift the validity and vitality of Paul's law-free mission to the Gentiles. The collection became a symbol for Paul of the right hand of fellowship (*koinonia*) originally extended to him and later, at Antioch, partly withdrawn.

Bassler then notes that most English translations lose the meaning of koinonia in describing this collection for the needy in Jerusalem. For Paul it was an essential core of his gospel mission. He carried out the earlier agreement with "the pillar" apostles in Galatians 2:10: "Remember the poor" (Georgi; Nickel). Likely the early Jewish Christian objection to the Gentile mission included a crucial concern: how would the new patterns of almsgiving and care for the poor and the widows be carried through? Paul spent his mission energy proving that the new believers would enter into this sacred circle. The circle is one of reciprocity: the Gentile Christians receive the salvation gift from the Jewish Christians, and the Jewish Christians receive the monetary gift from the Gentile Christians (Rom. 15:27).

> They were pleased and are in fact in debt to them. For if the Gentiles have become partakers with them (*koinonein*) of their spiritual goods (*pneumatika*), they ought also to perform a service for them with material goods.[7]

To imprint the point on our minds, let us imagine that this sharing of goods closes the circle of grace in early Christian thought. The gospel song, "Will the Circle Be Unbroken?" may evoke emotions when we think of loved ones and their condition before God. But apply that same motif and feeling to practical mutual aid: Will the circle of God's koinonia-grace be unbroken in our love and practice? That is the biblical challenge to mutual aid, rooted in God's grace poured out in Jesus Christ and through the Spirit-gift, of which we as believers all partake in common.

Because the early Christians knew they had a common fount for Spirit-life, they expressed their common experience in generous sharing. To be sure, as in Acts 6, problems arose in its practice. Whatever the circumstances, however, the deep and profound sense of common (koinonia) solidarity in Christ and in the Spirit moved the early Christian believers to practice mutual aid in various forms and circumstances.

Let us think of this "unbroken circle" in several ways. First, there is the issue of inclusion: are all the believers both givers and receivers of this charis-koinonia through practical mutual aid? Are all members included in mutual aid sharing? Second, we may make an inventory of all those experiences said to be part of the koinonia reality and show how mutual aid is one of them. If mutual aid is not on the tree, the koinonia reality is not complete; the koinonia tree will likely wither and die.[8]

Koinonia as foundation of mutual aid is evident also in Acts 2. Here koinonia marked the early Christian community and was accompanied by awe of the wonders and signs, praising God daily in the temple, and breaking bread in homes with joyful and generous hearts.

As González (1990:83) points out in his massive study of *Faith and Wealth in Early Christianity*, the imperfect verb (stressing past continued action) is used to describe their practice of selling and sharing what they had. He contends, I think rightly, that this process responded to the needs of the community. In contrast to the Greek Stoic idealizing of renunciation of goods, this practice in Acts was motivated by the needs of the community.[9] Further, "Koinonia means first of all, not fellowship in the sense of good feelings toward each other, but sharing" (p. 83).

Koinonia has also the meaning of partnership, as in business in Luke 5:10, used to describe Peter's fishing partnership with the sons of Zebedee. With this meaning of partnership-sharing, we grasp the force of the Pauline image and theology of one body and many members. In this partnership each contributes to the whole, enhancing the koinonia reality.[10] When one member suffers, all suffer; when one rejoices, all rejoice. Each part empowers the whole.

In Philippians, koinonia as partnership occurs four times: 1:5, partnership in the gospel; 2:1, partnership in the Spirit; 3:10, partnership in Christ's sufferings; 4:15, partnership in giving and receiving. Indeed, the first three aspects of koinonia-partnership are the foundations of the fourth, mutual aid. Clinching the koinonia argument is 1 John, which makes the horizontal (between people) koinonia the proof of the vertical (between people and God) koinonia. In 1:3 the writer speaks of koinonia between you and us; this "koinonia is with the Father and with his Son Jesus Christ." Later he concludes with this koinonia conviction: "How does God's love abide in anyone who has the world's goods and sees a brother or sister in need and yet refuses help? Little children, let us love, not in word or speech, but in truth and action" (3:17-18).

How foundational and pervasive this koinonia reality is to early Christianity! Without it, the church's mission, including witness to peace and justice, lacks the ring of truth.

## Biblical Koinonia in the Second Century

The developments in thought, instruction, and practice in the next three centuries further demonstrate koinonia at work, shaping the life of the church. The late-first- or early-second-century writing known as *The Didache* enunciates this central belief of early Christianity.

> Never turn away the needy; share all your possessions with your brother and sister, and do not claim that anything is your own. If you and he [or she] are joint participators in things immortal, how much more so in things that are mortal.[11]

Similarly, Eusebius reports that Dionysius, the bishop of Corinth, in writing to the Roman church, specifically to Soter the bishop, says,

> For this has been our custom from the beginning: to do good in diverse ways to all the brothers and sisters, and to send supplies to many churches in every city: now relieving the poverty of the needy, now making provision, by the supplies which you have been sending from the beginning, for brethren in the mines (forced labor imposed by the state).[12]

Clearly, sharing and not owning possessions was a basic Christian value (Johnson 1981). The theme continues in the early church. In the mid-second century, Clement of Alexandria wrote about money, wealth, and koinonia. He is best known for his essay on "Who Is the Rich Man to be Saved?" In his extensive treatment of wealth, based on reflection of Matthew 19:16-30, Clement argues that the wealthy Christian will find ways wealth can serve the needs of the community, especially the poor.

Clement reiterates the biblical warnings against wealth and love of money and finally stresses koinonia:

> God created our race for sharing (*koinonía*), beginning by giving out what belonged to God, God's own Word, making it common (*koinós*) to all humans, and creating all things for all (*pánta poiésas ypér pántōn*). Therefore all things are common (*koinà oûn tà pánta*); and let not the rich claim more than the rest. To say therefore "I have more than I need, why not enjoy?" is neither human nor proper to sharing (*ouk anthrópinon, oude koinonikón*). . . . For I know quite well that God has given us the power to use; but only to the limit of that which is necessary; and that God also willed the use be in common.[13]

In commenting on the use of koinonia in both Clement and Paul, Avila (1983:40) notes,

> The purpose of wealth is not only to achieve *autarkeia* [self-sufficiency] but also and equally to foster koinonia—equal fellowship that abolishes the differentiation between the few rich who wallow in luxury and the so many who labor in poverty.

Clement also warns against allowing wealth to become a hindrance and thus rails against luxury. He speaks of proper use defined in relation to necessity. Wealth is not evil but dangerous, like a poisonous snake,

> which will twist round the hand and bite; unless one knows how to lay hold of it without danger by the point of the tail. And riches, wriggling either in an experienced or inexperienced grasp, are dexterous at adhering and biting; unless one, despising them, uses them skillfully, so as to crush the creature by the charm of the Word, and himself escape unscathed.[14]

Another early-second-century writing, *Shepherd of Hermas*, addresses the issue of how rich Christians live before God. The prominent biblical issue of how the rich stand before God (especially in Luke and James) is taken up numerous times[15] and genially resolved by the remarkable parable of the sterile elm and fruitful vine (*Visions, Mandates; Sim.* ii). The rich man, poor in intercession and confession toward God because of his business, must lean on (give to) the poor, who are rich in prayer and faith; the poor must lean on the rich (*elm*) for material aid. In this way the rich are of service to God, and both together bear much fruit.

In this context Hermas uses the term koinonia, saying that the rich and poor are partners (*koinonoi*) in the work of justice. This view is based on the notion, derived from the Old Testament, that the poor are closer to God, that they pray more and their prayers are heard by God (see Pss.

72:2, 4, 12; 86:1-2). Further, in addressing the rich, Hermas says their wealth is useless unless shared with the needy (González 1990:100).

In another early writing, *Pseudoclementine Homilies*, the admonition to share possessions is correlated with a two-kingdom view. Those who choose to accumulate in the present will not have future goods. But those who choose the blessings of the future have no right to regard as their own the possessions and goods of this life. The so-called *Second Epistle of Clement* urges mutual compassion and regards almsgiving as better than fasting and prayer, of the same rank as repentance from sin.[16]

Most telling of its degree of importance, mutual aid practice was linked to the communion celebration itself. Justin, writing in Rome around A.D. 150, describes both the procedure for celebrating communion and the practice of mutual aid that concludes the celebration:

> Those who prosper, and who do wish, contribute, each one as much as he chooses to. What is collected is deposited with the one presiding, and he takes care of the orphans and widows, and those who are in want on account of sickness or any other cause, and those who are in bonds and the strangers who are sojourners among us. He is, in short, the protector of all those in need.[17]

As the church approached the end of the second century, more rich people, even a few aristocrats, became members. Irenaeus, writing in Lyon, assumes that wealthy Christians share with the poor and that their wealth has been taken from others, even when received in inheritance (cf. Jerome, cited in Swartley 1978:40). Thus it appears that Irenaeus believes the origin of wealth is unrighteousness. Even so, he does not counsel renunciation of possessions but generous sharing of them.[18]

## Third- and Fourth-Century Practices

Origen rarely addresses wealth, though he sold his extensive library on condition that the buyer give him a daily allowance, barely enough for subsistence. Defending Christianity against critic Celsus' charge that Christians are wicked, he speaks of "generosity and sharing [*koinonikon*]." As even pagans see, sharing is proof against wickededness.[19]

Defending Christianity against pagans, Tertullian denies that Christians have a common purse. However, he goes on to say that their sharing is voluntary, inspired by mutual love:

> Family possessions, which generally destroy brotherhood among you [pagans], create fraternal bonds among us. One in mind and soul, we do not hesitate to share our earthly goods with one another. All things are common among us but our wives.[20]

With Cyprian of Carthage (North Africa) a significant shift in emphasis occurs. Cyprian does hold that the bounties of creation are common to all and our resources are also to be shared. However, he calls for almsgiving as the chief way of sharing. And he introduces a new rationale—through almsgiving one can atone for sins committed after baptism. The blood and sanctification of Christ saves at baptism, but almsgiving saves from postbaptismal sin. [This notion seems to have had its basis in Judaism and became quite prominent in some of the second and third century Christian Fathers (Garrison: 46-59, 76-108)].

Cyprian also believes that almsgiving makes one's prayer and fasting more efficacious; the one who feeds Christ through almsgiving will be fed by Christ (the giver will be blessed). We are to give alms because Christ commanded it. Responsibility for our own children is no excuse for not giving alms. Rather, to deny alms is to deny true responsibility for our children, since we teach them to love their property more than God.[21]

Cyprian's emphasis on alms to atone for sins was conditioned by persecutions of that time. Many of his wealthy members defected from the church rather than risk death and loss of their wealth. When the persecution subsided, some wanted to return to the church, and the church needed them to be able to care for the many post-war widows and children. Further, the economic resources of the Christians were diminished by war. Cyprian allows them to come back on condition that they dole out large sums for the poor, and thus atone for their sin of defection.

Lactantius of Nicomedia in Northern Africa continues Cyprian's theme—that the way to secure wealth is to give it away and that liberality atones for one's sins. He holds that humans were "created for sharing, not as a matter of obligation, but as a matter of compassion."[22]

During this same time, in 251 A.D., the church in Rome had a massive program of care for the widows and poor. The church, consisting of many house fellowships throughout the city, had 1,500 people on its roll for support. Bishop Cornelius was aided by six presbyters, seven deacons, seven more subdeacons, and ninety-four people in minor roles.[23]

The bishop was responsible to oversee the administration of the church's properties and the massive program of distribution of money to these many widows and poor people. Although this assistance was mandated for church members, it was not limited to such. Other poor people outside the Christian community were also helped as resources were available. Although Rome was the largest Christian community, it is likely that other large Christian centers, such as Alexandria and Carthage, also had similar programs of caring for widows and the poor.

With Constantine a new chapter began in sharing and caring. Constantine saw himself as bishop of those outside the church. He enacted laws for the whole of society modeled on what Christians had been doing. Echoing Old Testament laws, the state took on the role of defending widows and orphans. The motivation for this is dubious, but it was most likely a means for maintaining the welfare and order of the empire. In later generations of the fourth century, laws were enacted against paganism. One had to be a Christian to be a soldier in the army, a complete reversal of earlier generations. Eventually most of society was cared for in a state-church pattern of support for widows and the poor. This was in effect a church-state welfare program.

Later bishops, especially the Cappadocians, continued to preach the themes of the earlier leaders, including sharing of goods because they, like creation's gifts, were common to all. Wealth was deemed good only if shared. Believers were not to charge interest on loans. Otherwise a person who came to you for medicine might actually receive poison.

Basil compared the rich to the man who arrives at the theater first and therefore claims it all as his. Rather, he should take only the space he needs and leave the rest for others. So should it be with money. Still later, the golden-mouthed preacher, Chrysostom, said that the truly rich are those who have no great needs and are free to give to others. Wealth is only true wealth when it moves out to others.

One of the better-known statements from Ambrose advocates sharing because our possessions are for the common good of all.

> The Lord our God especially wished this earth to be the common possession of all, and its fruits to be at the disposal of all, but avarice divided the rights of possession. Consequently it is just that if you claim anything as your personal property, which has been given to the human race and to all souls in common, you should at least give part of it to the poor. Since you owe them a share in your own rights, do not deny them their subsistence.[24]

Augustine addressed the issue of children's inheritance rights in a manner similar to Cyprian (above): "Make Christ a member of your family." However many children you have, add one for Christ. Christ's share then goes to the poor.[25] Augustine also indicated that non-Christians came to the church for help. "How many people there are nowadays who are not yet Christians who run to church and ask for the Church's assistance! They want temporal help for themselves, although as yet they don't want to reign with us in eternity."[26]

Both Augustine and Ambrose refer to almsgiving as wiping the Lord's feet with one's hair.

Anoint the feet of Jesus. By living well, follow in the footsteps of the Lord. Dry them with your hair. If you have superfluity, give it to the poor and you have dried the feet of the Lord; for hair is understood to be the superfluity of the body. You may do with your superfluities [as you desire]: they are more than you need, but they are necessary to the feet of the Lord. Perhaps on earth the Lord's feet are in need. For whom will he speak at the end if not of his members: When you did it to one of these least of mine, you did it to me? You bestowed your superfluities, but it was to my feet that you were gracious.[27]

## Problems in Early-Church Mutual Aid

Quoting Psalm 41:1, Jerome says a certain discernment is necessary in distributing alms: "Blessed is the one who understands concerning the needy and the poor."[28] While some poor should receive preferential treatment, for others one should be more hesitant to assist. Augustine writes, "One poor person searches you out, another you must yourself search out."[29]

But Shepherd of Hermas says,

You must not try to distinguish between the deserving and the undeserving. You may easily make a mistake, and, as the matter is in doubt, it is better to benefit the undeserving than, avoiding them, miss the good. We are told not to judge. We must open our generosity to all who are enrolled as disciples.[30]

Jerome also speaks of the problem of "real widows." Some merit being on the church's role and others should either remarry or serve as distributors of alms.[31] Further, their own families should assist as much as possible and certainly not interfere or deprive them of normal income through spinning.[32]

## Seven Lessons from the Early Church

This exploration shows how strongly early Christianity was marked by its views on material goods and its consistent testimony to mutual sharing of the goods and resources of its members. Scholars debate the early church's position on Christians participating in the military. But there is no debate on whether early Christianity held sharing of wealth to be an essential part of the community that marked its existence and growth in the Roman empire. The evidence is conclusive.

As Walsh and Langan (1977:114) indicate, this stance was rooted in a combination of basic Christian teachings: (1) Christian transformation of the values of the pagan world, (2) Christian criticism of the desires of the human heart, (3) God as Creator of the material world and the common purpose of material goods, (4) Christ and his identification with the poor, and (5) love and sharing in the Christian community.

Walsh and Langan conclude their study by summarizing the convictions that governed the lives and actions of early Christianity. I modify them here to apply directly to mutual aid in early Christianity.

(1) Christian commitment means that we will not place ultimate value on material possessions but will instead find our fulfillment in expressing our love for God through caring service to those in need.

(2) Our basic problem as Christians with wealth and possessions is not that we have or use them. The problem is our desire for them, especially as it leads to avarice, greed, and selfish use in which possessions lead to divisions and separations in the body of Christ.

(3) Material things are good as part of God's good creation. Because they are, like the bounties of creation, made available to all in common, our material resources are to be shared with all. They are to be viewed as a common blessing rather than regarded as our own.

(4) Based on Matthew 25:30-45 and other Christian teachings, Christ identifies with the poor in a special way. This identification provides a special motive for generosity and for wealthy Christians to help meet the material needs of the poor.

(5) Growing out of a koinonia experience in Christ that affects our total being, we become a community of sharing and support for each other because of who we are in Christ. This results in love and generosity in sharing of material resources.

(6) Our willingness to share this world's goods with those in need is a powerful witness to the world, to call people to Christ, just as it was for early Christianity in the Roman empire.

(7) By combining these convictions of the Christian faith with a realistic analysis of the socioeconomic world today and seeking to find fresh application of these teachings for society today, the church can be leaven and salt in the world, showing forth the light of Christ.

With devotion and joy, let us anoint the feet of Christ, in the practice of mutual aid.

## Notes

1. See here Gerhard Lohfink.
2. Mark 12:31; Matt. 22:39; Luke 10:27.
3. Matt. 19:16-22; Mark 10:17-22; cf. Luke 18:18-23.
4. For a close study of koinonia, and its variant forms as used in the New Testament, see Seesemann (1933), McDermott (1975), Panikulam (1979), and Hainz (1982).

5. Examples of Christ's sufferings occur in Phil. 3:10; Col. 1:24; 1 Pet. 4:13. Glory, as reward for suffering, is also promised (1 Pet. 5:1; 2 Tim. 2:12).

6. For the phrase, "participation/koinonia in the Spirit," see 2 Cor. 13:14; Phil. 2:1. J.G. Davies (1958:16-17) contends that the participation in the Spirit is a precondition to the possibility of participation (koinonia) in Christ: "We are only partakers of Christ in so far as we are partakers of His Spirit. The indwelling of the Spirit is for the specific purpose of affecting the indwelling of Christ—the 'Spirit in us' and therefore 'Christ in us.' " He further observes that the Spirit's work within the koinonia is to take the human nature of Christ and assimilate it into our nature so that we are transformed into the image of Christ, as in Col. 1:27; 2 Cor. 3:18. To become partakers of the divine nature is then the consequence of this process (2 Pet. 1:3).

7. Rom. 15:26-27; Koenig trans.: 74.

8. It is astounding to observe how koinonia is used without reference to mutual aid or giving money to one another. Of the ten essays in the World Council of Churches document to promote koinonia, none mentions mutual aid (Best and Granberg-Michaelson 1993).

9. Against the theses of Kraybill and Sweetland (1983) and Degenhardt (1965), and qualified dissent against Johnson (1977) also.

10. Rom. 12:3-8; 1 Cor. 12–14; Eph 4:7-16.

11. *Didache* 1.4.8.

12. Eus. *Eccl. Hist.* 4.23.

13. González: 116-17; Clement *Paid.* 2.13.

14. González: 115-16; *Paid.* 3.6.

15. *Vis.* iii. vi. 5-7; iii. ix. 2-9; *Mand.* x.i.4-6.

16. González: 101; 2 *Clem.* 16.4.

17. *Apol.* 1.67. For a discussion of the place of this in worship, see Kreider 1997:46.

18. González: 110-11; *Adv. haer.*4.30.1.

19. González: 118-19; *Contra Celsus* 3.78.

20. González: 129; *Apol.* 39.

21. González: 125-26; Cypr. *De op. et eleem.* 10-18.

22. González: 138; Lact. *Inst.* 5:6.

23. González: 133: Eus. *Eccl. Hist.* 6.43.11. See Lampe: 344. He says "über 1000 Unterstüzungsempfänger," but Eusebius clearly says 1500.

24. Ramsey: 237; Ambr. *Exp. in Ps.* 119[118]. 8.22.

25. Ramsey: 230; *De disc. Christ* 8.8.

26. Ramsey: 231-32; *Enarr. in Ps.* 47[46]. 5.

27. Ramsey: 228; Aug. *Tract. in Ioann.* 50.7.

28. Ramsey: 232; Jer. *Ep.* 120.1.

29. Aug. *Enarr. in Ps.* 147[146]. 17.

30. Walsh and Langan: 136; from *Quis Dives Salvetur?*, trans. R. B. Tollinton, 318.

31. Ramsey: 232; Jer. *Ep.* 123.5.

32. Ambrosi. *In Iam ep. ad Tim. 5:16.*

# References

Avila, Charles
  1983    *Ownership: Early Christian Teaching.* London: Sheed and Ward.

Bassler, Jouette M.
  1991    *God and Mammon: Asking for Money in the New Testament.* Nashville: Abingdon.

Batey, Richard
  1972    *Jesus and the Poor.* New York: Harper & Row.

Best, Thomas F., and Wesley Granberg-Michaelson
  1993    *Koinonia and Justice, Peace and Creation: Costly Unity.* Geneva: WCC.

Countryman, L. Wm.
  1980    *The Rich Christian in the Church of the Early Empire: Contradictions and Accommodations.* New York and Toronto: Edwin Mellen Press.

Davies, J. G.
  1958    *Members of One Another: Aspects of Koinonia.* London: A. R. Mowbray & Co. Ltd.

Degenhardt, H.
  1965    *Lukas Evangelist der Armen.* Stuttgart: Katholisches Bibelwerk.

Dupont, Dom Jacques
  1979    "Community of Goods in the Early Church," *The Salvation of the Gentiles: Essays on the Acts of the Apostles.* Trans. John R. Keating. New York: Paulist. Pp. 38-102.

Gager, John
  1976    *Kingdom and Community: The Social World of Early Christianity.* Englewood Cliffs, NJ: Prenctice-Hall.

Garrison, Roman
  1993    *Redemptive Almsgiving in Early Christianity.* JSNTSS 77. Sheffield: Sheffield Academic Press.

Georgi, Dieter
  1992    *Remembering the Poor: The History of Paul's Collection for Jerusalem.* Nashville: Abingdon.

González, Justo L.
  1990    *Faith and Wealth: A History of Early Christian Ideas on the Origin, Significance, and Use of Wealth.* San Francisco: Harper and Row.

Hainz, Josef
  1982    *Koinonia: "Kirche" als Gemeinschaft bei Paulus.* Regensburg: Friedrich Pustet.

Hengel, Martin
    1974    *Property and Riches in the Early Church: Aspects of a Social History of Early Christianity.* Philadelphia: Fortress.

Johnson, Luke Timothy
    1977    *The Literary Function of Possessions in Luke-Acts.* Missoula, Mont.: Scholars Press.

    1981    *Sharing Possessions: Mandate and Symbol of Faith.* Philadephia: Fortress.

Karris, Robert J.
    1978    "Poor and Rich: The Lukan *Sitz-im-Leben.*" In *Perspectives in Luke-Acts,* ed. C. H. Talbert. Danville, Va.: Association of Baptist Professors of Religion.

Koenig, John
    1985    *New Testament Hospitality: Partnership with Strangers as Promise and Mission.* Philadelphia: Fortress.

Kraybill, Donald B., and Dennis M. Sweetland
    1983    "Possessions in Luke-Acts: A Sociological Perspective." *Perspectives in Religious Studies* 10: 215-39.

Kreider, Eleanor
    1997    *Communion Shapes Character.* Scottdale, Pa. & Waterloo, Ont.: Herald Press.

Lampe, Peter
    1989    *Die stadtrömischen Christen in den ersten beiden Jahrhunderten.* WUNT, 2d series 18. Tübingen: J. C. B. Mohr (Paul Siebeck).

Lohfink, Gerhard
    1984    *Jesus and Community: The Social Dimension of Christian Faith.* Trans. J. P. Galvin. Philadelphia: Fortress.

McDermott, Michael
    1975    "The Biblical Doctrine of Koinonia." *Biblische Zeitschrift* 19:64-77; 219-233.

Meeks, Douglas
    1989    *God the Economist: The Doctrine of God and Political Economy.* Minneapolis: Fortress.

Nickel, Keith F.
    1965    *The Collection—A Study in Paul's Strategy.* London: SCM Press.

Panikulam, George
    1979    *Koinōnia in the New Testament: A Dynamic Expression of Christian Life.* Analecta Biblica 85. Rome: Biblical Institute Press.

Pilgrim, Walter
    1981   *Good News to the Poor: Wealth and Poverty in Luke-Acts.* Minneapolis: Augsburg.

Ramsey, Boniface
    1982   "Almsgiving in the Latin Church: The Late Fourth and Early Fifth Centuries." *Theol. Stud.* 43: 226-59.

Ringe, Sharon H.
    1985   *Jesus, Liberation, and the Biblical Jubilee.* Philadelphia: Fortress.

Rolston, Holmes
    1946   *Stewardship in the New Testament Church: A Study in the Teachings of Paul Concerning Christian Stewardship.* Richmond, Va.: John Knox.

Sampley, J. Paul
    1980   *Pauline Partnership in Christ: Christian Community and Commitment in Light of Roman Law.* Philadelphia: Fortress.

Seesemann, Heinrich
    1933   *Der Begriff KOINONIA im Neuen Testament.* Giessen: Alfred Töpelmann.

Sloan, Robert B.
    1977   *The Favorable Year of the Lord: A Study of Jubilary Theology in the Gospel of Luke.* Austin, Tex.: Schola.

Stegemann, Wolfgang
    1984   *The Gospel and the Poor.* Trans. Dietlinde Elliott. Philadelphia: Fortress.

Swartley, Willard M.
    1978   "Biblical Sources of Stewardship." In *The Earth Is The Lord's: Essays on Stewardship*, ed. Mary Evelyn Jegen and Bruno V. Manno. New York: Paulist.

    1994   *Israel's Scripture Traditions and the Synoptic Gospels: Story Shaping Story.* Peabody, Mass.: Hendrickson Publishers.

Thornton, L. S.
    1950   *The Common Life in the Body of Christ.* London: Dacre Press.

Walsh, William J., and John P. Langan
    1977   "Patristic Social Consciousness: The Church and the Poor." In *The Faith That Does Justice: Examining the Christian Sources for Social Change*, ed. John C. Haughey. New York: Paulist.

Yoder, John H.
    1994   *The Politics of Jesus.* 2nd ed. Grand Rapids: Eerdmans.

2

# Nehemiah: An Old Testament Model

## Wilma Ann Bailey

Mutual aid assumes reciprocity in the context of an ongoing community. The practice of mutual aid, however, is difficult and delicate in social settings with sharp differences in income and resources. Wilma Bailey proposes that a study of Nehemiah—especially chapter five—offers an instructive case study of mutual aid in settings of economic disparity. Following a careful description of the socioeconomic context, Bailey offers a penetrating interpretation of this text for the practice of mutual aid today.

## Mutual Aid in the Midst of Disparity

Mutual aid typically occurs in a closed set such as a community, congregation, or denomination. This is because there is an implicit assumption of reciprocity and continuing relationship between the participating parties. By definition mutual aid must be mutual, lest economic inequities harden, creating distinct and distant social groups within a community. Though one party may need immediate help, both parties must benefit, and the dignity, integrity, and equality of each must be maintained. The givers must not think themselves superior or the receivers inferior.

Mutual aid in its purest form is evident in small traditional societies where the principal form of economic exchange is (or was) barter.

Here most individuals or families function on the same socioeconomic level and have access to the same pool of resources. Mutual aid may also work well in congregations or communities where members are on the same socioeconomic level and share the same general attitudes about money, resources, and lending. The question this chapter explores is how mutual aid may be actualized in congregations or communities where there is disparity in income and resources.

In such cases, some have much wealth, others little. Moreover, attitudes and values in relation to money and material resources may differ between haves and have-nots. Mutual aid works best in communities where people function on the same social and economic levels, but if community is to be maintained, mutual aid is most necessary where they do not. These matters are examined here in the context of a model drawn from the Bible.

This study begins with an examination of the problem as outlined in Nehemiah 5. Attention is given to the concept of *shalom*; the social and economic situation; and, in broader biblical context, the issues of collection of interest on loans to the poor, debt slavery, and the function of the year of Jubilee and the sabbatical year as these apply to mutual aid in the covenant community.

## The Context of Nehemiah

Biblical Israel reformed itself several times, moving from a tribal society to a monarchic state to an ethnic-religious community under the political umbrella of a foreign empire. The need for mutual aid and the type of aid dispensed would have varied according to the political, economic, and social realities in each of those contexts.

According to the Bible, a portion of the people (mostly the elite) of the southern kingdom of Judah had been exiled to Babylonia following their defeat at the hands of that nation in 587-6 B.C.E. Babylon was in turn conquered by the Persians, who permitted the Judean exiles and their descendants to return to their homeland. They emigrated in waves over a period of a hundred years or more.

In the mid-fifth century B.C.E., Nehemiah, Jewish cupbearer in the Persian court, received permission to return to Jerusalem to rebuild the city. In Nehemiah 5:14 he refers to himself as a *pehām*,[1] a word usually translated as "governor." He is governor only over Judah (5:14) because the territory of the former Israelite kingdom is no longer a unit. This title carried with it some privileges and a measure of authority.

The book of Nehemiah[2] is a study in the formation of a new kind of Jewish community divorced from the monarchy, the larger political entity that formerly provided identity, structure, and boundaries. Those in the community are entitled to a level of protection and support to which (we might infer) those outside of the community are not. Members are so entitled because the welfare of each person in the community affects the welfare of the community as a whole. When Nehemiah's work of community building is frustrated by those working at cross-purposes, he calls them to account for their actions. Mutual aid, one could argue, is the only way to hold the community together when there is disparity in income and resources.

# The Text

According to chapters four and five of Nehemiah, the situation at the time is this: Amid rebuilding of the walls of the city of Jerusalem, conflict arises. A complaint is lodged by that part of the community identified as *ha`am* and *nesehem*, "the people and their wives," against *'ahehem hayehudim*, "their brother [kin] Jews" or "Judeans."[3] The problem is that there is a grain famine. Fensham (1982:190) blames the famine on a disruption of commercial activities due to the antagonistic relationship between the Judeans and their neighbors. In addition, the building of the wall is taking farmers away from their normal endeavors.

Fensham may be correct. The hilly country around Jerusalem is not conducive to grain farming. Probably denizens of that area bought wheat and barley from neighbors along the coast. Due to the famine, the poorer folk are being forced to pledge their fields, vineyards, and houses to buy grain (Neh. 5:3) and to borrow money (*kesep*) to pay the king's tax. They are using their fields and vineyards as collateral (5:4). As a result, they are not only forfeiting their fields and vineyards, but their children (especially the girls) are being forced into slavery. The poor argue that they and their children are human beings, members of the community just like the rich, but their children are not being treated as such. They are unable to stop the injustice because their resources are gone.

Nehemiah is outraged when he hears the cry (*s`q*) of the people.[4] He lays the offenses at the feet of the *horîm* and the *segagîm* (nobles and officials) (5:7). These are wealthy community members who are taking advantage of poorer kin. The precise nature of the charge is disputed. The NRSV follows the Massoretic text and translates it as "taking interest" (*massa'*) (5:7), but JPS uses the expression "pressing claims."[5] This language is connected to the sabbatical year instruction in Deut. 15:2.

Nehemiah does not make an immediate ruling. He calls together an assembly[6] and explains that he and others have been buying back their Jewish kin who have been sold beyond to foreigners. The nobles and officials are frustrating their task by selling other Jews who will in turn need to be bought back by them (5:8).

Nehemiah condemns these practices and offers two reasons why they should be changed. First, the people should live in fear of God. Second, they should want to avoid the taunt of the enemy nations (*goyim*). Although Throntveit (1992:123) suggests that the Israelites are picking up bad habits from their neighbors, this is not likely. The text indicates that the neighboring nations will taunt or shame Israel when they learn what is going on. The implication is that such practices are broadly recognized as wrong.

Nehemiah then reveals that he and his kin (literally "brothers")[7] have also been lending money and grain and charging interest. Notice that the wealthy have grain even during the famine (see also 5:11).[8] This may be why Nehemiah agonizes over how to respond to the poor folk in 5:7. Nehemiah calls for all to stop taking interest. He further demands that they return the property that they have taken from the people.[9] Blenkinsopp (1988:259) calls this an "emergency Jubilee" (see also Lev. 25 and Jer. 34:8-16). According to the text, the nobles and officials agree to do what Nehemiah asks.[10]

Nehemiah turns next to defending himself to his readers. He makes clear he has never extracted provisions (*lehem*, "bread") from the people, to which he is entitled by virtue of his office, even though he has to support many people for professional reasons (150 regularly, plus foreign visitors, 5:17). He provides for them all out of pocket because he does not want to burden the people and because he fears God (5:14-19). In contrast to him, he reminds readers, former governors took bread, wine, and silver from the people. Nehemiah also argues that he does not use his office for personal gain (5:16) or to build his own ego.

# Interpretation

Nehemiah's reactions to the situation probably are grounded in an understanding of shalom as the well-being of the community.[11] Shalom is the motivation for mutuality. Shalom cannot exist where there is community conflict or individuals and families deprived of the resources for full participation and productivity in the community. Fensham (cited above) may be correct that outside pressures affected the community; nevertheless, it had the ability to correct the immediate problem.

The wealthy people in the community may not be breaking the civil law (in the context of the Persian empire), but their economic practices are leading to impoverishment of others. Thus they are violating the Torah and its spirit. (For prohibitions against taking interest from the poor within the community, see Lev. 25:35-38, Exod. 22:25, and Deut. 23:19-20; for the return of property sold because of debt see Lev. 25:25-28; regulations on the length of slavery and manumission for an individual slave are in Exod. 21:2-11, Lev. 25:39-55, Deut. 15:12-18.)

Nehemiah's threat is that there will be divine (not human) revenge. God will shake away the property of the rich (Neh. 5:13). Significantly, Nehemiah does not appeal to his own authority as governor or to Persian law. This is a theological matter grounded in the covenant relationship God has with Israel. When the fields and vineyards are taken from the people, so is their livelihood. They are unable to be productive or contribute to the community. Children sold or forced away have also been lost to the community—not just in terms of numbers (though this is a concern, see 11:1-2) but in relation to their potential contributions to the community. By providing aid in the form of forgiveness of debt and restoration of property, the elite themselves will benefit in the long run.

Israel had earlier witnessed a rift in the community caused by one segment of the community forcing labor and taxes on others among them. After the death of Solomon (1 Kings 11–12), members of the northern tribes led by Jeroboam, who had witnessed the devastations caused by forced labor, asked Solomon's son and successor, Rehoboam, to ease the burden on the people. On the advice of his peers, Rehoboam took a hard line. According to 1 Kings 12:10-11, he replied to Jeroboam, "My little finger is thicker than my father's loins. Now whereas my father laid on you a heavy yoke, I will add to your yoke. My father disciplined you with whips, but I will discipline you with scorpions" (NRSV). At that point the northern tribes seceded, creating a rift in the Israelite community that lasted over 200 years.

Fortunately Nehemiah understood what Rehoboam did not about community formation and maintenance.

## The Socioeconomic Context

Joseph Blenkinsopp (1991:26) finds ample evidence that there was a close association between the temple elite and the propertied class in ancient Mesopotamia and Asia Minor during the Achaemenid period, from which sprang "an autonomous and privileged social entity which provided its members with the means for self-management and mutual economic assistance." Blenkinsopp assumes this to have been the case also in the western Levant (including Judah) (p. 24). He notes that Nehemiah controls the economic affairs of the temple (Neh. 13:13) and writes,

> The Babylonian immigrants imported, and succeeded in imposing the social arrangements with which they had become familiar in the Dias-

pora. They reconstituted their own assembly (*puhru*, *qāhal*, organized according to ancestral houses including free, property-owning citizens and temple personnel, under the leadership of tribal elders and the supervision of an imperial representative, in a cohesive social entity which, while allowing for additional adherents, was jealously protective of its status and privileges (1991:53).

Blenkinsopp believes Judah was an independent unit, separate from Samaria after the time of Darius. He cites the reference in Nehemiah 5:14-15 to the governors who were before him in Judah (1988:264).

Kenneth Hoglund proposes a different economic scenario. Noting the rise in small settlements in Judea and in the number of forts in the fifth century, he concludes Persian government policy was to decentralize the population and place the region under military control (1991:57-64). This supported a "tributary mode of production" that extracted resources from these villages and turned them over to the imperial authorities who also controlled trade (1991:59).

Hoglund cites Nehemiah 9:36-37, which tells of Ezra complaining that the people are "slaves" (or servants) to foreign kings (not chattel slaves; see Daniel L. Smith, 1991:78). Hoglund (1991:66) adds that these settlements were "administered, taxed and regulated as a corporate unit." Daniel Smith (1991:86) suggests that such treatment resulted in a "culture of resistance" that led to a theology of separation.

Responding to Hoglund and Smith, Halligan states that while such an imperial economy may have been functional during the early part of Persian rule, by the time of Nehemiah there is clearly private ownership. He proposes an economy based on credit. Collateral included future harvests, land, or offspring. Promissory notes "could be bought and sold among credit brokers" (1991:150). These notes could in turn be sold to people outside of the Jewish community who did not share its values or sense of covenant obligation.

The problem in Nehemiah 5, Halligan believes, is not excessive interest. The people could not "meet the principal that resulted in their loss of title to chattel and fixed assets" (1991:152). Halligan's analysis is that a sudden reversal in the economy as described in Nehemiah 5, involving the restoration of assets and a return of interest, would have dire consequences for the economy. He writes,

> The instant removal of the credit system would jeopardize all other dependent commercial transactions in progress, and no matter how distasteful to the deuteronomic palate they may be in character, these financial arrangements had to continue until relief for the economy arising from increase in production or trade occurred. These credit arrangements did not precipitate the famine but resulted from the peas-

ants' loss of power to produce salable goods and in turn to provide minimal subsistence for their dependents (pp. 152-153).

Nehemiah 5, however, indicates that a relatively small group of people are involved (the Jewish people in and around Jerusalem). The return of property may result in wealthy people being less wealthy but is unlikely to generate a total collapse of the economy.[12]

Money in the form of coins was introduced into Jerusalem around the time of Nehemiah (Betlyon 1992:1083). Money helped trade and was a boon to the economy of the ancient Near East. However, money as a regular means of exchange can make life more difficult for the poor if payment for goods or taxes must be made in hard currency. Even when a harvest is good, if it cannot be sold on the market the peasant will be cash poor and unable to pay taxes.[13] If taxes are due before a harvest comes in or if there is a poor harvest, they cannot be paid. One of these appears to have been the situation in Nehemiah 5. The people needed cash (*kesep*) to pay the king's tax.

Socially, there was significant stratification in Israelite society during the postexilic period. At least four major societal levels are evident in Nehemiah 5: *ha`am* and *nesehem, hayehudim, hapehâ,* and *hammelek. Hayehudim,* "the Jews" in this chapter, appears to refer only to the elite, to those who had experienced Babylonian exile (Blenkinsopp 1991:47). The common folk (*ha`am* and *nesehem,* "the people and their wives") were indebted to hayehudim, and the Persian king (*hammelek*). They could have also been forced to pay taxes to the governor (*hapehâ*) but Nehemiah waived his right to this to ease the burden on the people. The setting was ripe for a rift along class lines.

## Loans

Israel's law provided for interest-free loans to those in the community. In the earliest formulation of the law, such loans were for the poor only (Exod. 22:25-27). We may infer that loans to the poor were to be used to meet basic needs. (The example of the clothing in pawn supports this.) The wealthy members of the community were not to exploit the poor for financial or other advantage. They were rather to give up their right to interest and their profit from loans to provide aid to the poor. The Levitical instruction supports this same idea with an added reference to Egypt (Lev. 25:35-38): God brought Israel out of the house of bondage. As Chilton (1992:114) points out, the Israelites were not to let themselves or members of the community be re-enslaved through debt.

The Deuteronomic Code (Deut. 23:20) expanded the law to include not only the poor but all Israelites. Nehemiah assumes it is known that taking interest from members of the community is wrong (Neh. 5:7, 10). Interest is to be charged solely on loans to foreigners. Clearly the intent is to meet the needs of the community and make any profit from outsiders. If such a law were operational (likely it was not), the financial incentive favored lending to foreigners. Native Israelites would have been able to borrow solely from foreigners.

## Debt Slavery

According to Dandamayev (1992a:59), debt slavery was well-known in the ancient Near East but by the time of Nehemiah it was little practiced.[14] The more pragmatic approach of permitting people to work off their debt while remaining free was the norm. Earlier, when debt slavery was more common, it was regulated by law. Creditors were permitted to keep a debtor enslaved only for a limited period of time, according to Hammurabi's Code and the Nuzi texts.

The late texts of Leviticus, however, indicate that debt slavery was practiced to some extent in Israel even in the postexilic period. According to Leviticus 25:39-42, the term of service was set to end at the year of Jubilee. The debtor was to be treated like a worker, not a common slave, and the debtor could not be sold to a third party. This type of slavery was freely entered into by an impoverished person as a means of survival.

The earlier Deuteronomic Code specified that the term of service was to be limited to six years, though a slave could voluntarily stay longer (Deut. 15:12-17). If an Israelite is self-sold to a foreigner, the Israelite is to be redeemed by kin. It is clear that perpetual slavery of Israelites to other Israelites or to foreigners was not to be the norm for the theological reason that Israel is to be enslaved only to God (Lev. 25:47-55).

The situation in Nehemiah 5 is that impoverished Jewish people are being forced to sell their children into slavery. Jewish people, in turn, are being sold to third parties who are foreigners (Neh. 5:5, 8). Thus they may potentially be lost to the Jewish community forever.

## Sabbatical and Jubilee Years

The priestly authors of Leviticus included an injunction for sabbatical years (ch. 25). Mirroring the week, the sabbatical year was to occur every seventh year. The primary provision was that the land should rest (no sowing, pruning, harvesting) in observance of a "sabbath for YHWH." Specific reference is made to slaves, hired and bound laborers, livestock, other animals, and landowners who may equally consume what grows of itself. Thus every seven years there is a leveling of social classes in relation to food. Exodus 23:10-11 also refers to a seventh-year rest for the land to provide for the poor and wild animals (NRSV).

Neither this text nor the next uses the term "sabbath for YHWH." The seventh year may not have been conceived of as a single year in these texts. The former may simply refer to a seven-year period, which, if observed by the entire community, would likely yield a continuous supply of fallow land to provide for the poor (Wright 1992a:857). Deuteronomy 15:1-3 records that every seventh year there is to be remission of debts or perhaps suspension of debts owed by neighbors (Israelites). Deuteronomy 15:2b reads, "he shall not press his neighbor or his brother" (see Wright 1992a:859; Wacholder 1976:762). Wright (p. 858) suggests this refers not to the debt itself but to a pledge (Heb. *masseh*, land or children) used to secure debts. According to Wacholder (p. 762), the economic implications are that "lending money could never be a business transaction in Israel, but only an offer of assistance to the needy."

The sole reference to the year of Jubilee is found in Leviticus 25, where it is intertwined with the discussion of the sabbatical year.[15] The fiftieth year is a second sabbatical year following the forty-ninth year. The land is to remain fallow for two years in a row. The Israelites may eat only what grows of itself. Unique to the Jubilee is the notion that every one is to return to his or her family and land (Heb. *ahuzah*, possession) in that year. Land is to be returned to the original owners (Lev. 25:28). Israelites enslaved for debt are to be freed (Lev. 25:54). Wright (1992b:1027) explains the socioeconomic function of the Jubilee:

> The regular operation of redemption over time could result in the whole territory of a clan coming into the hands of a few wealthier families, with the rest of the families in the clan in a kind of debt servitude. The Jubilee was a mechanism to prevent this and to preserve the socioeconomic fabric of multiple-household land tenure with the comparative equality and independent viability of the smallest family-plus-land units.

Conceptually, the sabbatical and Jubilee years appear to be attempts, at least once every seven or fifty years, to radically reset economic and social factors that if not periodically corrected would have led to oppressive economic and social conditions for the masses of common people. In the words of Walter Harrelson (1996),

> They prevent some from becoming too rich at the expense of others who become too poor. Sabbatical and Jubilee provisions aim at the removal of crushing indebtedness, or self-imposed tenancy or debt-induced enslavement of oneself or one's children, while also helping to stem the amassing of fortunes at the expense of those who aren't as fortunate or industrious or clever as the wealthy.[16]

The sabbatical and Jubilee years represent mutual aid structured into the community's regular economic and social life. The theological rationale for these practices is that the land (which represents all resources, Lev. 25:23) and the people (Lev. 25:55) belong to God. They are only lent to the human community.

Does Nehemiah 5 describe an "emergency Jubilee," as Blenkinsopp suggests, or a sabbatical year? There is no reference to the blowing of the ram's horn, the proclamation of liberty, a fallowing of the land, or a general return. All of these are characteristic of the Jubilee. It is unlikely that the instructions in Nehemiah 5 are meant to be a kind of Jubilee. Neither are all elements of the sabbatical year found here. There is simply a call to practice mutual aid. When people are suffering, they need help immediately. It is neither necessary to wait for a sabbatical or Jubilee year nor to imitate them.

Nehemiah does not use his political authority as governor. He appeals to compassion and community spirit. There are positive incentives for compliance. Positively, this action is evidence that the people reverence God. Moreover, it will arrest the taunts of the *goyim* (those non-Israelite peoples and nations, Neh. 5:9). The latter implies that if the goyim look after their own, so should the Judean community .

## Conclusion

Mutual aid is a function of the community. The postexilic Jewish community as it appears in the book of Nehemiah was bound together by physical location, biological descent, and a commitment to Torah. The Torah itself contained instruction that ensured the stability of the community by building in periodic adjustments to the economic system. This plan aimed to prevent the permanent alienation of the poor due to indebtedness. It is clear that these precautions were not always instituted and other actions had to be taken. The request that the wealthy return what they have acquired from the poor is instructive on a social and spiritual level. It affirms the importance of all segments of society to the well-being of the community.

Can the model of Nehemiah 5 prove useful to late-twentieth-century Christian communities? The circumstances are distinctly different. Individual congregations are usually not economic units. Members of most congregations do not live, work, and worship in the same physical location. Most congregations will not be entirely socially and economically homogeneous. Even in wealthy or middle-class congregations there are likely to be elderly members whose retirement income is low and students or families undergoing temporary economic setbacks. There are also congregations where there is great disparity in income and resources, particularly in urban areas. However, a high degree of homogeneity is likely to characterize many congregations. But whether homogeneous or less so, Christian congregations do have boundaries that make mutual aid a viable option.

Mutual aid in congregations and communities where there is disparity in income and resources must place the shalom of the congregation or community above individual gain. There must be reciprocity of some sort, and the dignity of both parties must be maintained. It is crucial that attention be given to different ways segments of the community value and use money and resources. As a part of mutual aid efforts, long term solutions—such as jobs, education, health insurance, child care—should be sought or provided for community members who need them. Through mutual aid, a congregation or community in which there is disparity in income and resources can actualize God's love and be a model for the community beyond its boundaries.

## Notes

1. Literally coal, but more likely a *pehâ*, an Assyrian loan word; see also 5:15, 18.

2. The book of Nehemiah was separated from the book of Ezra in the Greek text during the third century of the Common Era by Origen. See Klein 1992:731. Before and after this time the Hebrew Bible maintained the unity of the work.

3. See Blenkinsopp 1988:256. It is perhaps significant that the poor themselves make their plight known to Nehemiah. They are suffering in the midst of a community, but no one seems to notice until they speak up.

4. A parallel may be found here between the cry of the Israelites in bondage in Egypt and their cries in economic bondage in Nehemiah 5. Compare 5:1, 6 and Exodus 2:23, where an alternate spelling of the same word is used.

5. See discussion below on the sabbatical year. The Hebrew word translated "press" is *ngs*. It is not present in Nehemiah 5:7.

6. The Syriac text indicates that he called with a "great voice" eliminating the assembly. Jephthah Gathaka points out that Nehemiah cannot use the normal court system because it is controlled by the elite who are the source of the problem (1992:198).

7. Fensham (1982:193, 197) assumes that this term refers to high officials though the word is used of a biological brother in Nehemiah 1:2. It likely refers to officials who are also his relatives, as it is clear he appointed his relatives to high positions (see 7:2).

8. JPS is probably correct. The sense of the text is that Nehemiah and his brothers are also lending at interest. The word *ns`*, "to lend at interest," is used (Brown, Driver, Briggs 1978:673).

9. NRSV says they are to return the property and interest on the money, grain, wine, and oil. The translation "interest" requires an emendation of the text. The Hebrew says *wm't*. JPS calls for a return of the property and the claims "for the hundred [*wm't*] pieces of silver, the grain, the wine, and the oil (5:11)." Constance Wallace (1987), however, provides the most logical explanation of the text. Comparing the Hebrew *wm't* to particles in cognate languages, she concludes it is

used here to divide "real from movable property." She translates, "Return to them, even this day, their fields, their vineyards, their olive groves, and their houses, and also their silver, the grain, the wine, and the oil" (p. 31). And so everything is to be returned.

10. Halligan (1991:153) argues that such an abrupt change in economic policy would have resulted in a collapse of the economy. If the economy were based on credit this might be the case. See below. The point here is to remedy the oppressive conditions under which the poor are forced to live, not to provide long-term solutions.

11. For a discussion of the term *shalom*, see Yoder and Swartley 1992; and Mauser 1992:13-35.

12. Businesses regularly write off debts owed to them and some first world nations have "forgiven" certain debts owed to them by third world nations. These practices have not led to a collapsed economy.

13. Alternately, the peasant may be forced to sell at a lower price to get the money to pay taxes.

14. Debt slavery and other forms of slavery grew during the Greco-Roman period for a variety of reasons (see Bartchy 1992:6.67-68).

15. The Jubilee year is mentioned solely in postexilic literature. It is likely that its origin was not grounded in theological understandings but pragmatic considerations. The exiled Judeans were first permitted to return home after about fifty years. They likely found others on land they considered theirs. The Jubilee may have originally been a means to get their land back.

16. Harrelson (1996) finds additional support in Isaiah 5:8 (amassing wealth isolates the community), Deuteronomy 15 (huge disparities in wealth are not permitted), Ezekiel 47–48 (a reordering of society will be the eschatological reality).

## References

Ackroyd, Peter
  1986  *Israel Under Babylon and Persia*. Oxford: Oxford University Press.

Bartchy, Scott S.
  1992  "Slavery: Greco-Roman." In *The Anchor Bible Dictionary*, ed. David Noel Freedman. New York: Doubleday.

Betlyon, John W.
  1992  "Coinage." In *The Anchor Bible Dictionary*, ed. David Noel Freedman. New York: Doubleday.

*Biblia Hebraica Stuttgartensia*
  1983  Stuttgart: Deutsche Bibelgesellschaft.

Blenkinsopp, Joseph
  1988  *Ezra-Nehemiah*. Philadelphia: Westminster.

  1991  "Temple and Society in Achaemenid Judah." In *Second Temple*. Sheffield: Sheffield Academic Press.

Bright, John
1975    *A History of Israel*. Philadelphia: Westminster.

Brown, Francis, S. R. Driver, and Charles A. Briggs
1978    *A Hebrew and English Lexicon of the Old Testament*. Oxford: Clarendon
        Press.

Buchholz, Todd G.
1988    "Biblical Laws and the Economic Growth of Ancient Israel." *The
        Journal of Law and Religion* 6 no 2:389-427.

Chilton, Bruce.
1992    "Debts." In *The Anchor Bible Dictionary*, ed. David Noel Freedman.
        New York: Doubleday.

Dandamayev, Muhammad A.
1992a   "Slavery: Ancient Near East." In *The Anchor Bible Dictionary*, ed.
        David Noel Freedman. New York: Doubleday.

1992b   "Slavery: Old Testament." In *The Anchor Bible Dictionary*, ed. David
        Noel Freedman. New York: Doubleday.

Durnbaurgh, Donald F.
1988    "Mutual Aid in Ministry to God's World." *Brethren Life and Thought*
        33:87-97.

Fensham, Charles R.
1982    *The Books of Ezra and Nehemiah*. Grand Rapids: Eerdmans.

Gathaka, Jephthah K.
1992    "Economic and Social Problems Created by Debt Crisis: A Bible
        Exposition on Nehemiah 5:1-13." In *The Church and the External Debt*,
        ed. Jan Harm Boer.  Jos, Nigeria: Institute of Church and Society.

Halligan, John M.
1991    "Nehemiah 5: By Way of a Response to Hoglund and Smith." In
        *Second Temple Studies: Persian Period*, vol 1, ed. Philip R. Davies.
        Journal for the Study of the Old Testament Supplement Series.
        Sheffield: Sheffield Academic Press.

Harrelson, Walter
1996    Personal Letter.

Hayes, John H., and J. Maxwell Miller
1977    *Israelite and Judaean History*. Philadelphia: Trinity International.

Herman, Barbara
1984    "Mutual Aid and Respect for Persons." *Ethics* 94: 577-602.

Hoglund, Kenneth
1991    "The Archaemenid Context." In *Second Temple Studies*, ed. Philip R.
        Davies. Sheffield: Sheffield Academic Press.

Holmgren, Frederick Carlson
  1987   *Ezra and Nehemiah: Israel Alive Again*. Grand Rapids: Eerdmans.

  1989   *Holy Bible Containing the Old And New Testaments with the Apocryphal/
         Deuterocanonical Books: New Revised Standard Version*. New York:
         Oxford University Press.

Klein, Ralph W.
  1992   "Ezra-Nehemiah, Books of." In *The Anchor Bible Dictionary*, ed. David
         Noel Freedman. New York: Doubleday.

  1988   "Nehemiah." In *Harper's Bible Commentary*, ed. James L. Mays. San
         Francisco: Harper and Row.

Koehler, Ludwig and Walter Baumgartner
  1994   *The Hebrew and Aramaic Lexicon of the Old Testament*. New York: E. J.
         Brill.

Maloney, R. P.
  1974   "Usury and Restrictions on Interest-Taking in the Ancient Near
         East." *Catholic Biblical Quarterly* 36:1-20.

Mauser, Ulrich.
  1992   *The Gospel of Peace*. Louisville, Kentucky: Westminster/John Knox.

Neufeld, E.
  1953/54  "The Rate of Interest and the Text of Neh. 5.11." *Jewish Quarterly
           Review* 44:194-204.

  1955   "The Prohibitions against Loans at Interest in Ancient Hebrew
         Laws." *Hebrew Union College Annual* 26:355-412.

  1992   "Sabbatical Year." In *The Anchor Bible Dictionary*, ed. David Noel
         Freedman. New York: Doubleday.

  1973   *The Ancient Near East: An Anthology in Texts and Pictures*, vol 1. Prince-
         ton: Princeton University Press.

Robinson, Gnana
  1978   "A New Economic Order: The Challenge of the Biblical Jubilee." In *A
         Vision for Man: Essays on Faith, Theology and Society in honor of Joshua
         Russell Chandran*. Madras: The Christian Literature Society.

Schökel, Luis Alonso, S. J.
  1976   "Somos Iguales Que Nuestros Hermanos: Para una exégesis de Neh.
         1-13." In *Mesianismo y Escatologia: Estudios en Memoria del Prof. Dr.
         Luis Arnaldich Perot*, ed. M. Cordero. Salamanca: Universidad Pontifi-
         cia.

  1992   "Jubilee, Year of." In *The Anchor Bible Dictionary*, ed. David Noel
         Freedman. New York: Doubleday.

Smith, Daniel
1991    "The Politics of Ezra: Sociological Indicators of Postexilic Judaean
        Society." In *Second Temple Studies*, ed. Philip R. Davies. Sheffield:
        Sheffield Academic Press.

Sutherland, John
1982    "Usury: God's Forgotten Doctrine." *Crux* 18 no 1:9-14.

1988    *Tanakh: The Holy Scriptures: The New JPS Translation According to the
        Traditional Hebrew Text.* Philadelphia: The Jewish Publication Society.

Throntveit, Mark A.
1992    *Ezra-Nehemiah.* Louisville: John Knox.

Wacholder, B. Z.
1976    "Sabbatical Year." In *The Interpreter's Dictionary of the Bible: Supplemen-
        tary Volume.* Nashville: Abingdon.

Wallace, Constance
1987    "WM- in Nehemiah 5:11." In *Eblaitica: Essays on the Ebla Archives and
        Eblaite Language,* ed. Cyrus H. Gordon. Winona Lake, Ind.: Eisen-
        brauns.

Williamson, H. G. M.
1988    "The Tyndale Biblical Archaeology Lecture 1987: The Governors of
        Judah Under the Persians." *Tyndale Bulletin* 39: 59-82.

Wright, Christopher J. H.
1992a   "Sabbatical Year." In *The Anchor Bible Dictionary*, ed. David Noel
        Freedman. New York: Doubleday.

1992b   "Jubilee, Year of." In *The Anchor Bible Dictionary*, ed. David Noel
        Freedman. New York: Doubleday.

Yoder, Perry B., and Willard M. Swartley
1992    *The Meaning of Peace: Biblical Studies.* Louisville, Kentucky:
        Westminster/John Knox.

# Part Two

# Theological and Ethical Perspectives

3

# Mutual Aid as "Practice"

## Joseph J. Kotva, Jr.

Addressing fundamental understandings of mutual aid, Joseph Kotva begins by reviewing early church mutual aid activities in Acts and the Apostle Paul's collection of funds for the Jerusalem church. Kotva concludes that these biblical examples differ from John Rawls' notion of mutual aid as a "natural duty." Mutual aid, in Kotva's view, more closely resembles Alasdair MacIntyre's concept of a "practice"—a shared pursuit of Christian community that requires virtues like generosity and justice. The final section of the essay applies this notion of mutual aid to the activities of Mennonite Disaster Service and Mennonite Mutual Aid.

## What is Mutual Aid?

Judging from ordinary conversations and scholarly sources, mutual aid is often poorly understood. In the scholarly sources, everything from communal living to music festivals, from church-based education to nonreligious cooperatives, and from care of the needy to assisting enemies, falls into the mutual aid basket.[1] The idea of mutual aid thus appears slippery and indeterminate. It becomes difficult to distinguish from notions of loving one's neighbor, doing good, providing stewardship, and so on.[2] Mutual aid can become an umbrella term for any helpful things the church may do.

This ambiguous use of mutual aid robs the concept of its critical edge and evaluative potential. A vague understanding of mutual aid

57

serves only as a blanket term of approval; it cannot tell us in sufficient detail why we favor certain behaviors over others or why some behaviors count and others do not. If the notion of mutual aid is to be useful or have force as an evaluative term, then we need a more adequate understanding of it.

Mutual aid, properly understood, can provide a ruler to measure some of our current engagements and institutions. However, to use mutual aid in this way requires that we better understand what it is and why Christians should be concerned about it. To move us toward this goal and offer an ethical analysis of mutual aid, I use Alasdair MacIntyre's (1984) idea of a "practice."

My argument develops in four sections, with the bulk of the analysis occurring in the third one. The first section sets the stage by looking to the New Testament to provide the touchstone for a Christian exploration of mutual aid. The next section looks at the understanding of mutual aid that emerges from John Rawls' *A Theory of Justice*. Rawls serves as an example of how mutual aid might be construed in a nonreligious, deontological framework. I will suggest, however, that his view of mutual aid as a "natural duty" is not well suited to the image that emerges from the New Testament.

Section three then recommends MacIntyre's notion of a "practice" as a more profitable approach to understanding mutual aid. I argue that the mutual aid envisioned by Scripture somewhat resembles MacIntyre's notion of a practice. When so viewed, mutual aid is seen as the shared pursuit of Christian community, a pursuit that requires and supports virtues like generosity and justice. The final section illustrates the evaluative potential of the developed notion of mutual aid by briefly comparing it with the activities of Mennonite Disaster Service (MDS) and Mennonite Mutual Aid (MMA). Although both MDS and MMA encompass many worthwhile activities, I will suggest that neither embodies true mutual aid.

# Seven Features of New Testament Aid

My focus in relation to the New Testament is primarily on the first two portraits of the new community's activities found in Acts and on Paul's discussions of his collection for the Jerusalem church.[3] Despite other relevant passages, these texts best illustrate what we have in mind when we talk about mutual aid. If there are New Testament examples of mutual aid, they are certainly found in the first community described as holding "all things in common" (Acts 2:44, 4:32) and in Paul's collection for "the poor among the saints at Jerusalem" (Rom. 15:26).[4]

Detailed exegesis of each passage is unnecessary. It is enough to note seven features visible in both Acts and the work of Paul:[5] (1) the centrality of Christian community, (2) the important role of material goods, (3) the primacy of grace, (4) the voluntary character of material sharing, (5) a concern with dispositions and attitudes, (6) the need for a sense of justice or fairness, and (7) the reciprocal nature of the sharing. These features are so closely related that the biblical texts do not always distinguish or treat them separately. Although the distinctions are artificial, they are used here for the sake of clarity.

(1) *Community.* The centrality of Christian community is the first key feature and is evident throughout the Acts passages. Acts 2 depicts "being saved" (v. 47), becoming a Christian, to mean joining a new, remnant people.[6] The passage begins with a reference to baptism (v. 38)—the ritual of initiation into the new community. Peter's hearers are then saved "from this corrupt generation" (v. 40). The implication is that they should leave the larger group for the remnant people (Johnson 1992:58). Those who join this new group participate in "fellowship" (koinonia, v. 42) and spend "much time together in the temple" (v. 46). Moreover, every day the Lord adds "to the community" (Johnson 1992:56, 60), to the "church fellowship" (Metzger 1975:304-305), "those who are being saved" (v. 47).

Acts 4–5 is likewise concerned with Christian community. Indeed, the relevant passage is bracketed by references to community (Johnson 1992:90). The passage begins by asserting the group's total unity—"All the believers were one in heart and mind" (4:32, NIV)—and ends by noting that "the whole church" (5:11) was seized by fear.

This focus on community was even more evident to Luke's first readers. The description of the community having all things in common (in 2:44 and 4:32) may be an allusion to the Greek ideal of friendship. As Luke T. Johnson (1981:119) points out, when Acts claims that

> the first Jerusalem believers were of "one heart and soul," Luke resonates the Hellenistic proverb, "friends are one soul"; and by saying that they "held all things in common," he echoed another traditional saying, for "friends all things are common."[7]

Luke thus portrays the first Christian believers as participating in a community that embodies the close links and intimate ties characterizing true friendship.

Paul's collection for the Jerusalem church also focuses on Christian community. He views this collection as an expression of Christian fellowship. This is underscored by the fact that he uses forms of the word *koinonia* ("fellowship") four times to refer to the collection.[8] Koinonia is among Paul's favorite terms for talking about the life of the Christian community. By applying that description to the collection, Paul plainly indicates that the collection itself is an expression of Christian fellowship.[9]

A comparable concern for Christian fellowship is evident in Paul's insistence that the collection is part of the reciprocal relationship between Jewish and Gentile believers. The Gentile believers have gained a share in the Jewish believers' spiritual blessings, so they are expected to help meet the material needs of the saints in Jerusalem (Rom. 15:27). Similarly, the Corinthians' abundance should be used to help meet the need of the Jerusalem saints so that, in turn, "their abundance may be for your need" (2 Cor. 8:14). Precisely this kind of sharing for Paul marks "the essence of the communal relationship in the Christian fellowship" (Nickle 1966:120).

This perspective underlies Paul's concern that the saints in Jerusalem accept the gift in a proper spirit (Rom. 15:31b). Offered as a symbol of solidarity, the collection is meant to demonstrate good relations between the Jewish and Gentile parts of the church.[10] By accepting the collection, the mother community in Jerusalem will affirm its unity with the newly founded Gentile churches (Achtemeier 1985:229-231). In short, Christian fellowship is, for Paul, central to the collection's meaning and significance.

(2) *Material Goods.* The second accent in these accounts is the fundamental role of material goods in bringing about Christian fellowship. Neither Luke nor Paul envisions Christian community solely on materialist grounds, as if the sharing of goods will by itself achieve Christian community.[11] Nevertheless, Luke and Paul view material sharing as an essential and probably primary symbol of Christian community.

Luke's allusion to friendship makes this clear. By saying that the early community "had all things in common" (Acts 2:44; 4:32), Luke is recalling the Greek ideal of friendship. But the startling aspect of this ideal is the centrality of material goods. The view of friendship to which Luke alludes carries a strong material component. Indeed, we are to recognize the early church as a community of friends precisely because of their shared possession of material goods.[12] Moreover, lest we think that the material question is incidental, Luke also offers us the positive example of Barnabas' generosity (4:36-37), followed by the chilling tale of Ananias and Sapphira (5:1-11). The latter case depicts the disposition of possessions for the community as a matter of life and death (Willimon 1988:53).

Paul's letters deal with the collection of money among Gentile churches for the poor saints in Jerusalem. It is not enough, he argues, to excel in faith, utterance, knowledge, and earnestness. Genuine Christian love must include sharing possessions (2 Cor. 8:7-8). This sharing between Christians is for Paul so central to Christian community, specifically to the unity of Jewish and Gentile believers, that he repeatedly uses the word koinonia in connection with the collection.[13] In this act of material sharing, Paul hopes to symbolize, embody, and, to some extent, affect Christian fellowship.[14] The sharing of material goods is for Paul at the heart of Christian community.

(3) *Grace*. Although community is important, the texts do not view the community solely as a human achievement. Thus the primacy of grace is the third significant feature. Acts insists it is God who summons one into the community;[15] it is God who saves (2:40; 2 47).[16] Those who join the community will receive the Holy Spirit (2:28). Acts also suggests that Ananias and Sapphira's "biggest mistake was to think they were dealing simply with another human gathering. They did not recognize that they were 'lying to God, not to humans' " (Johnson 1992:92; Acts 5:4; 5:9).

For Paul too, it is God's Spirit at work in dealings between believers. In talking about the collection project, Paul repeatedly uses the theologically rich expression "grace," or *charis* in the Greek.[17] He even sees the collection itself as an act of God's grace (2 Cor. 8:1). Paul contends that by participating in the collection, the believers from Macedonia are giving "themselves first to the Lord" (2 Cor. 8:5), not just to the brothers and sisters in Jerusalem (Georgi 1992:71). Moreover, it is the recognition of God's saving actions in Christ that provides the proper motivation for contributing to the collection (2 Cor. 8:9; 8:7).[18] Paul thus sees the collection as thoroughly intertwined with God's grace.

(4) *Voluntary Character*. The next feature is the voluntary character of the material sharing. Although Luke suggests that all things were held in common (Acts 2:44; 4:32), this level of sharing was clearly optional and voluntary, as seen in three ways. First, the positive example of Barnabas selling his field and placing the money at the apostles' disposal (Acts 4:36-37) "would hardly have been memorable if everyone was obliged to do the same" (Dillon 1990:738). Second, in challenging Ananias' deception, Peter reminds him that the sale of one's property and disposal of the resulting funds are voluntary (Acts 5:4; e.g., Johnson 1992:88). Third, subsequent to Acts 5 there are no more descriptions of possessions being held in common. This is hard to explain if Luke thought that a common purse was the only valid way for Christians to dispose of their possessions (Johnson 1981:128-129).

The voluntary character of the sharing is even more evident in Paul.[19] He points out that the churches of Macedonia gave "voluntarily according to their means" (2 Cor. 8:3), and he insists that the Corinthians' own gift be voluntary, "not as an extortion" (2 Cor. 9:5). Paul is unwilling "to command" their giving (2 Cor. 8:8), for that would neither please God nor provide a true expression of loving fellowship. Instead, each must make a free, personal decision as to participation.[20] Such a free act of giving will be honored by God and the saints in Jerusalem (2 Cor. 9:7-14).

(5) *Attitudes.* The voluntary character of sharing points to a concern with inner dispositions and attitudes. Luke considers it important that the new community not only ate together but did so with "glad and generous hearts" (Acts 2:46). Similarly, the problem with Ananias and Sapphira is not that they kept back some proceeds from the sale of their land. The problem is that their hearts (*kardia*, Acts 5:3, 4) were not in the right place. So, too, Paul is less concerned with the external act, with the amount given,[21] than with the "generosity" that produces the gift (e.g., 2 Cor. 8:2; 9:11, 13).[22] It is, after all, the "cheerful giver" who will meet with God's approval (2 Cor. 9:7; 8:12).

(6) *Justice.* Besides being voluntary and flowing from a sense of generosity, material sharing should reflect a sense of justice or fairness. This feature is visible in Luke's claim that goods were distributed according to need (Acts 2:45; 4:35) with the result that there were no needy among them (Acts 4:34). Whether this was literally achieved, it shows Luke's conviction that God's new remnant people evidenced a strong sense of distributive justice. Paul expresses a comparable conviction when he claims that the collection is a matter of "equality" (RSV) or "fair balance" (NRSV) between Gentile and Jewish churches (2 Cor. 8:13, 14). The collection is not intended to force one group into poverty so another group is enriched. Rather, the "abundance" of one group should help meet the needs of the other. Neither group should have "too much" nor "too little."[23]

(7) *Reciprocal.* The concern for just relationships leads us to a final feature: the sharing reflected in these texts is tied to relationships of mutuality and reciprocity. This is implicit throughout the Acts texts. Luke depicts a community that breaks bread together (2:42, 46), enjoys koinonia (2:42), and meets each other's material needs (2:45; 4:34). In so doing Luke presents a people bound together by their shared assent to the gospel who take responsibility for one another (Dillon 1990:734). While recognizing the apostles' authority, the image of mutual accountability emerging here does not permit great inequality or one-sided relationships. We are urged instead to think of friendship, of mutual giving and receiving.

What is implicit in Luke is explicit in Paul. The collection is to reflect and encourage relationships of mutuality and reciprocity. Since the Gentile churches have shared in the spiritual blessings of the Jerusalem church, the former should now help with the latter's material needs (Rom. 15:27). The Jerusalem church will respond in turn by offering intercessory prayers for the Gentile churches and by recognizing that these churches have also been graced by God.[24] The collection is thus part of the mutual recognition, care, and service that Christians owe each other.

In summary, the texts under consideration paint a rich picture of mutual aid. They focus on God-given Christian community. Within that focus, the sharing of material goods has a prominent place. This sharing is a symbol of Christian community, reflecting and encouraging relationships of mutuality and reciprocity. Such sharing is also voluntary, arising from a sense of gratitude and a concern for fairness.

## Mutual Aid According to Rawls

John Rawls' view of mutual aid provides an interesting contrast to the vision offered by Scripture. Rawls (1971:114) defines mutual aid as "the duty of helping another when he is in need or jeopardy, provided that one can do so without excessive risk or loss to oneself." Mutual aid is thus a minimal duty of beneficence: we should help others in need when the cost to ourselves is slight.

This, says Rawls (1971:115), is a "natural duty." It applies to us regardless of our institutional relationships or voluntary commitments. We need not have joined a specific organization or experienced the benefits of belonging to a particular group. The duty of mutual aid obtains "between all as equal moral persons." It is "owed not only to definite individuals, say to those cooperating together in a particular social arrangement, but to persons generally."

Viewing mutual aid as a natural duty fits well with Rawls' (1971:136) notion of the "original position." This position considers what duties, obligations, and principles would be chosen by fully rational agents who "are situated behind a veil of ignorance." That is, it considers what would be chosen by agents who had no knowledge of their particular social, cultural, or economic locations nor of their individual beliefs, abilities, or temperaments.

Rawls rightly argues that people so situated would acknowledge a duty to "mutual aid—a duty to help others in need when the personal cost is not great." Rawls (1971:338) offers two reasons for this. First, since the agents are behind a veil of ignorance and do not know their individual circumstances, they would affirm this duty on the probability that they would at some point need another's assistance (Herman 1984:582-583). Second, and in Rawls' (1971:339) estimation more importantly, they would affirm this duty because of "its pervasive effect on the quality of everyday life." It matters little if, as it turns out, we never need this assistance. What matters is the confidence and trust that come from knowing others are there if we do need them.

This, in short, is Rawls' account of mutual aid. I do not refute his contention that an ethic devised behind a veil of ignorance requires a general commitment to assist others in need. He is undoubtedly correct. However, when viewed from a Christian perspective instead of in relation to the veil of ignorance, Rawls' notion of mutual aid appears inadequate.

The problems with Rawls' account are apparent when we evaluate it in light of the New Testament vision discussed above. For example, mutual aid in the New Testament is clearly in the service of a voluntary association: the church. The sharing is not with just anyone but is specifically directed at fellow believers. There is an obligation to those outside the church as well, but priority is given to the needs of those within the believing community (Gal. 6:2, 10). This is at odds with Rawls' view that the duty of mutual aid is independent of all voluntary associations.

Similarly, Rawls' theory does not grasp the deep human connections and profound unity that the New Testament expects will be fostered by mutual aid. Rawls recognizes that mutual aid frees us from the fear of being totally alone. It teaches us to anticipate help from others if we are in need. This is important, but it can hardly compare to the New Testament images of friendship and koinonia. Where the New Testament sees profound bonds of Christian unity and mutual care, Rawls holds a generic confidence that strangers will aid each other in time of need. Where the New Testament sees people bound together by their mutual faith in what God is doing, Rawls sees no need for such shared pursuits.

Rawls' theory is also unable to account for the New Testament's concern with attitudes and dispositions. The New Testament is interested in one's "heart" and the generosity of spirit that undergirds the giving. In contrast, Rawls' conception is much less concerned with the spirit or disposition that accompanies an act of mutual aid. No doubt Rawls would commend a generous spirit. But such a spirit is unnecessary.

What *is* necessary, according to a Rawlsian strategy, is the recognition that mutual aid is the reasonable choice. From behind the veil of ignorance, choosing against mutual aid is virtually irrational. It is this moral point of view that generates the commitment to mutual aid. Whether that commitment coincides with a spirit of generosity is perhaps important but secondary.[25]

Another problem with the Rawlsian (1971:340-342) account is that it asks both too much and too little of us. It asks too much in that mutual aid, as a natural duty, is mandatory. Not only is it independent of voluntary associations, the giving of assistance is itself required. If someone is in need and I can provide help without great cost or loss to myself, I am duty-bound to offer it.

Of course, because this duty can conflict with other obligations and duties, there is some room for discretion. Not every *prima facie* instance of mutual aid is an actual occasion of moral duty. It is unclear, nevertheless, whether this duty-bound view of mutual aid can be reconciled with the biblical emphasis on voluntary giving. There may be a sense in which Rawls is demanding even more than Scripture.

But Rawls' (1971:117) account also asks too little: we are required to offer aid only if it is easy. If the cost is great, then "we are released from this duty." This does not fit well with Luke's picture of people selling everything so that others will not be in need. Nor does it fit Paul's commending the Macedonians as examples for the Corinthians to follow, for the Macedonians gave out of their poverty and beyond their means (2 Cor. 8:2-3).

Here again we see that the accents and emphases of the Rawlsian view are poorly suited to the biblical account. Where Scripture emphasizes voluntary giving, Rawls stresses duty. Where Scripture spotlights giving beyond means, Rawls releases from duty. Whatever the merits of Rawls' account, it is unable to give proper voice to the biblical examples.

Rawls' account cannot suffice for a Christian vision of mutual aid. His view of mutual aid, free from voluntary associations, fosters only the most general of human connections, inadequately ties the behavior to attitudes and dispositions, and simply stresses the wrong things at the wrong times. Christians seeking to understand the moral significance of mutual aid must look elsewhere.

# MacIntyre's Notion of "Practice"

What is a "practice"? I propose that Alasdair MacIntyre's notion of a "practice" provides a more appropriate understanding of mutual aid.[26] MacIntyre (1984:187) defines a practice as

> any coherent and complex form of socially established cooperative human activity through which goods internal to that form of activity are realized in the course of trying to achieve those standards of excellence which are appropriate to, and partially definitive of, that form of activity, with the result that human powers to achieve excellence, and human conceptions of the ends and goods involved, are systematically extended.

Examples of practices include chess and football, farming, medicine, scientific inquiry, and the work of historians, architects, painters, and musicians. But, says MacIntyre, activities like playing tic-tac-toe and tulip-planting are complex or cooperative enough to count as practices.

MacIntyre's notion of a practice has three central points. First, a practice is a cooperative human activity. Second, a practice concerns the realization of internal goods. Third, the realization of a practice's internal goods entails the extension of "human powers to achieve excellence"— that is, it requires that we acquire various skills and virtues.

The first point is clear: engagement in a practice involves us with others. Practices like medical care or football place us in continual, direct, cooperative contact with others. But even the more solitary practices like farming or scientific research tie us to others. Farming and research must be learned. Entrance into these practices means submitting to the experience and expertise of others farther along in that practice than we are. In addition, advancements in the practice—new farming methods or scientific discovery—are shared with others. And the products of the practices, whether fresh fruit or a new type of plastic, are seldom intended for the individual researcher or farmer alone. Practices are cooperative activities.

The point about internal goods is slightly more difficult. The basic notion of a good or goods concerns the aim, end, purpose, or goal of an activity. To say that something is good "is to say that it is under certain conditions sought or aimed at" (MacIntyre 1966:58). And since there are numerous activities, with numerous aims, there are numerous goods. In short, goods are those things that we aim at in and through our activities.

Given this basic understanding of a good or goods, the next step toward understanding "internal goods" is to look at the contrasting notion of "external goods." An external good is associated with an activity by mere happenstance; there is no intrinsic connection between the two. Suppose, for example, that I give my son candy (which he loves) or money (which he is just beginning to like) for playing baseball with me. Then in addition, suppose that I give him more candy or money whenever he hits the ball well or makes a good catch. This will provide only an external connection between candy or money and baseball. His aim or goal is candy or money, not something intrinsic to baseball. Outside of my stipulating a connection, there is no necessary or inherent relation between baseball and those things.

External goods—things like candy, prestige, status, money, the satisfaction of hunger or thirst or sexual desire—are contingently attached to practices. External goods do not belong to any particular activity or practice, and there "are always alternative ways for achieving such goods" (MacIntyre 1984:188). For example, money is not baseball's or jazz music's internal good. There are countless other ways to make money. I can love playing baseball or jazz without having any interest in making money from them.

By contrast, internal goods cannot be attained except by participating in a specific practice.[27] Internal goods concern a practice's point, purpose, and value as realized by those who participate well in the practice. Consider again my son and his reasons for playing baseball. If he continues to play only because he expects to get candy or money, then he is playing solely for an external good. But if, as he learns the game, he discovers the pleasures and satisfaction of baseball itself, then he has discovered the game's internal goods.

Internal goods are ends sought for their own sake and are difficult to specify without reference to the activity or practice with which they are associated. For example, internal goods are those things that make baseball or jazz or medicine worth pursuing, even if we never gain fame, wealth, or candy in the process. He loves baseball because he knows the drama of a close game well played and the value of the game's leisurely approach to time's passing. She seeks to excel in jazz because she understands the value of swing and the self-expression that can never be captured in words. They work to become good doctors or nurses because they recognize the good of caring for the sick.

These examples provide a window to what MacIntyre means by internal goods and why they are important for understanding social practices. External goods are also goods. We value and seek money, power, or status, but such goods have no internal or necessary relation to social practices like baseball, jazz, or medicine. We understand the good of money or status without needing to know anything about baseball or jazz or medicine. But we do not understand the goods of well-played games, swing, and caring for the sick without reference to their respective practices, nor do we truly understand those practices until we understand that it is their respective internal goods that make them worthwhile.

The third point concerns the acquisition of skills and virtues. MacIntyre rightly notes that the achievement of those goods internal to practices requires the cultivation of various skills and qualities of character. Said differently, skills and virtues are necessary to the realization of a practice's internal goods.

Consider, for example, Jeffrey Stout's (1988:269) discussion of the practice of medicine. He points out that medicine's internal good of caring for the sick

> requires the cultivation of various technical skills. But it also requires the cultivation of qualities that might be called the cardinal virtues of medicine . . . *practical wisdom*, the ability to exercise sound medical judgment and discernment; *justice*, the capacity to give everyone involved in or affected by the practice their due . . . *courage*, the strength of character required to risk danger, embarrassment, alienation from one's cohort, and so on . . . (as by opening a clinic in a high-crime area, admitting error in the treatment of a patient, or testifying against an incompetent col-

league); and *temperance*, a trait that keeps one pursuing goods internal to the practice, undeflected by goods of other kinds (as when a surgeon leaves a dinner early on the night before operating or a nurse spends evenings learning new diagnostic skills instead of out on the town).

What Stout says of medicine is true of all practices: they require the development of technical or physical skills and various qualities of character. If we were only interested in the external goods, then technical skills might suffice. But if we are to honor practices' internal goods, then we need to cultivate the qualities and virtues that will safeguard and promote those goods.

For example, consider what happens to baseball's internal goods if it is deprived of people who exercise the virtues of honesty and patience. Without honesty, we cannot know what it means to play a close game well. Without patience, we cannot play the game at all. Part of baseball's value has to do with its passage through time. Radically accelerating the game to suit the impatient would irrevocably alter the game. Baseball can be a wonderful school for qualities like honesty and patience, but deprived of these virtues, baseball's internal goods become impossible.

Achieving the goods internal to practices requires the cultivation of various virtues. Bereft of those virtues, practices are rendered pointless except that their institutional forms might remain as devices for achieving external goods. The dishonest and impatient may continue to play baseball, but they do so solely for fame or fortune. They deny themselves the game's internal goods and are themselves little more than parasites living off the virtuous performance of others.

In short, practices are cooperative activities aimed at internal goods. Attaining these goods depends on the cultivation of various qualities of character. We are familiar with many such practices and ought not underestimate their moral significance: they focus on those goods that we value for their own sake and are intrinsically tied to the kind of people we will become.

# Mutual Aid as Practice

The biblical vision of mutual aid resembles a practice more than a Rawlsian duty. Indeed, the biblical image of mutual aid includes all three facets of MacIntyre's concept of a practice.

For instance, practices are cooperative activities connecting people by their shared pursuits. This description far better reflects what we find in Acts and Paul than does Rawls' notion of duty, which is independent of voluntary associations. In Acts and Paul, mutual aid has to do with those who have joined the church in response to God's call. It arises out of and is directed toward other members of the church, toward others who share the Christian journey.

Furthermore, the biblical picture is not merely one of individual Christians helping other individual Christians. It also involves cooperative, coordinated sharing in the needs of others. In Acts, people's gifts are offered to the apostles for appropriate distribution (Acts 4:35). Paul not only advises the Corinthians on how to collect the money (1 Cor. 16:1-2), he also sends Titus to assist in its collection (2 Cor. 8:6 ), and he personally oversees its transfer to the Jerusalem church.[28] Thus, while mutual aid undoubtedly includes acts of sharing between individual Christians, it also includes more complex forms of cooperation. This is at least compatible with the notion of a practice.

Mutual aid, again like a practice, is also concerned with internal goods. Mutual aid is not about making money, gaining fame, or satisfying certain sensual desires. Instead, mutual aid aims at internal goods such as (1) the type of worship expressed through service to others, and (2) the formation and maintenance of Christian community.

The former good—worship—is shared with the closely related practice of charity. Acts of mutual aid, like those of charity, can be acts of worship and gratitude. Indeed, Luke sees mutual aid as a central expression of one's response to the gospel and links it to other forms of worship like communion and praise (Acts 2:44-47).

For Paul too, mutual aid is the appropriate response to having gained a share in God's blessings.[29] It is a way of giving oneself to God (2 Cor. 8:5), and it causes the recipients also to thank God (2 Cor. 9:12). Such worship is an internal good. It is valuable in its own right and attainable only through the practice of mutual aid or practices of that type (like charity).

The latter good—the formation and maintenance of Christian community—distinguishes mutual aid from charity. The centrality of Christian community was highlighted in our discussion of the biblical texts, where the sharing of material goods is a symbol of Christian community, intended to encourage relationships of mutuality and reciprocity. This is different from charity. Charity is directed to all without anticipation of reciprocity or even unity of spirit. Charity is not particularly concerned with Christian community.

In contrast, mutual aid not only arises from Christian community, it is intended both to symbolize and to engender genuine bonds of Christian unity. This is why Luke uses the sharing of goods to recall the ideal of friendship and why Paul was eager for the Jerusalem saints to accept the gift in a proper spirit.

Christian community is a good we value for its own sake without seeking to use it as a means to another end. In addition, it is hard to imagine how we would attain or maintain such community without mutual aid. It is not a good readily attainable by another means. The formation and maintenance of Christian community is, in other words, an internal good proper to mutual aid.

It must be admitted, however, that Christian community cannot be reduced to mutual aid. Although mutual aid is essential, full-fledged community also involves things like singing hymns together, listening to each other's stories, and putting up with each other's idiosyncrasies. Thus the good internal to mutual aid is more properly seen as that aspect of Christian community symbolized and engendered by reciprocal sharing, especially material sharing, among Christians.

Mutual aid is also like a practice in that it requires the cultivation of virtue. In discussing the biblical texts, we saw that material sharing should be a voluntary expression of love, flowing from a generous heart and a sense of justice or fairness. A scheme like Rawls' cannot account for this concern with attitudes and dispositions, but this concern makes sense from the perspective of a practice: mutual aid cannot attain its internal goods of worship and community without qualities like generosity and justice. A gift grudgingly offered or unconcerned with inequality can neither be an act of worship nor reinforce community. Such "gifts" can only undermine worship and community, causing resentment and reinforcing stereotypes.

These are not the only virtues essential to mutual aid. For example, mutual aid requires humility and honesty. These virtues enable candid evaluation of our various circumstances and prevent misuse of power or funds. Also important is the virtue of imagination. The need for this virtue is seen when Paul suggests that Gentile Christians owe Jewish Christians material assistance since the former received spiritual gifts from the latter. Paul suggests that their nonmaterial gifts may be more significant than our material ones. It takes imagination to see what others offer in exchange for our material assistance.

Imagination is also important in considering how my life might need to change if I am to more fully share with my brothers or sisters in need. Trust is likewise important: trust that God will honor the risk I take in sharing; trust in those who administer the larger projects of aid; trust that those who receive my assistance are not merely taking advantage; trust that those who offer me assistance are not merely exploiting.

There may be additional virtues necessary to mutual aid, but understanding it as a practice seems well-suited to the New Testament examples. Following those examples, I have argued that mutual aid is a cooperative activity aimed at the internal goods of Christian community and worship through service. Gaining these goods depends on the cultivation of the virtues of generosity, justice, honesty, humility, imagination, and trust. This argument makes better sense of the New Testament examples than does a duty-oriented approach like Rawls'. It also suggests why mutual aid is so important: our experience of Christian community and its concurrent virtues may well depend on our participation in authentic forms of mutual aid.

# Practical Implications

I conclude by briefly comparing the notion of mutual aid as a practice with the activities of MDS and MMA. This illustrates how mutual aid understood as a practice can be a helpful term for assessing contemporary activities. While brief, the following comments illustrate the evaluative potential of the concept.

At first blush the activities of MDS and MMA appear to be obvious candidates for mutual aid. On second thought MDS does not count as mutual aid. MDS's activities are not specifically directed toward members of the church, nor is there expectation of reciprocity. MDS does not enter disaster situations expecting that those helped will reciprocate. There is, in other words, an insufficient focus on Christian community for MDS to count as mutual aid. This is certainly not to disparage what MDS does. It is, instead, a reminder that MDS is more a reflection of charity, love of neighbor, or mission than a reflection of mutual aid.

The issue is more complicated when it comes to MMA, which provides Anabaptist-related church members with health insurance and administers a sharing program that aids needy individuals and congregations. Surely these are instances of mutual aid. I want to propose, however, that neither insurance nor the sharing program fits the definition of mutual aid developed in this chapter.

The central problem with health insurance is underwriting. To the extent that health insurance supports community, it does so by defining that community in terms of health status and income (Yoder 1992:60). The combination of risk management and rising premiums functions to exclude and/or to devalue those with existing health risks or lower incomes. Clearly this does not serve the good of Christian community.

Moreover, some of MMA's marketing strategies focus more on customers' self-interests than on forming community. Instead of promoting insurance as a way of spreading risk across the entire church, MMA sometimes appeals almost exclusively to desires for self-protection and good value. That is, the insurance policies are sold on the basis that they are competitively priced and will protect personal assets (Yoder 1992:63). Such strategies might be good marketing, but they are less than mutual aid: they promote neither Christian community nor the virtues of generosity and justice.

Obviously MMA is in a difficult position. Although it aims to serve the church, it also must function as a business. Financial viability and marketability are real concerns which can cause tension with MMA's churchly mission.

This tension is not unique to MMA. Most practices have corresponding institutions that support the practice. Whether baseball, football, medicine, or music, the practice is sustained by various institutions. Music is supported by the recording industry and night clubs; medicine is supported by hospitals and medical schools; football is supported by college athletics and the NFL, etc.

The difficulty is that most institutions focus on external goods like money, power, and status. While football, medicine, and music are practices, night clubs, hospitals, and the NFL are businesses necessarily preoccupied with money. The result is that the very institutions that support practices also can threaten them. The external goods with which the institutions are concerned "can compete with and even engulf goods internal to the practice."30 Thus, for example, major league baseball's focus on money and status now threatens to ruin the practice of baseball. It is therefore unsurprising that MMA sometimes adopts policies like underwriting that undermine the very practice it is meant to support. Practices and their supporting institutions are often in tension due to the institutions' focus on external goods.[31]

This does not mean that we must give in. It does not mean that we must allow the external goods to overwhelm the practice. The focus on external goods can be kept in check. Institutions are potential, but not necessary, corruptors of practices (McClendon 1986:176-184).

Consider, for example, that MMA could develop insurance or insurance-like plans in keeping with mutual aid. Plans that varied premiums according to family income, spread risk across the entire community, accepted members with preexisting conditions, and collected premiums only after the claims were incurred might be more consistent with true mutual aid. Instead of emphasizing individual self-protection and competitive premiums, such plans would emphasize sharing, accountability, generosity, and justice.

The initial market for such plans might be small. But unless our churches have entirely lost sight of the goods internal to mutual aid, there is already some market for such products. Moreover, as Scot Yoder (1992:63) notes,

> We should not underestimate the power of advertisement to shape the marketplace. Insurance can be promoted as a means for expressing social concern—a way of helping others as well as protecting yourself.

Publicity could focus on the good of Christian community, along with the virtues of generosity and justice. Plans could be marketed as expressions of solidarity with our brothers and sisters in Christ. Church members could be encouraged to subscribe to MMA insurance not because it is cheaper but because it provides a powerful symbol of Christian unity.

These are mere proposals, of course. And I readily admit I do not know all their implications or the difficulties of implementing them. I do want to suggest, however, that most of MMA's current insurance products are not truly mutual aid, and that we need alternatives if MMA is to help us participate in purer forms of mutual aid and thus realize the good of Christian community and its concurrent virtues.

If such alternatives are financially or legally unworkable, then perhaps it is time to ask about the real justifications for MMA's role as an insurance provider. In response to an earlier draft of this essay, Donald B. Kraybill suggested that "there may be a host of compelling reasons from a sociological perspective as to why Mennonites should operate their own health insurance programs." Maybe it is time to spell out those reasons. And maybe it is time to drop the "mutual aid" label from the current insurance products. Dropping this label would be an honest acknowledgment that, whatever their merits, the current insurance products are not mutual aid.

While most forms of health insurance do not qualify as mutual aid, the status of MMA's sharing program is less certain. This program, directed to meeting needs, is unencumbered by such features as risk management. And because it usually involves matching funds from local congregations, it includes a significant level of reciprocity and accountability. I wonder, nevertheless, if this is true mutual aid. Most of the program's money comes from MMA's status as a fraternal benefit association. This status allows MMA to provide members with certain benefits in lieu of paying certain corporate taxes. This is a good thing, but it means that there are few direct individual contributions to the fund.

Therein lies the difficulty. How does the program contribute to a sense of Christian community or encourage generosity, justice, and imagination without more direct, intentional, or purposeful participation by individual members? The pool of money from which this program draws does not depend on my generosity or my desire for Christian unity. All it depends on is my participation in MMA's other programs, mainly its insurance programs. Considering that those other programs do not fully embody the principles of mutual aid, is this enough?

Since the sharing program does not require the conscious involvement of most members, it seems inappropriate to regard it as a full embodiment of mutual aid. However, a rigorous campaign to solicit additional funds expressly to allow the sharing program to help local congregations meet member needs would help make it mutual aid. Such a program would be a powerful symbol of Christian camaraderie, would encourage virtues like generosity and justice, and would thus enable us to attain more fully the good of Christian community.

## Notes

1. Fretz (1939a:31, 37-38, 44, 54; 1939b:194-195, 198-208); Klassen (1963:93); Bender and Fretz (1957); Durnbaugh (1988); Peachey (1990).

2. I suspect that this expansive use of mutual aid stems in part from a fear of being viewed as selfish or sectarian. For example, if the discussion is limited to forms of assistance within a specific group (as I will suggest it should be), it might appear that the group has withdrawn from or is unconcerned with those outside the group. To avoid this appearance, articles on mutual aid mention assistance or charity given to those outside the group (e.g., Fretz 1939a:33; Klassen 1963:93; Durnbaugh 1988:89, 95-96). While this might allay fears of selfishness or sectarianism, it also clouds the meaning of mutual aid. Mutual aid ends up including forms of behavior that have no mutual or reciprocal element.

3. The references to Acts are found in 2:37-47 and 4:32-5:11, and Paul's discussion appears in Rom. 15:25-28, 31; 1 Cor. 16:1-4; and 2 Cor. 8–9.

4. A perusal of Durnbaugh (1974) and Hernley (1970) shows that dozens of New Testament texts have been used by Anabaptists and Mennonites to substantiate the call to "mutual aid." There is not enough space here to fairly treat even a representative sample of those texts. It is, moreover, unclear whether the numerous biblical texts cited in support of mutual aid actually share a common theme or vision. I therefore restrict my discussion to the two sets of texts that I believe virtually everyone will recognize as instances of mutual aid: Luke's vision of the new community sharing everything and Paul's collection for the Jerusalem church.

5. This is not to advocate conflation. Luke and Paul advance somewhat different views of the church, and they talk about quite different kinds of actions—communalism versus charitable collection. Nevertheless, there are important similarities in the visions of mutual aid that undergird these disparate texts. It is this shared vision that I will try to highlight.

6. Johnson (1992:56-63); Faw (1993:53-54).

7. Also see: Johnson (1981:128; 1992:58-59, 62, 86, 91); Dillon (1990:738).

8. Rom. 15:26, 27; 2 Cor. 8:4; 9:13.

9. Nickle (1966:105-106); Cranfield (1979:772-774). If Paul's agreement to "remember the poor" in Gal. 2:10 is a reference to the collection for the Jerusalem

church, then the collection project was a direct outgrowth of the "fellowship" (Gal. 2:9) achieved between Paul and Barnabas and the Jerusalem "pillars" of James, Cephas, and John (Nickle 1966:106; Georgi 1992:38-42).

10. Cranfield (1979:770); Fitzmyer (1990:867).

11. The texts under consideration do not allow us to focus exclusively on material goods. Luke's picture of early community life also includes the activities of teaching, eating together, worshiping God, and offering prayers (Acts 2:42, 45-46). Likewise, Paul's view of Christian fellowship includes mutual love, spiritual gifts, thanksgiving, and intercessory prayer (2 Cor. 8:7-8; 9:12, 14).

12. A parallel effect is achieved when Luke says that "there was not a needy person among them" (Acts 4:34). This is a reference to Deut. 15:4, which promises that there will be no more needy people in the land once the laws of almsgiving are perfectly kept (Johnson 1981:128). By alluding to Deut. 15:4, Luke suggests that the early church realized the best Jewish ideals about life together (Johnson 1992:91).

13. Rom. 15:26, 27; 2 Cor. 8:4; 9:13. A direct connection between fellowship and economic sharing is elsewhere evident in Paul's writings, especially Gal. 2:9-10 and Phil. 4:15. Murphy-O'Connor (1990a:814) also sees this connection in Paul's suggestion that the collection be taken on the first day of the week: "The fellowship expressed in the liturgical assembly was to serve as a reminder to be generous to others."

14. E.g., Johnson (1981:112); Rom. 15:27, 31b; 2 Cor. 8:19; 9:13-14.

15. Acts 2:39; Johnson (1992:58); Dillon (1990:734).

16. The passive phrase in 2:40 has the force of "let yourselves be saved" (Faw 1993:47; Johnson 1992:58), not the NRSV's "save yourselves." 2:47 says that it is "the Lord" who adds to the number being saved.

17. 1 Cor. 16:3; 2 Cor. 8:4, 6, 7, 9, 19; 9:8, 14.

18. Nickle (1966:110); Georgi (1992:83).

19. E.g., Nickle (1966:125-127); Cranfield (1979:771, 773); Murphy-O'Connor (1990b:824-825); Georgi (1992:54-55).

20. 2 Cor. 9:7; Rom. 15:26-27; 1 Cor. 16:2.

21. 1 Cor. 16:2; 2 Cor. 8:3, 11-12.

22. For example, the churches of Macedonia were probably too poor to contribute a large sum, yet Paul describes their gift as having "overflowed in a wealth of generosity" Nickle (1966:104 n. 45, 105, 126).

23. 2 Cor. 8:15; Exod. 16:18. Paul here appeals to Israel's experience of gathering manna in the desert. This has a double significance. First, Paul's choice of text, comparing the collection to God's gift of manna, reflects his conviction that the collection is itself an act of God's gracious providing for God's people. Second, Paul appeals to a text in which equality was achieved because God gave according to need. Thus, Paul's citation of Exod. 16:18 underlines both the grace-centered and justice-oriented dimensions of the collection.

24. 2 Cor. 9:14; Murphy-O'Connor (1990b:825); Rom. 15:31b.

25. Two further comments are in order. First, Rawls is concerned with "inner" matters like attitudes, desires, and dispositions. He says, for example, that the morally mature person will have developed a sense or sentiment of justice.

Rawls' (1971:478) argument for justice or mutual aid does not, however, depend on moral maturity or the sentiment of justice. Moreover, the sentiment of justice is itself defined in profoundly rational terms:

[T]he sentiment of justice is not a different desire from that to act on principles that rational individuals would consent to in an initial situation which gives everyone equal representation as a moral person. Nor is it different from wanting to act in accordance with principles that express men's nature as free and equal rational beings.

Second, generosity is probably a sentiment that belongs to the realm of supererogation. If so, it belongs to a morality that goes "well beyond our natural duties and obligations" and is "not . . . for ordinary persons" (Rawls 1971:478-479; 117).

26. The following discussion depends heavily on MacIntyre (1984:187-203; 1992:6-8) and Stout (1988:266-276). Also see McClendon (1986:162, 166-173). Robert Bellah's "practices of commitment" is roughly equivalent (1985:154, 157, 251-252, 335). Allen Verhey and Stanley Hauerwas use MacIntyre's notion of "practices" to analyze Christian prayer (Verhey 1992), the reading of Scripture (Verhey 1992; 1995), and the profession of medicine (Hauerwas 1986:39-62; 1994:158-163; Verhey 1992).

27. Some goods may be shared by closely related or similar practices. For example, some goods internal to chess may be shared with games that involve a similar level of sophisticated strategy, and some goods internal to football may be shared with other team sports.

28. Rom. 15:25-28; 1 Cor. 16:3-4.

29. Rom. 15:27; 2 Cor. 8:1; 8:9.

30. Stout (1988:274); cf. MacIntyre (1984:194).

31. McClendon (1986:173) is skeptical of too strong a distinction between practices and their institutions. He suggests that law or custom has fixed the social structure of some practices. Those structures should therefore be identified as the practices—e.g., hospital operation is both social structure and practice. McClendon (1986:173-176) is nevertheless keenly aware that such socially located practices can become severely corrupted and corrupting. The tension between external and internal goods thus remains, even as the institution versus practice distinction is downplayed.

# References

Achtemeier, Paul
    1985    *Romans*. Interpretation: A Bible Commentary for Teaching and Preaching. Atlanta: John Knox Press.

Bellah, Robert N., R. Madsen, W. M. Sullivan, A. Swidler and S. M. Tipton
    1985    *Habits of the Heart*. Berkeley and Los Angeles: University of California Press.

Bender, H. S., and J. Winfield Fretz
    1957    "Mutual Aid." *The Mennonite Encyclopedia*, vol. 3. Scottdale, Pa.: Herald Press.

Childress, James F.
    1986    "Mutual Aid." *The Westminster Dictionary of Christian Ethics*. Philadelphia: Westminster.

Cranfield, C.E.B.
    1979    *The Epistle to the Romans*, vol. 2, The International Critical Commentary. Edinburgh: T. & T. Clark.

Dillon, Richard J.
    1990    "Acts of the Apostles." In *The New Jerome Biblical Commentary*, ed. Raymond E. Brown, J. A. Fitzmyer, and R. E. Murphy. Englewood: Prentice-Hall.

Durnbaugh, Donald F.
    1974    *Every Need Supplied: Mutual Aid and Christian Community in the Free Churches, 1525-1675.* Philadelphia: Temple University Press.

    1988    "Mutual Aid in Ministry to God's World." *Brethren Life and Thought* 33 (Spring): 87-97.

Faw, Chalmer E.
    1993    *Acts.* Believers Church Bible Commentary. Scottdale, Pa. & Waterloo, Ont.: Herald Press.

Fitzmyer, Joseph A.
    1990    "The Letter to the Romans." In *The New Jerome Biblical Commentary*, ed. Raymond E. Brown, J. A. Fitzmyer, and R. E. Murphy. Englewood: Prentice-Hall.

Fretz, J. Winfield
    1939a    "Mutual Aid among Mennonites, I." *Mennonite Quarterly Review* 13:28-58.

    1939b    "Mutual Aid among Mennonites, II." *Mennonite Quarterly Review* 13:187-209.

Georgi, Dieter
    1992    *Remembering the Poor: The History of Paul's Collection for Jerusalem.* Nashville: Abingdon Press.

Hauerwas, Stanley
    1986    *Suffering Presence: Theological Reflections on Medicine, the Mentally Handicapped, and the Church.* Notre Dame: University of Notre Dame Press.

    1994    *Dispatches from the Front: Theological Engagements with the Secular.* Durham and London: Duke University Press.

Herman, Barbara
    1984    "Mutual Aid and Respect for Persons." *Ethics* 94 (July): 577-602.

Hernley, H. Ralph, ed.
    1970    *The Compassionate Community.* Scottdale, Pa.: Association of Mennonite Aid Societies.

Johnson, Luke Timothy
    1981    *Sharing Possessions: Mandate and Symbol of Faith.* Philadelphia: Fortress Press.

    1992    *The Acts of the Apostles.* Collegeville: Michael Glazier.

Klassen, Peter James
   1963   "Mutual Aid among the Anabaptists: Doctrine and Practice." *Mennonite Quarterly Review* 37:78-95.

MacIntyre, Alasdair
   1966   *A Short History of Ethics.* New York: Macmillan Publishing.

   1984   *After Virtue.* 2nd Edition. Notre Dame: University of Notre Dame Press.

   1992   "Plain Persons and Moral Philosophy: Rules, Virtues and Goods." *American Catholic Philosophical Quarterly* 66:4-19.

McClendon, James Wm., Jr.
   1986   *Systematic Theology: Ethics.* Nashville: Abingdon Press.

Metzger, Bruce M.
   1975   *A Textual Commentary on the Greek New Testament.* London and New York: United Bible Societies.

Murphy-O'Connor, Jerome
   1990a  "The First Letter to the Corinthians." In *The New Jerome Biblical Commentary,* ed. Raymond E. Brown, J. A. Fitzmyer, and R. E. Murphy. Englewood: Prentice-Hall.

   1990b  "The Second Letter to the Corinthians." In *The New Jerome Biblical Commentary,* ed. Raymond E. Brown, J. A. Fitzmyer, and R. E. Murphy. Englewood: Prentice-Hall.

Nickle, Keith F.
   1966   *The Collection: A Study in Paul's Strategy.* London: SCM Press.

Peachey, Loren
   1990   "Mutual Aid." *The Mennonite Encyclopedia,* vol. 5. Scottdale, Pa.: Herald Press.

Rawls, John
   1971   *A Theory of Justice.* Cambridge, Mass.: The Belknap Press of Harvard University Press.

Stout, Jeffrey
   1988   *Ethics After Babel: The Languages of Morals and Their Discontents.* Boston: Beacon Press.

Verhey, Allen D.
   1992   *The Practices of Piety and the Practice of Medicine: Prayer, Scripture, and Medical Ethics.* Grand Rapids: The Stob Lectures of Calvin College and Seminary.

   1995   "The Holy Bible and Sanctified Sexuality: An Evangelical Approach to Scripture and Sexual Ethics." *Interpretation* 49 (January 1995): 31-45.

Willimon, William H.
   1988   *Acts.* Interpretation: A Bible Commentary for Teaching and Preaching. Atlanta: John Knox Press.

Yoder, Scot D.
  1992    "Transplants, Justice, and Health Care Reform: What Can Health In-
          surers Contribute?" *Second Opinion* 18 (July): 49-67.

4

# Mutual Aid:
# Harbinger of the Kingdom?

Cornelius A. Buller

How is mutual aid tied to theological understandings? Cornelius A. Buller
argues that the practice of mutual aid reflects the very nature and image of
God. Human relationships are intended by God to be intimately and lovingly
interdependent. Mutual aid in Buller's view is both an aid and a witness to the
perfection of love in God's kingdom. The concrete enactment of love in the
practice of mutual aid makes a special contribution to contemporary life as
material goods become tools for realizing God's kingdom on earth.

## The Theological Context

The Bible offers a number of images that envision the fulfillment of
creation—a kingdom of lamb and lion in peaceful coexistence with
each person under her or his own fig tree, everyone's needs equally provided for, and no gender or racial tensions. All these images symbolize a
future kingdom. Although this is an eschatological hope, we are called to
live today as children of the King. We are called to be a community defined by the goal of shalom in the presence of God (Matties 1990:147-153).

Nonetheless, in the course of our lives we experience failures of the
mutuality that defines God's kingdom. Are women treated equally? Do
all persons have equal opportunities for education? Is racism prevalent?
Clearly we have goals unachieved and others unrecognized. It is possi-

ble to despair rather than celebrate. The following story of mutual aid shows the possibility of acting in accord with the kingdom of God.

In her examination of mutual aid among the Mennonites who emigrated from Russia to Manitoba in the 1870s, Hilda Anne Hildebrand (1989:139ff.) tells of the transfer of the Bergthal Waisenamt to Canada. The Waisenamt, an institution which served the Russian Mennonite communities, was intended to provide for the just division of estates and to safeguard the rights of widows and orphans unable to support themselves. The people of Bergthal, a daughter colony of Chortitza in European Russia, decided to move to Manitoba.

However, the Waisenamt had more liabilities than assets, and the colony included a number of poor families and persons. The Bergthal group decided that all who could would contribute toward eliminating the debt and meeting the travel expenses of those who could not afford the journey. Some donated up to one quarter of their assets. Thus the entire Bergthal community was able to make the trip to Canada and resettle in Manitoba.

Such acts of mutual aid provide signs of the spiritual mutuality toward which God calls us (Augsburger 1968:410). Those who are mature in faith and rich in worldly goods can use such riches to nurture faith, hope, and love in their weaker and poorer companions. And those rich in worldly goods but poor in faith may grow in faith and love through sharing their goods with those in need (Yordy 1962:145). In this way those who have little will lack nothing, as Paul states in 2 Corinthians 8:15.[1]

The following theological analysis of mutual aid is based on various Mennonite and Anabaptist positions as well as those of other thinkers, especially Wolfhart Pannenberg. The approach is rooted in faith that God is creator and redeemer of all reality and is working in history toward creation's eschatological goal, which is named and defined by Jesus and the apostles as the kingdom of God.

The title of this chapter raises the question of the relationship of mutual aid to the kingdom of God. I believe the answer lies in a theological conception of human nature that links creation with the expectation of an eschatological fulfillment. This connection has implications for our understanding of both the beginning and the end of creation as well as for our conception of human nature. Interdependence, mutuality, mutual love, community, and the inescapably social character of existence are all part of human nature and essential aspects of mutual aid.

J. Winfield Fretz (1958:5) states that "God has implanted the principle of mutual aid into the very nature of creation." Grant Stoltzfus

(1959:39) thinks of fellowship as the "oxygen of existence" and goes on to say that if we do not have it we perish. Several aspects of human existence correspond to the idea of an eternal hope and kingdom and its inherently social and moral character.

Generally accepted anthropological data point toward both the idea of mutuality and an eternal kingdom of God. The ideas of mutual aid, the image of God, and the kingdom of God are connected. Another way of saying this would be that God's goal in redemption is not completely strange to humans. It is the object of our inmost longing. It is that for which we were created and what we sometimes distort and destroy. To paraphrase Augustine's famous statement, we can say, Our hearts are restless until they together, in an inclusive community of mutual love, find their rest in Thee.[2]

## The Image of God: Interdependent Love

The Bible teaches that humans are created in the image of God (Gen. 1:27). How that image continues to be part of human existence in the context of sin has long been debated. Pannenberg (1985:74ff.) suggests that the image of God be thought of as the goal of perfect communion with God and with each other.[3] The aim of existence, rather than the current nature of the self, is what gives creaturely life its form and character.

This view offers a relational conception of the image of God and draws especially on the interrelationship of the eternal Father, Son, and Holy Spirit,[4] which finds historical expression in the relationship of Jesus to God. Jesus is the self-effacing and eternal Son of God, yet he is also one of us—a creature. By the Holy Spirit, Jesus is a son to God and an elder brother to creatures. In Jesus the human creature is made perfect and unsurpassable through the action of the Holy Spirit. The goal of God in creating a world is that creatures come to full participation in this inner-Trinitarian communion. This is the image of God to which creatures are created and called.

According to Janzen (1993:88, 177ff.) this intimate familial expression of divine and creaturely relationships underlies both the Christian and Jewish conceptions of reality.[5] In these images of the triune God, intimate familial and self-effacing love are the concrete expressions of the heart of God. Creation aims to achieve this relationship among creatures and between creatures and the Creator (John 17:26).

These relationships are not independent of each other. Interdependence is rooted in the relationship of all creatures to the Creator.[6] Thus the social characteristic of human existence is a reflection of the relational character of the image of God (Studer 1965:230). As argued below, it also expresses the open and needy character of human existence.

The image of God is the ultimate and controlling goal of creation—a goal that is and will be achieved in the kingdom of God (Hauerwas 1983:28ff.). Humans are created, in other words, to express the perfect and mutual love that the persons of the Trinity have for each other and all creatures (see Kauffman 1966:360ff.). We are to love God with heart, soul, mind, and strength and our neighbors as ourselves (Mark 12:29-31). The love of the Father, Son, and Holy Spirit for each other and together for the world is determinative for conceiving the character, destiny, and meaning of human life. This understanding of the image of God points explicitly to the creaturely enactment of mutual love as the final creative aim of God.

## The Self and the World: Needy and Needed

Humans are born incomplete.[7] Human infants need to learn appropriate responses to their environment. Their needs correspond with our freedom from instincts. It is a freedom that makes us open to our world.[8] It is, therefore, both possible and necessary for us to learn complex forms of interaction, even to manipulate the environment. Yet incompleteness makes human infants far more dependent than creatures born with ready responses to the world. Openness to the world and interdependence with other creatures fit together.

We are creatures who need others to succeed in life (Stoltzfus 1959:39). The converse also holds: others need us to live as well. Love recognizes the need of others and finds joy and fulfillment in helping them to a fullness of life. Each person depends on family, neighbors, friends, and teachers in this learning process. We are ensconced in a social world that bestows on us a cultural heritage.[9]

In the process of learning our culture, we also acquire freedom—freedom for meaningful action, freedom to participate in the interwoven social fabric. Each person internalizes a cultural heritage and sees its faults and strengths. Each person also possesses the potential to become an agent in the process of adapting to and remaking a cultural tradition. To be human is to participate in the process of history. Our human vocation is to adapt, renew, and affirm our cultural tradition.[10]

This dimension of human freedom can serve the community of creatures. Imagine a process of ever-widening circles of influence. The primary sphere of influence is family, friends, and backyard, but the impact of deeds and words moves quickly beyond this inner circle to the wider community of village, city, state, nation, and world.[11]

We are created for relationships with the whole of the created world and with the Creator. Our role in these relationships is a special one of mediating between creature and Creator. In the world of creatures, humans are the regents of God. We bring to most conscious and perfect fulfillment the creation's praises of its Maker and Redeemer. The world of creatures is intended by God to be a community of mutual love, freedom, praise, and joy. The role of humans, as representatives of God, is to facilitate these relationships.[12]

This interdependence includes the whole world. Our existence is one strand in an ecosphere that includes all life on this planet. The beauty and order of life on the earth depend on human agency. However, too often we use the nonhuman world for material gain rather than with respect. The ecological crisis is a consequence of this selfishness. Ecological abuse represents a special task in renewing the mutuality of our existence (Studer 1965:231ff.).

# Sin: Turning to the Self

Particularly in the first eleven chapters, the book of Genesis moves beyond the goodness of creation to show that the image of God does not define human existence. Sin quickly dominates human life. A great temptation faced by individuals, families, special interest groups, and nations is to aggrandize self-interests at the expense of others.[13]

We fail to love others. Both individually and collectively we turn from love and interdependent responsibility to selfishness. The life of sin is fundamentally selfish (Welker 1994:282ff.). Expressions of this self-centered existence include undue self-assertion, domination of others, individualism, and retreat from responsibility and action.

In a theological context, self-centeredness needs to be seen as a fundamental (even subconscious) refusal to acknowledge God as God. Humans possess the freedom to turn from God and from God's rule. Such sinfulness introduces oppositions and conflicts between creatures. The refusal of humans to acknowledge God is the root of evil (Rom. 1:21). In this refusal is the corollary refusal to acknowledge the claim of other creatures on our lives. Selfish love is able to love neither God nor neighbor.

Human sin frustrates the realization of the image of God, for in denying God, creatures become subject to death. The limited independence of personal existence is rooted in creaturely interdependence and ultimately in dependence on God. Sin is the failure to acknowledge God as God and oneself as a dependent creature. This failure brings the death of the self (Rom. 1:28; 2:12) and the destruction of community.[14] In other words, apart from the divine source of its life the creature must live in isolation and fear and finally come to a lonely end.

Sin is the denial of mutuality and the aggrandizement of the self. The reality of sin reinforces the idea that the image of God is not a possession but a goal toward which we are being created. Sin also reinforces the argument that our recreation in the image of God is fundamentally social. To restore fully the image of God, made possible by and disclosed in Jesus and (imperfectly) in the church, continues to be the goal of God in creation and recreation.

## Openness to God: Life's Eschatological Goal

Although sin distorts all relationships, an individual can never be so self-centered as to be completely independent of God and the world. We are social beings; our very survival depends on learning and receiving from others. No one is able to survive apart from the life-giving resources of the world and God.

But our imaginations always look beyond our current accomplishments and horizons. Forever seeking a horizon that encompasses all reality and makes existence meaningful, we are driven by needs beyond ourselves and our environments to the infinite. Utopian visions, political ideologies, and religious quests are examples of this striving for love, harmony, and meaning.[15]

Mortal creatures look for a future beyond the grasp of death. This search unfolds because we know that sin and death frustrate and ultimately annihilate human achievements of mutuality, love, and meaning. Even societies of mutual benefit and aid are unable to meet these deepest of human needs.

The philosopher Martin Heidegger argues that a moment of wholeness is necessary when all of life's events may be seen in their place, each in relation to all others and also to the whole (Pannenberg 1988:61-65). Heidegger suggests that the final moments before death offer this vantage point.

However, we know death as the dissolution and final destruction of this present existence, not as the ultimate moment to envision personal wholeness. In itself, death offers no sense of unity. Heidegger suggests there is no place this side of death from which everything can be structured and seen in its completeness. And if the last moments of existence offer no wholeness, then we must look for meaning beyond death.

The ideas of God and the kingdom of God intersect at the point of this restless need. The kingdom of God comes to us as the goal of existence and accommodates the need of each creature in the context of seeking the good of the whole creation (Pannenberg 1988:49). Wholeness is found in the resurrection of Jesus and in the hope of a kingdom of love, peace, and justice in which he is the preeminent witness and harbinger.

This hope is found in the One, the God of Israel, who is the author of the resurrection and the promise of the kingdom. What is implicit in this description, both of human existence and of the kingdom of God, is our orientation reaching beyond ourselves and human achievements, toward an eschatologically and socially complete wholeness. This is a future beyond history that moves and inspires in us faith, hope, and love.

In disagreement with the atheist position of his friend Sigmund Freud, the pastor Oskar Pfister (1993:562) argued that humans are fundamentally religious and oriented toward God:

> The goal and supreme good of all striving and longing do not lie in personal satisfaction, but in the kingdom of heaven, i.e. in the dominion of love, truth, and justice within the individual as in the universal community.

The point of Pfister's argument is that the greatest need of humans is to be transformed by love in its dual character—love of God and love of neighbor. The power of love is to draw individuals into the life of the kingdom of heaven, which addresses the questions of justice and truth in creaturely relations. The true good of individual existence is seen in its interdependent and eschatological character. It includes all created life in the universal community of God's creatures. Thus the character of all creaturely interaction is given form and purpose as it is embodied in the rule of God's eschatological love.

## Mutual Love: The Theological Roots

The love of the Father and Son for each other reaches out to redeem the dying creatures of God. Redemption seeks true communion of creatures with God and with one another (Klassen 1961:92). Jesus teaches us that God is love, holy, just, and our heavenly parent. He announces that God wishes us to be part of the divine family.[16] Jesus modeled the relationship of a child to the eternal Father with his cry of "Abba" and with his humble obedience to the will of God. He submitted himself to the will of God even to death on a cross. Raising him from the dead, God confirmed the divine sonship of Jesus.

God aims to create a new community in which every person, regardless of gender or race, is a full and equal participant (Gal. 3:28). This community is defined by the love of God and Jesus for each other and for the creation of God (John 13:34ff.; 14:21, 23, 31).

Consider Jesus' story of the rich man whose invited guests refused to attend his banquet. Outcasts and the marginalized of society were called to the table. During the course of his ministry, Jesus sat at the table with a motley assortment of such persons. In both his teaching and living, Jesus reveals the love of a Father who is gracious; he seeks the lost, offers true freedom, and opposes the tyrannies of sin created by religious and economic elites.[17]

We recognize this love in the willingness of Jesus to be scourged, beaten, and crucified for those who had no love for him (Rom. 5:8). We see it in the love that raised Jesus from death. We also view it in the image of Jesus washing the disciples' feet.

Through Jesus the love of God calls us to a new kind of life. To respond is to be drawn into God's holy love for the creation and for each creature. It is to be drawn into the self-forgetful love of Jesus (Phil. 2:1-11). The ecstatic joy of this God-centered love motivates the acts of mutual aid that abundantly supply the needs of others, for it trusts absolutely in God.[18]

This love overcomes all fears, including the fears that prevent us from giving and receiving concrete expressions of love. It seeks not direct returns but Christian growth and the maturity of the saints (Erb *et al.* 1978:5-6). Love seeks the ultimate gratification of our restless hearts through unity with Christ and in creaturely unity.

This outcome results from lives overcome by the power of God's Spirit. From Pentecost forward the Holy Spirit has energized the Christian community as the power of the coming kingdom of God. The Spirit, in the sense of "down payment" (2 Cor. 1:12ff.), "firstfruits" (Rom. 8:23), and "seal" (2 Cor. 1:21ff.; Eph. 1:13), also represents a foretaste of the eschatological kingdom for which we hope (Fee 1994:807). Most fundamentally, the Spirit of God is creating in us a new and eschatological life, a life as the children of the heavenly Father and ruler of the universe (Fee 1994:805ff.).

This new life is a corporate life of familial and self-giving love. Within this community it is possible for individuals to learn to love as they are loved by God, Jesus, and others (Snyder 1994:17). This love finds expression in the day-to-day realities of life together—in the process whereby the abundance of one fills the lack of the other (Acts 4:32-37). The concrete experience of love within the community of saints is a foretaste, a down payment, a harbinger of the ultimate perfection of love in the presence of God.

Thus the call of God in Jesus touches us in a way that corresponds most deeply with the goal toward which God has created us. We are created with the image of God as our goal, and the redemptive work of Jesus fulfills that very image. The image of God becomes fully explicit in Jesus and the faithful Christian community that is transformed by the gifts of the Holy Spirit (Fee 1994:881ff.). Drawing us into the power of God's love, the Holy Spirit makes a holy community out of individuals who would otherwise have explicit ties neither to each other nor God.[19]

To be human is to be challenged, commanded, and lured by God's faithful love "to trust and love God wholeheartedly (see Heschel 1965:111ff.). This involves us in God's love for the world. In this way we open ourselves to be perfected in the image of God. If we are drawn into God's love, then we are also drawn into God's faithful love for creation and especially for God's children.[20] We might ask where, apart from love's concrete expressions, is either faith or the love of God?[21]

# A Foretaste of God: The Presence of the Kingdom

Relationships with others, as they find their fulfillment in love, are the heart of personal existence.[22] Therein communion with God finds anticipatory expression in the day-to-day experiences of creaturely life.

Creaturely relationships are designed to express the divine love that unites Jesus and the Father. The foundation and structure of all life is the twofold love of Jesus that forgets the self in its love for God and selflessly reaches out to all creation. Humans are welcomed to participate in this operation of divine love. God's redemptive purpose draws all creatures into the love of God, of neighbor, and of the creation.

This essentially religious, hence moral, characterization of existence rests on the relational conception of the image of God described above.[23] True religion will allow God's love to express itself concretely in mutual acts of love. This love is not foreign to us as human creatures. Rather, it nurtures the Christian community of faithful sisters and brothers who witness to the redemptive action of God (Yoder 1969:258ff.).

The presence of the kingdom lends hope that the power to conceive a future transcends the limitations of historical causes and effects. It enables those who trust in God to be open to new and unexpected possibilities of action (Burkholder 1960:60). Love is a forgiving and creative power that overcomes our despair and hopelessness.

Hans-Jürgen Goertz suggests that those in the Anabaptist-Mennonite tradition might make a special contribution to contemporary society through their vision of a "fraternal society" in which acts of love rather than the forces of the marketplace guide human behavior (Goertz

1988: 10ff.). In this way the vision and hope for the kingdom of God would serve as the goal, motivation, and standard of behavior. Translated into action, these values are a critical force for the humanization of democratic capitalism (Goertz 1988:11).[24] Whether or not the church can have such a public impact, it is, nevertheless, vital for a robust church that the kingdom, not capitalism, define the horizon that gives meaning to Christian actions (Dyck 1963:165).[25]

The love and unity of the church is the primary vehicle of God's witness to the world.[26] The quality of the church's witness to the kingdom of God is directly related to the quality of its life as an extended family. In other words, the mutuality and love that characterize the church will determine the effectiveness of its evangelistic work—both locally and globally (Yordy 1962:143). The witness of a local congregation depends on the love—concretely expressed through mutual aid—of the members for each other. In addition, the witness of the church worldwide depends on the mutual love of Christians worldwide.[27]

Fretz and Bender (1957:796) suggest that an emphasis on simple frugality among the sixteenth-century Anabaptists helped thwart "jealousy, selfishness, and sophistication." This accent made it possible, according to Fretz and Bender, for these Christians to develop a special orientation toward familial mutuality. They argue that this understanding of Christian faith increased focus on the good of the group and reduced individualism.[28] The emphasis on collective welfare countered some of the usual sins of individualism.

In sum, when the love of God overflows from individual hearts into love for others, it transforms our perspectives on community and individual good and reduces greed and jealousy, which may corrupt the heart and mind.[29] Consequently, love and unity grow in an upward spiral of blessing (Graber 1964:209, 211).

The church as visible representation of the kingdom of heaven uses rituals to teach, enact, and reinforce the central features of its life and hope (Davis 1974:209). Footwashing and the Lord's Supper, for example, enact and teach the love and mutuality rooted in Jesus' loving action. The Lord's Supper expresses, among other things, mutual dependence on the grace of God in Jesus. Footwashing ritually expresses the mutual love and servanthood that characterize the life of the community of saints (Studer 1965:243-254).

# Practical Implications of Kingdom Love

This theological discussion provides a context for understanding the Christian practice of mutual aid. The presence of God's love is the creative and critical power of the coming kingdom of God, which energizes the practice of mutual aid. Furthermore, the concrete expression of mutual love in the form of aid is essential to Christian life (Raid 1967:401-404).

We dare not rely on the achievements of our Anabaptist ancestors, some of whom gave even their lives for others. Studer (1965:260) notes that whereas the first Christians and the Anabaptists joyfully contributed all that they had in order to meet the needs of their brothers and sisters, "We today are valiantly striving in our congregations to sometimes reach even the tithe." Christian love goes beyond the law of tithing (Sprunger 1994:28ff.).

How might the love of God in the community of believers find concrete expression? George Rupp (1991:215ff.) suggests that North Americans might think about shared responsibility and entrepreneurial teams. This shift might help to overcome the division of persons into a small class of creative entrepreneurs and a large class of drones. Rupp's suggestion might move the practice of Christian mutual aid beyond the idea of the rich aiding the poor and toward true mutuality between rich and poor.

Is it possible that those with sufficient financial resources might draw in the unemployed, for example, as partners in new and creative ventures? Is it possible for MMA to provide funds (in the form of matching grants and loans) either to individuals who wish to become partners rather than laborers or to groups that seek to achieve such mutuality within the context of an entrepreneurial venture?[30]

Suppose that a building becomes available at a fire-sale price. And assume that a successful Anabaptist-Mennonite entrepreneur or professional becomes aware of the opportunity. She or he alone could buy the building. On the other hand, such a situation may represent an opportunity to involve marginalized members of the congregation. Rather than aiming for further personal financial gain, well-established members might also seek the economic good of the less fortunate as well as their own. In other words, marketplace values are subsumed to love.

Such a venture could easily move beyond the material level. Marginalized members, experiencing the love of God through the actions of wealthier Christians, would be drawn more fully into the kingdom. Such tangible expressions of love become harbingers of the kingdom of peace and justice. They create possibilities for the transformation of lives and do so by transforming the community. Those who might have slipped away are drawn in (Fretz 1951:22ff.). The perfect love of the kingdom becomes physically real for a moment and touches all who see it.

Such actions of mutual aid shape the horizon of experience of all members of the congregation and beyond. Individually and collectively the stories of love in action teach us and help us to internalize the two-fold movement of love (Janzen 1993:57-64, 67ff.). They become part of the "cloud of witnesses" that encompasses and nurtures us into full maturity and participation in the historical embodiment of the kingdom of heaven (Heb. 12:1).[31]

Thus the children of God are prepared for the task of living already as citizens of the future kingdom. In more traditional theological terms, it could be said that the sanctification of the individual is achieved in the family of the faithful through the concrete operation of mutual love (see Davis 1974:192ff.).

Mutual aid is a harbinger of the kingdom to come. The practice of aid embodies God's love among us. It dramatically illustrates the words of 1 John 3:17-18: "But if any one has the world's goods and sees his brother in need, yet closes his heart against him, how does God's love abide in him? Little children, let us not love in word or speech but in deed and in truth." It is impossible to separate material and spiritual needs. These are interwoven just as human life blends physical and spiritual issues together (Niebuhr 1941:151ff.).

Mutual aid is an expression of love but also develops love. Mutual aid nurtures community spirit and energy in the dynamic movement of the community toward the kingdom of God (Hildebrand 1989:34). Love expressed in acts of mutual aid forms group identity and unity. It leaves none marginalized. In this unity of love there is a potent historical witness to the reality of the kingdom of God (John 17:22-23, 26).

How radical an application of love can Christians be expected to make? Is love a guiding principle for living or a critical principle, a utopian vision, by which our achievements are evaluated? In other words, do we need an interim ethic which relativizes the radical claim of the gospel of love? The traditional Mennonite and Anabaptist answer was an emphatic "No" (Yoder 1969:277).

But how is it possible to enact such love? Is this an ethic for rural communities only, or also for modern urban communities? How do we face economic stress and competition? Shall we retreat into urban or rural enclaves and ghettos?

Or shall we create new options for living that are truly shaped by the love of God? This option is costly. Whoever takes this route must be prepared to forsake his or her claim to independent wealth and security.[32] Along this path all possessions are placed at the disposal of the Holy Spirit. All is focused on the kingdom of God (Matt. 10:37-39). With the aim

With the aim of saving others, we sacrifice even our lives. Such love certainly opposes the ideals of (post)modern capitalism.

This is a tall order and can be achieved only when the Spirit of love fills our hearts to overflowing, when the Holy Spirit is unhindered by love of possessions. Jesus plainly promises that whoever abandons all for his sake "will receive a hundredfold, and inherit eternal life" (Matt. 19:29). That is the promise that propels us to serve the King of the new kingdom already breaking in upon us as a new order characterized by the practice of mutual love.

## Notes

1. All scripture quotations are from the RSV. In this context Paul dares to say that those who had much had nothing left over after sharing with the needy. In addition to reflecting on the miracle described in Ex. 16:18, perhaps he has Luke 12:48 in mind: of those who have much, much will be required. In other words, if one's excess in wealth is kept apart for the self and is not submitted to the passionate love of God that reaches out to those in need, then there is a surplus of selfishness. Therefore, the love of God will have found no room. The love of abundant possessions will have crowded the love of the neighbor from the heart (Burkholder 1960:55-57). Graber's (1964:213) interpretation of Matt. 25:14-30 is similar in spirit to this interpretation of Luke 12:48. LeMasters (1992:79, 88f.) points out that J. H. Yoder regards God's love (as revealed in Jesus' willingness to die for us) as the defining model of how the church is to exist in the world. Halteman (1995:83-85) has a good discussion of need and surplus.

2. Augustine (1960: Bk. 1, Ch. 1). If we keep this corporate characteristic in mind we can come closer to the simple grandeur of the original: "Our hearts are restless until they find their rest in Thee." The original speaks in the singular. This interpretation of human existence draws on the vision of Isa. 11 and on Ps. 42.

3. Pannenberg (1994:228) argues that this goal is not first of all present as a consciously chosen task but is already implicit "in the indefinite trust that opens up the horizon of world experience and intersubjectivity, and also in a restless thrust toward overcoming the finite."

4. I use these masculine images because they point beyond themselves to the Trinitarian God who is not a man, the misappropriation of these symbols by some men notwithstanding. The point of the images, which are drawn from the life of the biblical writers, is to elucidate the true nature of the relationship between creature and Creator. That the interrelationships of women and men have changed should not keep us from understanding the message of this imagery.

5. See also Matties (1990:153-159); Banks (1994:49-51); and Fretz (1958:10).

6. Matties (1990:147-153) argues that moral responsibility in Ezekiel is envisioned within an interdependency between individual, community, and Jahweh.

7. For fuller treatments of this argument see Berger (1967:3-7); Pannenberg (1985:43ff.); and Stoltzfus (1959:40), who speak of humans as searching for true community. Wolff (1974:10ff.) speaks of humans as needy. This is taken up by Janzen (1982:62).

8. Kraus (1969:448) uses the phrase "open to the world" to describe the necessary orientation of the early church in its servant and missionary characteristics.

9. See Matties (1990:192) and Halteman (1995:39f.), who both point out the centrality of household and family in the Old Testament. Halteman argues that this is intended as a political structure that is in fact countercultural in the Ancient Near East. The line of argument in this presentation would suggest that, while the biblical model may be politically countercultural, it corresponds to the fundamental realities of existence.

10. Unfortunately, various factors, such as the instrumentalization of the idea and experience of work as well as the concentration of power in the hands of small numbers of persons, can severely restrict the realization of this human vocation (see Rupp 1991:212). Much criticism could be leveled against the capitalistic developments, for example, in the liberal democracies of the modern West (see Grant 1974).

11. The thwarting of this openness and freedom is one of the aims of all who seek and enjoy privilege and power for their own sakes.

12. See Buller (1996:48, 70-73, 150-56, 160) and O'Donovan (1994:38). Stoltzfus (1959:41) connects mutual aid and care of the nonhuman world.

13. Dyck (1963:187) points out that in some instances mutuality has become ethnically focused so that "the brethren stick together in vice and virtue to protect their way of life." The international drug trafficking of some of the Mexican Mennonites and the silence of their communities suggests that, for them, "brotherhood" has become a *virtue* that is able to ignore that community's responsibility for the larger human community.

14. Gen. 1–11; Stoltzfus (1959:43, 47).

15. Ultimately, however, we know that all political achievements are limited and subject to abuse. They become oppressive. They marginalize and abuse the powerless and the alien. Visions of nationhood have the power to demand and justify such sacrifices. Nationalism easily becomes an idol which demands all kinds of sacrifices in war, diplomacy, and economics. True mutuality and love oppose narrowly national, political, and economic goals.

The notion in theoretical physics of a grand unified theory is another example of such searching. Examples can be given from many aspects of our existence, from theoretical and grand visions to simple and mundane attempts to find meaning. The innumerable attempts we make to transcend our limitations (e.g., space travel) also serve as examples. There are destructive implications of these scientific, technical, political, and economic activities. Not only is the unity of love and mutuality disrupted, but people, animals, and ecosystems are used and destroyed in the pursuit of these goals.

16. The modern notion of family must be corrected by the model given by Jesus in both his relationship to the Father and in his relationships with creatures. Raid (1967:402f.) implies that even among the descendants of the Anabaptists, family life has become focused on the self. Bumper stickers on some vehicles advertise the selfishness of modern parents as a means of exercising revenge on their children.

17. This point should not be ignored when interpreting the symbols of eternal Father and Son.

18. Augsburger (1968:414) suggests that Kant's categorical imperative (to treat every person as an end in him or herself) is the most clear expression of respect for individual human dignity. There are several problems with Kant's foundation for morals. First, it reverses the order of the Judeo-Christian foundation for morality in the faithful goodness of God by postulating God as the high-

est good on the basis of a rational conception of moral perfection (Kant 1969:29 and Pannenberg 1969:104; 1981:57f., 79f.). Second, it does not include nonhuman creatures (Kohák 1984:117f.). I follow Pannenberg in deriving moral thought from a theological conception of life. This is an inversion of the Kantian notion of the dependence of religion on morality. However, as both Pannenberg and Kohák acknowledge, Kant's moral thought should not be regarded as invalidated.

19. Fretz (1940:204f.) and Fee (1994:872).

20. Banks (1994:54) points out that such love is not a human possibility but is a reflection of the power of the Holy Spirit (Rom. 5:15; 15:30). It can be said with the Gospel of John (8:38) that "rivers of living water" flow out of the hearts of those who partake of the life of Christ.

21. Yordy (1962:124-130); Loewen (1987:197).

22. Fretz (1958:19) and Pannenberg (1970:232f.).

23. I believe that this depiction of human nature as fundamentally oriented toward the perfect realization of the image of God in the kingdom of heaven corresponds with all that we know and experience (Pfister 1993:561f.).

24. I agree with Goertz that the life of the church draws on a vision of a transcendent reality that is in a sense "utopian" (the word Goertz uses repeatedly). However, it should also be noted that the kingdom is not completely *oú topos*. It is present within history and is, if provisionally (or proleptically), visible in the church—especially in its tangible expressions of mutual love. Furthermore, the presence of the Holy Spirit indicates the reality of the *already* of the kingdom.

25. Hope for a transcendent kingdom frees us from slavish adherence to the status quo, which is always limited and subject to abuses. Hope creates freedom for new moral possibilities.

26. John 17:23; Klassen (1961:110).

27. It is worth noting that the unity of the family of God's children is rooted in love, not in dogma. This foundation would appear to be one consequence of taking seriously Paul's collection of a gift from the Gentiles on behalf of the Jerusalem believers. I believe that the Gospel and epistles of John would support this. Is there a role for Mennonite Mutual Aid in helping other groups to develop their own institutional applications of mutual love and in this way make a contribution to Christian unity?

28. Banks (1994:63) argues that mutual love seeks the good of the community. The metaphor of the community as one body highlights this.

29. Hauerwas (1983:32f.) argues that the Christian community provides a social horizon which contributes to the transformation of individuals. Mutual aid can help Christians to counter "the ravages of individualism, secularism, and materialism" (Driedger 1993:316f.).

30. This leaves aside, for the moment, questions that must be raised regarding the character of Christian participation in the current economic order. Not all entrepreneurial ventures can be blessed simply by the participation of Christians who love one another.

31. The recounting of the deeds of God's love in the community shapes that community. The stories are part of the mutual expression of love in the community. Collection and availability of the stories requires facilitation.

32. Halteman (1995:182f.) points out that countercultural decisions are enabled in the context of a supportive faith community. The lifeblood of this community is the Holy Spirit.

# References

Augsburger, Myron S.
1968    "Mutual Aid in the Congregation." In *The Compassionate Community*, ed. Hernley.

Augustine, Saint
1960    *The Confessions of Saint Augustine.* Trans. John K. Ryan. New York: Image Books.

Banks, Robert
1994    *Paul's Idea of Community*, rev. ed. Peabody, Mass.: Hendrickson Publishers.

Bender, Harold S.
1944    "The Anabaptist Vision." Mennonite Quarterly Review 18:67-88.

Berger, Peter L.
1967    *The Sacred Canopy: Elements of a Sociological Theory of Religion.* Garden City, New York: Doubleday.

1977    *Facing up to Modernity.* New York: Basic Books.

Brown, Dale W.
1979    "Communal Ecclesiology: The Power of the Anabaptist Vision." *Theology Today* 36 (April): 22-29.

Buller, Cornelius A.
1996    *The Unity of Nature and History in Pannenberg's Theology.* Lanham: Littlefield Adams Books.

Burkholder, J. L.
1960    "Love and Justice in Mennonite Mutual Aid." In *The Compassionate Community*, ed. Hernley.

Davis, Kenneth Ronald
1974    *Anabaptism and Asceticism: A Study in Intellectual Origins.* Scottdale: Herald Press.

Driedger, Leo
1993    "From Martyrs to Muppies: The Mennonite Urban Professional Revolution." *Mennonite Quarterly Review* 67 (July): 304-322.

Durnbaugh, Donald F.
1988    "Mutual Aid in Ministry to God's Word." *Brethren Life and Thought* 33:87-97.

Dyck, C. J.
1963    "Mutual Aid in a Changing Economy." In *The Compassionate Community*, ed. Hernley.

Erb, Allen, et al.
1978    "Mennonite Mutual Aid: A Plan for the Organization of a New Board to Carry on an Effective Program of Mutual Aid within the Mennonite Church." *Mennonite Historical Bulletin* 39/3:5-6.

Fee, Gordon D.
   1994   *God's Empowering Presence: The Holy Spirit in the Letters of Paul.* Peabody, Mass.: Hendrickson Publishers.

Fretz, J. Winfield
   1939   "Mutual Aid Among the Mennonites." I & II. *Mennonite Quarterly Review* 13: 28-58, 187-209.

   1940   "Mennonites and Their Economic Problems." *Mennonite Quarterly Review* 14/4 (October): 195-213.

   1947   *Christian Mutual Aid: A Handbook of Brotherhood Economics.* Akron, Pa.: Mennonite Central Committee.

   1951   "What Mutual Aid Can Mean to a Church." *Mennonite Community* 5/5 (May): 22-23, 29.

   1958   "Meditations on Christian Mutual Aid." In *The Compassionate Community*, ed. Hernley.

Fretz, J. Winfield, and Harold S. Bender
   1957   "Mutual Aid." In *Mennonite Encyclopedia*, vol. 3, ed. Cornelius Krahn, et al. Scottdale, Pa.: Herald Press.

Garrett, James Leo Jr.
   1971   "The Recovery of the Anabaptist Vision." In *Concern Pamphlet #18.* Scottdale, Pa.: Herald Press. Pp. 5-23.

   1979   "The Spirit of God and the Politics of Men." *Journal of Theology of Southern Africa* 29 (December): 62-71.

Goertz, Hans Jürgen
   1988   "The Confessional Heritage in its New Mold: What is Mennonite Self-Understanding Today?" In *Mennonite Identity: Historical and Contemporary Perspectives*, ed. Calvin W. Redekop and Samuel J. Steiner. Lanham: University Press of America.

Graber, O'Ray C.
   1964   "Why Christians Help One Another." In *The Compassionate Community*, ed. Hernley.

Grant, George
   1974   *English-Speaking Justice.* Toronto: Anansi.

Halteman, James
   1995   *The Clashing Worlds of Economics and Faith.* Scottdale, Pa.: Herald Press.

Hauerwas, Stanley
   1981   *A Community of Character: Toward a Constructive Christian Social Ethic.* Notre Dame: University of Notre Dame Press.

   1983   *The Peaceable Kingdom: A Primer in Christian Ethics.* Notre Dame: University of Notre Dame Press.

Hernley, H. Ralph, ed.
   1970   *The Compassionate Community.* Scottdale, Pa.: Association of Mennonite Aid Societies.

Heschel, Abraham J.
1965   *Who is Man?* Stanford: Stanford University Press.

Hildebrand, Hilda Anne
1989   "Mennonite Mutual Aid and the Concept of Social Welfare: A Case Study of the Bergthaler Waisenamt and the Co-operative Movement in the Rhineland Municipality." Master of Social Work thesis, University of Manitoba.

Janzen, Waldemar
1982   *Still in the Image: Essays in Biblical Theology and Anthropology.* (Institute of Mennonite Studies, No. 6). Newton, Kan.: Faith and Life Press.

1993   *Old Testament Ethics: A Paradigmatic Approach.* Louisville: Westminster/John Knox Press.

Kant, Immanuel
1969   *Foundations of the Metaphysics of Morals: With Critical Essays.* Ed. Robert Paul Wolff, trans. Lewis White Beck. New York: Macmillan.

Kauffman, Daniel
1966   "New Frontiers: Stewardship and Mutual Aid." In *The Compassionate Community,* ed. Hernley.

Klassen, William
1961   "Christian Realities in Mutual Aid." In *The Compassionate Community,* ed. Hernley.

Kohák, Erazim
1984   *The Embers and the Stars: A Philosophical Inquiry into the Moral Sense of Nature.* Chicago: University of Chicago Press.

Krahn, Cornelius
1982   *Menno Simons (1496-1561): Ein Beiträgzur Geschichte und Theologie der Taufgesinnten.* 2nd ed. Newton, Kan.: Faith and Life Press.

Kraus, C. Norman
1969   "Christian Sharing in the Mission of the Church." In *The Compassionate Community,* ed. Hernley.

Lapp, John E.
1944   "The Biblical Basis for the Christian Practice of Mutual Aid." *Gospel Herald* 37:241-242.

LeMasters, Philip
1992   *The Import of Eschatology in John Howard Yoder's Critique of Constantinianism.* San Francisco: Mellen Research University Press.

Loewen, Harry
1987   "Der Wahre Glaube: Zum Glaubensverständnis bei Menno Simons." In *Anabaptistes et dissidents au XVIe siècle,* ed. Jean-Georges Rott and Simon L. Verheus. Bibliotheca Dissidentium: scripta et studia, No. 3. Baden-Baden & Bouxwiller: Éditions Valentin Koerner. Pp. 191-199.

Martin, Ruth Hartzler
   1982   "What Makes Professional Service Christian?" In *Perils of Professionalism: Essays on Christian Faith and Professionalism*, ed. Donald B. Kraybill and Phyllis Pellman Good. Scottdale, Pa.: Herald Press.

Matties, Gordon H.
   1990   *Ezekiel 18 and the Rhetoric of Moral Discourse.* SBL Dissertation Series, No. 126. Atlanta: Scholars Press.

Mennonite Central Committee
   1947   "What is Mutual Aid?" Akron, Pa.: Mennonite Central Committee.

Menno Simons
   1956   *The Complete Writings of Menno Simons.* Trans. Leonard Verduin, ed. J. C. Wenger. Scottdale, Pa.: Herald Press.

Miller, Orie O.
   1961   "Operation Brotherhood." *Mennonite Observer* 7, 12 (March 254): 8, 11.

Niebuhr, Reinhold
   1941   *The Nature and Destiny of Man: A Christian Interpretation.* Volume 1: *Human Nature.* New York: Charles Scribner's Sons.

Niebuhr, H. Richard, ed.
   1989   *Faith on Earth: An Inquiry into the Structure of Human Faith.* New Haven: Yale University Press.

O'Donovan, Oliver
   1994   *Resurrection and Moral Order: An Outline for Evangelical Ethics.* Leicester: Inter-Varsity Press; Grand Rapids: Eerdmans.

Pannenberg, Wolfhart
   1969   *Theology and the Kingdom of God.* Philadelphia: Westminster Press.

   1970   *Basic Questions in Theology.* Vol. 1. Trans. George U. Kehm. Philadelphia: Fortress Press.

   1981   *Ethics.* Trans. Keith Crim. Philadelphia: Westminster Press.

   1985   *Anthropology in Theological Perspective.* Trans. Matthew J. O'Connell. Philadelphia: Westminster Press.

   1988   *Metaphysik und Gottesgedanke.* Göttingen: Vandenhoeck & Ruprecht.

   1993   *Systematische Theologie.* Band 3. Göttingen: Vandenhoeck & Ruprecht.

   1994   *Stematic Theology.* Vol. 2. Trans. Geoffrey W. Bromiley. Grand Rapids: Eerdmans.

Pfister, Oskar
   1993   "The Illusion of a Future: A Friendly Disagreement with Prof. Sigmund Freud." *International Journal of Psycho-Analysis* 74:557-579.

Raid, Howard D.
   1967   "Men, Materials and Mennonites in Mutual Aid." In *The Compassionate Community*, ed. Hernley.

Redekop, Calvin, Victor A. Krahn, and Samuel J. Steiner, eds.
1994  *Anabaptist/Mennonite Faith and Economics*. Lanham: University Press of America.

Rupp, George
1991  "Communities of Collaboration: Shared Commitments/Common Tasks." In *Theology at the End of Modernity: Essays in Honor of Gordon D. Kaufman*, ed. Sheila Greeve Davaney, pp. 210-218. Philadelphia: Trinity Press International.

Snyder, Arnold
1994  "Anabaptist Spirituality and Economics." In *Anabaptist/Mennonite Faith and Economics*, ed. Calvin Redekop, Victor A. Krahn, and Samuel J. Steiner. Lanham: University Press of America.

Snyder, John M.
1944  "Some thoughts on New Testament Mutual Aid." *Gospel Herald* 37:764-765, 772-773.

Sprunger, Mary S.
1994  "Dutch Mennonites and the Golden Age Economy: The Problem of Social Disparity in the Church." In *Anabaptist/Mennonite Faith and Economics*, ed. Calvin Redekop, Victor A. Krahn, and Samuel J. Steiner. Lanham: University Press of America.

Stoltzfus, Grant M.
1959  "Toward New Horizons in Mennonite Mutual Aid." In *The Compassionate Community*, ed. Hernley.

Studer, Gerald C.
1965  "Toward a Theology of Servanthood." In *The Compassionate Community*, ed. Hernley.

Swartzendruber, H. L.
1959  "Mennonite Mutual Aid." *Gospel Herald* 52 (48): 1058, 1069.

Welker, Michael
1994  *God the Spirit*. Trans. John F. Hoffmeyer. Minneapolis: Fortress Press.

Wenger, John Christian
1951  *Separated Unto God: A Plea for Christian Simplicity of Life and for a Scriptural Noncomformity to the World*. Scottdale, Pa.: Mennonite Publishing House.

Wiebe, Bernie
1977  "Biblical Mutual Aid: A Model for the 1980s." Baden, Ont.: Association of Mennonite Aid Societies.

Wolff, Hans Walter
1974  *Anthropology of the Old Testament*. Trans. Margaret Kohl. Philadelphia: Fortress Press.

Yoder, John Howard
1964  *The Christian Witness to the State*. Institute of Mennonite Studies Series Number 3. Newton, Kan.: Faith and Life Press.

# Part Three

# Historical Case Studies

# 5

# Mutual Aid Among the Augsburg Anabaptists, 1526-1528

## Jeni Hiett Umble

This intriguing case study profiles the practice of mutual aid in a sixteenth-century Anabaptist congregation faced with severe persecution. Based on a careful study of court records that document the interrogation of suspected Anabaptists, Jeni Hiett Umble shows that mutual aid in the Augsburg congregation entailed at least five aspects: the common purse, shelter, food and clothing, employment, and refuge. Umble argues that these expressions of mutual aid were anchored on theological understandings of stewardship and discipleship that characterized the Anabaptist movement from its very beginning.

## The Crime of Mutual Aid

On April 21, 1528, two men and four women were sentenced to be branded on the cheek, then roped onto a pillory and driven out of the city of Augsburg. They were condemned for the crime of rebaptism and for hosting "rowdy, evil, conspiratorial" gatherings of Anabaptist "rabble" in their homes.[1] Augsburg had a history of exiling Anabaptists, but branding (probably by burning a hole through their cheeks) was reserved for those who had especially angered the civic authorities. As records of interrogation make clear, the six heretics merited such severe

103

punishment because they had been rebaptized and had given housing, shelter, food, drink, and refuge to other Anabaptists.

One of the women was Susanna Doucher, wife of the prominent sculptor Adolf Doucher. She earned her punishment by giving money to a poor woman and hosting two other women in her home overnight. She also confessed to providing bread and wine for a large gathering of believers at her home on April 12, 1528 (Roth 1901:52). Although she was exiled, pregnancy saved Susanna from actually being branded on the cheek.

The remaining five were not so fortunate. Thoma Paur confessed to hosting his brothers-in-law, leaders of the Anabaptist movement. Caspar Schlosser also belonged to a family of believers who often met together. Dorothea Frölich and Scolastica Stierpaur each allowed the wife of an imprisoned leader to stay with them for several nights. For these crimes they were branded and exiled.

The most severe punishment, however, was reserved for Elisabeth Hegenmiller. Not only had she attended meetings and given both food and money to the poor, she had also publicly scolded her neighbor's maid for continuing to partake of the Catholic Mass. "How long will you eat the slimy bread of idolatry?" she cried out (Roth 1901:55). For this public denouncement of the Lord's Supper, Elisabeth had her tongue cut out. She was branded and exiled.

These six believers were not the only ones caught and punished by the Augsburg authorities. The summer and fall of 1527 had been marked by the arrest and subsequent imprisonment or exile of most of the local leaders.[2] Other believers escaped punishment by swearing that they would not attend Anabaptist gatherings, although permission was granted for two or three to meet together for Bible study.

The Anabaptists continued to meet in a variety of settings within the city and in a nearby forest or quarry. Their meetings were usually small, although most of them exceeded the "two or three" persons allowed by the city council.

On that Easter morning in 1528, however, as many as 200 believers and seekers made their way to Susanna Doucher's home. They quietly gathered behind Susanna's blanket-covered windows for worship. During the service someone noticed the presence of city guards in the vicinity. One leader warned the congregation that arrest was imminent. Some of the congregation chose to slip away, but eighty-eight persons were arrested and others were subsequently detained.

Those who were obviously nonresidents were immediately exiled and threatened with a beating should they dare to return. The remaining persons were native Augsburgers or residents of the city for some time. The civic authorities hired Konrad Peutinger, a humanist and secretary for the city of Augsburg, to question the believers about their Anabaptist activities. He meticulously recorded the details of each interrogation and noted the form of torture routinely applied to each prisoner.[3]

Peutinger's notes contain a wealth of information about mutual aid within the Augsburg congregation. Because the Augsburg authorities feared another outbreak of the so-called "Peasants' War," Peutinger specifically questioned the prisoners about the existence of a "common purse."[4] Such a collection could only be for the purchase of weapons, surmised the authorities. In their view, the Anabaptists were too closely linked to the rebellion of 1525 (Stayer 1991:6).

Peutinger not only asked about the common purse but also pressed for details about other assistance given to the believers. His questions reveal fear on the part of the civic authorities. Meetings of Anabaptists were therefore prohibited, and mutual assistance was viewed as a crime.

The answers of imprisoned Anabaptists reveal a community committed to caring for the needy among them.[5] Examples abound of both corporate and individual assistance among believers in the congregation. The records of interrogation depict theological commitments that emphasized the importance of caring for one's fellow believers. Indeed, mutual aid was at the very heart of the Anabaptist community in Augsburg.

## Mutual Aid Among the Augsburg Anabaptists

The words *mutual aid* were never used by the Augsburg Anabaptists, yet this term aptly describes the caring for needy brothers and sisters found in the congregation. Laban Peachey (1990:614) underscores the importance of the Anabaptists' radical following of the teachings of Jesus and how that led to a "rediscovery" of love for one's neighbor.

This understanding, combined with the severe persecution which forced the believers to provide for one another, led to the development of sharing and caring as "major elements of the Anabaptist movement." Mutual aid became "an expression of Christian brotherhood among members of a body of believers" (Studer 1965:39). The Augsburg Anabaptists understood that those with extra material resources would willingly share with those in need.

The phrase *community of goods* was sometimes used to describe the Anabaptist system of helping one another. However, this term should not be construed as holding everything in common. The term reflected the practice of the apostles to hold everything in common, as recorded in Acts 4:32. In sixteenth-century Augsburg, however, private property was not abolished, but one's own possessions were to be freely shared with those in need. As Balthasar Hubmaier, an early leader of the congregation, explained in 1526,

> Concerning community of goods, I have always said that everyone should be concerned about [the needs of] others, so that the hungry might be fed, the thirsty given to drink, and the naked clothed, etc. For we are not lords of our possessions, but stewards and distributors. There is certainly no one who says that another's goods may be seized and made common; rather, he would gladly give the coat in addition to the shirt (Durnbaugh 1974:12).

This attitude remained prevalent in the Augsburg congregation. Hans Leupold, a later leader, declared that he had always taught that not all things were held in common and that no one took anything from another by force. Nor did he compel anyone to come into the fellowship but allowed each one to follow his or her own will (Roth 1901:65).

Other Anabaptists also testified that no one was forced to contribute to the common purse, but when anyone had a need, others would provide. Anna Salminger emphasized that everyone worked, but those who could not work were given something.[6] Eitelhans Langenmantel, one of the wealthiest members of the Augsburg congregation, indicated that the desire to share grew out of the love each believer had for others. The needs of other members were therefore viewed as their own (Klassen 1963:81).

# Patterns of Mutual Aid[7]

The meticulous questioning by Konrad Peutinger has helped to preserve ample information about mutual aid in the Augsburg congregation. Peutinger methodically asked his prisoners about their baptism, where and when they attended meetings, what forms of mutual aid they had observed, and what assistance they had given to other Anabaptists. Although his exact questions have not been preserved, the answers reveal that he asked a standard list of questions. Peutinger used several questions to ferret out specific information about the common purse and other forms of assistance that were present in the community.

Mutual aid in the Augsburg congregation took on at least five different expressions. On some occasions, a collection was taken and then given to the deacons for distribution. Provisions were sometimes purchased to be shared when the believers came together for worship or study. When an individual's need became obvious, members of the congregation sometimes gave money or supplies directly to that person. These activities benefited both residents of Augsburg and the many foreign believers who sought refuge in the city. In addition, the foreigners received assistance in the form of extended housing, sustenance, and even employment from members of the faith community.

(1) *The common purse.* The many references to a common purse indicate that the congregation had a system for the collection and distribution of money to the poor. A box or purse might have been placed near the door or circulated during the meetings. Those who were able contributed money to be given to those in need. Usually the amounts were not large, although a goldsmith in the congregation reportedly gave generously.[8]

Word then spread that certain men in the congregation would distribute the funds. Dorothea Frölich, the widow of a tilemaker, testified that minister Georg Nespitzer had told her to go to Simprecht Wiedenmann, Laux Kreler, or Gall Vischer if she had any need for money. A weaver named Matheis Hieber had been told to go to Leonhard Dorfbrunner or Laux Kreler.

Some of the people questioned denied any knowledge of a common purse. Perhaps these persons were new to the community or had not attended meetings where such a box or purse was present. It is also possible that to protect the community they refused to reveal what they knew about such a purse.

Instead of revealing information about a common purse, some believers explained that whenever a brother or sister was in need others would share freely with that believer. In this way, members of the community managed to deflect attention from a common collection to the sharing of individuals with one another.

Anabaptists such as Mang Betz admitted that previously the fellowship had a common purse, but it had not been used during the time he had been with the believers. This account might be another attempt to avoid the question, but it might also be based in the reluctance of several men to assume the risks associated with such a purse (see below). Although clearly present at some times during the life of the congregation, the collection box or purse may have been used only intermittently.

(2) *Shelter.* The list of persons in the congregation who provided temporary shelter to other believers is long and tedious, yet this was an aspect of mutual aid. In most cases, shelter took the form of temporary lodging, probably a kind of bed-and-breakfast. For example, Els Knöll confessed that several times brothers and sisters stayed with her over-

night. On those occasions she also provided food for her guests. She did not serve wine but gave them only water to drink. Shelter appears to have been little more than providing overnight lodging and possibly a simple meal.

It is probable that housing assignments for refugees were made as the believers met together for worship. Dorothea Frölich kept two foreign women overnight following the Easter Eve meeting in the home of Gall Vischer. Although she claimed not to know their names, this may or may not have been true. Probably Frölich had simply been asked to provide lodging for the foreign sisters. Their presence at the meeting identified them as believers, and she asked for no further identification. Ignorance was certainly a form of mutual protection. Neither those who hosted nor those who lodged could then reveal the names of fellow believers.

The congregation also sheltered the many itinerant preachers who made their way through Augsburg. The maid of Konrad and Felicitas Huber indicated that many leaders, among them Melchior of Salzburg, had stayed in the home of her employers. Other leaders hosted by the Augsburg congregation included Georg Nespitzer, Leonhard Dorfbrunner, Bartholome Tuchheffter, Eukarius Binder, Claus Schleiffer, and Hans Hut.

(3) *Food and clothing*. Provisions in the form of groceries, supplies, and even clothing were distributed among members of the congregation. Often one member distributed goods directly to another. The grocer Elisabeth Hegenmiller provided needy Anabaptists with salt, lard, flour, and similar staples. At other times the provisions were delivered to a deacon for further distribution. This was probably the intention of Els Knöll when she took kraut and herring to the home of Hans Lauterwein.

Food was also distributed during the gatherings for study and worship. Some Anabaptists mentioned taking bread and wine during their meetings. Although these were clearly the provisions for communion, on some other occasions portions more substantial than a token bit of bread and swallow of wine were shared.

Other simple foods may have also been shared. Anna Salminger, wife of the imprisoned leader Sigmund, revealed that the host of a meeting sometimes provided soup, kraut, and other things. She specifically indicates that this was done to strengthen the bodies of weaker believers.

Susanna Doucher confessed that she had purchased wine, bread, and other items in preparation for the Easter meeting in her home. Hans Fesenmaier, a weaver, avoided telling what he knew about the distribution of money or other provisions. He had seen it happen only once during a meeting in a cellar after the celebration of communion. Even so, he claimed that he did not know who received the goods.

The items shared probably also included clothing. Thoma Paur testified that Anna Regel, a wealthy Anabaptist, provided coats for three of the leaders. According to Anna Butz, a Bavarian refugee named Elisabeth Sedelmair had told Anna's tenant Magdalena Seitz that if she were to be baptized, Elisabeth would bring her "an armful of clothing, as much as she could carry."

In this case it appears mutual aid was an incentive to join the Anabaptists. This example must be contrasted with the many instances of those who joined the movement and lost all possessions through fines, imprisonment, or exile. Surely Magdalena understood that the risks of joining the movement far outweighed any potential material gain. The Anabaptists were also careful to emphasize that those who did not work would receive nothing. This emphasis discouraged laziness and people who might join their ranks simply to receive food and clothing.

(4) *Employment.* Providing work for one another was common among the Augsburg Anabaptists. The fact that half of those arrested on April 12 were immediately expelled as foreigners suggests that the community was supporting a large refugee population. "Servant" or "maid" was the occupation listed next to the names of many foreigners. Often those servants found work in the households of fellow believers.

Jos Thoma, a blue-dyer, employed two women from Bavaria as maids. Caspar Schlosser reported meeting an old woman from Bavaria who worked for Benedict Schneider's wife for four weeks. The large number of these foreign believers who were also in domestic service indicates that employment was an essential aspect of mutual aid within the congregation.

Such employment was not unusual. Referrals from one Anabaptist to another indicate the presence of a network among the believers. Prominent Anabaptist Barbara Schleiffer instructed one foreigner to apply to work for Jos Thoma. Jos confessed to supporting the foreigner, a fellow believer, for several days.

Anna Butz testified that the innkeeper Hans Lauterwein employed many people and that all of them were among the believers. Presumably the many people needed to run an inn would allow Lauterwein to employ refugees without drawing attention to himself. Surely it was no coincidence that these believers all found their way to the Lauterwein inn.

The network of referrals also extended outside of Augsburg. Itinerant minister Georg Nespitzer had worked diligently to organize Anabaptists both within the city and in nearby towns and villages to provide for the many refugees (Schwab 1962:225). As they fled or were expelled, members of the Augsburg congregation also became refugees in need of employment.

The testimony of Ursula Schleiffer, the daughter of the above-mentioned Barbara, reveals that her husband found work for several weeks in the nearby village of Göggingen. This community was known as an Anabaptist stronghold; exiles from Augsburg were welcome.

The phrase *tentmaker ministry* aptly describes the combination of employment and ministry some Anabaptist leaders used. Local leader Hans Leupold plied his trade as a tailor as he lodged with Anabaptist families in Augsburg and its outlying villages. In this way Hans supported himself and his ministry. Working as a tailor may have also deflected the suspicion of local authorities, ever on the lookout for Anabaptist activities. In this case, employment provided a cover for ministry among the believers.

It appears that the local congregation and the extended Anabaptist community cared for Anabaptist refugees by providing work. They also tried to protect their leaders by portraying them as traveling craftsmen. Providing work—and thereby the means to support oneself and the ministry of the church—is another form of mutual aid.

(5) *Refuge.* Although all of the above—giving money, shelter, food, clothing, and employment—are forms of mutual aid, in some cases the long-lasting, extensive nature of the assistance can be construed as giving refuge. This deserves separate attention. Usually such help was given to those who had fled persecution and were in need of long-term housing, sustenance, and even employment.

Two women, both wives of imprisoned Anabaptist leaders, especially benefited from the extended care of the congregation. Veronika Gross, wife of Jacob, and Anna Salminger, wife of Sigmund, were recipients of much congregational care. Both found refuge in the homes of several Augsburg Anabaptists.

Veronika stayed at times with Eitelhans Langenmantel, several weeks with Dorothea Frölich, and with Afra Gabler. Anna stayed five weeks with a wealthy widow named Honester Krafter, three weeks with Laux Kreler, and several times with the family of a butcher surnamed Finder. Anna admitted that her hosts provided her with food and other necessities. She also acknowledged that on several occasions she and other sisters in the faith received money.

Both Veronika and Anna contributed to their own support, as they emphasized to Peutinger. Veronika sold her husband's books and worked as a seamstress. Anna earned twelve *gulden* through the sale of her household goods. She found work where she could. For example, while lodging with the Laux Kreler family she did some spinning. Konrad Miller testified that both women had done spinning for his wife. Mutual aid was clearly at work as these women assisted their host families.

Elisabeth Sedelmair, the wife of a farmer from Bavaria, also received extensive sustenance from the congregation. She stayed with Els Knöll for eight nights and spent an undetermined amount of time in the Hans Lauterwein household as maid and cook.

According to testimony of Anna Butz, Elisabeth Sedelmair knew much about the rich in the congregation because she often stayed with the wealthier believers. She apparently had connections among the leaders in the congregation and was therefore able to offer mutual aid to others.

As mentioned above, Elisabeth was in a position to offer clothing to at least one potential convert. As a refugee, she probably had few resources of her own. Her connections with the wealthy members of the congregation, however, put her in a position to distribute to those in need.

Mutual aid in its many forms was crucial to the survival of the early Anabaptist congregations. Persecution left many members dependent on their faith communities for assistance (Peachey 1990:614). Widows and orphans were often at risk. Congregations provided for the travel needs of itinerant ministers and also cared for the families left behind them.[9] Sharing their resources allowed the Anabaptists to care for the many needs within their own congregation and for the refugees who fled into the city.

## The Organization of Mutual Aid

The beginning of organized care for the poor among the Augsburg believers can be traced to the selection of Sigmund Salminger and Jakob Dachser as congregational leaders in February 1527. Later, Hans Kiessling and Gall Vischer were elected to the specific job of deacon. Their task was to administer funds gathered in the common purse. Following their arrest and banishment in October 1527, four other men were selected as deacons.

Simprecht Wiedenman, a cobbler, revealed that at a spring meeting held outside the city he had been elected to care for the poor.[10] The three other elected "keepers of the purse" were a goldsmith named Laux Kreler, an innkeeper named Hans Lauterwein, and a weaver known only as Spitzendrat. These deacons apparently represented both rich and poor in the congregation.[11] Presumably the goldsmith and the innkeeper were among wealthier members of the congregation, while the cobbler and weaver represented the poorer members. These men agreed to look after their needy brothers and sisters, especially since the actions of the city council had caused so much suffering.

As "servant[s] of the poor," Simprecht and the other deacons were responsible to distribute the money collected in the common purse. In his testimony, Simprecht accounted for some of the money he had collected and distributed. He reported that fellow deacon Laux Kreler had sent him twelve *patzen* (small coins) several days earlier. He had given three or four to the wife of Hans Leupold, who had many small children, and another three to his sister-in-law, who was also a widow and had many children. One coin was given to each of the poor who were exiled on April 13-14. Simprecht emphasized that all contributions for the needy were voluntary, that all money collected was distributed to the poor, and that the deacons kept neither "penny nor farthing" for themselves (Roth 1901:93).

Although only men were formally elected to the post of deacons, their wives were also active in the distribution of food, clothing, and money. Katharina Wiedenmann, wife of Simprecht, confessed to providing eggs, lard, and baked goods to various people (Roth 1901:97). The unnamed wife of Laux Kreler assisted the sick wife and child of Jakob Rotenstein and gave money to Els Knöll, who was hosting two refugees (Roth 1901:134, 86). Elisabeth Vischer, wife of Gall, hosted and fed ministers Georg Nespitzer and Augustin Bader. She claimed to have given no money but had contributed food and drink to other brothers and sisters (Roth 1901:76). John Oyer surmises that within the city women could distribute goods more easily and call less attention to themselves than men.[12]

Not all Anabaptists were willing to risk the wrath of the city authorities by holding the common purse. Konrad Huber, a lacemaker, reluctantly admitted to Peutinger that previously he had possessed a purse containing twenty gulden (Roth 1901:88). It happened in the beginning of the movement when some fellow believers brought the purse to his house and begged him to see to the needs of the poor. Although he opposed it, he kept the money for five weeks. During that time and "in the presence of others" he distributed no more than one gulden each to several brothers. No longer wanting to be responsible, he then took the purse to the local leader Hans Leupold and bound him to be responsible. The community subsequently elected Hans Kiessling and Gall Vischer as the first deacons.

In his testimony, Konrad Huber claimed that he did not know where the money came from except that Laux Kreler had contributed ten gulden and that he could not remember to whom he had distributed the money. Even his wife indicated in her testimony that Konrad had given up the purse a year earlier (Roth 1901:110). Both took great pains to minimize Konrad's involvement with the common purse. Although that is not unusual in such interrogations, the Hubers seemed genuinely reluctant to be responsible for this aspect of communal mutual aid. As persecution intensified and the common purse was targeted, men like Konrad Huber were less willing to take on the role of deacon.[13]

Electing deacons was one method the congregation used to organize aid to the needy among them. Another was the simple understanding that believers would reach out directly to those in need. A journeyman named Georg Mang, for example, confessed that whenever he learned of a needy brother, he assisted the man with whatever he could afford at the time (Roth 1901:28). Anna Klein knew that her mother and two other women had provided "travel money" when a few of the brothers were forced to flee (Roth 1901:44). Other members of the congregation indicated that whenever needy persons came to their home, they gave, as it was God's commandment to do.[14] Thus the burden of caring for the many needs among them was shared by the entire congregation.

## The Theology of Mutual Aid

Reading between the lines, one finds glimpses of which motivated these believers to help the less fortunate amo Of primary importance was the concept that a believer's posse were not his or her own. They were held in trust and were to be free shared with those in need. In the words of Ambrose Spittelmaier, "I should not work so that my house be filled, and my bowl be full of meat, but rather I should see that my brother has enough" (Durnbaugh 1974:25).

Els Knöll remembered that as believers were leaving a meeting held in a cellar, one leader had told them to support their poor brothers and sisters. She admitted she had sold her cloak and coat for the support of the community (Roth 1901:86). Anabaptists were encouraged to think of their possessions as resources that could be made available to others.[15]

Although the leaders emphasized giving, there was also an understanding among Augsburg Anabaptists that assistance to others would be reciprocated. Not all said it as clearly as the grocer Elisabeth Hegenmiller, who reported that she had been told "as she does to the poor, it will be done to her."[16] The practice of reciprocal sharing enabled later leader Menno Simons to write, "not one of the devout who have joined themselves to us, nor any of their orphaned children, have been left to beg their way" (Studer 1965:38).

Sometimes help was given even when reciprocal sharing was not expected. From Els Knöll we learn that an Anabaptist preacher admonished all to charitable acts toward the poor (Roth 1901:87). Local leader Hans Leupold did not limit assistance to members of the faith but said that "instruction, assistance, and help" should be given "whether or not he is a brother" (Roth 1901:65). This attitude no doubt reflects their understanding of God's will, yet it was also an effective tool for evangelism.

Klassen (1967:102) indicates that mutual aid was integral to the witness of early Anabaptist believers. He cites the example of the so-called Martyrs' Synod held in Augsburg in 1527, where the Anabaptists "virtually took the practice of mutual aid by the missioners for granted, [and] also stated that the movement would accept only members who were committed to mutual aid."

Durnbaugh (1988:90) notes that mutual aid was so important to the early Anabaptists that they considered it a hallmark of the true church. Scholars underscore the theological significance of Menno Simons' declaration that the voluntary sharing of goods was an integral part of the communion of saints.[17]

Because sharing was expected of those who joined the Anabaptist community, was it a "voluntary" practice?[18] Anna Butz testified that due to risk of oppression of the poor by the rich, they were careful within the congregation to insist that if a brother had too much he must distribute his goods.[19] Other comments also reveal tensions between the richer and poorer members of the congregation.[20] Possibly there was greater internal pressure for the rich to contribute. Certainly giving was voluntary in the sense that no one was compelled to join the Anabaptists. Once that commitment had been made, however, members were expected to share their resources.

Faith thus influenced the economic views of the Anabaptists. Peter Klassen (1963:79) uses the word *discipleship* to characterize Anabaptist understandings of property. He traces this view to Hans Hut, an early leader in the South German movement. Hut taught that a Christian had no right to selfishly enjoy his goods but should regard them as the means of helping those less fortunate.

John Oyer (1961:17) also uses discipleship to describe a faith community in which "sharing with the brother in need was done so frequently as to make it virtually impossible for one to call his own goods strictly private." Thus, *sacred trust*, *stewardship*, and *discipleship* are terms that characterized the Anabaptist understanding of property from the beginning. To care for others was to fulfill the will of God.

# The Legacy of Aid

The institutionalization of mutual aid in Augsburg broke down when virtually the entire congregation was arrested. Hans Leupold was beheaded, and the remaining leaders and deacons were banished. A few believers met several times in the woods outside the city, but by the summer of 1528 they had disbanded.

The seeds of corporate care had been planted in the wider Anabaptist community. By 1538 prospective members in one congregation were asked, "If need should require it, are you prepared to devote all your possessions to the service of the brotherhood, and do you agree not to fail any member that is in need if you are able to help?" (Verduin 1964:240). In roughly 1540, Leopold Scharnschlager, an associate of a later Augsburg leader Pilgram Marpeck, penned the "Communal Rules for the Members of Christ, Arranged in Seven Articles." The third article prescribed that

> a brother should always be at hand with a collection box or purse so that every member may know where to place the freewill offering if he is urged by the Lord to do so. Thus it will be possible at any time to minister to the poor according to what is available and what is the need of each one (Durnbaugh 1974:49).

In at least one instance, a covenant between congregation and missionary became part of a later commissioning service. The congregation promised to pray for the missionary and to continue caring for the poor and needy among them, especially the widow and children, should the missionary be executed (Kasdorf 1984:63). The early Anabaptist commitment to mutual aid thus continued and became a hallmark of the faith.

Historians of Anabaptism recognize that mutual aid was an early hallmark of the faith. Harold S. Bender identified three aspects of mutual aid—discipleship, the church as a brotherhood, and the ethic of love and nonresistance—as central to the "Anabaptist Vision" (Durnbaugh 1988:88). These themes are indeed found in the records of the Augsburg congregation. Believers belonged to a community where caring for one another was the natural expression of one's Christian faith. The needs were many because of the poverty of some and the toll that imprisonment, torture, exile, and even death placed on the congregation.

Corporate and individual assistance became essential components of Anabaptist self-understanding. By 1540 mutual aid was formalized in baptismal vows and membership expectations. Aid as a basic principle of Anabaptist faith is rooted in its earliest adherents, including those in Augsburg arrested in 1528 as they gathered for worship Easter morning.

## Notes

I gratefully acknowledge the guidance and resources provided by John S. Oyer, without whom this project could not have been undertaken, nor completed.

1. Roth (1901:44) transcribed the interrogations conducted under the direction of Konrad Peutinger, a humanist and secretary of the city of Augsburg.

2. For a concise history of the Augsburg congregation, see Christian Hege (1955:182-185) and Paul J. Schwab (1962:212-228).

3. Regarding torture, Donald F. Durnbaugh (1974:23) says the authorities "hoped to find confirmation of their fears of rebellion and heresy and to learn the names of other radicals, especially leaders, so that they could be hunted down as well."

4. Stayer (1991:121). The concern of the Augsburg authorities contrasts with Klassen's (1963:82) assertion that many times the economic activities of the Anabaptists were not given attention. In Augsburg, however, mutual aid was an issue of prime concern.

5. Other researchers also have documented the cruciality of mutual aid in the Anabaptist movement. See Durnbaugh (1974, 1988) and Klassen (1963, 1964, 1967).

6. Roth (1901:69). This was not, however, an invitation to sloth. Those who could work, but would not, were expelled from the community (Durnbaugh 1974:8).

7. Roth (1901:23-101) provides the primary source material for this section on "Patterns of Mutual Aid" unless otherwise cited.

8. Both Konrad Huber and Simprecht Wiedenman indicate that Laux Kreler contributed significantly to the common purse (Roth 1901:88, 93). As a goldsmith, Kreler apparently had sufficient means to share with others.

9. Roth (1901:44, 94); Durnbaugh (1974:7); Klassen (1963:81, 91).

10. Roth (1901:92). Oyer (1996:88) surmises that the traffic in and out of Wiedenmann's cobbler shop provided excellent cover for Anabaptist assistance.

11. Clasen (1972:326) notes that two of the four deacons were wealthy. Oyer (1996) highlights the wisdom of the congregation in selecting men who could relate to the various social classes of the Augsburg congregation.

12. Oyer (1996) has documented the activities of women leaders among the congregation. He notes a widespread pattern of women providing food and lodging for both ministers and refugees. They also helped distribute alms.

13. Stayer (1991:121). According to his testimony, innkeeper Hans Lautterwein also refused to take part in the organized distribution of funds to the poor. He admitted only to helping out when asked, as any good Christian would do. He did not assist in any distribution, so he said, because his wife was worried about the opposition of the city council (Roth 1901:99).

14. Because God had so commanded, Konrad Huber gave money and food to any who came to him for help (Roth 1901:88). Hans Lauterwein testified that he had always given gladly, as any Christian should (Roth 1901:100). Elisabeth Vischer fed those who stayed with her, as God commanded (Roth 1901:76).

15. Durnbaugh (1988:88); Klassen (1963:78; 1967:104).

16. Roth (1901:55). She therefore contributed ten *kreutzer* (small coins) to the common fund. Stayer (1991:121) also notes this concept.

17. See, for example, Durnbaugh (1974); Klassen (1963 and 1967); Sommer (1954).

18. Klassen (1963:89) indicates that "those who wished to join the persecuted radicals were expected to share their earthly possessions with others less fortunate."

19. Roth (1901:41). Clasen (1972:326-7) also noticed this tension in the congregation and speculated that the rich disliked associating with the poor. He noted that four of the nine who refused to attend meetings outside the city also refused to act as purse bearers. Oyer (1961:17) concludes that "in their practice of sharing there was something of a leveler attitude; they regarded riches with scorn. He who was rich must distribute to those who were less fortunate."

20. The testimony of Els Knöll and Simprecht Wiedenmann reveals a perception among some members that the rich did not want to meet with poor. Matheis Hieber complained to Peutinger that the poor were exiled but the rich got off. Simprecht Wiedenman also complained that the wealthy were exempt from the standard torture (Roth 1901:86, 93, 101).

## References

Clasen, Claus-Peter
  1972   *Anabaptism: A Social History, 1525-1618.* Ithaca: Cornell University Press.

Durnbaugh, Donald F.
  1974   *Every Need Supplied: Mutual Aid and Christian Community in the Free Churches, 1525-1675.* Philadelphia: Temple University Press.

  1988   "Mutual Aid in Ministry to God's World." *Brethren Life and Thought* 33:87-97.

Hege, Christian
  1955   "Augsburg." *The Mennonite Encyclopedia,* vol. 1. Scottdale, Pa.: Herald Press.

Kasdorf, Hans
  1984   "The Anabaptist Approach to Mission." In *Anabaptism and Mission,* ed. Wilbert R. Shenk. Scottdale, Pa.: Herald Press.

Klassen, Peter J.
  1963   "Mutual Aid Among the Anabaptists: Doctrine and Practice." *Mennonite Quarterly Review* 37:78-95.

  1964   *The Economics of Anabaptism: 1525-1560.* London: Mouton & Co.

  1967   "The Anabaptist-Mennonite Witness Through Mutual Aid." In *The Church in Mission: A Sixtieth Anniversary Tribute to J. B. Toews,* ed. A. J. Klassen. Fresno, California: Board of Christian Literature, Mennonite Brethren Church.

Oyer, John S.
  1961   "Anabaptism in Central Germany: II. Faith and Life." In *The Mennonite Quarterly Review* 35:5-37.

1996 "Anabaptist Women Leaders in Augsburg: August 1527 to April 1528." In *Profiles of Anabaptist Women: Sixteenth-Century Reforming Pioneers*, ed. C. Arnold Snyder and Linda A. Huebert Hecht. Waterloo, Ont.: Wilfrid Laurier University Press. Pp. 82-105.

Peachey, Laban
1990 "Mutual Aid." *The Mennonite Encyclopedia*, vol. 5. Scottdale, Pa.: Herald Press.

Roth, Friedrich
1901 "Zur Geschichte der Wiedertäufer in Oberschwaben: III. Der Höhepunkt der widertäuferischen Bewegung in Augsburg und ihr Niedergang in Jahre 1528." In *Zeitschrift des historischen Vereins für Schwaben und Neuburg* 28:1-154.

Schwab, Paul J.
1962 "Augsburg and the Early Anabaptists." In *Reformation Studies: Essays in Honor of Roland H. Bainton*, ed. Franklin H. Littell. Richmond, Va.: John Knox Press.

Sommer, Donald
1954 "Peter Rideman and Menno Simons on Economics." *Mennonite Quarterly Review* 28:205-223.

Stayer, James M.
1991 *The German Peasants' War and Anabaptist Community of Goods*. Montreal: McGill-Queen's University Press.

Studer, Gerald C.
1965 *Toward a Theology of Servanthood*. Scottdale, Pa.: Association of Mennonite Aid Societies.

Umble, Jeni Hiett
1995 "Meeting Around the Distaff: Anabaptist Women and Social-Economic Status in Augsburg, 1527-1528." Unpublished pages.

Verduin, Leonard
1964 *The Reformers and Their Stepchildren*. Grand Rapids, Michigan: Baker Book House.

# 6

# Mutual Aid Among the Swiss Brethren, 1550-1750

## John D. Roth

Scholarship on mutual aid among the early Anabaptists has focused primarily on the first half of the sixteenth century. John D. Roth's research extends the scope of inquiry among the Swiss Brethren by exploring the practice of mutual aid in the second generation and beyond. After sketching the theological understandings and actual patterns of aid, Roth shows how the very survival of the Swiss Brethren depended on help from outside their communities. The complex dependencies that often accompany such well-intended benevolence make this chapter a fascinating case study.

## Framing the Question

In the fall of 1526, Balthasar Hubmaier, one of the earliest leaders of the young Anabaptist movement in Switzerland, defended the Swiss Brethren understanding of wealth to Zurich reformer Ulrich Zwingli. "I have ever and always spoken thus of the community of goods," Hubmaier (1989:183) wrote, "that one person should always look out for the other—for we are not lords of our own goods, but stewards and distributors."

More than a century and a half later, Georg Thormann, pastor of a small Reformed congregation in the village of Lützelflüh near Bern, described the Swiss Brethren in remarkably similar language. The Brethren, Thormann (1693:preface) noted, "do not regard themselves as lords over their own possessions but share freely with their neighbors in need." Between the time of Hubmaier and Thormann, much had changed in the history of the Swiss Brethren. Yet it seems clear that the principle of mutual aid had survived as an enduring and distinctive feature of the group.

The history of mutual aid among the Anabaptists has attracted a fair amount of scholarly attention. Peter Klassen's (1964) seminal work, *The Economics of Anabaptism*, provided a general survey of Anabaptist attitudes toward property, wealth, and labor during the first two decades of the movement. More recently, James Stayer (1991)—in a book entitled *The German Peasants' War and Anabaptist Community of Goods*—has insightfully analyzed the social, political, and theological context within which various Anabaptist understandings of mutual aid emerged during the tumultuous years of the early Reformation.

As with most Anabaptist scholarship, however, these monographs focus almost exclusively on the first generation. Apart from several studies of Hutterian community of goods,[1] we know surprisingly little about the Swiss Brethren theological understanding of mutual aid or how the ideal found concrete expression within congregational life.

In this paper I will explore three related sets of questions, focused primarily on the history of the Swiss Brethren from 1550 to 1750.

(1) How did the ideals regarding mutual aid, so clearly and consistently expressed by the first generation of Anabaptists, become part of the theological tradition of the Swiss Brethren as it took shape in the last half of the sixteenth century? How were these convictions articulated from one generation to the next? What were the primary modes of theological transmission (e.g., hymnody, confessional and apologetic writings, sermons, and catechisms)?

(2) How did the Swiss Brethren embody the principle of mutual aid in congregational life? What institutions for mutual aid, formal or informal, emerged as the Swiss Brethren settled into somewhat more stable patterns of economic and community life?

(3) During times of persecution the Swiss Brethren were also grateful recipients of outside aid from various sympathetic groups. How did these relationships of dependency shape the long-term character of the Swiss Brethren church? What were unintended consequences of the benevolence which frequently accompanied expressions of mutual aid?

If the traditional scholarly emphasis on the first generation of Anabaptists has provided modern Mennonites with a sense of heroic possibility—with all of its accompanying drama of inspiration and challenge—my aim in addressing these questions is to inquire into the far less dramatic (but equally important) process by which the ideal of mutual aid became habitual for the Swiss Brethren.

# Theological Roots (1550-1750)

In contrast to the Protestant reformers—who wrote systematic apologetics, closely-reasoned confessions, catechisms, and devotional books to defend and preserve their reforms—Anabaptist leaders tended to articulate theological positions ad hoc. They forged convictions more often in the fires of interrogation and debate than in the calm reflection of the scholar's study. Such was clearly the case with mutual aid.

Throughout the first half of the sixteenth century, the Swiss Brethren position on questions of property and wealth emerged against the highly charged backdrop of the Peasants War of 1525 and the debacle of the so-called "Anabaptist Kingdom of Münster" in 1535. Both these events were closely associated with the Anabaptist movement, and both had dramatically focused attention on questions regarding wealth, property, and economic equality.

In the aftermath of these violent uprisings, government authorities throughout Europe assumed that the religious protest of the Anabaptists was inextricably linked to the specter of political and economic revolution. Thus, interrogators of captured Anabaptists routinely posed questions regarding their economic attitudes and practices. Put on the defensive, first-generation Anabaptists were forced to make their understandings of wealth and mutual aid part of the public record.

None of the most prominent early Anabaptist leaders in Zurich—Conrad Grebel, Felix Manz, and Georg Blaurock—advocated a revolutionary leveling of all economic wealth of the sort feared by authorities. But each of these leaders did insist that the true Christian could not own property without taking regard of the needs of others (Bender 1950:159, 205, 254).[2]

In 1527 Hans Hut, the primary representative of the movement in Southern Bavaria and Austria, argued explicitly that the Christian should regard private property as a trust from God which should be used as a means to help the less fortunate. Shortly thereafter, Abrosius Spittelmayr, a vigorous missioner in Upper Austria, Bavaria, and Franconia, denounced the hoarding of private possessions and argued instead that "the true Christian should not possess so much on the whole earth as a place on which to set his foot" (Klassen 1963:80).

Similar Anabaptist testimonies regarding the Christian's obligation to share abound in the records of interrogations, trial transcripts, confessions of faith, and apologetic writings. Not surprisingly, it was the Hutterites, with their distinctive practice of community of goods, who gave the most sustained theological attention to economic issues.[3] But other Anabaptist leaders—among them Hans Hut, Balthasar Hubmaier, and Menno Simons—also consistently addressed themes of wealth and mutual aid.[4]

Setting aside for the moment the debate over community of goods, let us look at how early Anabaptist teachings on mutual aid point toward a general convergence of convictions. Since all the earth belongs to God, the argument usually ran, Christians are merely stewards—not owners—of their material possessions; they have been entrusted by God to make the land productive, but they may not hoard their property for selfish purposes. Within the gathered community, the spiritual equality and mutuality suggested by the concept of the priesthood of all believers should include temporal possessions as well: each member of the congregation is responsible for the material welfare of the other members and should share freely wherever there is need. This sharing should not be done out of any sense of compulsion but as a voluntary and natural expression of one's love of neighbor.

On all of these basic principles, Anabaptists—who sometimes held widely differing positions on other doctrines such as the sword or church discipline—agreed. Regenerated believers, baptized in the body of Christ, should freely share of their material possessions if another member of the community is in need.

In the hostile setting of the courtroom, Swiss Brethren prisoners frequently emphasized to wary magistrates the *voluntary* nature of mutual aid. They thus distanced themselves from charges that they were advocating the elimination of all private property. These assurances seem to have made an impression.

By the second half of the century, as memories of the Peasants' War and Münster receded, authorities gradually lost interest in Anabaptist teachings on economics or their specific understandings of mutual aid. Questions regarding wealth, so central to earlier interrogations, become conspicuously absent in the court testimony and public debates after 1550.

Economic issues, for example, were not even broached at the Pfeddersheim Disputation of 1559 (Oyer 1986:304-351). Nor did they emerge as significant themes in the 1571 disputation at Frankenthal, where Swiss Brethren leaders debated for nineteen days with some of the leading Reformed theologians of South Germany.

The published transcriptions of the Frankenthal Disputation run to more than 700 pages. But Article IX, "Concerning Community of Goods:

Whether a Christian Can Buy and Own Property Without Violating Human Love," scarcely evoked a ripple of controversy between the two parties and was one of the few points on which both sides readily agreed. In their brief statement on Article IX, the Swiss Brethren defended the Christians' right to own property and explicitly sought to distance themselves from their Hutterian cousins. They "wished neither to praise or to defend" the practice of community of goods among the people of Moravia.[5]

But if authorities were losing interest in Swiss Brethren views on property and mutual aid, debate over these questions *within* the Anabaptist community was becoming far less measured. At stake was an issue that had festered in the Anabaptist movement almost from the moment of its beginnings in Zurich. Did genuine mutual aid, based on the model of the apostolic church in Acts 2 and 4, imply "community of goods" as a necessary and inevitable feature of the regenerated church? Or could the individual own private property that should then be shared voluntarily with needy members of the congregation?

As historian James Stayer has demonstrated, the Swiss Brethren had advocated a rule of economic sharing, which they explicitly linked to the biblical model suggested by Acts 2 and 4. Even though many of their earliest statements, including the Congregational Order of 1527, seemed to suggest that a common purse was biblically mandated, most Swiss Brethren were already qualifying the principle by arguing that the practice of mutual aid could not be coerced: sharing of possessions must be a *voluntary* decision on the part of the individual believer. "I don't reject property," insisted Hans Hausimann, an emissary from the Basel congregation commissioned to baptize in Bern. "In the beginning of Christianity everything was in common, but it is no command" (Stayer 1991:104).

Thus the Swiss Brethren argued that while community of goods was a fine thing, it should be a voluntary expression of Christian love, not made into an absolute principle of Christian faithfulness. Initially, as we have seen, the argument for voluntary mutual aid emerged as part of the Swiss Brethren defense against charges by the magistrates that they were advocating social and economic revolution. By mid-century, however, the focus of the debate shifted inward, pitting the Swiss Brethren against their Hutterian cousins.

Since 1528 the Hutterites, close spiritual relatives of the Swiss Brethren, had practiced a literal community of goods in the conviction that the gathered body of believers (*Gemeinde*) only became the body of Christ if it literally held all things in common (*Gemein*). As the Swiss

Brethren moved toward a clearer defense of private property in their encounters with state authorities, tensions with the Hutterites in Moravia over community of goods agenda inevitably escalated.

Fueling the bitter intensity of the debate was the mission strategy and zeal of the Hutterites. Every spring Hutterian communities in Moravia sent out teams of itinerant missionaries to recruit new members for the community. These missionaries quickly discovered that the best prospects for the Hutterite cause were to be found among the Swiss Brethren, so Hutterite mission efforts consciously targeted Swiss Brethren congregations. Since the two groups shared many of the same theological assumptions, the main point of Hutterite appeal focused on the controversial question of private property.

In 1556, for example, a group of Swiss Brethren in Bad Kreuznach joined the Hutterites. They explained, in the words of the *Hutterite Chronicle*, that the Swiss Brethren wrongly taught that each could "keep his own possessions and give to the poor whatever suited him." According to the new converts, the Swiss Brethren might have taught that everyone in the congregation *should* share, but in practice, if someone in the community was in need, he had to buy it from the other members (*Chronicle* 331).

In the course of the 1540s, 1550s, and 1560s, hundreds of Swiss Brethren left their congregations in central or southern Germany to join the community life of the Moravian Hutterites. For the Swiss Brethren who remained behind, the debate over private property and mutual aid was not merely a quarrel over abstract theological principles but a question linked to the very viability of their church.

One instructive exchange between the two groups occurred in 1567. Sometime the previous year, Swiss Brethren leaders had issued seven charges against the Hutterites. The first addressed the "Community as It Pertains to Possessions." Although the original Swiss Brethren document has not been located, the essence of their position can be reconstructed from the 376-page polemical response issued by the Hutterite community in Moravia in 1567 to defend its position. According to the Hutterites, the Swiss Brethren had claimed that they themselves "and all men are free in Christ without giving up temporal possessions." They wished to live and work independently, to raise their children in private, and to "share whatever whenever" as they saw fit.

The Swiss Brethren had cited scriptural references to defend their position. They noted, for example, that Philemon was a slave; therefore, members in the early church did indeed possess property. They also argued that the admonition of Christ to the rich young ruler applied only to the particular case and that the church of the apostles had given no explicit command to practice community of goods. The Swiss Brethren, implying that shared possessions inevitably led to tyranny, further charged the Hutterites with coercing members into giving up their property.

The Hutterites bristled at these notions, dismissing them as "a fine sermon for the uncommitted flesh." They recounted stories that had circulated about Swiss Brethren practice. As soon as baptism was given, so one story went,

> new converts go home to their possessions, give a trifle according to what they can afford, and at death leave their possession to unbelieving children or friends. . . . For the poor saints in the congregation to which they had offered themselves as a member they leave very little, or for the sake of appearances a small amount (*Abgeschrifft* 1567:17).[6]

Furthermore, the Hutterites had heard that the Swiss Brethren allowed some children of widows to go begging and forced them "to find their own poor food in the Netherlands before you took them in." In Aachen, a Swiss Brethren by the name of Jänekhus had a large stone house with plenty of furnishings and food while others lived in the woods because of persecution; even though one of the Swiss Brethren children had been eaten by wolves, he still did not take them in.

The Swiss Brethren church "had so declined in unity and love" that three or four married couples could not even live together in a large house,

> but each couple cooks separately, and without shame all eat at the same table divided into three or four sections, one eating well and the other poorly. . . . Even wood and ashes are not shared equally, each wants to be next to the fire, they argue over cattle . . . and finally, if they want peace, each must build a separate house or get rooms at an inn.

"What inequality," the Hutterites concluded, "what miserable community!" (*Abgeschrifft* 1567:17). Tensions between the Hutterites and the Swiss Brethren seem to have persisted through the end of the century.

By refusing to make community of goods an absolute principle, the Swiss Brethren added Christian voluntarism and pragmatic flexibility to their understanding of mutual aid, a stance they defended on the basis of Scripture. But the debate with the Hutterites also revealed the ambiguities of their position. If complete economic equality was not an absolute requirement for the Christian community, then one was forced to recognize and accept some measure of economic disparity in the congregation.

One partial response to this ambiguity was an effort during the second half of the sixteenth century to develop guidelines for regulating the economic activities of church members. Thus Hans Pauli Kuchen-becker, a Swiss Brethren in Hesse, included several articles related to mutual aid in his 1578 confession of faith. "Newborn Christians and children of God," wrote Kuchenbecker (1951:434-436), "can buy, own and use their own property as long *as they help the poor and extend aid.*"[7]

The article went on to denounce other economic activities widely accepted in early modern Europe, such as interest-taking and merchan-dising, and to defend the virtues of honest hand work in contrast to the ethically questionable labor of the merchant. The following article, "On The Poor," offered even clearer teaching on the congregation's responsi-bility "to support our poor members and comrades in the faith, old and sick, widows and orphans, and to show love to other needy people."

Kuchenbecker's confession, however, is among the last Swiss Brethren statements to address the question of private property and poverty in the church from an explicitly theological framework. By the end of the century, as the debate with the Hutterites reached a stalemate, positions on both sides had become firmly entrenched. Sources regard-ing Swiss Brethren attitudes toward mutual aid had fallen virtually si-lent. Indeed, surveying the catechetical and devotional literature be-tween 1600 and 1750, one could easily infer that the Swiss Brethren were simply not interested in mutual aid, at least not as a theological category.

According to some scholars, this silence in the sources should not come as a surprise since the Swiss Brethren supposedly did not engage in theological reflection of any sort. Unlike their Dutch counterparts, who published dozens of theological treatises, the Swiss consciously avoided theological argumentation and emphasized instead the existen-tial life of discipleship rooted in Christian ethics (Oyer 1984:218-229). While others may have been talking about mutual aid, the Swiss Breth-ren were quietly practicing it.

This argument does include truth. On the whole, the Swiss Breth-ren *were* less educated, more rural, more interested in ethics than theo-logical speculation. But recent archival discoveries suggest the Swiss Brethren were more creatively and actively engaged in theological re-flection than was earlier assumed. An extended theological defense of the use of the ban by Thomas Meyer, for example, has recently been brought to light in the Zurich archives, along with an eighty-page state-ment of faith attributed to Andreas Gut and an even lengthier (350-page) treatise offering a systematic Swiss Brethren response to the topics raised in the Frankenthal Debate, where they had not fared well.[8]

Although these recent archival finds have not been systematically studied, enough is known about them to report that the principle of mutual aid is not addressed in them. The predominant themes are arguments related to the ban, the relationship of the Old and New Testaments, and whether a Christian can serve in the offices of judge or magistracy. These themes—not mutual aid—seem to have been the issues that made the Swiss Brethren most distinctive or theologically troublesome in the seventeenth and eighteenth centuries.

Nor does mutual aid emerge as an explicit theme in the better known theological literature of the Swiss Brethren. By the early seventeenth century, the devotional repertoire of most Swiss Brethren households would have included a book entitled *Güldene Aepffel in Silbern Schalen* (*Golden Apples in Silver Bowls*). Published first in 1702, the book offered its readers a compilation of martyr stories, apologetic writings, and devotional materials, many of which had been circulating in the community for decades as independent tracts.

In addition, the Swiss Brethren borrowed heavily from the North German and Dutch catechal tradition in the seventeenth and eighteenth centuries. They particularly favored the catechism of the Hamburg leader Gerhard Roosen (*Christliche Gemütsgespräch*, first published in 1702), various hymns and prayers from Leonhardt Klock, and a popular children's catechism by Johannes Deknatel of Amsterdam entitled *Anleitung zum christlichen Glauben* (first German edition, 1756).

 absences continued

To this list one must add the Dordrecht Confession (*Christliche Glaubensbekenntnis*, with German editions published in 1691 and 1711), which had been a significant part of the Swiss Brethren canon since 1660 (Friedmann 1949:35-40, 154-202). Yet, surprisingly, in all of these writings mutual aid is mentioned only fleetingly or is absent altogether. To be sure, one can find scattered admonitions to care for the poor or to provide appropriate support for ministers in the congregation, but the principle of mutual aid was not a sharply defined article of faith along the lines of the oath or nonresistance.

Perhaps mutual aid was given more explicit attention in private Bible study or teaching. The sources are largely silent on this topic, but one interesting window into the Swiss Brethren use of scripture is offered by a 370-page concordance entitled *Conkordantz*.[9] Originating among South German Anabaptists in the 1540s, the concordance was reprinted several times in the seventeenth century and identified by authorities as representative of the theological orientation of the Swiss Brethren (Thormann 1693:375). Concordances need not be slavishly followed, of course, but they do provide a filter for reading Scripture. They selectively highlight particular themes and direct the reader to specific verses that support the theological bias of the compiler.

The *Conkordantz* explicitly addressed mutual aid only in two brief passages. Under the heading "Alms" (*Allmusen*), one finds several Old Testament references to tithing along with four references to wealth from the Gospels.[10] The one New Testament verse cited in full in the text comes from Matthew 6:20: "Store up for yourselves treasures in heaven, where moth and rust do not destroy, and where thieves do not break in and steal."

The second reference relevant to mutual aid is labeled "community" (*Gemeinschaft*). Here eight New Testament references are cited with the classic passages on mutual aid within the apostolic church from Acts 2 (v. 44-45) and Acts 4 (v. 32) reprinted in full. The larger point, however, is that these are the only apparent references to questions of economic life. Together, they total scarcely four pages (the entry for "separation" [*Absonderung*], by contrast, included ninety-one biblical references and ran for sixteen pages).[11]

Perhaps teachings on mutual aid were embedded more subtly or "organically" in the hymnody of the Swiss Brethren. If so, then one should find references to economic sharing in the *Ausbund*, a collection of versified martyr stories and edifying hymns compiled in the second half of the sixteenth century which served as the primary Swiss Brethren hymn book. The *Ausbund* was reprinted frequently for use among the Swiss Brethren during the seventeenth and eighteenth centuries. Like the *Conkordantz*, it was identified by various opponents as an authoritative text in the Swiss Brethren tradition (Wolkan 1965:33).

Interestingly, the earliest edition of the *Ausbund* (1564) did indeed contain three hymns which made explicit reference to community of goods. However, beginning in 1583 all these hymns were dropped from subsequent *Ausbund* editions, presumably as a part of the broader Swiss Brethren effort to distance themselves from the Hutterites. In my work with the hymnal, I have not found any clear references to the themes of mutual aid.

This survey of religious literature suggests that mutual aid was not a sharply defined or self-conscious principle of identity among the Swiss Brethren during the seventeenth and eighteenth centuries. It is possible that in a preindustrial cultural context the idea that a bounded community should provide for the well-being of its members was simply assumed.

Certainly basic mutual aid principles would have been commonplace themes in the framework of religious fraternities and guilds in early modern Europe. Most European villages of the day had their own community poor chests, long traditions of shared access to the "commons," and a deep sense of obligation to care for the physical well-being of widows and orphans in their midst.

Perhaps the Anabaptist principles of mutual aid became truly distinctive only in the industrial era of modern capitalism when these older traditions of community welfare began to break down. If this was so, then developing a theological rationale for mutual aid and a conscious pedagogical strategy for passing it down from generation to generation would have become relevant only in the modern era.

It is also possible that the Swiss Brethren were indeed teaching the principles of mutual aid even though their instruction was indirect rather than explicit. Thus, although the *Ausbund*—like virtually all of the devotional and catechetical literature noted above—does not highlight mutual aid as a distinct theme, a general theology of mutual aid might be inferred from other themes, which are more explicitly evident in its hymns. There is, for example, in many of the martyr hymns an explicit emphasis on the sovereignty of God and a keen awareness that temporal things have no spiritual value. Implicit in the stories of suffering is a call to show compassion to others who may also be suffering. And many of the hymns suggest that love of God is linked to the love of neighbor. In the end, it may be that such general theological themes are the most crucial underpinnings for a theology of mutual aid, a theology that persisted in an implicit, rather than explicit, form.

## Swiss Brethren Practice (1550-1750)

The absence of any self-conscious reflection on the principle of mutual aid—at a time of relatively great theological creativity among Swiss Brethren—is surprising. However, there can be no doubt that the Swiss Brethren continued to practice mutual aid in a variety of local settings. To be sure, none of these expressions were highly formalized. A strong congregational polity among the Swiss Brethren, along with repeated waves of persecution and upheaval, discouraged the creation of centralized institutions for mutual aid along the lines of the Prussian Mennonite "Tiegenhof Fire Ordnance" plan of 1623 or the "General Committee for Foreign Needs," which Dutch Mennonites established in 1710.

But Swiss Brethren leaders did recognize the need to establish basic guidelines for poor relief in their scattered congregations. In 1568 representatives from Swiss Brethren congregations throughout Switzerland and South Germany met at Strasbourg to seek a common position on a number of matters related to faith and practice. Eight of the twenty-three articles of agreement reached at the gathering addressed practical matters related to economic life.

Article 2, for example, seemed to encourage a perspective on mutual aid that extended beyond the local congregation: ministers were admonished to "visit neighboring congregations and, as much as possible, to supply them with whatever they lack." The following article called attention to the material needs of the leaders and their dependents. Ministers and elders were to

> visit, provide for and comfort the wives and children of those ministers who travel in danger or are in prison (or for the widows and orphans of those who have died) so that everyone in need might be provided for and those that are absent rest in the confidence that their loved ones are cared for.

Moreover, article 5 committed the Brethren to remember and to care for orphans "before other responsibilities" and to bring them up "in the fear of God, [to] discipline as one's own children and not [to] despise or cast [them] out." And Article 6 gave specific instructions as to how the care of orphan children of the brethren and elders of the congregation was to be funded. Those who were poor should be "brought up as opportunity affords from the common property; the well-to-do orphans however shall be brought up from their own property for a reasonable allowance" (Bender 1927:57-66). Subsequent conferences of Swiss Brethren leaders reaffirmed virtually all of these basic points.

Unfortunately, evidence of the actual implementation of these principles is scarce, especially for the seventeenth and eighteenth centuries. The *Taüferakten* do make occasional reference to Swiss Brethren *Armendiener* (deacons). This suggests the Swiss Brethren modeled their efforts at poor relief on the Acts 6 example. In this case the disciples collected money among believers for the poor members, then elected deacons to administer the funds. Followers of Hans Hut established a poor fund at St. Gall as early as 1526. And in the 1530s the Brethren in Strasbourg sent deacon Hans Frisch to collect tithes in a box (Bender 1927:189). Early Anabaptist congregations at Augsburg, Esslingen, Strasbourg, Kauibeuren, Passau, and the Tyrol also had common funds to provide for the poor in their midst (Clasen 1972:187-88).[12]

The first formal description of the office of deacon appears only in 1591. An ecumenical gathering of Anabaptists at Cologne (the group included Swiss Brethren, Dutch, and North German Mennonites) included in their summary statement a job description for the Armendiener:

> Deacons shall be chosen according to the example of the Apostolic Church, to whom is to be assigned the care of the poor. They are to distribute to the poor the gifts received for this purpose, so that the giver shall remain unknown as Christ teaches (Gross and Gleysteen 1991:xx).[13]

While ministerial records from the early eighteenth century make it clear that the office of Armendiener was firmly established within the leadership structure of Swiss Brethren congregations, we have only fragmentary evidence as to how the funds were actually administered. An entry in the church record book from the Montbeliard congregation in Alsace suggests that members of several different congregations cared for an elderly person on a rotating basis. This model of gifts "in kind" almost certainly supplemented a more systematic collection and distribution of alms by the deacon.

*elder care*
③

We know of one such fund through an episode told in the *Martyrs' Mirror*. In 1637 Swiss authorities in Knonau arrested Rudolf Egly, who had administered the poor fund of the Swiss Brethren congregation in that village. When soldiers threatened Martha Lindinger, Egly's wife, with the severest of tortures, she finally revealed the location of money (an act for which she later bitterly repented). Authorities confiscated 2,000 gulden.[14]

This seems to be a considerable amount of money if one takes as a frame of reference the fact that Swiss Brethren farms valued at 4,000-9,000 gulden were being confiscated by the government at the same time. It is difficult, however, to know whether this was a "typical" poor relief fund. Knonau was not a large congregation, but it was a center for Swiss Brethren activity in the Zurich region, and Egly was widely known and well-traveled. So it is possible that the amount of money gathered here was unusually large.

Certainly the stories of confiscations, imprisonments, and expatriation among the Swiss Brethren recounted in *Martyrs Mirror* underscore the need for a well-developed system of financial aid. Likely congregations assisted individual families when the head of the household was imprisoned or banished from the territory. The poor fund probably also supported travel costs for individuals and families who, in the face of persecution, emigrated to the Palatinate or to Moravia. Much more archival research remains to be done, however, before we can speak with any certainty about the administration of such funds.

*other examples of mutual aid*

In summary, patterns of mutual aid, especially in the form of poor relief, emerged quickly among Swiss Brethren congregations with the establishment of the office of the Armemdiener or deacon and the clear expectation that each group had an obligation to care for its poor. But these poor funds seem to be linked to specific local congregations and were not highly rationalized or coordinated in any centralized fashion.

*mutual aid tied to local congregation (not controlled)*

Other expressions of mutual aid within the congregation included economic support for ministers and their families, clearly stated commitments for the care of orphans, and travel funds to assist Swiss Brethren refugees. Although we know relatively few specific details of mutual aid, it is clear that fraternal assistance within Swiss Brethren congregations was crucial for the church's survival in a hostile environment.

## The Complexities of Giving and Receiving

Perhaps the most effective means of keeping the principle of mutual aid alive among the Swiss Brethren was the fact that they were themselves recipients of mutual aid. Indeed, their very survival as a community in the seventeenth and eighteenth centuries depended on the largesse of others.

In each instance, the Swiss Brethren were deeply grateful for the assistance given, but it is also clear that the act of receiving aid brought with it a set of complex consequences. These eventually led to a subtle but profound transformation in Swiss Brethren theology and identity.

The initial occasion for Swiss Brethren reliance on the mutual aid of others was a renewal of religious intolerance and governmental persecution in the 1630s and 1640s in Zurich and a second wave of persecution by Bernese authorities in the last half of the seventeenth century. Since the earliest years of the movement, the Swiss Brethren had lived under the shadow of intermittent persecution. Imprisonment, torture, expulsion, and even execution had virtually eradicated the movement in the urban areas of Switzerland by the middle of the sixteenth century. However, in the scattered hamlets and remote villages of the Bernese Oberland and the Emmental, small pockets of Swiss Brethren stubbornly persisted.

With time, an unofficial compromise slowly emerged between the Swiss Brethren and state authorities. On the one hand, the Swiss Brethren continued to face various forms of official persecution. They could not openly proselytize, for example, and all their worship services were held in secret. Since the state refused to recognize marriages within the Swiss Brethren congregations as legally valid, children born of these unions were considered illegitimate. They therefore had no legal status in regards to property ownership and inheritance. Cantonal authorities, particularly in Bern, would periodically issue a new round of mandates against the Swiss Brethren threatening them with fines, expulsion, and even death if they did not desist from their heretical beliefs (Müller 1895; Gratz 1953).

Yet underneath this official persecution, the Swiss Brethren appear to have been remarkably well-integrated into local community life. By many accounts, their non-Anabaptist neighbors regarded them as honest, upright, hard-working people whose eccentric religious customs did not seem to imperil the welfare of the community in any practical way. Much to the anger of civil authorities, many village pastors in the Reformed state church turned a blind eye to the presence of Swiss Brethren in their communities.

In addition, some friends and neighbors went beyond passive acceptance to various forms of active support. These people, known to the Swiss Brethren as the Truehearted (*Treuherzige*) or Half-Anabaptists (*Halbtäufer*), did not accept adult baptism or formally join the Swiss Brethren fellowship. However, they were deeply impressed by the spiritual integrity and ethical rigor of their Anabaptist neighbors and were sympathetic to their cause. In times of persecution, many of the Truehearted offered material assistance to Swiss Brethren families impoverished by fines. Some even sheltered Swiss Brethren hunted by state authorities.

The Swiss Brethren dependence on this help first became apparent in Zurich during the mid-1630s. In 1633 Zurich authorities took a census of the entire population of the Canton, in part to identify all of the Swiss Brethren living in the region. In 1635, following several unsuccessful attempts at public debate, authorities arrested some 300 Swiss Brethren and began to implement a policy designed to eradicate the Swiss Brethren population of the Canton. For the next ten years, the Swiss Brethren were subjected to house searches, arrests, confiscation of their property, imprisonment, occasional torture, and deportation (Bergmann 1916:68-135).

In the midst of these difficult years, the Swiss Brethren found support from two quite different sources. Locally, the Truehearted continued to supply beleaguered Brethren with food and shelter. On several occasions they actively interfered with governmental investigations, much to the anger of authorities. Though they remained members of the state church, the Truehearted were deeply sympathetic to the plight of the Swiss Brethren and assumed significant risks in their covert support for the Swiss Brethren cause.

At the same time, the Swiss Brethren also received aid from afar through the dramatic intervention on their behalf by the Dutch Mennonites. Late in the 1630s, rumors of Swiss Brethren persecution in Zurich had come to the attention of Mennonites in Amsterdam. In 1642 Godefridus Hottonus, pastor at an Amsterdam Mennonite church, wrote a letter to Zurich asking whether these rumors of Anabaptist persecution were indeed true. In response, the Swiss Brethren in Zurich gave a full account of their plight in a report written by Jeremias Mangold.[15]

The report provided a series of vignettes on the suffering that Zurich authorities had inflicted on specific individuals. It recounted in detail the precise nature of their punishments and the amount of money confiscated by authorities. According to a contemporary historian, J. H. Ottius (1672), Mennonites in Amsterdam immediately sent financial assistance in the form of 100 *rijksdalers* to the Swiss Brethren in Zurich in March 1645, along with a letter of encouragement and support.

The fullest expression of Dutch Mennonite generosity occurred several decades later in the 1660s, when authorities in Bern mounted a full-scale campaign to eradicate the Swiss Brethren from the region (Müller 1895:104-163). Throughout the 1660s, authorities imposed stiff fines on all who refused to have their babies baptized. They ordered Reformed pastors to preach regularly against the "pernicious sect" and renewed the threat of capital punishment for recalcitrant offenders.

These efforts culminated with a mandate of September 8, 1670, which demanded that all Anabaptists who did not swear a general oath of allegiance to the Bernese government were to be expelled from the country within two weeks. Those who refused to go were to be whipped, led forcibly to the border, and marked with a branding iron; if they returned they were to be executed. In several communities, non-Anabaptist village leaders were taken hostage until the village proved its compliance with the mandate. At least six Swiss Brethren men were sent to Venice as galley slaves.

In the face of these hardships, many Swiss Brethren fled their native country westward to Alsace or down the Rhine valley to the Palatinate in the north. Thus in 1671, more than 700 Swiss Brethren emigrants, many old, infirm, and completely impoverished, flocked to the Palatinate seeking religious toleration. In the next decades, hundreds more Swiss Brethren left home searching for solace in the Alsace and Palatinate.

Estimates vary, but in the early 1690s as many as 400 more refugees flocked to the Alsace region. There they joined established Swiss Brethren congregations in the villages of Markirch, Jebsheim, and Ohnenheim under protection of the lords of Rappoltsweiler. In 1709 the Bernese government made yet another attempt to rid the land of all Swiss Brethren, prompting in 1710 the exodus of another wave of refugees.

With each new wave of persecution and emigration, the Dutch Mennonites responded with astounding energy and generosity.[16] The effort began on October 24, 1659, with a letter of protest and intercession from Hans Vlaming, deacon of the Amsterdam Mennonite congregation, to city officials in Bern and concluded in 1717 with the last settlement of Swiss refugees in Sappemeer.

The full details of that relief effort to the Bernese Brethren cannot be told here. It is important to note, however, the broad scope of Dutch aid to the Swiss. It included direct financial gifts (eventually amounting to at least 500,000 guilders), moral support in the form of letters of encouragement, direct political lobbying by Dutch diplomats and influential businessmen in an effort to persuade Swiss authorities to mitigate their persecution, and logistical support in the relocation of hundreds of Swiss refugees to settlements in the Alsace, Holland, or North America.

The story of this massive relief effort deserves a broader hearing. The systematic and sustained benevolent efforts of Dutch Mennonites undoubtedly spared the lives of hundreds of Swiss Brethren. Such aid left a legacy of compassion which surely inspired the descendants of those Swiss refugees to respond in kind to the plight of Russian Mennonites in the 1870s, the 1920s, and the 1940s.

It might be tempting to end the story here with the warm image of the Dutch Mennonite generosity poured out to their suffering fellow believers. But acts of charity are never simple deeds: even the most benevolent gesture of charity establishes a relationship of hierarchy and dependence. This can have consequences far beyond the act itself. As recipients of mutual aid from both their Truehearted neighbors and the more distant Dutch Mennonites, the Swiss Brethren community was not immune to these complexities.

The first of these complexities focused on the Truehearted, those sympathetic villagers who continued to attend the state church and refused to accept adult baptism but nonetheless frequently attended Swiss Brethren meetings and offered active support for the Swiss Brethren movement. The Truehearted were deeply impressed with the Swiss Brethren and willing to offer much needed material support in times of persecution. However, they were not prepared to put their lives or livelihoods in jeopardy by publicly committing themselves to the church.

From a pragmatic perspective, the Swiss Brethren were deeply grateful to the Truehearted for their many secret acts of kindness and support. Yet from a theological perspective, gratitude toward the Truehearted created a dilemma the Swiss Brethren did not know how to resolve. At the heart of the Swiss Brethren religious outlook was a view of the world that divided all of creation into two spheres: the fallen world ruled by Satan and characterized by violence, selfishness, and enmity; and the gathered, visible community of the redeemed who lived together in accordance with Jesus' standard of forgiveness and love.

Expressed most succinctly in the Schleitheim Confession of 1527, this dualistic view of life lived on in the sixteenth- and seventeenth-century hymnody, martyrologies, and devotional literature of the Swiss Brethren. The constant threat of persecution only reinforced this view of the church as a distinct society set apart from a hostile and alien world.

The most important religious ritual in the Swiss Brethren tradition was believers baptism. Baptism marked the great divide between the fallen world and the gathered body of the redeemed. This understanding, grounded in scripture and theologically consistent, technically left no place for the Truehearted within the Christian community. Since they refused to be baptized into the fellowship, the Truehearted were, logically speaking, part of the fallen world and outside the salvation of Christ. At the same time, however, their acts of kindness to the Swiss Brethren—often at great risk to themselves—made life bearable in the midst of persecution. Thus many of the Swiss Brethren were loath to make an issue of whether the Truehearted were saved or not.

In the early 1690s, amid intense persecution in Bern, this latent tension surfaced as part of a reform movement led by Jakob Ammann (Roth 1993). Ammann and his supporters were troubled by the casual and generous attitude of some Swiss Brethren ministers toward the Truehearted. While one could be grateful for material assistance, Ammann pointed out, the Truehearted had not made a commitment to baptism and had not submitted to the discipline of the congregation. Since they were not a part of the church, they were still part of the world and therefore in need of salvation. To pretend that the Truehearted were saved made a mockery of the Anabaptist understanding of adult baptism and the integrity of the gathered church.

Others in the Swiss Brethren church, led by Hans Reist, refused to disassociate themselves from the Truehearted or to make any absolute pronouncements on their salvation. In language reminiscent of the Swiss Brethren attempt to compromise on the question of community of goods in the debate with the Hutterites, Reist and others sought some sort of middle ground. On the one hand, they shared with Ammann a view of the church as being distinct from the world, and they too were committed to the exercise of church discipline. But they recognized, often implicitly and out of the painful reality of their experience, that the absolute boundaries between the fallen world and the church described in Schleitheim were not always relevant.

Even Christ, they argued, fellowshipped with tax collectors and sinners. The Truehearted should not be permitted at the communion table, but social avoidance had never been part of the teachings of Christ or the Apostles. Moreover, who could say with certainty whether, in the providence of God, the Truehearted would be saved or not? For Reist and his supporters, refusal to declare the Truehearted as part of the fallen order was a compromise they thought could be accommodated in the mystery of God's redemptive love and grace.

Ammann had a legitimate point. According to the logic of the Swiss Brethren understanding of the church—as a gathering of adult believers who publicly expressed commitment through the ritual of baptism—the Truehearted were indeed part of the fallen world. Nevertheless, in light of the generous help the Truehearted offered, the majority of Swiss Brethren were willing to duck the logical implications of their own theology. The result was deep division in the Swiss Brethren church.

Relations with the Dutch were at least as complex, if not more so. The Dutch clearly considered themselves faithful co-representatives with the Swiss Brethren of the same Anabaptist family. Their support had been crucial to the very survival of so many Brethren. At one level, the pitiful plight of the Swiss refugees had created at least a hint of critical self-reflection among the well-established, wealthy Dutch Mennonites. Thielman van Braght, for example, eagerly included the stories of persecuted Zurich and Bernese Brethren as a contemporary continuation of the ancient drama of suffering Christians. In van Braght's reading, the Swiss Brethren experience served as a mirror in which Dutch Mennonites could reflect uneasily on their own comfort and security.

In an even more explicit critique, Pieter Langendijk, a Dutch Mennonite poet, composed a stinging satire in 1713 entitled "Swiss Simplicity, Lamenting the Corrupted Manners of Many Dutch Mennonites or Nonresistant Christians," in which he contrasted the unaffected style of Swiss Brethren faithfulness to Christ with the lavish extravagance of the upper class Dutch Mennonites (Horst 1955:129-131).

But these stories are exceptions. In the end, the relationship of economic dependency suggested that it would be the Dutch who set directions for the Swiss Brethren church, not the other way around. To be sure, the Dutch were rarely if ever heavy-handed in their paternalism. But throughout the eighteenth century, progressive Swiss Brethren leaders turned to the Netherlands for new tastes in religious style and new models of church renewal and reform. The pietistically inclined writings of Johannes Deknatel of Amsterdam, for example, became widely popular in South German congregations. In the late eighteenth and early nineteenth centuries, Swiss Brethren leaders explicitly followed Dutch models in replacing their outmoded "meetinghouses" with fashionably designed churches. The idea of a trained and salaried pastorate, schooled in the subtleties of the biblical languages and systematic theology, clearly emulated a leadership pattern pioneered by Dutch Mennonites.

The Swiss Brethren also followed the Dutch lead in the establishment of church-supported high school and seminary, the founding of a mission society, the creation of a church paper, the awakening of a historical consciousness, and a new openness to ecumenical initiatives. All these innovations in the Swiss Brethren tradition reflected, at least in part, a new sense of filial dependence on Dutch Mennonites nurtured by a century of Dutch largesse.

These initiatives were not inherently at odds with Swiss Brethren theology. However, the long history of charity almost certainly predisposed the Swiss Brethren to accept Dutch models less critically than they might have otherwise. That conclusion seems confirmed by an eighteenth-century incident in the Palatinate. In 1759 Peter Weber, a reform-minded revivalist preacher in Höningen, spoke against the spiritual deadness he saw in Palatinate Swiss Brethren congregations. An angry bishop sought to silence him, not because Weber's criticisms were untrue, but because they put the South German churches in a bad light and could imperil the generous subsidies they were receiving from the Dutch for constructing their new churches (Neff 1930:65-101). Granted, the incident was isolated—but it suggests relations of economic dependency can affect ability to speak truth.

In summary, the Swiss Brethren experience of receiving outside aid highlights complexities of paternalism and dependence that frequently accompany well-intended benevolence. Beholden to the Truehearted and to the Dutch Mennonites for their very survival, the Swiss Brethren appear to have deferred to both groups in several key areas of theological conviction and identity. At the least, the example of the Swiss Brethren suggests there are important differences between fraternal aid, which is genuinely mutual, and benevolent assistance, which implies a hierarchy of power and dependency.

# Mutual Aid and Theological Identity

The Swiss Brethren were a marginalized people between 1550 and 1750. They lived under the constant threat and frequent reality of persecution. The disruptions to community life entailed by this persecution inevitably had economic results. Thus mutual aid in the Swiss Brethren community and help from outside were essential to their survival.

In light of this, it remains somewhat surprising that the Swiss Brethren did not reflect at greater length on a theological rationale for mutual aid, especially since they were energetically engaging a range of other theological issues at the time. Once they resolved the question of "community of goods" in their debates with the Hutterites, economic questions seem to have become less important to them. Possibly the need for mutual aid was so obvious and its practice so deeply ingrained in the habits of the Swiss Brethren community that it required no theological defense or self-conscious justification. In any event, it seems the principle of mutual aid was "caught rather than taught" during the period under study.

As a marginalized, persecuted people, the Swiss Brethren lacked the material resources and civic space needed to create highly rationalized institutions of mutual aid. Each congregation had its own fund with money raised through voluntary contributions. The money appears to have been distributed ad hoc as needs emerged. The local character of mutual aid persisted in Swiss Brethren congregations until the early nineteenth century, with the emergence of foreign mission societies, state-regulated fire insurance policies, and "widows and orphan funds."

Offering tangible expressions of compassion to the needy is a basic Christian virtue. Yet as the Swiss Brethren experience suggests, acts of compassion bring in their train relationships of power and dependence. A striking feature of the story of Swiss Brethren mutual aid is the way in which benevolent aid helped reshape theological identity.

## Notes

1. Sommer (1954); Gingerich (1985).

2. For references to Grebel's view on property; *TA, Zürich*, 216 for Manz and *TA, Zürich*, 217 for Blaurock.

3. Friedmann (1956:259-266); Stayer (1991:139-159).

4. References to Hut and Hubmaier have already been cited; for a glimpse into Menno's views, see his "True Christian Faith" and "Reply to False Accusations" (1986, 368-69 and 559, respectively).

5. Yoder (1962); Fast (1971:28-38).

6. The Hutterite authors of the polemic went on to name Theobold's sister at Lamsum, Theobold Schweiningen at Eibeschitz, Hans Bechk at Oberwisternitz and Michael Schneider at Unterwisternitz—"all of them wealthy, yet what came to the church from them?"

7. Emphasis added.

8. Meyer (1575); Gut (1588/89). A manuscript translation of selected writings of Menno Simons, written in Swiss dialect and interspersed with commentary has also been found in the Bernese archives. Menno's *Fundamentboek*, first published in 1539, was available in German translation by 1575. The manuscript version is noted by Heinold Fast, "Wie sind die oberdeutschen Täufer 'Mennoniten' geworden?" 43/44 (1986/87), 93. Further study of the manuscript, located at the Burgerbibliothek in Bern, is still needed. In Menno, the Swiss Brethren might have found a more systematic defense of mutual aid. Menno's works were cited in the course of the Amish Division, but there he is mined for proof-

texts regarding the ban, and it is not clear whether he exerted a broader influence on Swiss Brethren thought.

9. For a description of the entire book, see Robert Friedmann (1942:95-98). The only known version of this presumably first edition is found at the Mennonite Historical Library (Goshen, Ind.). According to Friedmann, the booklet of tracts found its way onto the *Index librorum prohibitorum* of 1570 and was also known to the Hutterites as evidenced by several Hutterian manuscript copies.

10. The other New Testament references were to Mark 10 (the story of the rich young ruler); Luke 11 (negative example of the Pharisees tithing mint leaves) and Matthew 19 (rich young ruler).

11. In all, the concordance addressed a total of sixty-six different topics.

12. Poor funds are also mentioned at congregations at Appenzell, Zurich, and Basel, at Grossenbach in Fulda in 1528 and 1529, and at Alzey in the Palatinate in 1608. At Strasbourg the believers decided in Oct. 1528 either to administer the money themselves or to hand it over to Lucas Hackfurt, director of the Poor Administration of the City (Krebs and Rott, Elsass, I: 185). The fund Passau never amounted to more than two pounds. A peasant near Ansbach who had only one child sold a meadow for ninety-six florins to aid needy fellow believers who had many children. Since he then lacked fodder for the animals, the peasant also sold three oxen, seven cows, and three horses (189).

13. According to Clasen (1972:189), at Esslingen a hat was put upside down on a table during meetings to prevent people from seeing how much each believer contributed. The fund never exceeded one florin.

14. Van der Zijpp (1991:843); Van Braght (1985:1110); Bergmann (1916:120-21).

15. The report was entitled, *Ein wahrhaftiger Bericht von den Brüdern im Schweitzerland in dem Zürcher Gebiet wegen der Trübsalen welche über sie ergangen sind, um des Evangeliums Willen, von dem 1635sten bis in das 1645sten Jahr.*

16. Dyck (1962:136-158), Müller (1895:164-194).

## References

"Abgeschrifft der Gegebenen Antwort von den Brüdern"
    1567    Archives of the Mennonite Church, Hist Mss 1-447.4, Box 1.

Bender, Harold S.
    1927    "The Discipline Adopted by the Strasbourg Conference of 1568." *Mennonite Quarterly Review* 1 (January): 57-66.

    1950    *Conrad Grebel.* Goshen, Ind.: Mennonite Historical Society.

Bergmann, Cornelius
    1916    *Die Taüferbewegung im Kanton Zürich bis 1660.* Leipzig: M. Heinsius Nachfolger.

*The Chronicle of the Hutterian Brethren*
    1987    (vol. 1) Rifton, New York: Plough Publishing House.

Clasen, Claus-Peter
    1972    *Anabaptism: A Social History, 1525-1618.* Ithaca, NY: Cornell University Press, 186-200.

*Concordans-Büchlein oder Zeiger der namhafften Spruch aller Biblischer Altes und Newes Testament, sampt einem ordentlichen Register am End dieses Büchleins. Jetz auff ein Newes fleissign übersehen und in Truck verfertigt* (s.l., 1693 and 1709).

*Conkordantz und Zeiger der nahmhafftigsten Sprüch aller Biblischen Bücher . . . auffs kürzest verfasset und zusammengebracht sampt einem ordentlichen register am end dis Büchlins* [a.l.: s.n.].

Correll, Ernst
  1925   *Das schweizerische Taüfermennonitentum: Ein soziologischer Bericht.* Tübingen: J. C. B. Mohr.

Durnbaugh, Donald F.
  1974   *Every Need Supplied: Mutual Aid and Christian Community in the Free Churches, 1525-1675.* Philadelphia, Pa.: Temple University Press.

Dyck, C. J., ed.
  1962   *The Heritage of Menno Simons: A Heritage of Faith.* Newton, Kan.: Faith and Life Press.

Fast, Heinold
  1971   "Die Frage nach der Autorität der Bibel auf dem Frankenthaler Taüfergespräch, 1571." Mennonitische Geschiehtsblätter: 28-38.

Fretz, J. Winfield
  1939   "Mutual Aid Among the Mennonites." *Mennonite Quarterly Review* 13 (January): 28-58, 13 (July): 187-209.

Friedmann, Robert
  1942   "The Schleitheim Confession (1527) and Other Doctrinal Writings of the Swiss Brethren in a Hitherto Unknown Edition." *Mennonite Quarterly Review* (April): 82-98.

  1949   *Mennonite Piety Through the Centuries: Its Genius and Literature.* Goshen, Ind.: Mennonite Historical Society.

  1956   "Economic Aspects of Early Hutterite Life." *Mennonite Quarterly Review* 30 (October): 259-266.

Gingerich, Barbara N.
  1985   "Property and the Gospel: Two Reformation Perspectives." *Mennonite Quarterly Review* 59 (July): 248-67.

Gratz, Delbert
  1953   *Bernese Anabaptists and their American Descendants.* Scottdale, Pa.: Herald Press.

Gross, Leonard and Jan Gleysteen
  1991   Trans. "The Concept of Cologne." *Mennonite Yearbook.* Scottdale, Pa.: Mennonite Publishing House, 8-10.

Gut, Andreas
  [1588/89] "Einfaltig bekanntnus," Staatsarchiv Zurich, EII, 443: 121-197.

Hernley, H. Ralph, ed.
1970    *The Compassionate Community*. Scottdale, Pa.: Association of Mennon-
        ite Aid Societies.

Horst, Irvin and Ava
1955    "Simplicity Laments Corrupted Manners." *Mennonite Life* (July):
        129-131.

1984    *Dutch Aid to Swiss Brethren*. Amsterdam: Doopsgezinde Historische
        Kring.

Hubmaier, Balthasar
1989    "Dialogue with Zwingli's Baptism Book." In *Balthasar Hubmaier: Theo-
        logian of Anabaptism*, ed. John H. Yoder, trans. Wayne Pipken. Scott-
        dale, Pa.: Herald Press.

Klassen, Peter J.
1963    "Mutual Aid Among the Anabaptists." *Mennonite Quarterly Review* 37
        (April): 78-95.

1964    *The Economics of Anabaptism*. The Hague: Mouton & Co.

Klaassen, Walter, ed.
1981    *Anabaptism in Outline*. Scottdale, Pa.: Herald Press.

Krebs, Manfred and Hans Georg Rott, eds.
1959    Elsass, I. Teil: Stadt Strassburg, 1522-1532 (Quellen zur Geschichte der
        Täufer, Bd. 7). Gütersloh: G. Mohn.

Kuchenbecker, Hans Pauli
1951    "Des Bekenntnis der Schweizer Brüder in Hessen." *TA, Hesse*, Mar-
        burg: G. Braun, 434-436.

Menno Simons
1986    *The Complete Works of Menno Simons*. Scottdale, Pa.: Herald Press.

Meyer, Thomas
ca. 1575 "Vonn dem Christen Ban unnd unschluß der unghorsammen und
        loosen menschen von den frummen und gloubigen in der gmein got-
        tes, wie unnd warumb er solle brucht werdenn [ca. 1575]," STAZ, EII
        444: 143-163; (other versions also found on pp. 227r-240v and pp.
        242r-259r).

Müller, Ernst
1895    *Geschichte der bernischen Taüfer: Nach den Urkunden dargestellt*. Langnau.
        Frauenfeld: I. Huber.

Neff, Christian
1930    "Peter Weber, ein mennonitischer Pietist aus dem 18. Jahrhundt."
        *Christlicher Gemeinde-Kalender* 39:65-101.

Ottius, Johann Heinrich
1672    *Annales Anabaptistici, hoc est, historia universalis de Anabaptistarum orig-
        ine, progressu, factionibus. . . .* Basel: Jacob Werenfels.

Oyer, John
1984  "The Strasbourg Conferences of the Anabaptists, 1554-1607." *Mennonite Quarterly Review* 58 (July): 218-229.

1986  Ed. and trans. "The Pfeddersheim Diputation, 1557." *Mennonite Quarterly Review* 60 (July): 304-351.

Roth, John D.
1993  *Letters of the Amish Division. A Sourcebook.* Goshen, Ind.: Mennonite Historical Society.

Snyder, C. Arnold
1994  "Anabaptist Spirituality and Economics." In *Anabaptist Mennonite Faith and Economics,* ed. C. Redekop, V. Krahn, and S. Steiner. Lanham, Md.: University Press of America. Pp. 3-18.

Sommer, Donald
1954  "Peter Rideman and Menno Simons on Economics." *Mennonite Quarterly Review* 28:205-223.

Stayer, James
1991  *The German Peasants' War and Anabaptist Community of Goods.* Montreal: McGill-Queens University Press.

Thormann, Georg
1693  *Probier-Stein, oder Schrifftmäsige und auss dem wahren innerlichen Christenthumb hargenommene gewissenhafte Prüffung des Täuferthums.* Bern: Andreas Hügenet.

Van Braght, Thieleman J.
1985  *Martyrs Mirror.* Scottdale, Pa.: Herald Press; originally published in Dutch in 1660.

van der Zijpp, N.
1962  "The Dutch Aid the Swiss Mennonites." In *A Legacy of Faith: The Heritage of Menno Simons,* ed. C. J. Dyck. Newton, Kan.: Faith and Life Press. Pp. 136-158.

1991  *Ein Wahrhaftiger Bericht von den Bruder im Schweitzerland . . . Von den 1635sten bis in das 1645sten Jahr.* Reprinted as an appendix to the *Ausbund.* Lancaster, Pa.: Amischen Gemeinden.

Wolkan, Rudolf
1965  *Die Lieder der Wiedertäufer.* Nieuwkoop: B. de Graaf.

Yoder, Jess
1962  "A Critical Study of the Debate Between the Reformed and the Anabaptists Held at Frankenthal, Germany in 1571." Ph.D. dissertation, Northwestern University.

7

# Mutual Aid Among Dutch Waterlander Mennonites, 1605-1668

Mary S. Sprunger

Scholars have often noted the contribution of wealthy Mennonites to seventeenth-century Dutch society. In this chapter Mary S. Sprunger shows that there were also many poor Dutch Mennonites aided by highly institutionalized programs of material relief. Using a wealth of primary sources, Sprunger describes mutual aid in the large Waterlander Church of Amsterdam, where some fifteen percent of the members were receiving material aid from the congregation in the mid-seventeenth century. This insightful case study demonstrates the complicated issues in any system of care and raises again the distinction between charity and mutual aid.

## Sixteenth-Century Precursors

The prosperity of Mennonites in the seventeenth-century Netherlands was long used as an example of the kind of worldliness that North American Mennonites should avoid. Rarely mentioned, however, was the fact that there were also many poor Dutch Mennonites and that the churches in the Netherlands had a long history of spending thousands of guilders a year to support hundreds of needy families in their midst. These highly institutionalized forms of poor relief had their origins in

144

more informal, sometimes radical, types of mutual aid practiced by first generation Anabaptists in the Low Countries.[1]

Early Dutch Anabaptism received its distinct flavor from Melchior Hoffman, who brought believers' baptism to the Netherlands in 1530. Hoffman's message was infused with apocalyptic visions predicting the establishment of a godly kingdom on earth in preparation for the Second Coming, which he expected in a few years. When Anabaptists took over the city of Münster in 1534, Dutch Melchiorites flocked to the New Jerusalem.

In Münster, partly to help cope with the influx of immigrants and partly for theological reasons, a forced community of goods was implemented. Deacons were in charge of confiscating property and valuables and redistributing them as needed (Stayer 1991:135). Excitement about events in Münster was widespread in the Netherlands. In Amsterdam some Anabaptists twice attempted their own takeover and managed to hold the city hall for one night in May 1535.

During that same year, there were at least three ordained deacons responsible to give help to needy Anabaptists in Amsterdam (Grosheide 1938:96). Apparently demand for aid sometimes exceeded available funds among the 3,500 to 5,000 Anabaptists in the city (Waite 1990:37-38).[2] This disparity is not surprising, for there was probably much poverty in Amsterdam in the 1530s. Recent research shows that the vast majority of Amsterdam Anabaptists were craftsmen or wives of craftsmen. While some of these, such as goldsmiths and bookbinders, were highly ranked artisans and may have enjoyed financial security, economic crises in the 1520s and 1530s had impoverished the lives of numerous artisans in the Netherlands.

Many Anabaptists migrated to Amsterdam in search of economic opportunity. These immigrants likely depended on help from the resident Anabaptists, some of whom were relatively prosperous.[3] Unfortunately, we know almost nothing about the deacons and their work during the period of persecution or about other forms of mutual aid. Since all Anabaptist activities had to be clandestine, mutual aid was probably conducted in an informal manner without written accounts, which could have too easily fallen into the wrong hands.

Other sixteenth-century evidence about mutual aid among Anabaptists comes from the writings by Menno Simons. He wrote about mutual aid in the community of believers in response to opponents' accusations that Anabaptists rejected private property. In his staunch refutations to these charges, Menno stressed that truly regenerated Christians obeyed the biblical mandate to care for the poor and to offer food, shelter, and clothing to strangers, enemies, and anyone in need (Menno Simons 1956:558-60).

This practice was quite different from holding property in common. While the apostolic church did practice a community of goods, the New Testament did not make it a universal requirement for Christians. Dirk Philips, like Menno, wrote that the fellowship of communion obliged the members of the community to look out for each other's temporal as well as spiritual needs. Dirk taught that a member of the congregation should not have to beg, for this violated the true meaning of fellowship (Keeney 1968:136).[4]

Menno does not give details about precisely how sharing should be organized. In an undated letter of comfort to some women recently widowed, Menno encouraged piety, modesty, and virtue. He called the widows to care for "needy saints" but not for those "who have enough, because these do not need your aid and services."[5] He continued, "True Christians ought not to burden each other with unnecessary expense."[6]

Menno found the model for this devout life of service in the biblical widow Sarepta in Sidon who served Elijah. This reference is Menno's only one to people in the church specially commissioned to carry out mutual aid. While Menno (1956:402, 974) mentioned "deacons" twice in his writings, it was only in passing; he provided no description of their function in the church.

In the early decades of the Reformation, much of the fear about Anabaptism stemmed from tales of radical economic behavior—some true, but most rumored. In reality, only one Anabaptist group, the Hutterites, advocated and practiced true economic equality among believers through absolute renunciation of private property.

James Stayer has demonstrated that noncommunal Anabaptists in Switzerland also strove to practice the economic principles of the apostolic church in more radical fashion than historians and theologians have previously admitted. Some Swiss Brethren went so far as to advocate selling houses and land for redistribution to anyone among them in need (Stayer 1991:8-12, 95-106).

In 1535 two brothers, Jan and Thoenis Elbertsz, were preaching true community of goods in Amsterdam (Grosheide 1938:96). They wanted Anabaptists to pool all their resources, then redistribute them equally in the community of believers. Whether or not any Dutch Anabaptists actually followed through with this remains a secret of the past.[7]

Early Anabaptists everywhere wrote and preached under the shadow of persecution. Not only might their property be seized, but Anabaptists were also in danger of losing their lives. Furthermore, in tune with the times, almost all first generation Anabaptists believed the end of the world was near. With the Second Coming imminent, the value of property seemed immaterial. Could this same open sharing find expression in the tolerated church after several generations of Anabaptism, particularly in an urban, capitalist setting?

## Waterlander Mennonite Poor Relief

Severe religious persecution in Amsterdam ended in 1579, when Holland joined a loose union of Dutch provinces determined to gain independence from Spanish rule. The union agreed to protect freedom of conscience but declared that the privilege and preferred religion was Calvinism, even though the Reformed were a minority in the Netherlands.

Still, Mennonites could now worship without fear of arrest and loss of property. The way was clear for Mennonites to participate fully in the opportunities offered by Amsterdam's booming economy as it entered into a golden age of prosperity, world influence, and cultural achievement that continued through most of the seventeenth century.

The Mennonites experienced their own golden age. They were active in almost all areas of commerce and industry, some becoming very prosperous already by the end of the sixteenth century. Mennonites were especially prominent in the textile industry but were found in all kinds of other trades as well (Sprunger 1994:137-147). A number of Mennonite painters, writers, architects, and engineers contributed to the great artistic output and technological advances of the late sixteenth and seventeenth centuries (Krahn 1957:227-233).

It was not, however, a golden age for everyone in the Netherlands. There were just as many Mennonites who were poor enough to require material aid as there were Mennonites who could be called rich. And of course there were many more in between, ranging from those barely making it on their own to Mennonites counted among the upper rungs of the middle class. The prosperous Mennonites shared from their wealth to help their less fortunate brothers and sisters. Already by 1600, and probably before, Mennonites were taking care of each other through a well-organized system of congregational poor relief.

One congregation of about 1,000 to 1,500 members, the Waterlander branch of Mennonites in Amsterdam, offers an example of how poor relief worked (Sprunger 1993:36). About ten percent of the congregation's members were considered wealthy by contemporary standards.[8] At least fifteen percent were on the opposite end of the social and economic scale and needed material help from the congregation.[9] This situation was probably typical of other large Mennonite congregations in Dutch cities.

## The "Ministers of the Poor" at Work

At three o'clock on a Thursday afternoon in January 1658, the "ministers of the poor," or deacons of the Waterlander Mennonite Church of Amsterdam, met in their special chamber for a weekly meeting. Presiding was Jan Gerritsz Schouten, a silk merchant, who probably called the meeting to order with prayer. The minute-taker, another merchant and a ship owner, assessed fines for any deacons who were tardy or absent.

On this day, nine out of ten were present. Two of the deacons were new to the office. Others had served for many years. The cloth merchant Anthony van Hoeck the Elder had twelve years of experience, and the iron merchant Arent Dircksz Bosch, who had served as deacon intermittently since 1612, had over forty years.[10] In fact, the large table was surrounded by successful merchants who were probably attired in sober black clothes of the finest quality fabrics. It must have been a daunting sight to the needy members of the church who came to request help. Although all Waterlander Mennonites were brothers and sisters in the faith, the diaconal chamber reflected the upper social levels.

Anabaptists upheld the office of deacon as an important ordained ministry to oversee the material affairs of the church and care of the poor, the sick, and the elderly.[11] Like other Protestants, the Waterlander Mennonite deacons cited Acts 6 as the biblical precedent for their office. Seven men "of good repute" were ordained to "serve tables" and care for needy widows so the disciples could focus their energies on preaching.[12]

In seventeenth-century Amsterdam, it was only logical that the deacons were almost always merchants. The task of funding and administering a complete social welfare system required strict organization, careful accounting, and financial prudence, qualities found in successful businessmen. It was a weighty responsibility for volunteers. In 1658 the deacons controlled, to a large extent, the quality of life for the 152 households (365 individuals) on the poor relief rolls.[13]

During the meeting, the deacon's servant (also church janitor) was downstairs handing out cash to those who received weekly alms. He also controlled the flow of petitioners to the deacons' chamber. The diaconate needed a full-time servant to help with the heavy workload. Besides delivering goods and messages and keeping the church clean, he knew more about the poor members' living conditions than any of the deacons or ministers. He often reported cases of desperate poverty or shed light on the character of a person requesting help. He made the rounds with the visitation deacon because he knew where all of the alms recipients lived.[14] Also in the church during the meeting, but in separate quarters, were three respectable widows—the deaconesses of the congregation—and their helper. Their chief duties were procuring and distributing clothing and bed linens.[15]

Simke Harings made the first request of that day.[16] He needed help paying his rent and announced plans to move to a cheaper apartment in May. The deacons told him not to take out a new lease without their advice and approval. Sixteen-year-old Jan Pietersz was next. He had been an apprentice with the same tailor for three years but had begun to work for a different clothier. The deacons warned him sternly that if he left his current apprenticeship, they would discontinue his financial support.

Next was the wife of Gillis Seis. She wondered if the deacons could figure out a way to provide lighting for her husband's loom, located in their apartment. The deacons promised to send someone to look into the matter. Christina de Roo, an older woman from England who had lived in Amsterdam for many years, requested a weekly stipend and help with the rent for her small house, which she had been paying by herself. The deacons told her to come back the next week. Neeltje Jans came on behalf of a sick woman who could not manage on her own. The visitation deacon promised to visit her on his next rounds.

A thirteen-year-old girl, Weintje Pieters,[17] requested new underclothing. The deacons agreed that a change of clothes was certainly in order, so they directed her to the deaconess chamber. The distribution of underclothes and linens was considered women's work and therefore the domain of the deaconesses. Next came a request for help on behalf of a sick woman who needed a doctor. The deacons gave instructions to contact a former deacon, doctor François Verschagen, for medical help. The visitation deacon promised to check on the sick woman during his rounds.

Daniel Eggertsz requested money to buy a flat-bottomed riverboat to replace one that had capsized. The boat represented the family's livelihood, and Daniel and his wife were willing to put up their house, worth 600 guilders, as collateral for a 200-guilder loan.[18] Rather than loaning him money, the deacons instead gave Daniel thirty guilders for his barge, with advice that his family henceforth "manage on their own." The last matter of the day was a disagreement between two parties regarding some borrowed money. After the deacons cleared up that matter, the meeting was adjourned until the same time the next week.

## Waterlander Mennonite Poor Relief

In this typical meeting, the deacons handled a broad range of requests. Their main responsibilities, however, were rather basic: providing shelter, food, clothing, and fuel to all church members in need.[19] To provide free housing, the church owned or operated seven residential complexes of different size and quality, most of which were located in an artisan quarter of the city (the Jordaan).

The Lindenhofje, for example, was a home for widows. A unique Low Countries' institution, a *hofje* is a cross between an almshouse and a home for the elderly. A quiet courtyard was surrounded by small rooms and apartments where the elderly or poor lived independently but secluded from the outside world. The Lindenhofje consisted of houses and apartments on the street as well as "good second-story rooms above" and provided space for about eighteen women.[20]

The so-called Bakehouse was another Mennonite institution. This housing complex, originally a large dried biscuit bakery with rooms for some of its employees, contained twenty-two apartments for widows, couples, and some families. The residents were a colorful group of Mennonites whose lifestyles were often in stark contrast to their more prosperous sisters and brothers in the faith.[21]

Some of these clusters of apartments were built or bought by the church; others were founded by wealthy Mennonite individuals as independent institutions, yet the deacons had the authority to choose who lived in the private hofjes. The best-known is the Anslohofje, today the Claes Claesz Hofje. Dating back to at least 1616, it is one of the oldest hofjes in Amsterdam. Its founder, Claes Claesz Anslo (d. 1632), was a prosperous cloth merchant and deacon (Wijnman 1971:481). Poor Mennonites lived in all eight of the apartments, and it appears that the deacons, rather than the regents of the hofje, decided who would live there.[22]

Thirty years later another merchant and deacon, Arent Dircksz Bosch, built a home for Mennonite widows. Established in 1648, the Boschhofje had eight small apartments (four downstairs and four upstairs) running along one side of a narrow passageway (Wijnman 1971:489).

The above residences were reserved for those unable to pay their own rent. If one became vacant, it was the deacons' privilege, without advice or consent of the family or person in question, to decide who could move into the hofje. As nonpaying residents, the poor had no right to make final decisions about where they lived, and the deacons sometimes moved residents from one place to another to accommodate as many people as possible.[23]

If no apartments were available for a needy family, the deacons would work out some arrangement, paying either all or some of the rent of an inexpensive dwelling. Such decisions were left to the good judgment of the deacons. Persons falling under this arrangement were not to sign or renew leases without consent of the deacons.

In addition to shelter, the deacons provided the have-nots of the congregation with basic foodstuffs, fuel, and petty cash. Rye bread was the staple of the northern European diet, so the deacons handled most food requests by supplying bread to needy families. For example, in May 1656 Trijntje Victoors explained to the deacons that she could not earn much with flax work during the summer; rather than asking for money, she requested two loaves of bread per week to help tide her over.[24]

The deacons gave each needy household a tally stick (*kerfstock*), which gave the family a right to a certain number of loaves per week from a specified baker usually assigned according to neighborhood. The baker would notch each stick for every loaf received. Periodically, to settle the accounts, the bakers would bring in the tally sticks along with their records of how many loaves they had baked from the congregation's rye.[25]

The other food staples for the poor were distributed only once annually in the winter, when shorter days and harsh weather resulted in less work and more illness. In 1663 the deacons distributed 2,703 pounds of cheese, 18 *mudden* of gray peas and 12 1/2 of white peas, 9 tons (1,440 kilograms) of butter, 56 sides of bacon weighing 3,034 pounds, and 22 sacks of groats. Often the deacons paid for these food staples themselves, each donating certain amounts to cover part or all of one foodstuff.[26] In the summer those on poor relief received allotments of turf or peat, which by the seventeenth century was the most common source of fuel in Holland.[27]

To take care of other needs, depending on size of household and income, most of the poor members received a weekly dole that ranged from fifteen stuivers a week for a widow to fifty stuivers or more for a large family. Ideally, the deacons intended this *weekgeld* to supplement a household's other sources of income. A family member or designated representative would come to the church every Thursday to pick up the money. Deacons took seriously individual requests for increases in this weekly money. Both bread and money might have been granted temporarily in light of some crisis, such as extended illness or lack of work due to winter weather or some other reason (Sprunger 1993:181-182).

The deacons also provided medical care to any of the congregation's poor who were ill or injured. Despite their relative ineffectiveness during the seventeenth century, medical services were expensive. In 1661 Annetie Meijnders received thirty guilders from the deacons to pay a barber-surgeon (not a real doctor) to cut a stone from her four-year-old son, who died during the process.

To minimize costs, the deacons sometimes had a surgeon in their service. He would be paid a flat fee for a year to treat the church's needy. The barber-surgeon was to provide his own "salve, plasters, gargling fluid, waters and cooling-draughts," whereas the deacons would pay for any other medicines the poor might need from the apothecary.[28] When the plague struck, such as in the early 1660s, the deacons hired a special person to comfort and help the sick.[29] When it seemed as though grave circumstances called for a real medical doctor, the deacons tried to secure the services of a former or current church board member.[30]

Deacons placed the infirm or physically or mentally handicapped members who were unable to live alone, such as Blind Geesie or Jan Huijbertsen the Cripple, under care of other poor members. Since the widows' hofje served only single women who could take care of themselves or required only occasional help, a disabled member might be boarded with a relative or congregational member, usually poor, for a sum that varied according to the severity of the infirmity. As for orphans, an enterprising member might take in several persons, for each boarder brought extra money into the household.

In 1658 Trijntje Martens was running her own little nursing home. She kept an elderly widow and an unmarried woman who was either handicapped or infirm, each for twelve guilders per month. For an additional twelve guilders and ten stuivers monthly, she cared for "a man very miserable of body" who had been bedridden for many years but was "of pious heart and patient in his suffering." Trijntje received a total of 438 guilders annually to care for and feed her three boarders (more than the deacons' servant earned per year).[31]

Orphans were handled in much the same way as the infirm, until the 1670s when the Amsterdam Mennonites founded two orphanages. Keeping siblings together was not a priority for the deacons. More important was providing the children with a good home, training so they could eventually support themselves, and education.

For example, in 1652 two young sisters were placed in different homes. Wittier Martens went to live with Trijntie Jans for seventeen guilders, ten stuivers per quarter-year. There she would also "be taught the handwork of sewing linen and reading." (Her sister Kuier was sent to live with a different woman.) The quarterly payment of sixteen guilders was to include room and board as well as instruction in handwork and washing. The deacons added an additional one-and-a-half guilders so she could learn to read.[32]

Besides these basics—weekly money, bread, food staples, fuel, linens, some medical care, burial, and perhaps a free residence—the needy of the congregation requested, and mostly received, much extra money for special needs. Goods made up about one-quarter of requests for aid, such as shoes, stockings, shirts, bread allotment, or extra turf. Far more common, however, were requests for money. Sickness, a harsh winter, an accident, lack of work, childbirth—all could place an extra strain on the household budget so that a family required extra funds from the deacons. Sometimes a member would ask for money to pay specific debts, such as to the grocer or baker, for a doctor's bill, or for back rent. One woman requested three years of back rent.[33]

A common kind of debt was money owed to Lombardeers, the informal term for loan banks or pawnshops, which could legally charge up to 32.5 percent annual interest (Van Deursen 1991:59-62). As much as they hated to pay these loan sharks, the deacons almost always retrieved a member's goods from the pawnshop, but an admonishment and warning against resorting to the Lombardeer went hand in hand with return of the goods. Occasionally the deacons would hold the articles themselves for a week or two as a lesson and warning against this short-sighted practice.

The deacons preferred that members in their care come to them first, before pawning their clothes or household items. Perhaps in recognition of this fact, Annetje Harmens made a convincing appeal in April 1656 when she told the deacons that unless they gave money for rent due, she would have to visit the pawnbroker.[34] Some people denied responsibility, such as the man who returned from a sea voyage to find that his wife had pawned his net and clothes, then died before reclaiming them.[35] And these were not small sums: sometimes the deacons had to pay as much as seventy guilders to buy back the pawned goods of one person (enough money to pay apartment rent for one year).

Money was of course required for many other needs, such as travel to another city or province to claim an inheritance. There was also a fee required to become a burgher of Amsterdam.[36] These miscellaneous requests were the kind most often denied. One other unusual request was ransom money for seafaring men imprisoned by Barbary pirates. It was the policy of the diaconate not to spend the money of the poor on ransoms, but well-off members of the congregation, including individual deacons, might be solicited for contributions to buy a poor Mennonite out of slavery.[37]

The supplemental and total support of these many poor individuals and families was costly and required prudent management of funds to keep the church running in the black. Fortunately, the corporate financial expertise of the diaconate was substantial. The emphasis put on carefully-kept account books and wise stewardship of money suggests that the diaconate was dominated by businessmen. The bookkeepers carefully recorded every stuiver spent or received and totaled the amounts at the end of each month.[38]

Like good merchants, the deacons sought to minimize expenditures when possible, such as buying wholesale, requesting price reductions, or petitioning for exemption of excise tax on foods and turf bought for charity.[39] Rather than buying ready-made underclothing and bed linens or fabric, the diaconate hired needy women of the congregation to make them. Deaconesses oversaw the entire production, including spinning, weaving, dying, and sewing.[40] This in turn provided supplemental income for some of the women supported by the diaconate. To minimize the cost of bread, the deacons bought their own rye wholesale, stored it in a church warehouse, and distributed it to individual bakers. In this way they only had to pay the bakers for milling and baking.[41]

## Filling the Poor Chest

Despite the careful use of the poor funds, the church still had to raise large sums of money to provide the help described above. Unlike the Reformed deacons who went door to door soliciting funds or the Jewish synagogues that taxed members for support of the poor, the Mennonites relied on the voluntary generosity of their members. Yet the Waterlander diaconate of Amsterdam seemed free of the severe budgetary problems suffered by many diaconates—Mennonite and other—throughout the Netherlands.[42] From the time of the first surviving financial records of the church in 1605 until it merged with another Mennonite congregation in 1668, the Waterlander diaconate always had an ample surplus in its poor chest.

Where did all the money come from? Undoubtedly many prosperous Mennonites were generous. Furthermore, as prudent businessmen, the deacons made every effort to maximize income through investments. They collected money in several ways. Members could drop money into iron poor boxes in the church.[43] They could give money directly to an individual deacon or elder (some of these gifts were anonymous and often amounted to several hundred guilders at one time).[44]

Members could also remember the needy in their wills.[45] Wealthy Waterlanders might leave substantial amounts, such as the medical doctor and Waterlander elder Johannes Reijersz, whose will of 1680 bequeathed 1,000 guilders to poor Mennonite orphans throughout the Netherlands and 2,000 guilders to the poor of the Waterlander and Flemish congregation in Amsterdam.[46]

More modest folk also left money to the work of the diaconate. The self-written will of the Englishman Robbert Pandert, which he gave to a deaconess in 1652, is evidence that not only prosperous Waterlanders gave to charity.

> I ask that you give all that you find in my house, which is not for any children nor for any friends, but only for the congregation, and do not let one from all take this or that, but sell everything to the profit of the congregation. Everything that there is I earned with my work and because my child Tomas Robbertsz is dead I give also his earnings to the congregation, as much as my part is, and you will also find [in my house] the *maentseel* [certificate of monthly income, probably from the Dutch East India Company].[47]

Besides money, people might also bequeath clothing or other goods to the poor. In the seventeenth century, clothes were very expensive and maintained a substantial value even secondhand.[48]

Any surplus in the poor funds was invested.[49] As successful merchants, the deacons knew that an idle penny was a wasted one. They recognized the potential profits from excess alms. The deacons preferred to invest the surplus money rather than have it collect dust in the poor chest. They loaned out various sums, ranging from several hundred to several thousand guilders, to individuals at (as the deacons were careful to stress) reasonable interest rates. The preferred borrowers were the deacons or elders themselves who pumped the money into their own business ventures. The diaconate also lent out money to other "good people" in the church, but individual deacons had to guarantee the loans.[50] Both the individual and the congregation could profit from the diaconate's policy of loaning out funds. Indeed, the Waterlanders had one of the most bounteous poor chests in Holland.

## Problems in Dutch Mennonite Poor Relief

The Waterlander Mennonite deacons provided the poor members of the church with a substantial quantity of material support, but to what extent did they model New Testament and Anabaptist principles in their administration of poor relief? Was this in fact mutual aid? Or might charity be a better designation? To answer these questions, it is necessary to look at several problems in the administration of congregational poor relief: (1) the relationship between church membership and alms, (2) the relationship between discipline and alms, and (3) the extent to which the diaconate tried to promote self-sufficiency and break the cycle of poverty from one generation to the next.

## Membership and Alms

Seventeenth-century observers and some later historians have suggested that while competing for souls in the Netherlands, Calvinists, Catholics, and Mennonites offered generous poor relief programs as one way to attract new members and boost the size of their churches.[51] Around 1620, a Calvinist preacher at Rotterdam accused the Mennonites of "handing out gifts and charity" to gain adherents "whose belly is their God" (cited in Groenveld et al. 1981:122).

While this may sometimes have been the case before about 1625, the increasing numbers of rural poor moving to the cities (Nutseling 1985:164-165) led diaconates in the Netherlands to reassess the fiscal prudence of bringing in the poor to boost membership. There is no evidence that Mennonites in Amsterdam were trying to attract the needy with promises of large handouts. Indeed, just the opposite was true.

By the mid-seventeenth century, the ministers and deacons concerned about additional burdens on the church poor box carefully screened new candidates for membership to weed out the insincere. One reason for deacons to help examine new baptismal candidates was to see "whether their request comes out of a just fear of God, and whether they have good witnesses, and have brought them along, so that one understands and is assured that the matter does not revolve around bread." The church board had to consider carefully each application for membership, so that "through carelessness, one does not burden the congregation with unvirtuous people."[52] Clearly, the elders and deacons realized that persons might be motivated by hope of alms rather than by faith.

Mennonite "foreigners"—those not born in the city of Amsterdam —had to undergo even more careful scrutiny than new converts. When in 1652 the deacons codified their duties and policies, no less than ten articles focused on Mennonite immigrants moving to Amsterdam. This was testimony to the leadership's worry about "poor people from abroad, coming from Friesland or other lands, to live here, who cannot make it on their own."[53] A thriving urban center, Amsterdam attracted many immigrants who sought their fortunes in the big city. But those who came poor usually stayed poor. They soon learned opportunities were not so plentiful as they had hoped.

The church leaders carefully checked out new arrivals who petitioned for church membership to prevent a stream of Mennonite poor from moving to Amsterdam and becoming dependent on financial support. The burden of proof lay on the newcomers. Besides presenting a letter of testimony from their home congregations, the "foreigners" had to convince the deacons that they had better chances to earn living wages in Amsterdam than in their previous places of residence. In fact, Waterlander Mennonites throughout the Netherlands agreed that poor members would not receive letters of testimony without credible demonstration that the émigrés could better support themselves in a different city.[54]

Without doubt this ordinance was the initiative of the Amsterdam church, which felt threatened, with good reason, by the influx of poor immigrants. A single congregation could not absorb the cost of supporting every Waterlander Mennonite family who moved to town.

If satisfied with the applicants' plans for earning a living, the deacons would admit the immigrants on a provisional basis. If not satisfied, the deacons would admonish the applicants for moving in the first place. They were told "that they had done very wrong to come here so lightly, where not only rent, but everything that one eats, drinks, or wears is so extremely expensive."[55]

The deacons then advised the immigrants that it would be best for them to return to their hometown where the cost of living was much cheaper. Those who took this advice immediately were given some money for the trip home.[56] Eventually the deacons instituted a one-year waiting period for would-be alms recipients coming from outside of Amsterdam. Thus a double standard is evident in church membership policies. Newcomers without financial security were less likely to be able to join the church than those who were clearly self-sufficient.

## Discipline and Alms

This same double standard, based on economic status, was at work in the practice of church discipline. Mennonites believed the congregation should be a community of believers who, on their own faith, voluntarily committed themselves to a life of discipleship. Having joined the church, members were accountable not only to God but each other. The elders of the church strove to keep members in line, preferably through use of the "small ban"—temporary exclusion from the Lord's Supper—or the "big ban," excommunication, for sinners who refused to show repentance.

For the Waterlander Mennonites, discipline was a spiritual matter; they never advocated avoidance in marital, business, or social ties. Stricter Mennonites believed that the faithful should shun the "separated" in all areas of life (Visser 1988 1:114-15). Reasons for preventing a member from taking communion included holding office in the government, swearing oaths, carrying weapons, working on or owning shares in an armed ship, marrying someone of a different faith, going bankrupt, getting drunk, having domestic quarrels, or engaging in sexual relations outside the bonds of marriage.[57]

About one-third of the discipline cases to come before the Waterlander elders involved members on poor relief. These members made up about fifteen percent of the total congregation—a significant over-representation.[58] Worried that Mennonites from the lower classes might fail to meet the church's high standards of behavior, the elders and deacons kept a close eye on the alms-receivers. A duty of the deacons was to report to the elders matters of misconduct "by any of the brothers, or sisters, be it from drunkenness, unauthorized marriages outside the community, fighting between man and wife, between brother and brother, between sister and sister, or between neighbors, be it women or men."[59] The elders could then take steps to admonish and, if need be, ban the sinners.

The deacons made church discipline their business because alms could be suspended or cut off completely when a pauper was banned from the congregation.[60] Poor relief was a privilege of membership rather than a social right. Thus for the poor, church discipline could have serious economic ramifications. For the self-sufficient, banning could be embarrassing but not financially threatening.

In 1652 the deacons withheld the weekly alms of Rykge Douwes. She had struck her daughter's sewing mistress so severely that the woman could not sleep because of the pain. More often than not, the threat of losing alms was an incentive strong enough to produce repentance on the part of the wrongdoers. Two weeks later Rykge brought several witnesses to the elders to testify that she had made peace with the woman and could be reinstated as a member of the congregation in good standing.[61]

In September 1618 the ministers instructed Freerck the Peat Porter and his wife Mijntje to move out of their apartment, supplied by the diaconate, as soon as possible. They had had a long history of quarreling and had made too much merriment at their daughter's wedding, drinking to excess and dancing. The approaching winter, however, moved the ministers to allow Freerck and Mijntje to stay in the congregational housing until May, when the couple would undergo reevaluation. More complaints arrived in February, but the record does not show whether or not Freerck and Mijntje had to move.[62] Only in a few dire cases were alms recipients turned out on the streets, but it did happen.[63]

Marrying someone of a different faith could have economic consequences for a poor person. Marriage outside of Mennonite groups was considered sinful for both the rich and the poor, although the economics of welfare again created a double standard. For the financially independent, marriage to a non-Mennonite would usually result in a period of temporary banning, but for an alms recipient it might mean the loss of some or all poor relief. The deacons expected the non-Mennonite spouse, particularly if male, to find support for the family from his own church (Sprunger 1993:213-214).

Poor relief was not only contingent on proper conduct but also on proper use of the alms that were given. The diaconate kept watch over how the poor were using the alms received from the congregation.[64] Those who misused what they received were admonished, encouraged to improve, and instructed as to the proper use of their alms.

On a visit to one apartment in 1649, the deacons discovered that bargeman Obbe Vrericks and his wife Annetge Barents "kept an ample house" (*ruym huyshielden*). Among other grievances, the couple's lack of frugality caused the diaconate and elders great consternation "because one does not intend the poor money to be spent thus." The deacons revoked Obbe's and Annetge's weekly stipend and ordered them to move out of their apartment. In the middle of January, after Obbe and Annetge asked for forgiveness, the deacons agreed to reinstate their alms and find them a new place to live on condition that their conduct remain acceptable.[65] The Waterlander elite cherished thrift as well as cleanliness, orderliness, domestic harmony, chastity, and sobriety.

## Promoting Economic Independence

The Waterlander diaconate controlled distribution of gifts to the poor and attempted to control how the poor used them. What steps did they take to alleviate causes of poverty? One irony is that the deacons' servant did not earn enough to support his family and had to receive additional aid from the office for which he worked. The deacons wanted to see needy members become self-sufficient, so they supported education, job training, and small business ventures. However, these initiatives probably represented the least total expenditure from the poor chest.

The deacons usually supported self-help ventures, no matter how modest or ultimately unsuccessful. They often loaned or contributed small amounts of money to finance new trades. The prospects were usually bleak, especially for large families. Roelofje Harmens and her husband Jan Evertsen, for example, made various abortive attempts to make ends meet. Roelofje was forty-two in 1658 when her family was first recorded in the diaconal poor book.[66] Her husband, six years younger, was then not a member of any congregation but later joined the Waterlanders. By 1660 they had five children who ranged from ages one to twelve.

Jan and Roelofje were trying to sell fabric when in September 1662 they decided to try making mustard. Initially the deacons gave Roelofje money with which to purchase some vats and a month later an advance on her weekly stipend to get her little business off the ground. Early in 1663 they provided another cash advance for mustard seed. In December of 1663 Roelofje appealed to the deacons for a year's cash advance, about seventy-five guilders. She hoped to get ahead and thereafter not burden the congregation. The deacons gave her the money but on condition that she also give up her two weekly loaves of bread.

She was back half a year later asking for fifty guilders to pay back rent. She claimed her children, now six of them, had been sick. Thus the business was "greatly weakened." In October 1664 she asked to live in an apartment owned by the church because the family was having problems paying rent. Roelofje also announced plans to sell butter and other goods for a living. In the next month the deacons gave her a substantial sum to stock the shop. Jan and Roelofje continued to make mustard and also sold bricks, ventures financed by extra money from the diaconate.

By 1669 the two youngest boys, Dirk and Evert, were in school, but the rest of the children worked. Luytje, twenty-one, sewed wool, while the other children worked for a silk manufacturer. Harmen, eighteen, was a weaver. The two youngest girls spun silk. Despite a rent-free apartment, however, the combined incomes were still not enough to support the family, and the parents continued to make frequent requests for extra money for the rest of their lives.

The deacons realized the real key to breaking the cycle of poverty lay in job training, yet the education of poor relief recipients was minimal. Some but not all young children went to private school masters to learn reading and sometimes writing, which required an additional fee. Both girls and boys between the ages of about seven and ten might attend school but not all the Waterlander children did. The deacons usually paid for the school fees at the parents' requests.[67]

More significant in the long run, however, were efforts to train young people in lucrative trades, in order to help them reach economic independence. The deacons tried to see to it that older children learned a useful skill. They sometimes offered advice about suitable trades and paid for apprenticeships. In 1661 the deacons visited a woman with five sons, and "since most of her children work in the ropewalk, she was advised to let her children learn other handwork, so that when they reach their majority, they can support their own homes."[68]

Similarly, in 1665 the deacons found fault with Maeijke Reurs for putting her son out to make silver thread. Now fourteen, he had been drawing thread at least since the age of ten. The deacons recommended that she and her husband have him learn a better trade. Furthermore, they admonished her for letting the two oldest sons (aged sixteen and twenty) join crews on ships sailing to Spain. "She acted carelessly to let her children sail on such perilous journeys."[69]

Although the deacons may not have approved of the risks that seafarers underwent, especially if they had families to support, they nevertheless frequently helped young men pay for the provisions needed to embark on a long voyage, such as to the East Indies. In many cases the mother or wife promised to reimburse the poor chest from the sailor's income, which could be collected monthly in Amsterdam by a family member or other authorized person.[70]

Success stories were few. Only occasionally did poor relief recipients voluntarily give up their alms, and most attempts at self-subsistence were short-lived. In 1656 four different members thanked the diaconate for what they had received from the congregation and announced they no longer needed material help; three of these returned for aid less than one year later. One was Gerritje Jacobs, a widow with one child who returned her baker's tallystick in the summer but was back in the winter asking for rent money and additional help.[71]

Willem Verbeeck, a young leatherworker, was more successful, supporting himself long-term without alms. He explained that he could now earn three-and-a-half guilders per week with his trade. The deacons advised him against plans to marry, either because they felt his income was not yet high enough or because they did not approve of his choice of a spouse. Nevertheless, Willem does not reappear in the diaconal records.[72]

The story of this young man is an exception. Most long-term poor relief recipients, try as they might, were not able to support themselves and their families. More often than not, poverty was perpetual and passed from one generation to the next.[73] Only in the next centuries would a conscious structural rather than bandage approach to poverty emerge in Mennonite poor relief.

## Mutual Aid or Charity?

Were the Mennonite leaders overly sensitive to the problems of the immigrant poor? Was suspending alms for church members who were under the ban in line with New Testament ethics? Was applying double standards according to economic status a biblical practice? Could the deacons have made more of an effort to find well-paying jobs for the alms recipients, to help them become financially independent?

Pragmatism characterized Waterlander poor relief. Some of the diaconate's practices—evicting people from their homes for moral lapses and not warmly welcoming poor immigrants who wished to join the congregation—may seem cold by twentieth-century standards. But the times demanded harsh measures. When the goal of caring for every member of the congregation also carried a financial obligation, then the elders and deacons had to be sure they could, if necessary, actually support everyone they let in. The deacons faced a dilemma inherent in any system of parochial social welfare: how to exercise compassion and carry out the Christian mandates of brotherly and sisterly love, which included caring for anyone in need, without bankrupting the church coffers so no one could be helped.

Although the Mennonites in Amsterdam as a whole were probably the wealthiest in the Netherlands, the congregation correctly feared the balance tipping too far to the lower end of the economic scale. The earliest surviving congregational ledgers suggest that in 1605 the deacons provided some kind of material aid to about thirty individuals or families.[74] By 1658 when the first list of poor relief recipients organized by heads of households appeared, the number had increased to more than 150 needy families—three times as many.[75] The congregation probably grew slightly during this time, but the figures are nevertheless striking. They reflect general societal trends of rural pauperization and migration to the cities.

Whereas some members were becoming more wealthy and were generous, a shrinking percentage of members had to support the growing percentage of poor. In 1658, fifteen to eighteen percent of the members "By the Tower" may have been alms recipients (Sprunger 1993:35-40; 133 n. 8).

The Amsterdam church did not want to replicate the position of the Delft Waterlander Mennonites, who had been several hundred guilders in debt already in 1614. Attributing this to the many poor, elderly, and orphaned in their congregation and to their dearth of benefactors, they appealed to the Amsterdam Waterlanders for funds.[76]

After examining the complexity of Dutch Mennonite poor relief, can this system of congregational welfare still be labeled mutual aid? The church used the resources donated by some members to serve the needs of others. Although the aid was very complete, it was in many ways paternalistic rather than mutual. Those dependent on church welfare were not allowed to make decisions regarding their own aid. They were subject to unsolicited advice about marriage, their children's careers, and lifestyle issues. They were at the mercy of deacons and elders who moved in some of the highest social and intellectual circles of Amsterdam. The element of mutuality and reciprocity was obscured in such a hierarchical system. This form of congregational welfare differed little from Reformed, Catholic, Lutheran, and Jewish poor relief found in Amsterdam at the same time (Van Deursen 1991:63-66).

The theology of the seventeenth-century Dutch Mennonites did not include restructuring society. After all, God had created both the rich and the poor. Those who were prosperous had a Christian duty to help provide for the less fortunate, but they were not expected to give all to the church in a radical community of goods. In fact, to do so would have been a folly, for in an urban, commercial, and capitalist setting, financial security meant having a surplus. Without comprehensive government welfare, workers' compensation, and medical insurance, a prolonged illness or the death of the major breadwinner could mean destitution for a family without investments and savings.

The welfare provided by Dutch Mennonites was one of the most complete examples of mutual aid practiced by Mennonites anywhere at any time. However, it was also one of the most flawed if our yardstick is the economic model of the apostolic church or the radical community of goods practiced by some early Anabaptists. If we consider the urban context of the Dutch Mennonites, however, we may forgive some of the flaws and admire the efficient institutions they developed to deal with poverty in their midst. They were simply trying to follow New Testament teachings about wealth, poverty, and charity as they best understood them.

## Notes

1. The archival sources used for this research are found in Amsterdam in Archief van de Verenigde Doopsgezinde Gemeente te Amsterdam (Particular Archive [PA]1120), Gemeentearchief Amsterdam, the Netherlands.

2. Jan Paeuw wrote a brother, Cornelis Vlaminck, that there was need in the congregation. His response was one of disbelief that all ten or eleven pounds had already been used up. Apparently he thought the money had not been used wisely (Grosheide 1938:96).

3. Waite (1990:28-31, 34-37), Grosheide (1938:75-85).

4. All Protestant religions abhorred mendicancy.

5. Letter from Menno Simons to some widows, May 18 [ca. 1549], in the Doopsgezinde Bibliotheek, Universiteitsbibliotheek Amsterdam. My translation, with help from Piet Visser's transcription, "Brief van Menno aan enkele bedroefde weduwem," 1988.

6. Translation from Menno Simons (1956:1028).

7. A small, short-lived Mennonite movement advocating community of goods emerged in Amsterdam in the early seventeenth century, but little is known about its scope. Most Mennonites were horrified by this reappearance of

radical Anabaptism (Theunisz. 1627:7-8, 22-28).

8. PA 1120 nr. 152: "Rekenboeck voor de gelden tot subsidie van sommige leeraeren" (May 13-15, 1642).

9. PA 1120 nr. 136: "Armen-boeck" (Jan. 1, 1658), first section, 0v-70v.

10. PA 1120 nr. 134: "Resolutie van extraordinari assistentie aen den Armen— (Jan. 10, 1658).

11. For a short discussion of the office of deacon in the Protestant and especially Mennonite traditions, see *Mennonite Encyclopedia*, s.v. "Deacon." For how Luther differed from Calvin and Anabaptists on the role of deacon, see McKee (1984:177-78).

12. Although these original seven men had broader responsibilities than financial duties and serving the poor, such as teaching—they functioned more like bishops or presbyters—most church traditions consider them to be the first deacons. As this ministry developed, at least in the Dutch Mennonite tradition, it came to include the maintenance of church property, the administration of finances and salaries, and the authority to advise preachers and elders. But a statement of purpose by the deacons themselves in 1652, in which they outlined their duties, left no doubt about their primary function: "to provide for and serve the poor of the congregation in their daily needs, so that none shall suffer want." PA 1120 nr. 118: "Resolutieboek van de kerkeraad of diakenen," article 1:1. In 1652, the deacons set down in writing the policies and regulations of their office, which they had been practicing for many years. These 137 resolutions, dealing especially with poor relief and administration of funds, offer the modern reader a uniquely detailed picture of the deacons' duties and an insight into the rationale behind many of their policies.

13. PA 1120 nr. 136, first section: 0v-70v.

14 PA. 1120 nr. 118, additional articles 1-15 under "Knecht van's Armenkantoor:" 1516.

15. It is difficult to name these women, since their books did not survive.

16. All primary information from this day, unless otherwise noted, taken from PA 1120 nr. 134 (Jan. 10, 1658).

17. See also PA 1120 nr. 136:60.

18. PA 1120 nr. 134 (Jan. 3, 1658).

19. PA 1120 nr. 118, art. 14:2.

20. PA 1120 nr. 118, art. 15:2.

21. PA 1120 nr. 136, first section, 1-10. For more on the Bakehouse, see Sprunger (1993:134-38).

22. PA 1120 nr. 136: 23v-26v, 62v.

23. PA 1120 nr. 118, art. 20:3.

24. PA 1120 nr. 134 (May 11, 1656).

25. PA 1120 nr. 118, arts. 88-91:9-10.

26. PA 1120 nr. 144.

27. PA 1120 nr. 118, arts. 26-28:4.

28. PA 1120 nr. 140, ff. ii (July 13, 1617).

29. PA 1120 nr. 134 (Nov. 1, 1663, Oct. 16, 1664, Nov. 13, 1664).

30. E.g. PA 1120 nr. 134 (Jan. 6, 1656).

31. PA 1120 nr. 136:51, 50, 50v.

32. PA 1120 nr. 118:31 (March 12 and 17, 1652).

33. PA 1120 nrs. 133-35, "Resolutie van extraordinari assistentie aen den Arrnen," 1649 and following.

34. PA 1120 nr. 134 (Apr. 27, 1656).

35. PA 1120 nr. 134 (Apr. 6, 1656).

36. PA 1120 nr. 134 (Mar. 13, 1664): Sjou Sibbels was given 2 guilders, 10 stuivers for *poorterschapsgeld*.

37. PA 1120 nr. 134 (Oct. 22, 1654).

38. PA 1120 nr. 118, art. 35:5.

39. PA 1120 nr. 118, arts. 26-28:4

40. PA 1120 nr. 118, arts. 106-110:12.

41. PA 1120 nr. 118, arts. 85-87:9.

42. Neither of Waterlander congregations in Leiden or Delft could raise enough of their own money to support their poor.

43. PA 1120 nr. 118, arts. 33, 34, 40:4-5.

44. PA 1120 nr. 118, art. 36:5.

45. PA 1120 nr. 118, art. 37:5.

46. PA 1120 nr. 431: Will of Dr. Johannes Reijersz. (Sept. 28, 1680).

47. PA 1120 nr. 172: bundle of wills; nr. 117:36v (Dec. 7 [?], 1619).

48. In 1606 Hendrick van Seevenbergen left his clothes to the congregation, which then divided them among the poor. Rather than all going to the poor, however, the best coat, jacket, and pants, as well as a pair of leather leggings, a pair of linen underleggings, and a pair of socks were first given to the preacher Lubbert Gerritsz. PA 1120 nr. 140:7v, 1606.

49. PA 1120 nr. 118, art. 38:5

50. PA 1120 nr. 118, arts. 42, 45:5,6; nrs. 148-49: Schuldboeken, 1620-76.

51. Geyl (1948, 1:308), Van Deursen (1974:124-27), Roodenburg (1990:114).

52. PA 1120 nr. 118, art. 116:16.

53. PA 1120 nr. 118, arts. 92:10.

54. PA 1120 nr. 118, arts. 99-101:11.

55. PA 1120 nr. 118, arts. 92-94, 96-98:10-11.

56. *Ibid.*

57 PA 1120 nr. 131: Reinier Wybrantsz., "Wet reden datmen can by brengen, deer van datmen yemandt, die beispelyck is, vermaent dat hy vande tafel des heren voor een tyt sal blijuen" (n.d.).

58. Disciplinary notations are contained in the minutes of the congregation, PA 1120 nr. 117 (1612-41); minutes of the *dienaren*, nr. 116 (1612-20; 1640-68); and the so-called "ban book," nr. 125 (1646-79). Although the lack of systematic poor relief rolls prior to 1658 makes it difficult to form definite conclusions about the relationship between economic status and frequency of the ban, of the seventy-nine recorded cases of discipline between 1658 and 1668, at least twenty-nine or about one third were also on the regular relief rolls during these same years. While several more can be identified as belonging to lower occupational groups, others in the ban book included merchants or wives of merchants and families of members of the church board. PA 1120 nr. 125:1-26; nr. 136:1-115v.

59. PA 1120 nr. 118, art. 117:13.

60. One church elder, Reynier Wijbrantsz., explained the relationship between alms and good conduct. Paul had instructed, "if any would not work, neither should he eat," nor should anyone eat who "walketh disorderly" (2 Thess. 3: 6, 14, 15). Therefore, concluded Reynier, some kind of "withdrawal" was necessary from "the enjoyment of alms" or from "the community of the Lord's Supper" until improvement occurs. PA 1120 nr. 131:[2] .

61. PA 1120 nr. 116, part B:21 (June 12 and 27, 1652).

62. PA 1120 116:25v-26v (Sept. 20, 1618 and Feb. 7, 1619).

63. PA 1120 nr. 117:53v (Feb. 8, 1626).

64. PA 1120 nr. 118, art. 7:2.

65. PA 1120 nr. 116, part B:[fo. 17] (24 Nov. 1649): B:[18] (Jan. 12, 1650).

66. The information about Roelofje Harmens and her family comes from the following sources: PA 1120 nr. 136:58v, 112v, B28v, B68v; nr. 134 (Jan. 24, 1658; Feb. 5 and Oct. 28, 1660; Aug. 24, Sept. 7, Oct. 5, and Dec. 28, 1662; Feb. 8 and Dec. 13, 1663; Aug. 28, Sept. 18, Oct. 2, and Nov. 27, 1664; Jan. 27 and Feb. 5 and 26, 1665).

67. PA 1120 nrs. 134, 136.

68. In 1662 the woman informed the deacons that she could support herself, but no further explanation is given. Either she or her sons were supporting the family, or she had remarried." PA 1120 nr. 136:42.

69. PA 1120 nr. 136:44.

70. PA 1120 nr. 134 (March 29, 1657), Annetje Teunis.

71. PA 1120 nr. 134 (July 27, 1656; Dec. 21, 1656).

72. PA 1120 nr. 134 (July 6, 1656). He does not appear in the poor book lists of 1658 or 1668.

73. Rensien Alberts is an example of generational poverty. Her father, Albert Janssen, had been the custodian of the church but did not earn enough to support his family. The family lived in the Bakehouse. When Rensien died at the age of seventy-one, she was still living in the Bakehouse under the care of the deacons. PA 1120 nr. 136:4v; nr. 117, 25 (Sept. 6, 1617); nr. 140: Kasboek vol. 1 (1605-1620), e.g. 3v, 4v, 6-8.

74. PA 1120 nr. 140 (May 1605-May 1606).

75. PA 1120 nr. 136 (1658).

76. PA 1120 nr. 117:11 (Apr. 27, 1614).

# References

Geyl, P.
   1948    *Geschiedenis van de Nederlandse stam.* 3 vols. 2nd ed. Amsterdam: Wereldbibliotheek.

Groenveld, S. et al.
   1981    *Wederdopers-menisten-doopsgezinden in Nederland 1530-1980.* 2nd ed. Zutphen: Walburg Pers.

Grosheide, G.
   1938    *Bijdrage tot de Geschiedenis der Anabaptisten in Amsterdam.* Hilversum: J. Schipper Jr.

Keeney, William Echard
   1968    *The Development of Dutch Anabaptist Thought and Practice from 1539-1564.* Nieuwkoop: B. de Graaf.

Krahn, Cornelius
   1957    "Anabaptism and the Culture of the Netherlands." In *Recovery of the Anabaptist Vision: A Sixtieth Anniversary Tribute to Harold S. Bender,* ed. Guy F. Hershberger. Scottdale, Pa.: Herald Press.

McKee, Elsie Anne
    1984    *John Calvin on the Diaconate and Liturgical Almsgiving.* Geneva: Librairie Droz.

*Mennonite Encyclopedia, The*
    1956-1990  Five volumes. Scottdale, Pa.: Herald Press.

Menno Simons
    1956    *The Complete Writings of Menno Simons c. 1496-1561.* Ed. J.C. Wenger, trans. Leonard Verduin. Scottdale, Pa.: Herald Press.

Nutseling, H. P. H.
    1985    *Welvaart en werkgelegenheid in Amsterdam 1540-1860. Een relaas over demograftie, economie en sociale politiek van een wereldstad.* Amsterdam: De Bataafsche Leeuw.

Roodenburg, Herman
    1990    *Onder censuur. De kerkelijke tucht in de gereformeerde gemeente van Amsterdam, 1578-1700.* Hilversum: Verloren.

Sprunger, Mary S.
    1993    "Rich Mennonites, Poor Mennonites: Economics and Theology in the Amsterdam Waterlander Congregation during the Golden Age." Ph.D. diss., University of Illinois, Champaign-Urbana.

    1994    "Waterlanders and the Dutch Golden Age: A Case Study on Mennonite Involvement in Seventeenth-Century Dutch Trade and Industry as One of the Earliest Examples of Socio-Economic Assimilation." In *From Martyr to Muppy. A Historical Introduction to Cultural Assimilation Processes of a Religious Minority in the Netherlands: the Mennonites,* ed. Alastair Hamilton et al. Amsterdam: Amsterdam University Press.

Stayer, James M.
    1991    *The German Peasants' War and Anabaptist Community of Goods.* Montreal: McGill-Queen's Univ. Press.

T[heunisz.], I[an]
    1627    *Der Hanssijtsche Menniste Geest-drijveren Historie. Ofte kort Verhael van de ghepretendeerde Ghesichten, Inspraken, Openbaringen, ende haer Acten, by onse tijden. . . .* [Amsterdam]: Jan Theunisz.

Van Deursen, A. Th.
    1974    *Bavianen en slijkgenzen. Kerk en kerkrolk in Holland ten tijde van Maurits en Oldenbarnelvelt.* Assen: Van Gorcum.

    1991    *Plain Lives in a Golden Age,* trans. Maarten Ultee. Cambridge: Cambridge University Press.

Visser, Piet
    1988    *Broeders in de geest. De doopsgezinde bijdragen van Dierick en Jan Philipsz. Schabaelje tot de Nederlandse stichtelijke literatuur in de zeventiende eeuw.* 2 vols. Deventer: Sub Rosa.

Waite, Gary K.
    1990    *David Joris and Dutch Anabaptism 1524-1543.* Waterloo: Wilfrid Laurier University Press.

# Part Four

# Organizational Case Studies

8

# Changing Patterns of Mutual Aid in Ontario, 1864-1994

## E. Reginald Good

In this study of changing economic patterns in Ontario, E. Reginald Good shows how the emergence of mutual aid organizations departed from traditional understandings of Gelassenheit. Good traces the emergence of several mutual aid efforts in Canada and notes the important influence of J. Winfield Fretz. In assessing the impact of these efforts, Good concludes that although individual leaders were committed to the ideology of mutual aid, this did not reflect the experience and commitment of many rank and file members of the church.

## Traditional Values and Social Arrangements

Recent understandings of mutual aid do not adequately reflect the lived reality of the majority of nineteenth- and twentieth-century Mennonites in Ontario.[1] Traditional patterns of economic interdependence among Mennonites in Ontario were rooted in the ideology of Gelassenheit—total nonresistance to God's will—and its undergirding social practices. Gelassenheit was perceived to be the principle by which the whole natural order functioned.

Mimesis, the process of imitation, linked the ideology of Gelassenheit to practice. Mennonites reproduced and maintained social arrange-

171

ments that reflected patterns perceived in the larger, living cosmos. As Mennonites modernized, the ideology of Gelassenheit gave way to the ideology of progress, which provided the rationale for social change. Mennonites gradually became involved in defensive/offensive restructuring to resist social assimilation and to compete with non-Mennonites in the public arena. This paper contextualizes the origins and development of the so-called mutual aid organizations among Mennonites in Ontario within this changing ideological ethos.

Premodern Mennonites believed that "the creatures, rightly understood and used, teach [Gelassenheit] the total surrender to God out of which new life comes" (Klaassen 1991: 29). In the words of J[ohn] B[aer] (1867:116), nature

> shrinks back from death. Vegetation forces its way to the light: animals seek their food and with surprising instinct avoid that which is injurious. . . . All things desire life, are glad of their existence, and aspire after a better and higher state of life.

By an intricate hierarchical arrangement, each species serves to support others as it earns its own living in an enduring community of peaceful coexistence. As Barbara Sherk (1896:227) has written,

> Look at nature, in all its beauty and grandeur, how everything fulfills the purpose for which it was created, in its proper sphere and assigned place. The violet, even though it was a humble flower, still fulfilled the purpose that had been established for it; as such it was to be the example for Christians, who were to search out the will of God and carry it out as was done in the natural order. There is a place, a work for everyone, and to find that place and to do that work which God has assigned to each, should be the whole aim of our lives.

"Natural phenomena in their created integrity," argues Klaassen (1991:33), provide a model for all people to be "what they were created by God to be, and not what they themselves imagine they should be." According to David Sherk (1867:115), God created man as a social being

> with power and authority to subdue the earth and have dominion over the fishes of the sea and over the fowls of the air, and over every living thing that moveth on the earth; but man was not to subdue man and to have dominion over his fellowman, his own kind and brother.

Then came the fall. Satan broke the social bond through the transgression of Adam and Eve and instilled selfishness and self-willfulness in them and their descendants.

Thereafter, humans subjected themselves to and served the creatures rather than, as God intended, ruling over them and serving God.

Only Jesus Christ can empower humans to detach themselves from dependence on "everything that constitutes human life in this world" and attach themselves to "the eternal, uncreated God who lives in light unapproachable" (Klaassen 1991:34).[2] "Thus," in the words of Mennonite preacher Elias Weber, "the omniscient God reinstated the order [*Ordnung*] of a social life into the plan of salvation, whereby we shall be united with God and each other, already here on earth."[3]

Mennonites reproduced and maintained a social hierarchy, based on work as *the* common denominator, that mimicked the natural order. Every healthy, able-bodied person was assigned an appropriate place and sufficient work in the community (*Gemeinschaft*), which Ecclesiasticus 2:5 (Froschauer edition) describes as "the furnace of Gelassenheit." Church leaders "controlled the rituals that guarded community boundaries and clarified hierarchical structures" (Yoder 1983:345).

Mennonites learned patience or fatalism from the water and air which suffer "monstrous abuse without crying or threatening" (Klaassen 1991:33). Tests of poverty, sickness, toil, and pain were believed to come "not by chance but by the hand of a merciful and altogether unerring Providence, which permits it for wise purposes" ("Suffering" 1865:57).

> Since Christ, who is the head of the church and without sin had to suffer so grievously to pay the whole guilt of Adam, He desires that all His members shall share in the cup of suffering and the baptism of affliction, and pass through many forms of suffering and trouble (D. Sherk: n.d.).

Most church members chose to experience this suffering vicariously through "afflicted" coreligionists who were urged to "pray for patience and strength to bear the imposed suffering as God wishes" (D. Sherk: n.d.). Thus the worthy poor in Mennonite communities, particularly widows and orphans, became Christlike and able to breathe new life into all members through their burden of suffering. "Do not, then, murmur," an anonymous writer in the *Herald of Truth* admonished, "but rather give him thanks that he has counted you worthy of this calling."[4]

Charity and compassion were qualities to be cultivated in the face of the uncertainty of God's cosmic plan. It was part of the process of working out one's salvation on an individual level. But the creatures of nature taught the renunciation of control (*Wehrlosigkeit*) or nonresistance, the abandonment of attempts to impose solutions on the issues of the present. There was no expectation that Christians should redistribute their wealth because "God has so ordained in his unsearchable decree that rich and poor shall dwell together. . . . The grave will make us all equal" ("Rich" 1865:2).

## Mutual Aid Challenges Traditional Values

The ideology of Gelassenheit was exposed to a sustained critique by progress-minded Mennonites in Ontario. They lobbied for systematic relief for fifteen thousand coreligionists who migrated from New Russia to Canada and the United States in the 1870s. C. F. Detweiler (1873:151), for example, argued that Christians should redistribute economic burdens rather than passively accept human suffering as the will of God. He deplored it as a

> sad fact that the great aim of many of our brethren, is, or seems to be, to add wealth to wealth, and acre to acre, while they show little inclination to help the needy. Not even to lend, lest the thing lent is spoiled, or lest their neighbors are encouraged to be pesterous.

David Sherk (1874:51) admitted that systematic relief for Russian Mennonite immigrants did not seem to fit Jesus' teaching that in almsgiving the left hand should not know what the right was doing. But, he argued that "under the present circumstances, where the distress is so great, and the amount required so much, we must . . . unite prudence with benevolence."

Other progress-minded Mennonites obliquely challenged the traditional conception of salvation which sacralized vicarious suffering. John M. Brenneman (1874), for example, acknowledged that God was responsible for leading the Russian Mennonites through severe trials, "but who can say that it is not the purpose of God, through the sad calamity of the Russian brethren also to try us here in America, whether we will sympathize with and show mercy towards them, or not. . . ." In other words, Brenneman suggested that salvation was linked to responsible stewardship.

Contributors to funds set up for the relief of Russian Mennonite immigrants did not necessarily share the progressive views of C. F. Detweiler, David Sherk, and John M. Brenneman. They typically desired to loan their money at a reasonable rate of interest and thereby profit from the misfortune of the immigrants. David S. Holdeman condemned this attitude: "Is it in accordance with the word of God to take interest from these poor people?" he rhetorically challenged readers of the binational Mennonite newspaper, *Herald of Truth*.

Readers did not attempt to justify charging interest. However, John F. Funk commented that "the loaning of the money with interest, is, no doubt, the best that we can do, under the present circumstances" (Holdeman 1875:75). In August of 1874 an ad hoc immigration committee in Ontario, subsequently organized as the Committee of Management of Mennonites in Ontario, set a standard rate of six percent—the common prevailing rate of interest on primary mortgages—and eight years for the payment of loans to Russian Mennonites. The Board of Guardians based in Elkhart, Indiana, followed suit by setting guidelines of six percent and seven years.

Contributors to Russian Mennonite relief also looked on the immigrants as a potential source of indentured labor. They recalled that their own forefathers had once been immigrants.

> The brethren who already lived in America paid their passage until they could repay it with their labor, and through the blessing of God became in easy circumstances. The same thing can again be done for the needy Russian brethren (Basinger and Steiner 1874:53).

This plan subsequently was implemented. Unfortunately, some Russian Mennonites felt exploited by their North American sponsors. Peter Unruh and David Holdeman (1875:158) lamented that some North American Mennonites

> pay such small wages that we do not know how they can expect to meet the approving smiles of a just God. . . . It is frequently said that it is better for them to work for small wages than to remain idle, to which we also assent. But how are they to support their families, and secure seed under such circumstances?"

Bernard Warkentin believed that Mennonite sponsors "wanted to keep healthy, able-bodied immigrants while letting the old and weak go West" (Schlabach 1988:276). Theron Schlabach maintains that the idea of scattering individual members of a family "was logical but it overlooked immigrants' desire to stay together and reestablish their communities" (1988:276). Mennonites traditionally defined the family as a farm-based household under patriarchal control. If the family lost its patriarch or the patriarch failed to meet its economic needs, ministers typically sanctioned and even helped dismember the household so members could join other legitimate families.

Traditional Mennonite values came under scrutiny and criticism in the 1870s when progress-minded Mennonites lobbied for systematic relief to destitute Russian Mennonite immigrants. This lobbying resulted in the creation of a temporary relief organization, the Committee of Management of Mennonites in Ontario, to provide assistance for the immigrants. However, many Mennonites contributed to such relief organizations for traditional reasons. These included a sense of charity as well as desire to generate interest income to meet nepotistic obligations and to secure indentured labor to expand farm production above daily subsistence requirements. Gelassenheit survived intact as the dominant Mennonite ideology.

# Preserving Social Hierarchy

As the nineteenth century progressed, urbanization, commercialization, and industrialization led Mennonites to devise divergent strategies to reproduce patriarchal, farm-based households, the bulwark of the traditional Mennonite social hierarchy. In highly developed areas such as Waterloo Township, Waterloo County; and Markham Township, York County, rising land costs and declining commodity prices made it difficult for less affluent farmers to provide farms for their children who came of age. Dissolution of social boundaries provided opportunities for young people to interact socially with the host society, seek livelihoods in nonagrarian activities, and abandon the Mennonite church community.

Some blamed this exodus on "rich ministers" with fatalistic attitudes. They appeared too busy with their own business affairs to provide the leadership required to keep Mennonite young people down on the farm and in the church.[5] As L. J. Burkholder complained, "we see men of a ripe experience appointed by God as caretakers of the flock, who stand at a distance and look on with indifferent eyes."[6]

One reason for this indifference was that ministers typically were chosen from among the most affluent ten percent of the Mennonites, who owned about a quarter of the church community's land area. They secured generational succession of the farm-based household by exploiting the labor of the poorest ten percent of Mennonite landowners, who owned less than two percent of the church community's total land area. Mennonite youth from the poorest families faced "greater restrictions in establishing separate households, married later, practiced greater fertility control, and more often left the community" (Loewen 1994:195). They worked as servants for wealthier Mennonite farmers until they could afford to marry and establish independent households.

Satisfied as they were with this arrangement, ministers made no effort to mobilize community resources to aid poor families in establishing separate farm-based households. Money occasionally was loaned to members of the extended kinship network by childless couples or single adults. But usually, prosperous Mennonites invested surplus cash in land for themselves to be handed down later to their own children.

Poor families turned to "private individuals, usually non-Mennonites," for loans to purchase farms. These men were "retired, wealthy farmers" who "often held several mortgages on farms for Mennonites" (Laurence 1980:AB-2). They demanded that their mortgagers purchase fire insurance to secure their investment. Voluntary canvassing of members for money and labor, which Mennonites had previously relied on for compensating losses due to fire, was considered inadequate. The cash donations fire victims received were unpredictable and usually did not cover the cost of materials required to repair or rebuild one's damaged property. In addition, the value of labor contributed to install the materials was more than offset by the cost of food and whiskey with which the victim was expected to supply the workers.[7]

At the local Waterloo conference of September 9, 1864, members expressed a need for a Mennonite organization which would provide the benefits of a commercial fire insurance company without involving subscribers in those subrogated legal actions which undermined the nonresistant ideology of Gelassenheit. A resolution was passed that approved, in principle, "a plan . . . which would be helpful in guiding the person in the amount which he should reasonably give in case of a brother suffering loss by fire" (Burkholder 1935:156-57).

The rhetoric of those laymen involved in the subsequent establishment of a Mennonite farmers mutual insurance organization, the Waterloo-area Mennonite Aid Union, often referred to the charitable aspects of the undertaking. However, most of the initial subscribers were moderately wealthy. In the Weber (now Pioneer Park) congregation, for example, only five out of twenty-one subscribers were from among the poorest ten percent of the landowners. Ministers, on the other hand, were covered by the plan even though they were not required to contribute financially to annual levies under it (according to Section VIII of the first Mennonite Aid Union Constitution dated 1866).

The Mennonite Aid Union soon became widely accepted among modernizing Mennonites in Ontario. From an initial membership base in the Waterloo area, the Union gradually expanded. By 1876 members of all Mennonite congregations in the Ontario district conference were permitted to subscribe.

Other district conferences of the Mennonite Church perceived the Union to be an expedient venture as well. At the Indiana district conference sessions of October 13, 1882, it was agreed that an "arrangement or system of collection similar to that which has now been maintained already some twenty years in Canada" be established to "obviate the necessity of brethren identifying themselves with the general Insurance companies to which many of the brethren are opposed."[8] The Illinois district conference followed suit in 1883 as did the Lancaster district conference in 1886.

Mennonite farmers mutual fire insurance organizations purported to provide the benefits of a commercial company without undermining the nonresistant ideology of Gelassenheit. However, insurance in any form undermined the mimetic aspects of Gelassenheit by looking to actuarial science rather than the creatures of nature for inspiration to reproduce and maintain social arrangements. It also protected subscribers from providential exposure to the vulnerability of need and thereby threatened to destabilize God's social order. What begins in this period as an organized calculated means to meet communal need prevails in the next period, in the context of widespread economic depression.

## Depression Prompts Changes

Mennonite relief giving in the 1930s did not reflect the severe depression taking its toll in North America and all the Western world (Schlabach 1980:125). However, Mennonites were not ignoring the economic needs of destitute members in their own congregations. In the 1930-31 budget year, the Ontario district conference Charity Fund Committee received seventeen requests for help from the $1,000 of annual interest gained from the district conference Poor Fund for such members.

A request from Jesse B. Martin, pastor of Erb St. Mennonite Church, was probably typical of those received. He observed that widower Addison Erb's children, Helen, Frederick, and Ruth, had been taken from their father and placed in Christian homes. "They are needy children. There is no support here for them. We must look to the Heavenly Father to care for them."[9]

Another request came from Lewis Weber, employed by the General Mission Board at the Mennonite Gospel Mission, an Ontario district conference congregation in Toronto. Weber had just received a medical bill of $301.23 for services rendered his wife since 1927. The General Mission Board could not afford to pay. He had sufficient personal savings to cover the bill but was hesitant to eliminate his nest egg when the General Mission Board provided no retirement benefits for its workers.

The flood of requests for assistance in 1931 could not all be met. George Weber, chairman of the district conference Charity Fund committee, reported at the Ontario district conference sessions in June 1931 that his committee expended their resources by contributing $100 to the Ministers' Aid Fund and $50 to a family in Haldimand County. This inability to respond to the vast majority of requests may have led to the appointment of an ad hoc study committee by the Ontario district conference to investigate the whole question of "Government investments and Government support."[10]

At the conference sessions of June 1932, the study committee delivered a report recommending that

> those interested in Canadian Government Annuities are not acting out of harmony with the Church's position and attitude to Life Insurance, this system of investment having eliminated the features which make insurance undesirable to the Mennonite Church.

The study committee in addition recommended that members be allowed to take "government support" as represented in Mothers' Allowances and Old Age Pensions, the latter of which had only been available since 1929.

## A Proposed Benefit Association

Both recommendations were accepted. However, neither responded to the needs of people like Lewis Weber, who faced the prospect of spending his life savings on medical bills. He did not qualify for financial assistance either from the conference Charity Fund or secular welfare systems. Consequently, A. C. Kolb proposed that the Ontario district conference establish a "Mennonite Benefit Association," a church-sponsored social insurance plan "in no way out of harmony with Scriptures or the tenets of the Church."[11]

Ministers acknowledged that secret societies and life insurance companies were making

> persistent inroads among the Mennonite Churches, presuming to offer something better than anything the Church provides, having under their system definite methods whereby provisions are made so that the needy may never be left in suspense and anxiety.[12]

However, many ministers failed "to see the need of such an elaborate organization for a group of people who claim to live by faith and trust in a heavenly father." The majority of the ministers felt that "the Church in general is not ready for a step like this."[13]

Not until the eve of Canada's declaration of war against Germany on September 10, 1939, would Ontario district conference delegates reconsider Kolb's recommendation to create a church sponsored social insurance plan. At the conference sessions of June 1939, an ad hoc study committee appointed by the Executive Committee of the Ontario district conference reported on "the possible avenue of service of a Mennonite welfare organization." The committee expressed alarm at

> the ever-increasing number of our membership who apparently find it necessary to appeal to civic and provincial governments for financial

assistance" [and the] extent to which such a situation would ultimately affect the privileges we are now enjoying as a nonresistant body."[14]

Conference ministers immediately responded to the concern by authorizing the formation of a Welfare Board with power to levy per capita assessments on church members semiannually; also, an ad hoc study committee was appointed to consider anew the matter of government annuities and pensions.

The Welfare Board devoted most of its resources during the ensuing war years to meeting the needs of dependents of alternative service workers. However, not everyone was satisfied with the level of support thus extended. One alternative service worker wrote to his bishop, J. B. Martin, "I don't know what happened to the promises that were made to us before we left as far as support for our wives goes or that they would be looked after."[15]

At the Ontario district conference sessions of 1943, a committee of investigation was appointed to act as a liaison between congregations with needy dependents of alternative service workers and the conference Welfare Board. The policy of the committee of investigation was that dependents should maintain themselves with their own labor and resources as much as possible. In effect, women had to prove their own need to get help.

Also at the 1943 Ontario sessions, the annuities and pensions committee submitted a plan for the organization of a "Mennonite Mutual Aid or Welfare Association." It was designed to "make some provision for extended illness, extended unemployment, and operations. These three and the death benefit would meet the situation, and would end the pressure for other means of protection."[16] Conference ministers adopted the plan in principle, but they suggested that the administrative structure of the association be revised in consultation with the Welfare Board and that it be reconsidered at the conference sessions the following year in 1944.

The Benefit Society subsequently was placed on hold at the conference sessions of 1944 because the Family Allowance Act, which the Government of Canada had recently enacted, demanded immediate attention. If conference ministers were going to proscribe that assistance to its constituents, revisions were required in the proposed social insurance plan to offset the influence of the Act.

## The Family Allowance Act

The Family Allowance Act of 1944 was designed to assist families in lower income brackets by providing monthly benefits for each child up to sixteen years of age in graduating amounts (according to age) from five to eight dollars. Although the allowances were made regardless of need, upper-income wage earners paid for them through personal income taxation. The primary concern of some Ontario district conference members "in accepting such allowances was based on the feeling that somehow the children benefiting would be under some additional, although undefined, obligation to the government" (Good 1951:21).

An ad hoc study committee was appointed to study the matter of Family Allowances; it brought a report to the conference sessions of 1945. The committee condemned the acceptance of assistance under the Family Allowance Act because "the Bible standard of home life can best be maintained when the parents of the home accept the responsibility of family finances."[17]

Ministers vigorously debated this report and finally passed a resolution "that we allow individual members to be guided by their own conscience in accepting or rejecting benefits under Family Allowances."[18] Probably most ministers would have agreed that the better the Church "can meet its needs without the aid of the state, the less the danger that the state will encroach upon those areas where it ought not to operate" (Hershberger 1969:166). But at the time, Ontario Mennonites found themselves "without the resources for the practical solution" (Good 1951:21).

The official acceptance of Family Allowance benefits sensitized ministers to the "lack of Christian provision for meeting the needs" of indigent members, and the proposed Mennonite Mutual Benefit Society was now reconsidered as a means to provide some measure of economic security to them. Some ministers, who had previously opposed an organized plan for mutual assistance in times of death or impairment of health, now changed their minds. They recognized that, although such a system was not the ideal method of expressing the Christian spirit of charity to those in need, it would be preferable to leaving all responsibility in the hands of the state.

## *The Mutual Benefit Society*

Beginning in 1945, then, the Ontario district conference took earnest steps to implement a social insurance plan for its members. The annuities and pensions study committee examining the question was increased from five to eight members and instructed to consider again the feasibility of implementing the proposed Mennonite Mutual Benefit Society. At the Ontario district conference sessions of June 1946, the enlarged committee reported that "the economic factor looks satisfactory to us" and recommended that ministers put the plan into action.

By June 1948 the plan was operative under the title Mennonite Benefit Association, Inc., with a charter "which practically gives us the privilege of operating . . . as the conference, membership, and directors deem fit."[19] The administrative structure was the same as that proposed in 1944, except that the Welfare Board had no direct representation. The benefits offered were substantially the same as proposed in 1943.

The Mennonite Church General Conference was motivated by the example of Ontario Mennonites to organize a social insurance plan for United States Mennonites under the auspices of Mennonite Mutual Aid and named Mennonite Mutual Aid, Inc. The organization was modeled along the basic "lines followed by the Mennonite Benefit Association of Ontario."[20] It was chartered in Pennsylvania where "an association similar to the one in Ontario and for practically the same purposes could be incorporated."[21] M. R. Good, Secretary-Treasurer of the Mennonite Benefit Association, was elected first president of Mennonite Mutual Aid, Inc., and served 1949-1954.

Mennonites in Ontario, as their coreligionists elsewhere in North America, did not develop a vision for relief and service or mutual aid prior to World War II. Their social conscience was "chained to, and limited by, a rather formalized dissent from actual war" (Schlabach 1980:125-26). The catalyst, which finally resulted in the founding of social insurance institutions in Ontario and the United States, was not the widespread hardship experienced by many Mennonite families during the depression of the 1930s. Rather, the motivation was the desire of Mennonites to preserve those political privileges that enabled them to live out pacifist convictions in wartime without recrimination.

Official church sponsorship of social insurance plans inadvertently undermined the stoical ideology of Gelassenheit by intervening to prevent human suffering which might have resulted from the loss of political privileges. Social insurance also represented a positive initiative to improve the quality of life for all subscribers—conflicting somewhat with the fatalistic ideology of Gelassenheit, which aspired to complete trust and hope in God. It also cultivated dependence on, rather than detachment from, the very human institutions which tradition-minded Mennonites believed would separate them from God.

# The Influence of J. Winfield Fretz

When World War II broke out in 1939, Mennonites in Ontario still preserved their traditional, hierarchical social order. Wartime and postwar economic opportunities led to the disintegration of traditional Mennonite society and the abandonment of the ideology of Gelassenheit, which undergird its existence. Ontario Mennonites left their farms by the thousands after 1940 and assimilated into the middle class of urban Ontario society. A professional Mennonite intelligentsia helped them link their old world to middle-class respectability by articulating and marketing new symbols of Mennonite identity. These fit the "new, conservative middle-class Canada" (Loewen 1993:182). One new symbol of Mennonite identity was mutual aid, and its most ardent promoter was J. Winfield Fretz (author of the foreword to this volume).

Fretz concluded his graduate studies in sociology at the University of Chicago in the depths of the Depression. He then sought "a place . . . in the Mennonite Church" where he could study the institutions of "the Mennonite people from the standpoint of a Christian sociologist."[22] He hoped his findings would transform Mennonite society from a despised, passive object of history into a dynamic and active subject shaping its own destiny in harmony with "its historic religious principles and . . . its God-given function" (Fretz 1940:209). He believed that "among the techniques or characteristic practices within our tradition none have played a more vital role than have the practices of colonization and mutual aid" (Fretz 1955:F1). He saw these as the building blocks of Mennonite society.

Actually, although Fretz "came from a strong Mennonite family and an old and traditional Mennonite Church," he had never been "consciously . . . aware" of the ideas and principles that held Mennonite communities together until his doctoral supervisor, Arthur Holt, "carefully and repeatedly pointed it out." Prior to entering a doctoral program, Fretz had "fallen in love" with the Rochdale principles of cooperation and the cooperative movement, which he viewed as an alternative to "the selfish aspects of capitalism" (Fretz 1985).[23]

At Holt's instigation, Fretz wrote his doctoral dissertation on Mennonites' historical contribution toward a cooperative commonwealth. Carl Landes suggested that Fretz entitle it "Rochdale Principles of Cooperation Operating in the Mutual Aid Societies of the Mennonite Church."[24] However, Fretz settled on "Mennonite Mutual Aid: A Contribution Toward the Establishment of a Christian Community" (Fretz 1941). The title proper was derived from Peter Kropotkin's *Mutual Aid: A Factor of Evolution*. Fretz concluded that Mennonite "emphasis on Christian brotherhood is preparing the soil for cooperation."[25]

Following the conclusion of his doctoral program, Fretz labored to establish a united program of colonization and mutual aid among Mennonites in North America.[26] He believed that keeping Mennonite young people established "on land and in economically stable rural communities" was vital to "prolonging and strengthening the life of the Mennonite Church." Furthermore, "it would be a direct fulfilling of one of the traditional principles of the church, namely, providing for the poor and needy of its members and looking after the welfare of all" (Fretz 1940:199, 213).

Fretz proposed the establishment of a central mutual aid committee, "organized in the same manner and the same spirit in which the central committees on relief and peace were created," to coordinate colonization and community development activities (Fretz 1940:210). Unfortunately, Fretz perceived "a lack of interest, in fact almost total apathy, on the part of the Mennonite constituency to the whole idea of mutual aid" (Fretz 1985).

Further, he noted that in

> all too many cases within the brotherhood of the Mennonite churches the standards of the secular world have been adopted with regard to financial matters. Many of the congregations have completely denied that they have any responsibility for the economic welfare of their members.

He attributed "the great annual loss of members" to "the neglect of the principle of social responsibility within the Mennonite Church, that is, the idea that the welfare of one member becomes the concern of all" (Fretz 1940:199, 207).

Fretz began to feel that mutual aid was a lost cause, something akin to footwashing, the holy kiss, the devotional covering, and other traditional Mennonite practices. In 1963, Fretz moved to Waterloo County, Ontario, to become the first president of Conrad Grebel College. Fretz discovered "a new generation of [urban] Mennonites" attending seven large churches in the twin cities of Kitchener-Waterloo who were "growing up unaware of the mutual aid aspect in their tradition" (Fretz 1989:269-71). Many "were not involved in any enterprises that were contributing to the welfare of the Mennonite community."

Howard Snyder, general manager of the Bell Telephone Employees Credit Union in Toronto, Ontario, persuaded Fretz that the founding of a Mennonite credit union would resurrect the old principle of mutual aid in a contemporary form. Such an institution would "perform mutual aid services for urban people that parallel the barn raising, field plowing, and harvesting traditionally performed only in rural communities" (Fretz 1985).

At Fretz's initiative, twenty-one men from Mennonite congregations in Kitchener-Waterloo met on February 25, 1964, to discuss the possibility of "grafting . . . the young twig of the credit union . . . to a branch of an old mutual aid tree" (Fretz 1989:280). The favorable response led to an organizational meeting on March 12, 1964, at which time temporary officers were elected. Howard Snyder, elected president, was an (Old) Mennonite. The other officers were Russian Mennonites who attended General Conference or Mennonite Brethren churches.

The temporary officers applied for a provincial charter under the name of Waterloo County Mennonite Credit Union Limited. Fretz wrote a cover letter with the application. There he made a case to include all Mennonite bodies in Waterloo County in a common bond of association for the purposes of the Credit Union Act. He maintained that "congregational government" was a "historic characteristic" of Mennonite polity that accounted for their organizational pluralism. However, "Mennonite differences are more sociological than theological." They have "always strongly emphasized three aspects of Christianity, namely, the church as a brotherhood, a life of Christian discipleship, and the governing of all relationships in life by the ethics of love."[27]

The Province of Ontario accepted Fretz's argument and issued a charter in May 1964. On 1 June 1964 a full board of nine directors was elected along with a Credit Committee and a Supervisory Committee.

Unfortunately, Fretz found that most area Mennonites were "unacquainted with the Rochdale principles . . . on which the credit unions are based. For this reason most of our coreligionists are indifferent or only mildly interested in the Credit Union."[28] Therefore, "credit unions will need to be 'sold' to our people and this over a period of time."[29]

By the end of the first year of operation in 1965, membership in the Credit Union stood at ninety-three. Not until 1970 were there over 200 members, and not until 1976 did membership reach 1,000. Then membership quadrupled over the next four years until it reached 3,996 in 1980.

This rapid growth in the late 1970s was due in part to a shift in marketing strategy that assumed

> the genius of the credit union movement lay in certain major economic advantages, such as higher returns on investment and lower rates on loans. . . . This shadow blocked real understanding of credit union philosophy and the founding concerns about mutual aid (Bender 1984:24).

A recession hit the Canadian economy in the late 1970s. Businesses failed, interest rates skyrocketed, and the Credit Union was not able to offer competitive financial advantages to its members. "By 1980, it had become clear that divergent perceptions of both mission and procedures existed." Two Special Sessions of the Board were called—one in July and a second in November—to initiate a process for rationalizing the operation of the organization, developing new market strategies, and ensuring long-term membership loyalties.

# The Credit Union Comes of Age

At the annual meeting of the Credit Union in 1981, Lloyd Martin, president of the Mennonite Credit Union, sounded a call for the organization "to represent more fully the principles of the credit union movement as well as the fundamental principles of the Mennonite Church." A detailed Statement of Philosophy, approved by the membership in 1984, "brought the Mennonite Credit Union . . . full circle" by "confirming the traditional commitment to a clear reflection of biblical stewardship and firmly-established patterns of mutual aid" (Bender 1984:26).

J. Winfield Fretz was pleased with this development. Fretz entitled his address to the Annual Meeting of the Credit Union in 1985 "The Mennonite Credit Union Comes of Age." Now that the Credit Union "is headed into its twenty-first year," he said, "it has developed a full rounded body in size and strength and is ready to perform its God-given service for which it was created" (Fretz 1985:10).

Urie Bender, director of communications (1979-1991) and communications consultant (1991-1994) of the Mennonite Credit Union, was less enthusiastic. Writing to the president of the Pennsylvania Mennonite Federal Credit Union in 1991, Bender confided that "our Mennonite credit unions do not yet have an adequate sense of selfhood; we don't really know yet who we are. . . . ," he noted. Were they "just a credit union in the movement sense? or some kind of Mennonite bank? or a strange hybrid flirting with both theology and high finance[?]"

Bender believed that most Mennonites were not committed to mutual aid principles. For that reason, the most difficult part of providing leadership to Mennonite credit unions was "the Mennonite factor in the field of membership." Mennonite credit unions had a mission to sell the ideology of mutual aid to Mennonites who "are being integrated into the cultural milieu."[30]

The Mennonite Credit Union was founded by persons committed to the ideology of mutual aid, but they thought mutual aid, rather than Gelassenheit, had been the dominant ideology in Mennonite life. They attempted to use the Mennonite Credit Union as a vehicle to sell the ideology of mutual aid to urbanized Ontario Mennonites seeking symbols of Mennonite identity to link their old traditions to middle class respectability. These efforts, however, met with only checkered success.

The ideology of mutual aid does not adequately reflect the lived experience of the majority of nineteenth- and twentieth-century Mennonites in Ontario. So-called mutual aid organizations, including the Committee of Management of Mennonites in Ontario, the Mennonite Aid Union, the Mennonite Benefit Association and the Mennonite Credit Union, were byproducts of efforts to preserve the traditional ideology of Gelassenheit or promote the modern ideology of progress in the changing social and economic contexts in which North American Mennonites lived. Some individual founders of these organizations, such as David Sherk, A. C. Kolb, and J. Winfield Fretz, personally were committed to the ideology of mutual aid. However, many individual subscribers did not share the same commitments.

## Notes

1. See for example the ideology of mutual aid articulated in the "Statement on Christian Mutual Aid," Smithville, Ohio, June 4-6, 1964 (Hernley 1970:569).

2. By created things Klaassen means "ourselves, time, science, religion, theologies, structures of thought, institutions, church, programs, five-year-plans of all sorts, calls to kingdom-commitments, MCC" (Klaassen 1991:34).

3. [Elias Weber], letter to fellow ministers [1873], Early Correspondence Collections, Archives of the Mennonite Church (hereafter AMC).

4. "Suffering," 1865:100. Dissident voices occasionally challenged how Mennonites treated their widows and orphans. Preacher John Baer, for example, wrote an article for the *Herold der Wahrheit* in 1867 concerning "the Christian's duty regarding collections for the poor as described in 1 Corinthians 16:1." Baer explained in his cover letter to the editor of the *Herold*, John F. Funk, that he was motivated to write the article in response to a heart-rending case of a widow's treatment by the church:

"We have a poor widow among us, a sister from Germany, who has for quite some time been staying with one of our neighbours while she was able to work actively. Afterwards she went around our neighbourhood, staying as much as half a year with us, and thought of appealing to our church about it. For some time she was with one of our people who lives with his son. This son appealed to the church. She was required to contribute her property, which reduced her to a state of beggary; and it is now doubtful whether the desired money will be collected—so I thought I would present the necessary charitable duties through the *Herold*." John Baer letter to John F. Funk, February 16, 1867, John F. Funk Correspondence, AMC.

Baer believed that the treatment of this "poor widow" illustrated a systematic disregard of "charitable duties" among (MC) Mennonites in Canada and the United States, which he intended to address in his article. What is perhaps equally revealing is that Baer's article was printed in neither the *Herold* nor its English-language counterpart, *Herald of Truth*. Baer was a regular contributor to the *Herold* during the 1860s and one can only assume that Funk objected to the tenor or substance of this particular submission. Possibly Funk returned it to Baer because it has not been located among Funk's extant papers.

5. Daniel Brenneman letter to John F. Funk [1863], John F. Funk Correspondence, AMC.

6. L. J. Burkholder, letter to the Mennonite ministers of the Markham District, Sept. 1894, quoted in Friesen (1995:173).

7. Garland and Talman (1931:344-45); Abraham Break Sherk, "Early Recollections," 1904, Abraham Break Sherk Fonds, Mennonite Archives of Ontario (MAO).

8. "Conference in Indiana" 1882:330.

9. J. B. Martin to Bro., February 2, 1931, Secretary's Correspondence, Mennonite Mission Board of Ontario, MAO.

10. *Calendar of Appointments*, 1931-1932, pp. [16 and 26], Ontario Mennonite Conference.

11. A. C. Kolb letter to S. F. Coffman, June 14, 1932, S. F. Coffman Family Fonds, MAO.

12. *Mennonite Mutual Benefit Association Constitution*, [1933], Mennonite Benefit Association Collection, [A. C. Kolb], MAO.

13. J. B. Martin, letter to A. C. Kolb, March 17, 1933, Mennonite Benefit Association Fonds, MAO.

14. *Calendar of Appointments*, 1939-1940, pp. 22-23, Ontario Mennonite Conference.

15. B. S. to J. B. Martin, March 1, 1943, J. B. Martin Family Fonds, MAO.

16. *Calendar of Appointments*, 1942-43, pp. 33-36, Ontario Mennonite Conference.

17. *Calendar of Appointments*, 1945-46, pp. 22-23, Ontario Mennonite Conference.

18. *Calendar of Appointments*, 1945-46, p. 43, Ontario Mennonite Conference.

19. *Calendar of Appointments*, 1947-48, p. 25, Ontario Mennonite Conference.

20. Orie O. Miller letter to Samuel S. Wenger, March 21, 1949, Mennonite Aid Inc. Collection, Orie O. Miller Correspondence, III-29, AMC.

21. Orie O. Miller letter to MMA members, May 23, 1949, Mennonite Aid Inc. Collection, Orie O. Miller Correspondence, III-29, AMC.

22. J. Winfield Fretz letter to J. J. Hildebrand, May 21, 1938, J. Winfield Fretz Fonds, MAO.

23. Fretz (1964) defined these principles as follows:

a) To promote the economic betterment of its members.

b) To promote thrift habits.

c) To promote wise use of credit.

d) To counter the usury of many lending agencies.

e) To provide education—invaluable in today's problems of

1) Installment buying

2) Comparison of interest rates

3) Exposing dangerous sales practices.

f) Provide a friendly and capable counselling service to members in financial distress.

g) Provide members with loan service at reasonable rates.

h) Receive members' deposits and provide best possible interest rates.

24. Carl Landes letter to J. Winfield Fretz, February 17, 1937, J. Winfield Fretz Fonds, MAO.

25. J. Winfield Fretz letter to Carl Hutchinson, March 10, 1939, J. Winfield Fretz Fonds, MAO.

26. He worked directly with the General Conference Mennonite Church Board of Mutual Aid and the Mennonite Central Committee Mutual Aid Section.

27. J. Winfield Fretz letter to Ralph Crough, March 24, 1964, Mennonite Credit Union Fonds, MAO.

28. J. Winfield Fretz letter to the Board of Directors, the Mennonite Credit Union, [1975], Mennonite Credit Union Fonds, MAO.

29. J. Winfield Fretz letter to Vincent Harding, January 12, 1966, J. Winfield

Fretz Fonds, MAO.

30. Urie Bender letter to Larry Miller, October 24, 1991, Mennonite Credit Union Fonds, MAO.

# References

B[aer], J[ohn]
  1867   "An Affecting Incident." *Herald of Truth* 4:115-116.

Bainbridge, John
  1952   *Biography of an Idea: The Story of Mutual Fire and Casualty Insurance.* Garden City, N.Y.: Doubleday.

Basinger, David and Abraham Steiner
  1874   "Our Views." *Herald of Truth* 11 (March): 53.

Bender, Urie
  1984   *Working Together: The Story of Mennonite Credit Union (Ontario) Limited, 1964-1984.* Kitchener, Ont.: Mennonite Credit Union.

Brenneman, John M.
  1874   "Let Us Have Compassion on the Poor." *Herald of Truth* 11 (January).

Burkholder, L. J.
  1935   *A Brief History of Mennonites in Ontario.* Toronto: Mennonite Conference of Ontario.

"Conference in Indiana"
  1882   *Herald of Truth* 19 (October): 330.

Detweiler, C. F.
  1873   "Appeal from the Russian Brethren." *Herald of Truth* 10 (September): 151.

Fretz, J. Winfield
  n.d.   "[Altona, Manitoba:] The Renaissance of a Rural Community." Unpublished.

  n.d.   *Meditations on Christian Mutual Aid.* Association of Mennonite Aid Societies.

  1938   "Christian Mutual Aid Societies Among the Mennonites." M.A. thesis, University of Chicago.

  1939   "Mutual Aid Among the Mennonites, I." *Mennonite Quarterly Review* 13:28-58.

  1939   "Mutual Aid Among the Mennonites, II: Mutual Aid Activities in a Single Mennonite Community." *Mennonite Quarterly Review* 13:187-209.

  1940   "Mennonites and their Economic Problems." *Mennonite Quarterly Review* 14:195-213.

  1941   "Mennonite Mutual Aid: A Contribution Toward the Establishment of a Christian Community." Ph.D. dissertation, University of Chicago.

1947    *Christian Mutual Aid: A Handbook of Brotherhood Economics.* Akron, Pa.: Mennonite Central Committee.

1955    "Colonization and Rehabilitation: An Area of Christian Mutual Aid Activity." Address to a Conference on Mennonite Mutual Aid Sponsored by Mennonite Central Committee, Chicago, Illinois, July 14-15, 1955.

1964    "The Credit Union Brings 'Christianity to the Marketplace.' " Unpublished.

1985    "The Mennonite Credit Union Comes of Age." Address to the Twenty-First Annual Meeting of the Mennonite Credit Union. Unpublished.

1989    *The Waterloo Mennonites: A Community in Paradox.* Waterloo: Wilfrid Laurier Press.

Friesen, Leonard G.
1995    " 'A Lamb Born of God': L. J. Burkholder and the Ontario Mennonite Church, 1894-1940." *Ontario History* 87:173-92.

Garland, M. A., and J. J. Talman
1931    "Pioneer Drinking Habits and the Rise of Temperance Agitation in Upper Canada Prior to 1840." *Ontario History* 27:341-64.

Good, E. Reginald
1984    "War as a Factor in Mennonite Economic Policy: A Case Study of Insurance Institutions Sponsored by the Ontario Conference, 1864-1954." M.A. thesis, University of Waterloo.

Good, Milton R.
1951    "Canadian Public Welfare and the Mennonite Church in Ontario." *Mennonite Community* 5:20-21.

Hernley, H. Ralph, ed.
1970    *The Compassionate Community.* Scottdale, Pa.: Association of Mennonite Aid Societies.

Hershberger, Guy F.
1969    *War, Peace and Nonresistance.* 3d ed. Scottdale, Pa.: Herald Press.

Holdeman, David S.
1875    "A Letter from Kansas." *Herald of Truth* 12 (May): 75-76.

Klaassen, Walter
1991    "Gelassenheit and Creation." *Conrad Grebel Review* 9:23-35.

Laurence, Hugh Getty
1980    "Change in Religion, Economics, and Boundary Conditions Among Amish Mennonites in Southwestern Ontario." Ph.D. dissertation, McGill University.

Loewen, Royden
1993    "Rurality, Ethnicity, and Gender Patterns of Cultural Continuity during the "Great Disjuncture" in the R.M. of Hanover, 1945-61." *Journal of the Canadian Historical Association* N.S. 4:161-82.

1994    "The Mennonites of Waterloo, Ontario and Hanover, Manitoba, 1890s: A Study of Household and Community." *Canadian Papers in Rural History* 9:187-210.

"Rich and the Poor, The"
    1865    *Herald of Truth* 2 (January): 2.

Schlabach, Theron F.
    1980    *Gospel Versus Gospel: Mission and the Mennonite Church, 1863-1944.* Scottdale, Pa.: Herald Press.

    1988    *Peace, Faith, Nation: Mennonites and Amish in Nineteenth-Century America.* Scottdale, Pa.: Herald Press.

Sherk, Barbara
    1896    "Thy Will be Done." *Herald of Truth* 33 (August): 227.

Sherk, David
    n.d.    "Farewell Admonition." Early Correspondence. Archives of the Mennonite Church.

    1867    "Subjection to the Higher Powers." *Herald of Truth* 5 (March): 37-38.

    1874    "Concerning the Russian Affairs." *Herald of Truth* 12 (May): 51-52.

"Suffering"
    1865    *Herald of Truth* 2 (December): 100.

Unruh, Peter and D. S. Holdeman
    1875    "To the Readers of the *Herald*." *Herald of Truth* 12 (September): 158.

"Use of Affliction, The"
    1865    *Herald of Truth* 2 (August): 57.

Yoder, John C.
    1983    "True Watchers: A Study of Social Order Among the Mennonites in Eighteenth-Century Pennsylvania." *Mennonite Quarterly Review* 13(57): 339-53.

9

# My Brother's Keeper: Origins of Mennonite Mutual Aid

## Albert N. Keim

In this fascinating account, Albert Keim tells of the birth pangs of Mennonite Mutual Aid as a formal organization. After sketching the historical forces that catalyzed interest in churchwide mutual aid, Keim describes the tumultuous 1944 special session of the Mennonite General Conference. This conference endorsed a churchwide aid organization contingent on ratification by six district conferences. Keim describes how church leaders organized Mennonite Mutual Aid despite having the support of only five conferences.

## A Difficult Birth

"CONFERENCE APPROVED MUTUAL AID WITHOUT OPPOSITION. FEELING HAPPY."[1]

The telegram captured the mood of Chris Graber. He had sent the message only minutes before he and Guy Hershberger caught the Friday night Rock Island train from Lincoln, Nebraska to Chicago. Graber and Hershberger were headed home to Goshen, Indiana. They had just attended the annual meeting of the Iowa-Nebraska conference of the Mennonite Church (MC), where they proposed creating a new organiza-

192

tion called Mennonite Mutual Aid.

The telegram was addressed to Orie Miller and reached him as he was leaving to catch an overnight westbound train out of Lancaster, Pennsylvania. He too was going to Goshen, Indiana. The next evening Miller, Hershberger, and Graber met in an office at Goshen College to develop plans to implement a new Mennonite Mutual Aid organization ratified the day before by the Iowa-Nebraska conference.[2]

The upbeat character of the telegram from Chris Graber put the best gloss on a difficult situation facing the Continuation Committee on mutual aid that Saturday evening in September 1944. The problem was that the 1944 special session of the General Conference had stipulated that the creation of Mennonite Mutual Aid could go forward only after six of the nine (Old) Mennonite district conferences in the United States approved the program. The action of the Iowa-Nebraska conference on September 8 was only the fifth of the six needed. Four other district conferences had deferred approval for a year, stalling the Mutual Aid project. What could be done?

Frustrated by the delay, the committee told its chairman, Orie Miller, to write to the leaders of the four recalcitrant conferences and ask them to hold a special session to ratify the plan.[3] The hope was that at least one conference might do so. Unfortunately, nothing happened.

After waiting five months for action to free it to organize mutual aid, the Committee decided to move ahead without the sixth district conference ratification. Fortunately, Allen Erb, moderator of the Mennonite General Conference, also the enterprising director of the Mennonite Hospital at La Junta, Colorado, believed strongly in the mutual aid plan. He agreed to call a meeting of his General Conference executive committee, the Mutual Aid Committee, and two representatives from each of the nine district conferences. That meeting on May 31, 1945, formally—if a bit unofficially—established the Mennonite Mutual Aid organization.

But to tell the story correctly, we must start at the beginning, for this prelude only hints at the persistence with which a few leaders supported the idea and the languid support it got from most Mennonites. The formation of Mennonite Mutual Aid is the story of the triumph of a modernizing vision over the apathy and inertia of an inherited tradition.

## The Historical Setting

Mutual aid among Mennonites was not a new idea in 1944. During their several-hundred-year history, Mennonites had lived in tightly bound rural communities where communal care for each other was normal and continuous. Mennonite mutual aid took on modern forms in the nineteenth century as Mennonites and Amish in the United States began borrowing fire and storm insurance plans from their American neighbors. One of the first was an Amish Aid Society organized in Eastern Pennsylvania before 1850. Mennonite leader John Funk organized a flourishing fire insurance society in the 1890s. By 1940 there were twenty-four local and regional property aid insurance societies and three Mennonite automobile insurance associations. Insurance as a form of cooperative help was thus not foreign to most Mennonites.[4]

Life insurance was another matter. In its first report in 1930, the new Mennonite General Problems Committee noted that while many Mennonites were participating in various property-loss insurance plans, it was good that all (Old) Mennonites opposed life insurance. The Problems Committee hoped Mennonites would remain faithful in God's promise to take care of his children. But the committee also admitted that conventional congregational help was less adequate than in earlier eras.[5]

The Committees addressed the insurance issue in 1930 and 1931 because of the Great Depression. Although the effect of the Depression on Mennonites varied greatly from community to community, its economic impact was clearly felt. The collapse of wheat and corn prices was catastrophic for farmers—and most Mennonites were farmers. But the hardships did not generate new church initiatives in mutual aid.

In fact, when the first major New Deal program, the National Recovery Act, began in 1933, the Mennonite General Conference passed a resolution that supported moves to "alleviate poverty and unemployment" but was clearly meant to warn Mennonites against government entanglements. The resolution applied the "unequal yoke" understanding to the New Deal programs.[6]

Given the economic difficulties during the early 1930s, one might have expected some effort to offer a Mennonite alternative, but the Mennonite General Conference took no action until 1935. That spring the Ohio district conference petitioned the General Conference to "furnish a means whereby our people would be able to lay away for the future, money to be properly invested by some of our able brethren and paid back by way of annuities, funeral expenses, etc. . . ." In June the Pacific Coast district conference asked the General Conference to consider creating a "Churchwide plan to care for needy widows and thereby eliminate the need of accepting State relief."[7]

In response the executive committee of the General Conference appointed a five-person Stewardship committee to

> make a study of Christian stewardship as it affects our financial obligations and practices, and bring plans, if advisable, for an organization that

would provide for necessary medical care, hospital bills, funeral expenses, etc., of the worthy poor of the Church, to the next General Conference.[8]

The secretary of the new Stewardship Committee was Christian (Chris or C. L.) Graber, the real force behind the committee. In the 1930s Graber was the pastor of Goshen College Mennonite church; business manager of Goshen College; owner of Goshen Electric, Inc.; part owner of E. Z. Gas, Inc.; secretary-treasurer of the Mennonite Educational Finance Corporation; and treasurer of the Peace Problems Committee. Graber possessed a genuine entrepreneurial drive, good humor, and extraordinary energy. Graber was without peer among Mennonite leaders as an astute money manager. In 1945 he became the first executive officer of Mennonite Mutual Aid.

Graber had seen the effects of the Depression firsthand in Wayland, Iowa. There, nearly single-handedly, he had nursed the Wayland State Bank back to health after it crashed in 1929. More than anyone else, he had managed to steer Goshen College out of near economic collapse during the difficult years 1930-35. In 1936 he turned his hand to the Stewardship Study Committee agenda. Unfortunately, his chairman was Jacob (J. C.) Frey, a deacon and retired farmer from Archbold, Ohio. Frey had little knowledge of money management and high regard for thrift. Like all Mennonite leaders in the 1930s, he was extremely cautious. As a result, the 1937 "Report" of the Stewardship Study Committee was a conservative and cautious document.[9]

The Mennonite General Conference met in Turner, Oregon, in 1937. It was a landmark conference in several respects. It was the first conference where the three men who would be the pivot of a new generation of Mennonite leaders first made their influence felt. One was Graber. Another was Harold Bender, present by virtue of his new chairmanship of the Peace Problems Committee and his dominant role on the Historical Committee. Third was Orie Miller, chairman of no committee but member of several. He was a gray eminence whose good judgment, business success, and devotional piety made him an emerging force in Mennonite circles, though at the time his legendary reputation had not yet been established. In 1937 Orie Miller and Harold Bender shared one serious handicap in their emerging roles as church leaders: they were not ordained. At Turner, Oregon, they were the only two lay delegates in a sea of bishops, ministers, and deacons.

The Turner General Conference was a landmark in another way. The conference received and acted on three historic documents. The General Problems Committee presented "A Statement Of The Position

Of The Mennonite Church on Unionism," a response to the new pro-union environment created by the New Deal and the growing numbers of Mennonite workers in industry. The General Conference accepted the paper on unionism. Of particular consequence for the future of mutual aid was the paper's proposal to create a committee that soon drew into its purview Goshen College professor Guy Hershberger. Soon Hershberger would be the creative Mennonite voice regarding industrial matters. He would develop strong convictions regarding the need for a Mennonite mutual aid organization.

The second document came from the Peace Problems Committee, now chaired by Harold Bender. Orie Miller was the committee's secretary, and in 1937 Chris Graber became its third member. The three crafted "A Statement Of Our Position On Peace, War and Military Service," the first official statement on the Mennonite position on war ever adopted by the Mennonite General Conference. When World War II began several years later, the (Old) Mennonites had a well-crafted statement they could use as they witnessed to government and drew up their response to the military draft.

The third document of historic note was the "Report" of the Stewardship Study Committee, which had five points. The committee began by telling ministers to teach against the "spirit of the age," defined as "getting rich by spending" and of "paying debts by borrowing." This behavior was contrary, the Report insisted, to the New Testament, which teaches "thrift, economy and saving." Mennonites should use savings banks and postal savings to lay money aside for their old age and for emergencies. The Report also warned against careless investment: Mennonites should only consider investments that were "conservative and sound." The advice matched what any Chamber of Commerce might have suggested. There was nothing specifically Mennonite about it.

The committee recommended against a churchwide automobile accident aid plan. Their advice was to continue to use district conferences as settings for such aid plans. They applauded the numerous property loss aid plans already in place at district conference levels and urged large districts to help small ones in the spirit of "bearing one another's burden."

To aid the poor and indigent, the committee recommended using the Mennonite Relief Committee, which in the 1930s was a largely moribund arm of the Mennonite Board of Missions and Charities. Its purview had always been overseas relief, and in a year it would open work in Spain behind the lines of the Spanish civil war. The committee recommended that the church establish for "all poor in the Church" an Emergency Relief Fund which the MRC would administer. The concept was a rather standard "poor relief" model rather than a more dynamic notion of mutual aid.

Finally, the committee acknowledged that

> life insurance is making inroads in our Church, and it is the feeling of many that some systematic help be given by our church to provide benefits such as people expect to receive from life insurance companies in times of sickness, death, and burial. The committee feels that an effort should be made to affect an organization in such a way as to give such aid to the brethren and sisters in the church who need it and want it.

The committee recommended that a churchwide organization be established as a buffer against worldly life insurance companies. "We believe," the committee told the General Conference delegates, "that such an organization could fulfill the injunction of the Scriptures to "Bear one another's burdens" and to be "our brother's keeper." The General Conference approved the recommendations and asked the committee to prepare a plan of operation for action by the 1939 General Conference.[10]

The 1939 General Conference was hosted by the Allensville Mennonite congregation in the Kishacoquillas Valley in central Pennsylvania. With nearly one of every ten (Old) Mennonites in the United States in attendance, it may well have been the largest gathering of (Old) Mennonites in their history to that time. It nearly capsized the logistical support system of the Mennonites in the Valley. But it also reflected a rising tide of interest and support for General Conference and highlighted how important a General Conference action on mutual aid would be to the success of any mutual aid plan.

It was to this historic gathering that the Stewardship Study committee brought their final best recommendation. They proposed the formation of two churchwide associations, one a "Fire and Storm Loss Association" and the other a "Death and Burial Aid Association." Each organization should be buttressed with a $25,000 reserve fund to meet minimal state insurance laws and be chartered to do business across the country. The organizations would be administered by the Mennonite Board of Missions and Charities.

The recommendation showed Chris Graber's hand at work, for it was much more audacious than his fellow committee members would have proposed. But it was also too aggressive for the General Conference delegates. They moved to "accept the recommendation . . . for further study."[11] The farmer ministers of the (Old) Mennonite Church in 1939 were not yet ready to support such a legally and financially complicated churchwide mutual aid organization.

# A New Concept

The 1939 report of the Stewardship Committee used the term "mutual aid" for the first time. The appearance of this term was surely a result of the work of a young GC Mennonite graduate student at the University of Chicago. In 1938 J. Winfield Fretz completed a masters thesis entitled "Christian Mutual Aid Societies Among the Mennonites," and by the fall of that year he had found an enthusiastic reader in Dean Harold S. Bender at Goshen College.[12]

Bender was also editor of the *Mennonite Quarterly Review (MQR)*, a scholarly journal that published material on Mennonite life and thought. He immediately arranged to publish two segments of the thesis in the *MQR*.[13] Thus by the time Chris Graber wrote the 1939 Report, he had read the Fretz articles and borrowed a new term to describe what he was trying to promote. He called it mutual aid.

The timely character of Fretz's thesis was not merely that it offered a new label to describe what the Stewardship Committee had been working on but that it also legitimized the idea. In an exhaustive survey, Fretz demonstrated the continuous and integral quality of mutual aid during every era of Mennonite history. To the persistent quartet of mutual aid boosters—Chris Graber, Harold Bender, Guy Hershberger, and Orie Miller—Fretz's work provided powerful support for the mutual aid idea. In making the argument to the cautious and conservative bishops, ministers, and deacons in the (Old) Mennonite Church, having history on their side was a great advantage.

Fretz's work offered one other argument to Graber and his colleagues: mutual aid was not like insurance, which, he pointed out, was based purely on selfish considerations to achieve security and autonomy. Fretz argued that mutual aid was a fundamental element in any vital Christian community, for its purpose was not self-aggrandizement but promotion of the physical, social, and spiritual well-being of everyone in the community. Through mutual aid each member could become a guarantor of every other member's well-being. For the first time, the poor relief and alternative life insurance proposals, begun at the 1935 General Conference, had a historical, sociological, and theological foundation on which a vision could be built. With his practical cast of mind, Chris Graber immediately began using the new material.

One other factor made the Fretz material attractive to Bender and Graber. Neither of them was a friend of the New Deal, and in his introduction to Fretz's material in the *MQR*, Bender commented,

> In these days when the desire for what is known as social security has
> become almost overwhelming and is leading to significant changes in

our American social order, it is most interesting and profitable to note how Mennonites have attempted to solve this problem on the basis of a Christian social philosophy.[14]

By the end of the 1930s Bender and Graber, pushed by the challenge of New Deal social security, had moved beyond a search for a workable poor relief system for "worthy Mennonite poor." Now they were aware of the need for a broad-based system of social security to cope with the vicissitudes of modern life. More people than just the poor needed a safety net.

While such an awareness grew out of the changes Bender and Graber observed in American society, it was buttressed by the new social analysis being done by their colleague at Goshen College, professor Guy Hershberger. In April 1939, Harold Bender's Peace Problems Committee sponsored a "Mennonite Conference on Applied Non-Resistance." Guy Hershberger read a paper on "Nonresistance and Industrial Conflict." He explained why labor unions had grown so powerful during the 1930s and why nonresistant Mennonites could not be members of unions. Underlying everything was Hershberger's concern that the new industrial economy was spoiling the rural Mennonite communities by drawing Mennonites into the new industrial orbit.

At the end of the essay, he invoked Thomas Jefferson's idea that farm life was essential to "healthy social living." Mennonites, he told the audience, should "remain in their small rural communities where their warm religious faith can have an opportunity to bind them together into closely knit, intimate community relationships." He described what he called "our ideal Mennonite community." It would have "a well organized system of mutual aid," he told his listeners.

> This community would have its own social security program, well organized and carefully financed. In case of sickness or death in any family this system [would] function so as not to leave any destitution. For only so can life insurance and the need for government social security be obviated in our Mennonite communities."[15]

To preserve this ideal community, he urged the creation of a

> carefully managed financial organization to help young people in getting a start in farming for themselves. Brethren with money to spare, instead of investing it in industrial stocks—where it is likely to be used in industrial conflict, should place it in custody of this organization which would use it to help those in need of help.[16]

Furthermore, incentives should be offered to young Mennonite teachers to teach in rural Mennonite community schools, and Mennonite community hospitals should be created. Staffed by Mennonite doctors and nurses, these institutions would offer their communities cooperative medical services.

Such Mennonite communities would be permeated with the non-resistant spirit of Christ, Hershberger observed. They would be oases of "happiness and contentment and a security so great as to prevent any appreciable drift of our population to the large urban centers of industrial conflict." It was quite a vision.[17] By 1939 Fretz and Hershberger had established both the rationale and the need for a broad-based Mennonite mutual aid organization. But the time was not yet ripe for its creation.

## A Dramatic Moment

At daybreak on Friday, September 1, 1939, Chris Graber was pulling weeds in the family garden before walking across the street to his office at Goshen College. Straightening to rest his back, he was suddenly aware of Harold Bender striding across the yard from the Bender home next door. By the look on Bender's face Graber knew something was wrong. "The Germans just invaded Poland," Bender told Graber. Bender had just heard the report on the radio.[18]

It was a moment of truth for the two men. Suddenly the press of work waiting for them at the college across the street—preparing for the arrival of the students in a few days, arranging for a groundbreaking ceremony for the new library, and preparing the orientation for the new personnel director (Ernest Miller)—seemed less urgent. For the next six years, helping fashion a Mennonite response to the war and military conscription would occupy much of their energy.

The coming of World War II also put in new perspective the General Conference rejection, just one week earlier, of their proposal for a churchwide mutual aid plan. In its report to the 1941 General Conference, the Stewardship Committee admitted that the war had generated prosperity, which "lessened the need for relief" because "our people [have] more dollars."[19] With the formation of the alternative to military service program (Civilian Public Service), it was also clear that the time, energy, and funding for a mutual aid program was not available.

Actually, there were several other factors deflecting the plan to create the two mutual aid associations that the Stewardship Committee had proposed in 1939. In early 1940 the Mission Board "declined," as Graber diplomatically put it, to become the administrative unit for the new associations. Further research had also made clear that such mutual aid associations would have to get state-based charters. This suggested that perhaps such mutual aid organizations should be based in the district conferences. Already Indiana-Michigan, Ohio, Pacific Coast, Ontario, and Missouri-Kansas district conferences had expressed interest in setting up some conference mutual aid systems. In light of those developments, the Stewardship Committee decided to let things coast and see what came of such initiatives.

If one effect of the war was to generate prosperity among Mennonites, another was to create a deep sense of vulnerability and stress. The war highlighted how interactive Mennonite communities had become with the United States culture and economy.

Military conscription heightened that awareness of vulnerability. It soon became apparent that a high percentage of Mennonite young men were electing to do military service, despite the relatively easy option of Civilian Public Service. The Draft Census study showed that ten percent chose noncombatant service and twenty-nine percent went into military service. Only sixty percent elected CPS. The study reinforced misgivings, especially among conservatives, that the assimilative forces of American culture were breaking down the boundaries of Mennonite belief and practice. The apparent weakness of Mennonite convictions regarding nonresistance seemed to offer confirmation that Mennonites were drifting into conformity with the national ethos. Something had to be done to stem the tide and remedy the situation.[20]

The discontent with trends in the Mennonite church took on combustible form in the General Problems Committee of the General Conference in 1943. Established in 1929, the Committee had become a main force in an attempt to forge a general consensus on nonconformity. The Committee had some heavy hitters such as bishops Daniel Kauffman of Scottdale, Pennsylvania; Oscar Burkholder of Ontario; Harry Diener of Kansas; D. A. Yoder of Indiana; and J. L. Stauffer of Virginia.

After a dozen years of biennial exhortations to greater nonconformity, the Committee came to the 1943 General Conference at Goshen with an action plan. Nonconformity and nonresistance should be made tests of membership. A member could violate the doctrine of nonconformity by

> holding life insurance, membership in labor unions, immodest and worldly attire (including hats for sisters), the wearing of jewelry (including wedding rings), and attendance at movies and theaters.

But the real dynamite was a resolution requiring that any district conference unable or unwilling to enforce the Resolution's conditions be dropped from General conference membership.[21]

Unable to deal with such a volatile resolution in the 1943 conference, a special General Conference session was held in 1944 to address the General Problems Committee report. At issue was whether General Conference had the authority to impose nonconformity on the church. A specific case was whether Illinois district conference should be allowed to continue membership in General Conference, given lax dress standards.

The special General Conference session of 1944 was clearly an attempt by the General Problems Committee to impose churchwide discipline. It nearly succeeded. The two-day session began on a blistering hot Tuesday evening in the administration building auditorium at Goshen College. A hundred and twenty-four delegates answered the roll call. Among them was Harold Bender, ordained only two months earlier, and thus able for the first time to be an official delegate to General Conference. Orie Miller and Guy Hershberger were the only "lay delegates" present.

All day Wednesday and Thursday, the delegates heard sermons on nonconformity, conference authority, and the power of the Holy Spirit. The climactic session came on Thursday evening, when the General Problems Committee Resolution was put forward for discussion. The meeting quickly lapsed into incoherent wrangling as the discussion focused on point five of the Problems Committee Resolution. It read, "Should any conference definitely decide that they will not work in harmony with General Conference in maintaining the standards of the same, they forfeit their place in General Conference."

Conservatives saw this as a way to place the burden of proof on the conferences, forcing conferences to take action on nonconformity issues. Progressives saw it as preemptive and lacking in pastoral and brotherly process. The meeting became tense as confusion over how to resolve the impasse overwhelmed the delegates.

It was one of those climactic moments that required a special gesture. Bishop Sanford Yoder rose to the occasion. Guy Hershberger remembered the event vividly forty years later.

> In response to questions and statements as to the reason for the current distrust, Sanford [Yoder] quietly rose to the full length of his 6 feet 3 and, in his soft-spoken voice, said words to this effect: "You ask the reason for our situation? I'll tell you the reason. It is because fellowship has broken down. There was a time when we experienced the finest of Christian fellowship [in a certain community which he mentioned by name] but for some time this has no longer been possible. Today the feeling experienced is one of ostracism. The fellowship is gone. This is the reason for distrust and tension in the church.

Hershberger remembered the effect of Yoder's words.

When the speaker sat down there was deathly silence. Had a pin been dropped one could have heard it—until a brother suggested a time for prayer. Then, after a long season of prayer the conference rose from its knees and discussion was resumed. . . ."[22]

It was a dramatic episode. The spontaneous prayer meeting lasted an hour and a half. Again Hershberger caught the significance of what had happened.

As the meeting drew to a close it was announced that the Friday morning session would be receiving a report from the Resolutions Committee, followed by action on the 1943 report of the General Problems committee. Following the benediction a brother said to me: "Whatever is done tomorrow will have little meaning. The purpose of the special session of General Conference was achieved this evening." The brother was right. The dramatic evening session had given birth to a new Mennonite General Conference. The old had died. The new was born in 1944.[23]

Hershberger was right. During the night the Resolutions Committee softened the preemptive point five, requiring the General Problems Committee to work with an errant conference to avoid forfeiting membership in General Conference. Conservatives, disappointed with the change, were somewhat mollified by the addition of a second resolution devoted specifically to a reaffirmation that "the Scriptures enunciate clear principles concerning simplicity."[24]

Both resolutions passed easily, but as so often in history, at the very moment of victory new forces for change had already taken over. Only J. B. Smith and S. F. Coffman of the original founding generation of General Conference were at the special 1944 session. Daniel Kauffman had died six months earlier in the first week of January. In a year, an ailing Aaron Loucks would die. Eighty-year-old D. D. Miller was gravely ill. George Brunk Sr., A. D. Wenger, and John H. Mosemann had all died in the late 1930s. The lifework of these men was embodied in the 1944 Resolutions, but their implementation would rest with a new generation. These men born at the turn of the century were now, in the middle of the century, managing the institutions and caring for the life of the church.

Less than two weeks after the special session, forty-seven-year-old Harold Bender became dean of the new Goshen College Biblical Seminary. Just six months earlier, fifty-year old Paul Erb had become editor of the *Gospel Herald*. His titular boss at Mennonite Publishing House was forty-one-year-old A. J. Metzler. The forty-four-year-old J. D. Graber had just begun two months earlier his decades-long tenure as the first full-time executive secretary of Mennonite Board of Missions. Ernest Miller, president of Goshen College, was fifty-one. His brother Orie Miller, executive secretary of MCC, was fifty-two. The President of Hesston College was forty-six-year-old Milo Kauffman. J. L. Stauffer was the "old" man among top Mennonite institutional leaders in 1944; he was fifty-six. For the next two decades these were the men who would shape the institutional life of the Mennonite church and preside over the changes set in motion by the second World War.

That Mennonite Mutual Aid, so long in gestation, should be born at this pivotal moment of leadership change was no accident. Both the war and the new generation of leaders made it happen.

# The Impact of Civilian Public Service

By 1943 Harold Bender's Peace Problem's Committee, Guy Hershberger's Committee on Industrial Relations, and Chris Graber's Stewardship Committee all began to worry about the welfare of Civilian Public Service conscientious objectors when they returned to civilian life. Since the men received no pay during their service, most would be indigent when they were discharged.

That awareness was heightened by national debate about how a grateful nation might reintegrate its returning servicemen into the civilian economy after the war. In June 1944 Congress passed the "GI Bill of Rights," which offered servicemen liberal educational and economic help, something Mennonite CPS men would not be eligible for. Could Mennonites do anything less for their men?

In preparation for a presentation to the 1943 General Conference, Bender, Hershberger, and Graber persuaded Milo Kauffman, General Conference moderator, to call a meeting that included members of the three committees and representatives from most of the district conferences. Out of the meeting came a consensus that the church must develop a churchwide aid plan designed, in the first instance, to help CPS men. In his report Harold Bender summed up their intentions.

> Some men will have been away from normal life . . . for five years. . . .
> Meanwhile the rest of us have had good incomes and normal home life.
> It will be not merely a matter of justice and fairness but of the obligation
> of genuine Christian love and brotherhood that we share the load . . . of
> the returning C.P.S. men. The United States government . . . plans to
> provide generously for the returning soldiers and is already preparing
> rehabilitation programs. . . . The Mennonite church needs to prepare . . .
> to render similar needed services to its returning C.P.S. men for whom
> no government aid will be available.[25]

Unfortunately, the 1943 General Conference was so preoccupied with CPS and nonconformity difficulties that mutual aid matters were deferred. The three committees were told to meet and prepare a plan to be presented to the next conference; the special session was scheduled for August of 1944. On October 16, 1943, P. L. Frey, Orie O. Miller, John R. Mumaw, Guy F. Hershberger, Harold S. Bender, and C. L. Graber met in Akron, Pennsylvania, to draw up a mutual aid plan. Orie Miller chaired the meeting. After a long afternoon of discussion, the group took action: "That the committee favors the creation of a new organization to be known as Mennonite Mutual Aid. . . ."[26]

They decided Mennonite Mutual Aid should be of "church wide service . . . be incorporated as a nonprofit, no-stock corporation," and be funded "through borrowing from brethren who desire to invest their money in the welfare of the Mennonite church." The governing board should be twelve "men," six to be elected by General Conference and six by the Board itself. Its first order of business should be to establish a fund to help discharged CPS men get a new start in civilian life.

After having their mutual aid proposals sidelined for further study four times over eight years by General Conference, a primary concern of the group was to design a presentation strategy that would assure the proposal's passage at the 1944 General Conference. By this time the Graber, Miller, Bender, and Hershberger quartet was becoming more adept at Mennonite church committee politics. With the election of Allen Erb as moderator of General Conference, the task became somewhat easier: Erb supported churchwide mutual aid. The group decided to try to persuade the Interboard Committee (which comprised all the chairs of General Conference standing committees) and the Executive Committee of General Conference to approve their plan before the August 1944 General Conference meeting.

At a December 1943 meeting, the Executive committee and the Interboard Committee approved the mutual aid plan "in principle." The Executive committee then appointed a mutual aid committee to prepare the presentation of the plan to General Conference. Allen Erb, Aaron Mast, Guy Hershberger, C. L. Graber, and Orie Miller became the committee. Moderator Erb was chair; Miller was secretary.

The committee quickly agreed on a two-pronged campaign to gain General Conference assent. In one prong, C. L. Graber would attend each of the district conferences during 1944 and present the Mennonite mutual aid plan. The hope was that by the August General Conference meeting many of the district conferences would have endorsed the mutual aid idea. At a second level, Hershberger would write a series of short pieces on mutual aid for the *Gospel Herald*, the (Old) Mennonite paper. From March through April, Hershberger prepared and published seven articles explaining the mutual aid plan. The intention was to build support for the idea among the rank and file in the church.

To Hershberger's chagrin, his articles generated several spirited articles in the *Gospel Herald* by minister John M. Snyder, who argued that true New Testament mutual aid would require that those who "have no need share their goods with those who have need, not expecting to receive again." Snyder was critical of the "insurance" dimension of the plan.[27] Hershberger complained that Snyder's idea of "need" was too narrow. Christians, Hershberger argued, "have a responsibility for taking good care of that which God has entrusted to them." Spreading losses so that all can be secure is the point of mutual aid, he explained.[28]

In June, Graber presented the plan to both the Virginia and Pacific Coast conferences. He was dismayed when both conferences failed to endorse the plan. "It looks to me perhaps I did not quite high-pressure them enough to get it through," he complained to Hershberger.[29] Do not worry about it, Hershberger told him. "Virginia . . . and Oregon . . . are afraid of everything new as being something worldly."[30]

Both men's spirits were buoyed when the Indiana-Michigan and Ohio conferences approved the plan before the General Conference. Unfortunately, two districts approving and two tabling the plan did not constitute the strong support they had hoped for.

The special session of General Conference endorsed the new mutual aid plan "in principle." The vote was seventy yes, twenty-one no. A Mutual Aid Committee was appointed, with the proviso that the program could not begin until ratified by six district conferences.[31] At the time, this condition did not seem a problem. During the fall Graber attended five more district conferences, where Illinois, Missouri-Kansas, and Iowa-Nebraska all ratified the plan. Unfortunately, Southwestern Pennsylvania and Dakota-Montana both denied approval. The committee had five districts but not the required six. The process stalled.

By February 1945 the Allied armies were converging on the German heartland. It was clear the war would soon come to an end. Worried about how to meet the needs of an expected flood of discharged CPS men in need of help, the new Mutual Aid Committee, now organized with Orie Miller as chairman and C. L. Graber as executive secretary, sought for a means to get the program underway. When a letter from Orie Miller to the four nonratifying district conferences asking them to act on the mutual aid program failed to get action, the Committee decided to take a different tack. In March, citing the extreme urgency to get Mutual Aid organized, Orie Miller persuaded moderator Allen Erb to call an organizing meeting to create Mennonite Mutual Aid. It was a gutsy decision, but, from the perspective of mutual aid supporters, it needed to be done. The extreme inertia of the General Conference committee system had nearly ruined the prospects of the new plan.

Thus on May 31, 1945, the new Mennonite Mutual Aid (MMA) organization was born. Twenty-seven persons gathered in Adelphian Hall at Goshen College for the historic event. Present were the Mutual Aid Committee, the General Conference executive committee, representatives of all nine district conferences, and representatives from the two eastern Pennsylvania conferences not members of General Conference. Bishop John E. Lapp represented Franconia; Bishop Amos Horst represented Lancaster. Orie Miller chaired; C. L. Graber was secretary.

The Mutual Aid Committee had drawn up Articles of Incorporation and a Constitution with bylaws, which it presented to the group. A three-hour discussion ensued. After lunch the Mutual Aid Committee met with the General Conference executive committee to allay any qualms the executive committee had about moving ahead and to write a resolution to take to the entire group for action. With that completed, the entire group convened at 3:00 p.m., and in two hours Mennonite Mutual Aid was born.

The new organization was authorized to "immediately arrange its offices" and raise $5,000 for operating expenses. Its first efforts were to be in "CPS rehabilitation." Then, as needs appeared, it would move to other aspects of mutual aid service. The meeting also authorized the new organization to "assemble $100,000" in capital to begin its program of help.

At 5:00 p.m. the Mutual Aid Committee met to complete its organizational tasks. Graber, functioning as secretary, was made administratively responsible for the new organization. Since Orie Miller was going on a long around-the-world trip for MCC, Guy Hershberger was appointed chairman of the MMA in his absence.[32]

A few weeks later, the new organization had a room in a house on South Eighth Street in Goshen, Indiana, and stationery with which to begin business. In July the state of Indiana granted the new organization a charter. By the end of October 1945 Graber reported receipts in loans and contributions of $8,750. He also reported spending $254.91 in startup costs, which included $160 for the first eight months of office rent.[33]

In September Guy Hershberger wrote three articles for the *Gospel Herald* announcing the formation of Mennonite Mutual Aid, Inc. Hershberger was at his best as he explained that mutual aid was a simple device by which Mennonites with means could connect with Mennonites who had needs. Mennonite Mutual Aid, he assured his readers, would help them find each other.

# Hesitations and Reservations

The organizational good sense of the new generation of leaders looked to some of their contemporary Mennonites like a worldly trend. In one of his first editorials after he became editor of *Gospel Herald* in 1944, Paul Erb offered a ringing endorsement of mutual aid then in the planning stages.

He was quickly chided, however, by minister Clarence Fretz. The new plan is not as claimed, Fretz told Erb, "a return to scriptural Mennonite principles." Not only was the plan based on "novel" ways of providing mutual aid, but it really had "no precedent in scripture." Fretz was sure the New Testament Christians had no system "whereby they paid in at a certain rate and were given any kind of assurance that they might receive a certain amount of help in the time of need."[34] Fretz was also sure they would not have agreed to a charity system that also assured them of protection for their property at the same time. To many Mennonites the insurance features of the aid plan seemed to have more to do with clever means of risk reduction than with New Testament mutual aid.

Bishop O. N. Johns of Ohio, present at the May 31 meeting that formed Mennonite Mutual Aid, Inc., reflected another concern shared by many of his fellow Mennonites. He did not like its churchwide character.[35] Rank and file Mennonites were suspicious of such bureaucratic organizations. Bishop Johns would have agreed wholeheartedly with Clarence Fretz when Fretz told Paul Erb that the "early Christians had [no] church wide organizations." Fretz found such organizations problematic because they short-circuited the role of ordained church leaders in managing the help for the needy. The reluctance of the ordained brethren, who managed (Old) Mennonite General Conference, to endorse the new bureaucratic and rational mutual aid system was a hesitation by leaders grounded in charisma (ordination by lot) to a system based on professional expertise.

One other factor made some conservative leaders reluctant to support the mutual aid plan. It had to do with the nonconformity politics of the early 1940s. Bishop John L. Stauffer of Virginia explained to Orie Miller why C. L. Graber was not able to persuade district conferences to support mutual aid. "If the General Conference will stand by its standards [of nonconformity] . . . then I think Mutual Aid will look better to the conferences, otherwise they will continue to be reluctant to become involved in another organization."[36]

Many eastern district conference leaders were deeply suspicious of the Bender-Hershberger-Graber-Miller quartet's leadership. Not only did they seem too compliant on nonconformity issues; they were also directing the Civilian Public Service program, which many conservatives considered a serious violation of nonconformity. Mutual aid was thus a hostage of those conflicts over nonconformity during World War II.

In the end, the 1945 formation of Mennonite Mutual Aid was a response to the needs of CPS men for whose welfare Mennonites of all persuasions had deep concern. The broad-based skepticism most Mennonites felt for large-scale organization gave way to that larger concern. But it was also the product of a small handful of new leaders who had mastered modern organizational techniques and believed deeply that the Mennonite community needed a new approach to the social welfare of its people. More than anything else, they saw Mennonite Mutual Aid as a new and better way to help preserve the fragile and changing Mennonite community they feared would soon disappear.

## Notes

1. C. L. Graber to Orie Miller, "Telegram," September 8, 1944, file 1, box 1 MMA, AMC. The following primary source materials used in this chapter are located in the Archives of the Mennonite Church (AMC) located in Goshen, IN: Records of the Committee on Industrial Relations; Records of Mennonite Mutual Aid; Records of the Peace Problems Committee; and the Papers of Guy Hershberger, C. L. Graber, Orie Miller, and Harold S. Bender.

2. Minutes, "Continuation Committee," September 9, 1944, file 1, box 1, MMA, AMC.

3. Letters, passim, 1944, file 1, box 1, MMA, AMC.

4. J. W. Fretz and H. S. Bender, "Mutual Aid," ME 3:796-801.

5. "General Church Problems (As seen through the eyes of our General Problems Committee): Insurance," *Gospel Herald* 23 (August 14, 1930): 434-435. See also "Report of the General Problems Committee: the Insurance Problem," Mennonite General Conference: Report of the Seventeenth Mennonite General Conference held near Archbold, Ohio, August 26-28, 1931:85.

6. *Ibid.*

7. Mennonite General Conference, Report of the Nineteenth Mennonite General Conference held near Kitchener, Ontario, August 27-29, 1935:8.

8. *Ibid.*

9. Report of the Twentieth Mennonite General Conference held at Turner, Oregon, August 25-27, 1937:37, 38.

10. Report of the Twentieth Mennonite General Conference held at Turner, Oregon, August 25-27, 1937:37, 38.

11. Report of the Twenty-First General Conference held at Allensville, Pennsylvania, August 23-25,1939:33-35.

12. Harold S. Bender to J. Winfield Fretz, October 1, 1939, file 1, box 7, Bender Papers, AMC.

13. Fretz (1939a:28-58) and Fretz (1939b:187-209).

14. Harold S. Bender, "Editorial," *Mennonite Quarterly Review* 13, 1 (1939): 4.

15. Hershberger (1939:153).

16. *Ibid.*

17. It was a vision that was being talked about, at least at Goshen, by Graber, Bender, and Hershberger. Bender told J. Winfield Fretz that "Hershberger's paper together with discussions which have centered around some points which he mentioned, plus a thought or two generated by some of your statements, has led me to think seriously about urging the establishment of a Mennonite rural community in terms of a mutual aid cooperative Christian society. I intend to work on this with our own folks within the next few months." Bender to Fretz, October 11, 1939, file 1 box 7, Bender Papers, AMC.

18. Gladys Graber Beyler and Millie Graber Stoltzfus, Oral Interview, January 2, 1994, Harrisonburg, Virginia.

19. Report of the Twenty-Second Mennonite General Conference held at Wellman, Iowa, August 26-29, 1941:9.

20. Paul Erb, Editorial, *Gospel Herald* (August 11, 1944): 371. See also Sanford Shetler, "The Mennonite Church Today," *Gospel Herald* (August 11, 1944): 369-370.

21. Report of the Twenty-Third Mennonite General Conference held at Goshen, Indiana, August 18-24, 1943:51-52.

22. Guy F. Hershberger, Introduction, in *Edward: Pilgrimage Of A Mind* (Wadsworth, Ohio, 1985), XIX.

23. *Ibid.*

24. Cf. Report on "The Meetings In Indiana," *Gospel Herald* (August 25, 1944): 409, 412, 420.

25. Report of the Twenty-Third Mennonite General Conference held at Goshen, Indiana, August 18-24, 1943: 42.

26. Minutes, Committee On Industrial Relations, October 16, 1943, CIR Collection, AMC.

27. Snyder (1944:477).

28. Guy F. Hershberger, "Mutual Aid For Sharing Of Losses In Case Of Calamity, Sickness or Death" (n.p., 1944), file 1, box l, MMA, AMC.

29. C. L. Graber to Guy F. Hershberger, July 21, 1944, file 1, box 1, MMA, AMC.

30. Guy F. Hershberger to C. L. Graber, July 7, 1944, file 1, box 1, MMA, AMC.

31. Report of the Special Session of the Mennonite General Conference held at Goshen College, Goshen, Indiana, August 15-18, 1944, 3.

32. Mutual Aid Committee Meeting, May 31, 1945, file 1, box 1, MMA, AMC.

33. Mennonite Mutual Aid, Inc., Treasurer's Report, October 24, 1945, file 1, box 1, MMA, AMC.

34. Clarence Fretz to Paul Erb, April 24, 1944, file 1, box 1, MMA, AMC.

35. O. N. Johns, Minutes, Ohio Mennonite and Eastern A.M. Conference, June, 1945, file l, box 1, MMA, AMC.

36. John L. Stauffer to Orie Miller, July 1, 1944, file 1, box 1, MMA, AMC.

# References

Burkholder, J. R., and Calvin Redekop, eds.
  1976   *Kingdom, Cross and Community.* Scottdale, Pa.: Herald Press.

Fretz, J. Winfield
  1938   "Christian Mutual Aid Societies among the Mennonites." M.A. thesis, University of Chicago.

1939a "Mutual Aid among the Mennonites, I." *Mennonite Quarterly Review* 13:28-58.

1939b "Mutual Aid among the Mennonites, II." *Mennonite Quarterly Review* 13:187-209.

1940 "Mennonites and Their Economic Problems." *Mennonite Quarterly Review* 14:195-213.

1942a "Mennonite Mutual Aid, A Contribution Toward The Establishment of a Christian Community." Ph.D. diss., University of Chicago.

1942b "Rural Life Problems And The Mennonites." *Mennonite Quarterly Review* 16:167-173.

1945a "Mutual Aid Strengthens the Local Congregation." *Gospel Herald* (October 5): 506.

1945b "Principles Of Mutual Aid In The Local Congregation." *Gospel Herald* (October 12): 532.

Hershberger, Guy F.
1939 "Nonresistance and Industrial Conflict." *Mennonite Quarterly Review* 13:135-154.

1940 "Maintaining the Mennonite Rural Community." *Mennonite Quarterly Review* 14: 214-223.

1942 *Christian Relationships to State and Community.* Scottdale, Pa.: Herald Press.

1944 *War, Peace and Nonresistance.* Scottdale, Pa.: Herald Press.

1944a "What is Meant By Mutual Aid?" *Gospel Herald* (March 16): 1075.

1944b "On What Problem Has the Stewardship Committee Been Working?" *Gospel Herald* (March 23): 1091.

1944c "What Are Some Changes Taking Place in Mennonite Community Life?" *Gospel Herald* (March 30): 1107.

1944d "What Is the Relation of Nonresistance To The Mennonite Community?" *Gospel Herald* (April 7): 4.

1944e "What Is the Proposed New Organization: Mennonite Mutual Aid?" *Gospel Herald* (April 14): 36.

1944f "How Is the Proposed Mennonite Mutual Aid Expected To Function?" *Gospel Herald* (April 21): 52.

1944g "What Are To Be the Policies Of The Proposed Mennonite Mutual Aid?" *Gospel Herald* (April 28): 68.

1945a "Mennonite Mutual Aid Is Now Organized." *Gospel Herald* (September 21): 474.

1945b "How Will Mennonite Mutual Aid Obtain Its Working Capital?" *Gospel Herald* (September 28): 492.

1945c "How Will Mutual Aid Assist the Person Who Needs Help?" *Gospel Herald* (October 5): 508.

1945d *Mennonite Quarterly Review 19:* Entire Issue.

1951 *The Mennonite Church In the Second World War.* Scottdale, Pa.: Herald Press.

Johns, Lois
1945 "Mutual Aid In Panorama." *Gospel Herald* (September 21): 474.

Snyder, John M.
1944 "Is Mutual Aid Scriptural?" *Gospel Herald* (September 15): 477.

Toews, Paul
1996 *Modernity and the Persistence Of Community.* Scottdale, Pa.: Herald Press.

10

# Fifty Year Partners: Mennonite Mutual Aid and the Church

### Steven M. Nolt

In this essay Steven M. Nolt traces the growth of five decades of partnership (1945-1995) between Mennonite Mutual Aid and the Mennonite Church. Nolt explores three topics that illustrate the evolving nature of the partnership: life insurance, the development of investment services, and the expansion of services to other Anabaptist-related denominations. He also explains how MMA came to enjoy the good fortune of being recognized as a fraternal organization in 1965—a legal status with certain tax exemptions that benefit the church.

## The Growth of a Partnership

American history brims with examples of mutual aid in action. Immigrant communities, ethnic enclaves, and religious bodies of all sorts have regularly banded together in organized—sometimes fully bureaucratized—efforts to assist one another.[1] Whether they faced life on the frontier or an equally formidable urban existence, groups of Americans joined in providing one another with economic advice, loans, and working capital. They also formed burial aid societies, mutual insurance associations, and fraternal benefit organizations in which financial, social, and religious concerns mixed freely. Some observers have even argued that the urge to create voluntary mutual aid federations is a defining characteristic of American life.[2]

Despite their well-known proclivity for separation from and nonconformity to the larger society, North American Mennonites proved no different than their neighbors when it came to forming mutual aid societies. In the later nineteenth and early twentieth centuries, Mennonites and Amish Mennonites of virtually all stripes organized dozens of fire and storm protection associations, burial aid societies, and property insurance plans.[3]

Aside from their specific constituency, these groups were hardly distinguishable in purpose, function, or organization from many similar non-Mennonite aid societies. Much as other aid agencies, Mennonite voluntary societies guided and encouraged benevolence, strengthened in-group identity, and supported ethnic and religious community cohesion.[4]

Mennonite Mutual Aid (MMA), organized in 1945 on a continent-wide denominational scale, soon became the largest and most diversified of the rationalized Mennonite efforts at mutual assistance. Founded toward the end of the American heyday of mutual aid societies,[5] MMA, nonetheless, exhibited all the traits of the wider movement. Like other Mennonite aid plans, MMA's fifty-year institutional story shares many similarities with those of other fraternal benefit groups based on ethnic, immigrant, or church-based identities. What makes such an organization distinctive, however, is its ongoing relationship with a particular community—in MMA's case, its Mennonite constituency. Examining that interactive partnership illustrates MMA's story and offers insights into the people who created and rely on the institution today.

Mennonite Mutual Aid grew from deep concerns and convictions in Mennonite communities. Drawing on historic traditions of mutuality and sharing, yet aware of social and economic shifts in a fast-changing world, MMA's organizers sought to develop means to offer organized, systematic financial help to fellow church members in unsettled postwar economic circumstances. MMA first offered farm and small business start-up loans to demobilized Mennonite conscientious objectors following World War II.[6] Later the agency offered insurance-style programs and financial services to a rapidly professionalizing people.

As Mennonite social and economic contexts evolved, Mennonite Mutual Aid responded. "In this changing situation," MMA's first board chair Orie O. Miller (1892-1977) wrote, "the church means (intends) to go along with its members and help them wherever in good conscience they need to go."[7]

Yet MMA's relationship with the church was not simply reactionary. Mennonite Mutual Aid also led the Anabaptist family of believers in thinking about issues of stewardship, ethical investment, and wholistic health and wellness. Throughout its fifty-year history, MMA has had an interactive partnership with the church. At times MMA has taken the lead, such as in sponsoring discussions on the Christian and litigation.[8] In other cases MMA has followed the church. When Mennonites moved toward full-time, salaried ministry in the 1950s and 1960s, MMA responded with church employee pension plans.[9] Occasionally, MMA and church groups came down on different sides of an issue, as in the 1994 debate on U. S. health care reform, which appeared to set voices in the church at odds.[10] Nevertheless, throughout MMA's history dialogue has been central.

Indeed, the interactive relationship between MMA and the Mennonite community is the most salient feature of its five-decade life. It is also one of the few constants in a history marked by expansion and change. Begun in 1945 with minimal staff in several rented rooms, MMA now manages an office with some 235 employees as well as 160 counselors across the country.[11] When the board of directors first met in the fall of 1945 they had $7,700; by 1994 the organization had an annual operational budget of $16 million and managed assets of 950 million.[12]

From a young institution carrying out limited activities on behalf of one Mennonite body, MMA has become a highly diversified operation serving a whole family of related denominations. Against this background of rapid development, the continued close relationship between Mennonite Mutual Aid and the church is all the more striking.

Three developments detailed below explore the relationship of the church and its most prominent mutual aid agency. Taken together, these incidents do not create a complete institutional history of Mennonite Mutual Aid.[13] They do, however, involve several key turning points and developments in MMA's fifty-year pilgrimage. Most important, they suggest the type of interactive relationship that has kept MMA vital and distinctive—a relationship to which both MMA and the church must continue to tend for their mutual well-being.

## From Burial Aid to Fraternal Life Plans

No issue better illustrates MMA's interactive partnership with the church than the controversies over life insurance. Life insurance was never a major part of MMA's panoply of services; arguably, other aspects of the institution's past are more central to understanding its everyday operations. Nevertheless, the decades-long discussion around survivors aid highlights the dialectical relationship between the institution and its constituency—especially during MMA's early years.

Historically among (Old) Mennonites, life insurance was taboo.[14] Church leaders opposed life policies for several reasons, often charging that such plans betrayed a lack of trust in God and the care of the church, or that policies would "unequally yoke" buyers with non-Christian commercial companies.[15] Less frequently, church pronouncements focused on the supposed bad business practices of insurance firms, the fact that companies excluded poor risk buyers, or that the concept of life insurance "made merchandise" of human life.[16] After the 1921 influential "Garden City Statement of Fundamentals," church leaders enshrined the prohibition as doctrine.[17]

Nevertheless, actual (Old) Mennonite practice was never as unified as its official pronouncements sounded. Repeated ecclesiastic denouncements also admitted that members were purchasing—and selling—such plans. From the late nineteenth century onward, peddling life insurance was a popular part-time job in America. Mennonites were not immune to the lure of extra cash such franchises promised.[18]

By the 1940s church members found themselves caught between a tradition of opposing life insurance and emerging economic realities that grounded a family's livelihood in an individual's ability to work, rather than in land or animals. In such a world, life insurance was no more or less commonsense protection than fire and storm plans had been in the past. As an institution created to serve the changing social and economic needs of the church, MMA could hardly avoid the smoldering issue of life insurance.

Indeed, MMA's original 1944 four-point authorization from the church hinted at the topic. One of the new agency's purposes was "Providing for aid in case of property loss, sickness, or death."[19] Exactly what that meant in practical terms was an open question, but MMA directors such as Guy F. Hershberger (1896-1989) wasted no time exploring the matter. In February 1947 Hershberger argued that MMA should move beyond its original small enterprise loan program and offer insurance-like plans for hospital-surgical and burial costs.

Board chair Orie Miller, along with MMA's founding manager Christian L. Graber (1895-1987), agreed that insurance-style offerings needed "the organization's major attention."[20] Sudden talk of insurance troubled MMA's assistant manager John M. Snyder (1907-1977), who resolutely opposed life insurance and feared the church taking any steps in that direction. Office tension increased, and Snyder ultimately resigned.[21] His departure symbolized the broader church's divided opinion. MMA needed to work closely with the church if it hoped to keep such tension from erupting openly.

Informally testing ecclesiastical opinion, MMA directors spoke with church leaders and lay members. Hoping "to assure itself still more fully as to the wish of the church," the board conducted a denomination-wide survey. A summer 1947 questionnaire went "to at least one minister (including all active bishops) in every congregation of each conference affiliated" with the Mennonite Church.[22] The survey queried attitudes toward MMA's organizing various property, sickness, and death benefit plans. Of 187 respondents, seventy-five percent (140) believed there was "a need for an organized program to provide aid in case of death," and fifty-three percent (100) thought MMA should waste no time establishing it.[23]

Survey results in hand, Guy F. Hershberger prepared a report for the 1947 biennial (Old) Mennonite gathering. He requested authorization to begin plans for "mutual help concerning losses in cases of calamity, sickness, and death."[24] Two days before the resolution was due for a vote, however, the proposal hit a snag. MMA board member and bishop Simon Gingerich (1882-1971) of Wayland, Iowa, began to have second thoughts. He feared the proposal looked too much like commercial life insurance.

Hershberger was worried. "I was sweating. So I said, 'You wouldn't be opposed to helping a widow or her family if her husband dies.'" The bishop acquiesced. "I'll go along with it if you put the word 'burial' in there," he told a relieved Hershberger.[25] A hastily rewritten text mentioned only "burial expenses," and the resolution passed, although church leaders halved the proposed $1,000 benefit.[26]

The question of how MMA was to fulfill its mandate to provide adequate aid "in case of death" was still far from settled, however. At MMA's request the same church gathering appointed a five-member committee "to make a comprehensive study of the Life Insurance question and its implications."[27] Granting the church "the responsibility to decide whether our recommendations are . . . [in] harmony with the Word,"[28] MMA waited six years for an answer.

In large part, the delay stemmed from deep differences in the church itself, as reflected in the committee's divided opinion.[29] Having outlined his views in book-length form years earlier, member Herbert N. Troyer (1889-1954), a Hartville, Ohio, minister and schoolteacher, was perhaps the church's most vocal opponent of life insurance (Troyer 1932). While Simon Gingerich shared Troyer's misgivings, other members—Goshen College dean Carl Kreider and Hesston College dean Ivan R. Lind—took the opposite view.

Especially Lind argued that changing economic circumstances all but necessitated life insurance for nonfarm families. In contrast to Troyer's calm assurances that survivors could look to the church for sustaining—though unsystematic—support, Lind was angry. "I have not seen the church step out to help our widows [adequately]. . . . Commonly, we see them let alone to struggle alone and hope they make it, and sometimes accuse them if they don't."[30]

Meanwhile Princeton-trained economist Kreider argued that much of the opposition to life insurance was based on outdated information gathered before tougher government control had put the business on sounder footing.[31] Moreover, he pointed out that, since the coming of workers compensation in the 1910s and social security in the 1930s, growing numbers of Mennonites were already covered by government-run insurance against untimely death. This was especially true of urban mission congregations.[32]

As the committee's work dragged on, Kreider left to teach in Japan, and Guy Hershberger took his place.[33] As he would often do in MMA's history, Hershberger managed to assemble a consensus and move forward. By 1953 a report was ready for church consideration.[34]

That statement suggested that simple term policies, which were neither greater than an individual's actual earning power nor connected to fantastic investment schemes, fit within the bounds of responsible Christian stewardship. In fact, such insurance—which was to be for "survivors," not the deceased's "life," constituted a "desirable form of insurance . . . which could be so administered [`by organizations in the brotherhood']." Simple term life insurance was not an ethical issue. What was problematic was for church members to buy such plans from commercial companies which acted unethically. If MMA would establish survivors' aid plans in a commonsense manner, the church could destroy the legitimate lure of term policies.[35] The report asked the church to give MMA such authorization.[36]

Following discussion, delegates to the Mennonite biennial conference approved the statement. They did not, however, approve several closing paragraphs, which appeared to strip the church of authority to discipline members holding nonchurch policies of almost any sort.[37] Some feared such a move would give backhanded endorsement to the many types of life insurance and investment they still considered beyond the pale. Retaining the committee for another two years, the church asked for a final report in 1955.

That proposal was a ringing endorsement of MMA. It called on congregations to acquaint members with the agency's plans and to urge participation "as the scriptural and brotherly means for the bearing of one another's burdens." Furthermore, where members believed MMA's coverage was not adequate, the wider church now asked them to call for MMA's expansion rather than buy commercial plans.[38] The church, giving MMA the nod to begin developing a full-fledged survivors' aid plan, affirmed the report.

During the next two years, MMA staff worked to develop a term life plan that would provide sufficient "rehabilitation" for survivors without compromising Mennonite commitments to stewardship and simple living. Guy Hershberger was again part of the drafting team, as was economist Kreider, MMA director H. Ralph Hernley, and the agency's new general manager, Harold L. Swartzendruber.[39]

Settling on a maximum $10,000 benefit and terms up to age sixty-five, the plan fell within Mennonite parameters of approval. Still, as manager Swartzendruber emphasized, the mutual aid agency wanted to work with the church at every step. In December 1957, retired MMA chief C. L. Graber took the outline to the General Council meeting and received final approval.[40]

## A Fraternal Organization

Along the way, however, MMA had run into a different sort of dilemma. Venturing into survivors' aid plans suddenly brought the board face-to-face with state law. Since 1950 MMA had been operating its hospital-surgical and burial aid plans under a nonprofit Pennsylvania charter. The state's law was quite flexible, which had given MMA room to experiment and grow, but increasingly the state was tightening the reigns.

Swartzendruber and others knew that their Pennsylvania charter would never support expansion into survivors' insurance. To launch the church-approved survivors' aid plan, MMA would have to form a full-scale, incorporated Indiana mutual insurance company.[41]

The process was time-consuming and complicated. One stipulation, for example, required 400 signed survivors' aid membership applications in a given time period. Although applicants could come from outside Indiana, all needed to sign in-state. Since the 1959 Mennonite biennial conference was set for Goshen, Indiana, MMA made a concerted effort to obtain sign-ups there yet feared appearing too pushy or hard-selling among a people still unaccustomed to church-related survivors' aid. It was a delicate balancing act.[42]

By September 1960 matters were in order. The following spring an MMA survivors' aid subsidiary, Mennonite Aid Insurance, Inc. (MAII), was running.[43] Apparently the life insurance question was solved. An extended conversation between MMA and the (Old) Mennonite church had resulted in a sensible survivors' aid plan under the auspices of MAII.

Nevertheless, a whole new chapter lay just around the corner. This time it was MMA, not the church, which called for reconsideration. Being a mutual insurance company, it turned out, was not quite what Swartzendruber, Hershberger, and others had anticipated. MMA soon discovered "that such a legal structure is basically incompatible with the general mutual aid approach."[44]

For its part, the state had ruled that MMA engaged in unfair and discriminatory business practices by extending extra aid to families or individuals whom church leaders identified as particularly needy. MMA had regularly reserved one percent of assessments in a catastrophic aid sharing fund from which they offered special help to hurting members. From the perspective of MMA staff, that sort of activity was what Mennonite Mutual Aid was all about.

Regulators in Indianapolis, however, saw things quite differently. As a mutual insurance company, MMA needed to treat each case with exacting similarity. This approach put MMA in a serious quandary. After years of waiting, the agency had finally received church approval for chartering a legally sound survivors' aid program—then its church efforts seemed to have short-circuited. Pursuing life insurance appeared to have been unwise after all. Could the church help work through this impasse? Ultimately, the Mennonite historic practice of mutual aid played an important role in the resolution.

After one of several frustrating meetings with insurance regulators in Indianapolis, MMA manager Swartzendruber received an unexpected phone call from the state's chief actuary. Speaking quickly, the official told Swartzendruber MMA would get nowhere if it insisted on actually practicing mutual aid—which the actuary was sure was what Mennonites wanted to do. "My father knew your people, and how they help each other," he said. He told Swartzendruber to explore provisions for establishing a fraternal benefit organization that could provide insurance *and* help to members as it wished. "The position of the Indiana insurance department is against forming any new fraternal, so I can't say much more to you in this call," he concluded, "but it would work beautifully for you."

Soon thereafter the MMA office received an unexpected visitor. Edward J. Peters, an established Indianapolis actuary, stopped in Goshen on his way to a vacation cabin in Michigan. The phone caller, it turned out, had told Peters about the Mennonites' situation and urged him to offer his legal and technical help. Peters had grown up in Maryland, where Mennonite neighbors had impressed him with their commitment to mutual aid. He asked if he could help keep the church's organized efforts alive. Suddenly the aid agency was itself the recipient of generosity. Swartzendruber recalled, "If I ever saw any miracles in my life, that was one of them."[45]

By 1965 MMA had reorganized as a fraternal benefit organization.[46] Allowed to sell and manage insurance policies much like a chartered insurance company, a fraternally arranged MMA association was also free to offer help to members in any way it saw fit. Since fraternals were exempt from most insurance industry taxes as long as they used their tax liability for charitable purposes, MMA could offer grants, gifts, and emergency aid to families and congregations hit by catastrophe or finance special church projects. A new Fraternal Benefits Fund distributed the money through a network of regional representatives and local contacts. The arrangement intensified MMA's church connections, since the agency now had to dispose of thousands of dollars a year through denominational channels for congregational needs.

Ironically, being a fraternal organization put MMA in the same legal category as lodges and so-called "secret societies," which Mennonites had long opposed as fiercely as they had life insurance. Indeed, the state now required MMA to declare itself a "lodge" with a central office, branches, and rituals.[47] While general manager Swartzendruber noted some church people raising "Objections . . . to the connotations of a 'lodge system' with 'rites' and 'rituals,' " he assured them that local congregations qualified as branches and that prayer sufficed as ritual.[48]

As MMA approached its twenty-fifth anniversary in 1970, its fraternal benefits operations were running smoothly. Nevertheless, staff wondered if the survivors' aid plan, which had unwittingly led them down a distinctive road, should be revisited. Although a decade had passed since MMA survivors' aid first became available, fewer than 1,000 persons had signed up for the plan—far less than the group's other plans for health and burial. As the aid agency considered whether "the program [should] be expanded, retained basically as at present, or even phased out," it acted in what was by now a predictable fashion: it consulted the church.[49]

Convening a September 1970 gathering of Mennonite pastors, teachers, lay people, and its own staff, MMA asked what to do with its survivors' aid program. Participants discussed merits and flaws of MMA's plans. In conclusion they urged MMA to promote survivors' aid in congregations, emphasize the need for women to obtain coverage, and communicate the unique features of a fraternal benefit organization. "We can't help in a barnraising if our people don't have a barn," one representative noted. "Maybe the needs are not as evident as when a barn is destroyed, but it may be just as real." The pastor of a small, low-income Chicago congregation explained that his members had few reliable resources when death took a wage earner; MMA survivors' aid program could connect his people with the support of the broader church.[50]

Accepting the group's advice, MMA moved toward promoting its survivors' aid programs. Brochures, such as *Why Survivors' Aid?*, acknowledged life insurance as a relatively new MMA endeavor but highlighted advantages of coverage through a Mennonite fraternal benefit organization. MMA's "Informant" newsletter, sent to congregational representatives and pastors, defined life insurance terms and explained MMA's offerings.[51] By 1979 a new brochure asked provocatively, *If You Die, Can They* [i.e., your children] *Count on Your Neighbors?*

More positively, four years earlier MMA had prepared an educational film strip on survivors' aid. "The Pleasant Valley Story" told the experience of the Harper, Kansas, Mennonite congregation that experienced some twenty deaths—several quite unexpected—in less than five years. The script recounted how Pleasant Valley formed a survivors' aid group that worked to plan wills and buy group survivors' aid coverage from MMA.

"In another age," the story explained, "when relatives lived in close proximity. . . . when land, livestock, and machinery represented financial security, life insurance was superfluous. But the answers that worked so well in the past do not work so well today."[52] That same year, MMA had also begun introducing the term "life plans" in place of survivors' aid.[53]

By 1980 MMA was still fine-tuning its approach to and philosophy of life plans, but the major questions had been resolved.[54] Shifting Mennonite attitudes and changing economic realities would likely have reshaped the church's attitude toward life insurance in any case. Yet MMA never forced the issue, but worked with the church to discern their mutual course of action.

At times MMA seemed the progressive partner; at others, the agency provided the voice of caution—such as questioning the ethical merits of its briefly held mutual insurance company charter. Furthermore, in the process of sorting through the "life insurance question," MMA developed the fraternal benefits arrangement, which ultimately became the agency's most remarkable feature and tied it ever closer to the church's congregational heartbeat. With what could have been a highly contentious issue, MMA and the church fashioned a dialogue that challenged both parties to faithfulness and highlighted fraternal bonds.

## From Deacons to Investment Advisers

Although mutual aid had historically been an unbureaucratized affair among Mennonites, it was not leaderless. Traditionally, an ordained deacon in each congregation managed the group's financial affairs, including handling and distributing alms funds as material needs arose. In many cases the deacon was an established farmer whose economic success had won wide respect and to whom church members could turn for monetary advice and opinion. Sweeping social and economic changes of the twentieth century disrupted this historic pattern and at the same time increased the need for new types of Christian financial counsel. MMA helped close the resulting gap and provided leadership for church stewardship efforts.

MMA's deaconing activity is another illustration of the church and its aid agency working together to address pressing needs in a changing environment. During the decade in which MMA was born, more than sixty percent of Mennonite congregations had active deacons. But not many years later, one historian noted that "the office . . . is in a transition period and the older patterns are changing somewhat."[55] As new congregations began with less sense of tradition and as Mennonites began to downplay the role of distinct leadership roles, deacons' ranks began to shrink.[56] By the mid-1950s deacons served fewer than half the church's congregations, and after 1965 the portion was always closer to a quarter.[57]

The office of deacon also withered due to Mennonites' changing financial situations. As increasing numbers of the church members entered business or professional job markets, they faced new economic issues, which the older, rurally oriented deacon system was often less equipped to handle. And as a land- and commodity-based pattern of life gave way to a salaried or cash investment economy, the church's traditional avenues of advice offered less concrete help.

In his conversations with Mennonite business people, for example, MMA's first general manger, C. L. Graber, noted that many were frustrated with charitable giving. If they converted investments into cash for the church, they needed to pay heavy capital gains taxes, reducing their contributions. They were sure there were ways around this problem, but who in the church could explain or find it? After investigating, Graber suggested that the church create a foundation to receive donations tax free, then manage investments and distribute the monies at donor direction. Receiving encouraging responses in the fall of 1952, Graber then took the proposed Mennonite Foundation (MF) to the MMA board, then to denominational leaders before moving toward incorporation at year's end.[58]

In less than a decade, MF had serviced twenty-four gift depositors and dispersed about $20,000 a year—mostly to Mennonite institutions. Such creative financial investigation, implementation, and service was only the beginning of MMA's new role as the church's professional diaconate. This role would keep MMA and the church in conversation for decades to come.

Larger donors, it turned out, were not the only ones who needed help and advice in the changing economy. Increasingly, as Mennonites thought about the future, they needed to plan to pass on more than a farm to their children. Estate planning involved special care, and most Mennonites were first-generation novices when it came to such efforts.

Appreciative of MMA's work with larger businesses through the Mennonite Foundation, the Mennonite Coordinating Committee asked MF in 1959 to expand its services to include general estate planning for all members.[59] Such work required much personal contact and local, one-on-one counseling. In 1960 MMA hired John H. Rudy, a pastor from near Gettysburg, Pennsylvania, as a half-time traveling consultant. A former chemical engineer and corporate manager, Rudy had strong interests in bringing faith and economics together.[60] In many cases his presentations were joint affairs with financial counselor Daniel Kauffman.

Rudy found an openness in congregation after congregation as church members welcomed him and asked for financial advice of all kinds. Clearly the need for stewardship education and mutual aid teaching was great. As MMA discussed these opportunities in the early 1960s, the agency was also undergoing a thorough self-evaluation and reorganization.[61] That process, culminating in 1965, allowed MMA to create new staff positions, including Rudy's full-time assignment as director of financial services. In addition to its administrative tasks, the new financial division also prepared educational materials, such as the pamphlet *The ABC's of Making a Will, How an IRA Can Help You Retire*, as well as the teaching kit *Money: For Better or Worse*, which MMA distributed to congregations.[62]

With churches asking for more help in defining and addressing economic issues, MMA expanded structurally, opening MF branch offices in 1968. The first was in Hesston, Kansas. Bringing estate planning and stewardship offerings to a local level, regional staff soon serviced other larger Mennonite communities. By the mid-1970s, MF grew to include services, such as offering personal financial guidance, arranging expert legal and tax counsel, and conducting special educational conferences and seminars on a range of topics.[63] Meanwhile MMA encouraged congregations to revive and transform the diaconate at the local level.

"They might be known as financial ministers or financial counselors," MF's John Rudy announced, but in any case the local church needed to spend more time examining economic issues.[64]

MMA's work sparked new church initiatives even as church urgings directed the aid agency's plans. Spurred by MMA's challenge to take economics seriously, the 1973 Mennonite Church General Assembly appointed a Work Group on Economic Issues.[65] The group's observations and recommendations called for more church attention to financial concerns and produced a six-point "Call to Faithful Stewardship." In 1985 the General Assembly incorporated the "Call" into its ten-year evangelism and stewardship goals.[66]

MMA in turn affirmed the larger church's effort and in 1980 co-sponsored a year-long "Special Project on Money and Economic Concerns" in eleven congregations to follow up the General Assembly's challenge. Headed by John Rudy and Daniel Kauffman (by now with Hesston College), the project asked churches how MMA could help them in breaking the silence on money and stewardship.[67] Although the church had originally "asked MMA to develop and promote mutual aid tools and plans to implement the strongly held mutual aid concepts," the staff discovered that "Today the opposite situation exists." Mennonites in 1980 had "a variety of mutual aid tools, but . . . have failed to maintain a strong mutual aid conceptual base in our value systems as a church."[68]

In response MMA named John Rudy Stewardship Minister in 1981 and Laban Peachey Mutual Aid Minister the following year, commissioning them to teaching, writing, and consciousness-raising.[69] Their service included initiating the first churchwide Mutual Aid Sunday in 1982 and publication of a significant congregational resource, *Christian Stewardship: Faith in Action.*[70] Under the heading "Money Matters," Rudy also prepared regular financial advice and thought pieces for *The Mennonite Weekly Review.*[71] Increasingly in the 1980s, MMA's financial counselors sought to place their economic concerns in a wholistic framework which included stewardship not only of material goods, but also of spirituality, health, and environmental resources.[72]

Despite its heavy commitment to education and advocacy, MMA's work in stewardship and financial counseling was not a one-way street. While the aid agency provided valuable help to church members, it also returned to the church for ethical advice. As MMA invested its own funds and those entrusted to it through the Mennonite Foundation, it sought to fashion ethical guidelines in harmony with church teaching and tradition.

Although the process underwent periodic refinement, the 1972 and 1979 guidelines statements were the most comprehensive to date. In those documents MMA pledged "to participate only in enterprises which appear to be in harmony with the nature and mission of the Church as generally understood by Mennonites."[73] Since the church traditionally eschewed the military, gambling, and tobacco and alcoholic products, MMA would avoid these firms as well. Additionally, MMA would seek investments that promoted social betterment or directly advanced religious work. Moreover, the board pledged to review the guidelines every five years and continue testing them with the church.[74]

In addition to drawing on general church counsel, MMA solicited direct church input when facing particularly difficult investment predicaments. One such case involved discussion of MMA's investment in companies doing business in apartheid-era South Africa.[75] As the western business community responded to calls to divest from South Africa to put pressure on the country's white minority government, MMA looked at its own investment scheme. In 1986 MMA began to review its economic commitments and established a task force composed of business people and ethicists from across the church. That group recommended withdrawing investments from all businesses operating in South Africa with the exception of food, medical, and educational publishing firms. Such a step would have involved divesting up to $7.5 million in MMA funds.

In 1987 the board asked the task force to solicit more counsel and offer several ethical alternatives. The study process drew on a variety of resources in the church community—not all of whom shared the same convictions. While some stressed divestment as the clearest expression of Christian justice, others suggested working for change as shareholders in companies. Questions of justice, however, could have become muddled when direct action such as divestment would have in turn lowered MMA's operating capital, driving up premiums and forcing some members to lose coverage.

Ultimately, the church counseled that "Justice issues in the community need to be addressed first, before there is credence in addressing justice issues outside the community."[76] The whole process resulted in MMA's divestment of its South African portfolios and also led to MMA's preparing a five-step model for dealing with future ethical investment quandaries. The process stressed discernment in the community— signaling MMA's continued interest in maintaining close ties of accountability with the church.

Questions about proper investment surfaced again in 1991 when MMA investigated the possibility of opening its own mutual funds. Fifteen months later, the MMA Praxis Funds were born.[77] The funds screen investment possibilities to eliminate firms which fail to meet ethical criteria, as well as to locate prospects that enhance their communities and treat employees fairly. Additionally, the funds offer investors the possibility of automatically tithing their earnings directly through the Mennonite Foundation. Praxis seeks to offer church members the opportunity "to join belief and deed in the area of investment."[78]

Some Mennonites enthusiastically supported the establishment of the Praxis funds. Others were more reserved. They believed the funds were too oriented toward producing wealth for the already well-heeled. MMA acknowledged the church's divided response but moved forward with Praxis nonetheless, believing the response was generally supportive.

At the end of the twentieth century, some observers believe social and economic acculturation pose a serious challenge to North American Mennonites. If so, Mennonites have few needs more pressing than thoughtful attention to economic ethics and stewardship of money as well as material and environmental resources.[79] MMA's dialogue with the church on these issues will likely be among its most critical in the years to come.

# From MC Mennonites to Other Anabaptist Churches

The ideas and ethos that produced Mennonite Mutual Aid fifty years ago grew out of broad inter-Mennonite discussions on economics, social change, and mutual care in the 1930s and 1940s. The mutual aid movement's leadership was not confined to a single group: General Conference (GC) Mennonites, such as J. Winfield Fretz and Howard D. Raid joined (Old) Mennonites Orie Miller and Guy Hershberger as well as Mennonite Brethren Peter C. Hiebert (1870-1963) and Martin A. Kroeker (1900-1973) in providing inspiration for one another's early efforts. Cooperative activities during World War II also fostered these intergroup discussions of help and community caring. Mutual aid was a topic which brought Mennonites together.[80]

Despite this broad background, MMA's initial mandate came from a specific Mennonite body: the (Old) Mennonite Church.[81] As an agency, MMA was to work with and serve a single group. Fifty years later its constituency is anything but narrow. The story of Mennonite Mutual Aid's widening arc of church relationships highlights another fifty-year dialogue between the institution and its parent body.

The Mennonites who formed MMA approached the second half of the twentieth century both outward-looking and somewhat defensive of their cultural borders. For some sixty years (Old) Mennonites had been aggressively involved with mission and service work in the larger society. Since 1920 they had cooperated with other Mennonite branches in the interchurch relief agency Mennonite Central Committee.[82] Yet (Old) Mennonites were also decidedly cautious about their direct institutional ties. Contact with outsiders had only heightened their sense of distinctiveness and occasional anxiety over being a separate, sectarian people. That other subgroups in the Mennonite family did not share identical convictions about matters such as plain dress only increased (Old) Mennonite suspicion of their spiritual kin. Often comfortable with inter-Mennonite efforts in distant settings overseas, they were more reticent to cooperate with other Mennonites closer to home.

Still, MMA directors and staff never lost their sense of mutual aid's expansive implications. In time they would nudge their founding body to expand its vision of mutuality to include an ever wider network of people.

Already during its first year of operation MMA's board bent its mandate to include the (Old) Mennonite's more conservative cousins— the Conservative Amish Mennonite Conference and the Old Order Amish—who expressed interest in supporting MMA's loan program.[83] These less acculturated folks were not as threatening to the (Old) Mennonite self-understanding, and the aid agency heard no calls to exclude their conservative kin. Moreover, these potential members provided a helpful financial boost to the young organization.

By 1950, however, with the inauguration of the hospital and burial plans, the board faced more difficult questions of inclusion and exclusion. Although only approved (Old) Mennonite church members were eligible for MMA's health and burial plans, what of nonmember spouses— especially those who were members of bodies such as the General Conference Mennonite Church? Could MMA decline them enrollment and benefits? Board members finally decided that such individuals could receive benefits as dependents, provided the full-fledged member paid a double membership fee.[84]

Despite such cautious rulings, MMA's leadership was interested in increasing communication among all Mennonites engaged in organized aid efforts. In 1954 MMA's Harold Swartzendruber responded to a request from the GC Mennonites' Board of Christian Service to attend a mutual aid get-acquainted meeting in Newton, Kansas. So successful was this session that participants formed a continuation committee and invited staff from other Mennonite aid plans to join them later.

Soon the group—now calling itself the Association of Mennonite Aid Societies—elected Swartzendruber chair and met annually to pool experience and explore the formation of the continent-wide reinsurance program, Mennonite Indemnity, Inc. Certainly MMA was not solely responsible for the creation of the Association or the reinsurance corporation, but it was a firm supporter and active participant of both efforts. MMA had long favored some type of reinsurance plan, and board chair Orie Miller was active in Mennonite Indemnity.[85]

These sorts of cooperative engagements only fueled MMA's desires to see organized mutual aid placed on a more interdenominational footing. Good relationships with Mennonites of diverse backgrounds allowed them to see their work in broader terms. Nevertheless, MMA's primary relationship was with its sponsoring (Old) Mennonite body, a group much less sure of cooperation's value, and MMA did not force the issue of expanding services.

In the end, though, concrete requests to broaden MMA's constituency came not from within the organization but from other aid groups. In 1955, as the (Old) Mennonite biennial gathering assembled in Hesston, Kansas, representatives of the 3,000-member Mennonite Hilfs-Plan of nearby Moundridge approached the MMA staff. The Hilfs-Plan covered property losses for church members of GC Mennonite, Mennonite Brethren, and related backgrounds. Their staff wanted to offer hospitalization benefits and asked whether Hilfs-Plan members could join MMA even though they were not (Old) Mennonites. Retired general manager Chris Graber diplomatically presented the request to the (Old) Mennonite General Council, which held a special noon caucus and issued a cautious "yes."[86]

By December, Hilfs-Plan participants were signing on to MMA's hospital-surgical rolls. MMA reported an "excellent working relationship" with Hilfs-Plan director Jacob A. Wedel (1899-1967).[87] Wedel was a longtime friend of MMA board member Albert Weaver. In the long run, friendships like theirs proved more important to the cause of cooperation than official contacts and pronouncements.[88]

Still, MMA relied on official words from its parent body. Committed to the (Old) Mennonite church, MMA asked for counsel before proceeding further. When other Mennonites complained that they too would like to enroll in MMA hospitalization and burial plans but without first joining the Hilfs-Plan, MMA chair Orie Miller asked the (Old) Mennonite Executive Committee for permission to provide MMA services to members of all Mennonite bodies who requested them. Though they lacked enthusiasm, (Old) Mennonite leaders were slowly coming to accept the idea of greater interaction with their spiritual cousins.

MMA received the go-ahead, but cautious elements in the denomination still insisted "that we retain the organizational structures and administration in our own brotherhood." Furthermore, they instructed Miller to see to it that MMA amend corporate constitutions to ensure all directors would continue to be (Old) Mennonites.[89]

Yet with the opening of MMA programs in the mid-1950s to a broader Mennonite family, the mutual aid agency would never be the same. Already by 1957 an amazing forty-three percent of its nearly 11,000 hospital-surgical plan enrollees were members of other Mennonite groups—primarily GC Mennonites and Mennonite Brethren.[90] That year general manager Harold Swartzendruber told the board that other Mennonite bodies would likely desire voting or observer status on MMA's board or subsidiary boards.[91] Control would have to be more flexible.

Beginning in 1959, Howard D. Raid represented GC Mennonites at MMA meetings; however, he did not vote. Several years later MMA underwent a major reorganization that consolidated its several corporate boards into a single body and provided for the co-opting of members.[92] In 1963, sensing a growing acceptance of inter-Mennonite work on the part of their church leadership, MMA's elected (Old) Mennonite directors co-opted two GC directors and a Mennonite Brethren representative as full voting members of the board.[93] By 1969 "increasing relationships with . . . other Mennonite groups" prompted MMA to propose amendments to its constitution to ensure voting representation of GC and MB constituencies on the seventeen-member board. The (Old) Mennonite delegate body meeting that year approved the change.[94]

Meanwhile the (Old) Mennonites were reorganizing themselves under the name *Mennonite Church* (MC). Part of the new scheme called for MMA itself to become one of five new "program boards" responsible to the new Mennonite Church General Assembly.[95] The reorganization heightened the relative importance of MMA in the new denominational structure as well as reaffirm the church's interest in its aid agency. While MMA welcomed the support and prominence, the new arrangement raised the question of how closely the organization should be tied to its parent group while attempting to serve a much broader constituency.

For Mennonite Mutual Aid, even a subject as mundane as office location could become a political matter. Another part of the MC restructuring scheme called for integrating facilities. Would MMA now join the other four program boards in searching for common office space, church officials asked?[96] The request was a serious consideration since MMA's rapid 1960s growth had put tremendous stress on its increasingly crowded building. Nevertheless, MMA was wary.

Knowing the symbolic importance of locations, manager Swartzendruber held back. Might the growing GC and Mennonite

Brethren constituency see the relocation as a sign of continued MC domination of the mutual aid program? "The way that our Mutual Aid services have been accepted on an inter-Mennonite basis, and the way in which these groups are working together . . . is vital and very important," the general manager wrote to the church restructuring committee. "For this reason, MMA is concerned about its image and facility sharing with any one [Mennonite] group even though it respects and desires its relationship as presently structured."[97] Thus MMA went ahead with its own building project on Goshen's North Main Street. Apart from other MC program boards, the location symbolized the distinction its interchurch constituency necessitated.

Throughout the 1970s and 1980s, MMA tended its church relationships with care. Accountable to the MC General assembly, MMA took its parent body's counsel seriously and reported regularly. In addition, MMA increased communication with its expanding constituency. Office staff and field representatives increasingly came from a variety of Mennonite backgrounds. In 1977, GC Mennonite William E. Dunn became board chair. Activities stemming from Fraternal Benefits programs spanned the diversity and helped congregations across the entire latter-day Anabaptist spectrum.

Indeed by the early 1990s MMA increasingly used the term *Anabaptist* instead of *Mennonite* when describing its participant base. That base currently includes some twenty-six groups—from the Evangelical Mennonite Church and the Apostolic Christian Church to the Amish and Old Order River Brethren.[98] In fact, defining MMA's constituency in broad terms has become a stated goal. According to president Howard L. Brenneman, "Our vision is that every eligible Anabaptist will be touched by an MMA program or service by the year 2000."[99] Nevertheless, the MC retains majority control of MMA, and the denomination's members remain the agency's most loyal constituent block.[100]

Given that the early impetus behind MMA came from broad inter-Mennonite discussions on community, stewardship, and mutual help during the 1930s and 1940s, MMA's half-century journey toward greater inclusiveness has, in one sense, brought its dialogue full circle.[101] By 1995 MMA was arguably one of the largest and most broadly inter-Mennonite organizations in existence.[102] For MMA the challenge now is to balance an increasingly diverse body of participants and maintain the type of accountability and communication each segment expects. The Mennonite Church has grounded MMA in a particular tradition of responsibility while freeing its institutional servant to meet needs beyond its own bounds, even when this involves giving up some control.[103]

# Into the Future

Each of the themes discussed in this chapter is part of MMA's current and future growth frontiers. In 1995 the MMA board began considering new efforts to increase the aid agency's life insurance membership. Again survivors' aid intersects with MMA's fraternal benefits status, since the urge to expand life insurance grows in part from a desire to bolster membership and increase fraternal benefits funds, which currently distribute more than $2.5 million annually.[104] Meanwhile, the activities of the Mennonite Foundation continue to expand, as does MMA's entire constituency.

In recent years, for example, MMA officials have been working closely with the Missionary Church—a denomination with historic ties to the Anabaptist family—and have found that denomination increasingly receptive to the aid institution's activities. Additionally, MMA responded to requests from Quaker bodies and recently approved the Religious Society of Friends as an eligible fraternal constituency.[105]

Critics both outside and in the organization regularly point out MMA shortcomings, missed opportunities, and unfulfilled ideals. Nevertheless, a fifty-year partnership between an aid agency and a specific constituency is a remarkable achievement in the world of North American voluntary societies—church or otherwise. For both MMA and the church, the challenge of the next fifty years will be to maintain their historically close relationship.

## Notes

1. The literature is enormous. Representative titles include Baird (1982), Clawson (1989), Henderson (1990), Hernandez (1983), Kauffman (1992), Shreve and Vecoli (1981), and Weisser (1985).

2. Such observers included de Tocqueville and James Bryce. Academic histories of the United States have long cited voluntary associations as a hallmark of American life. See, e.g., Beard and Beard (1929).

3. See Fretz (1941 and 1957).

4. In a June 2, 1995 address, J. Winfield Fretz noted that in the early twentieth century, Mennonite groups with which he was associated did not think of their mutual aid activities as unique to their faith communities. His observation bears the point that Mennonite efforts along these lines were quite similar to those of their non-Mennonite neighbors.

5. With the end of mass immigration (1925) and the coming of the modern welfare state (1935), the founding of new mutual aid societies in America dropped off. Nonetheless, such societies continued to remain important for more recently arriving immigrants (e.g., Hernandez [1983]). One could argue that the (Old) Mennonites who organized MMA were in fact recent *social* immigrants of sorts, as they moved into what was for them a profoundly different postwar social and economic world. On this point see also Shreve and Vecoli (1981). More

recently, with the return of mass immigration (since 1965), there has been a revival in the founding of immigrant mutual aid societies and organizations in the United States. Thus, in a broader sense, the movement's midcentury decline was more of a lull than a demise.

6. Burkholder (1981) offers a brief review of this phase of the program. Early MMA board minutes are comprehensive; XII-9 MMA Board of Directors collection (hereafter Board minutes), located in the Archives of the Mennonite Church, (AMC) Goshen, Ind.

7. Third of three points in a Miller-prepared summary of the April 10, 1943, meeting of the Committee on Industrial Relations, Chicago, Ill., I-3-7 (Committee on Economic and Social Relations), AMC.

8. From 1959 to 1965 MMA sponsored a study on litigation and Christian ethics that included a major 1961 consultation. Referred to Mennonite General Conference in 1965, the matter languished. In 1975 MMA general manager Harold L. Swartzendruber reminded Mennonite Church general secretary Ivan J. Kauffmann that MMA was still interested in having the church examine the issue. The Mennonite Church responded with a task force which eventually proposed "The Use of the Law: A Summary Statement," approved by the 1981 Mennonite Church General Assembly. See Consultation on Litigation Problems, a 57-page booklet of papers from 1961 meeting, in-house historical files, Mennonite Mutual Aid office, Goshen, Ind. (Hereafter HF); Paul N. Kraybill to litigation task force members, October 14, 1976, HF; *Use of the Law* (1982); and Swartley (1982), which was published with MMA financial support.

9. "Christian Principles to Guide the Church in the Remuneration of Church Workers," *Mennonite General Conference Proceedings, 1961*, pp. 92-95, summarizes a two-year discussion on the trend toward salaried ministry. The same report booklet (pp. 41-42) included MMA's proposed "Retirement Plan for Mennonite Church Workers," which the church then adopted and MMA incorporated in 1963 as Mennonite Retirement Trust. Also Board minutes, August 4, 1960. The church had approached MMA as early as 1954. See M. M. Troyer to Orie O. Miller and Christian L. Graber, December 31, 1954, "Ministerial Study," Mennonite Mutual Aid Correspondence Files (hereafter CF), presently housed at two locations: Mennonite Mutual Aid offices, Goshen, Ind., and Archives of the Mennonite Church, Goshen, Ind.

10. *Gospel Herald* 87 (May 24, 1994): 9.

11. MMA headquarters through the years have always been in Goshen, Ind.: several rooms at 1413 South Eighth Street (1945-1954); 1202 South Eighth Street (1954-1958); 111 Marilyn Avenue (1958-1971); and 1110 North Main Street (since 1971, with additions in 1979 and 1985).

12. Board minutes, October 24, 1945. The 1945 dollar figure represents total donated assets minus travel expenses to date. Total income donated to begin MMA was $8,750. Of this amount, Orie and Elta Miller had given $6,000, or more than two-thirds. Without the Millers' generosity, it is doubtful MMA could have started operations that fall. The 1997 figures were provided by Dean Preheim-Bartel in a telephone conversation on December 30, 1997.

13. No complete institutional history exists; however, a lengthy "Historical Sketch of the Development of Mennonite Mutual Aid and Its Subsidiaries," apparently prepared by Harold L. Swartzendruber around 1961 or 1962, includes helpful information on the agency's early years. See also in-house historical files HF and CF.

14. Convictions on the topic were considerably more diverse if one defines Mennonitism more broadly. Despite their 1897 resolution opposing members purchasing life insurance, the Mennonite Brethren prohibition fell away quietly by the mid-twentieth century. See Janzen and Giesbrecht (1978:80-81). For their part, General Conference Mennonites never opposed life insurance in any systematic or regular way. By 1939 the Defenseless Mennonite Church (now Evangelical Mennonite Church) had even spawned its own church-related life insurance company—see Ringenberg (1992:21-22). The Old Order Mennonites and Old Order Amish, however, joined (Old) Mennonites in opposing life insurance.

15. See, for example, Daniel D. Miller, "Life Insurance," in Kauffman (1914:575-87); Bender (1916); Diener (1928); Kauffman (1928:532-44); and Troyer (1932).

16. See the compilation, "Life Insurance Resolutions," in V-7-33, Mennonite Research Foundation, Project 10, Archives of the Mennonite Church, Goshen, Ind. Melvin Gingerich amassed resolutions on life insurance from the mid-nineteenth century through the 1940s for each (Old) Mennonite and Amish Mennonite district conference. Other than the arguments based on nonconformity/ unequal yoke reasoning, the Mennonite rationale for rejecting life insurance was clearly *not* unique. Many religious groups opposed life insurance for the same reasons Mennonites did (although in most cases their opposition did not stretch much beyond the 1930s)—see Albree (1870). Zelizer (1979) offers an excellent intellectual history of life insurance and its opposition in the United States with selected European comparisons.

17. The prohibition was part of article thirteen. See Report (1921).

18. Interview with Carl Kreider, June 28, 1995. Kreider's father was not opposed to life insurance, although he neither purchased nor sold policies out of respect for church teaching. Nevertheless, Kreider knew persons who did both. Indeed, church leaders were as concerned with the trend toward members selling life insurance as they were with members buying plans. By 1960 MMA staff members were surprised to discover that even in "conservative congregations, a large share of the young married folks have life insurance." Board minutes, June 30, 1960.

19. "Mennonite General Conference Report of the Special Session . . . 1944," pp. [2-3]. The actual text of the four points appears on p. 54 of *Mennonite General Conference Report, 1947*.

20. Board minutes February 14, 1947; Orie O. Miller to A. J. Metzler, April 8, 1947, 1947 Board book. Also Graber (1982:56).

21. Board minutes, December 31, 1947. Interview with Guy F. Hershberger, 1986, transcript, p. 6, HF.

22. Although the wording is vague, it implies that surveys were not sent to ministers in the Lancaster or Franconia conferences, which operated as independent Mennonite bodies at the time.

23. *Proceedings of Mennonite General Conference, 1947*, pp. 55-56.

24. Interview with Guy F. Hershberger, 1986, transcript, p. 6, HF. Board minutes from April 18, 1947, and July 11, 1947, record very lengthy discussions of life insurance and the similarities of MMA's proposed death benefit plan. The board was clearly aware that they were drawing up a plan which would amount to *de facto* life insurance coverage, but they were not agreed on their support for it. Likely Simon Gingerich, cited by Hershberger, below, (note 25) was not the only member with reservations.

25. Interview with Guy F. Hershberger, 1986, transcript, p. 6, HF.

26. See Graber (1982:56-57), who felt the approved figure was too low but was at least glad to have the measure passed. Contrary to Graber, however, the amount was $500. The board increased the burial benefit to $750 only in 1956. See Board minutes, March 26, 1956.

27. Proceedings of Mennonite General Conference, 1947, p. 56. The special 1946 session of General Conference held at Souderton, Pa., had discussed life insurance at the request of the Problems Committee, which noted with alarm the increasing number of commercial policies in church members' hands, but the body produced no new statement. See Mennonite General Conference Program and Proceedings, 1946, p. [1].

28. Board minutes, April 18, 1947, minute 16.

29. Committee work was also delayed on occasion because chair John L. Horst's ill health and extensive responsibilities as a Mennonite Publishing House editor drained his energy to organize meetings and manage correspondence (passim, XII-6, Box 1, MMA Insurance Study Committee of General Conference, 1947-1955, (ISC) AMC. His actual opinion on the subject under consideration is difficult to decipher.

30. Ivan R. Lind, "Statement on Life Insurance," ISC.

31. Carl Kreider, "Reactions to Questions Submitted to the General Conference Life Insurance Study Committee," ISC. Carl Kreider to Ivan R. Lind, January 11, 1950, ISC. Kreider told Lind he would refuse to sign a report that included what he believed to be Troyer's inaccuracies and ill-informed half-truths.

32. In 1908 Congress instituted Workers Compensation for federal employees. States began passing similar comprehensive and mandatory laws after 1911. Social Security insurance for widows, orphans, and the aged began in 1935. It was not mandatory for the self-employed or employees in some sectors until the 1950s, but many Mennonites actually signed on before they were forced to. Interview with Carl Kreider, June 28, 1995. Opposition to Social Security lingered in Virginia, however. See J. Ward Shank to John L. Horst, October 3, 1953, ISC.

33. Hershberger's appointment is interesting, given his having worn many institutional hats at the time. A Goshen College history professor, he was also an MMA board member and chair of the church's Economic and Social Relations Committee (ESRC). As a Life Insurance Committee (renamed Insurance and Investment Committee after 1951) member, he was to represent wider church concerns via his ESRC work.

34. The committee had submitted an interim "analytical" report in 1951, which discussed and defined terms and reviewed Mennonite history but proposed no specific action. See *Mennonite General Conference Report, 1951*, pp. 67-75.

35. Lancaster County, Pa., attorney Samuel S. Wenger made the same point when he told MMA that "increasingly . . . our Mennonite folks even here in conservative Lancaster County are taking out life insurance `under cover,' and that it would be wise for the Church to get its own institution ready for action at the earliest possible time." Samuel S. Wenger to Harold L. Swartzendruber, December 12, 1958, HF. The idea that church-sponsored agencies could and should offer services similar to their secular counterparts was at the core of Mennonite redefinition of nonconformity during the period. See Nolt (1995).

36. *Mennonite General Conference Report*, 1953, pp. 71-81. Term life insurance was discussed, among other places, in ISC minutes February 23, 1952, ISC.

37. John L. Horst to Ivan R. Lind, Herbert N. Troyer, Guy F. Hershberger,

and Simon Gingerich, September 23, 1953, discusses the objections to the report's concluding sections. Apparently, Hershberger had also suggested deleting the prohibition against life insurance from the 1921 Garden City Statement. See mimeographed substitute wording in ISC, and Simon Gingerich to Guy F. Hershberger, August 24, 1953, in which Gingerich protests Hershberger's move.

38. "Report of the Investment and Insurance Study Committee," July 2, 1955, ISC. Also Guy F. Hershberger to John L. Horst, July 2, 1955, ISC. MMA had received another important endorsement from Wenger (1951:234-44), which strongly implied that Mennonites should eventually expect reasonable insurance plan from MMA.

39. "Report of the Widows and Survivors Rehabilitation Sub-Committee to Mennonite Mutual Aid Board, August 23, 1957," HF.

40. Harold L. Swartzendruber to Board of Directors, November 20, 1957, and attached report of Graber to Mennonite General Council, 1958 Board book. Franconia Conference—not a full member of General Council—was not part of the approval process. On Franconia's 1960 approval of MMA survivors' aid, see John E. Lapp to Harold L. Swartzendruber, October 11, 1960, CF.

41. Interview with Harold L. Swartzendruber, June 30, 1995.

42. *Ibid.* See also Board minutes in 1959.

43. The charter was broad enough to include the hospital-surgical and burial plans, since MMA hoped to consolidate its organization.

44. Reports Submitted to Mennonite General Conference, 1965, p. 92. AMC.

45. Interview with Harold L. Swartzendruber, June 30, 1995. Another important figure who provided MMA with extensive expert advice of organizing as a fraternal benefit agency was Edward J. Mulleins, Skokie, Illinois, Allstate Insurance actuary, whose favorable impressions of Mennonites from his childhood in Pennsylvania made him eager to assist.

46. Although the new arrangement ultimately absorbed MMA's health plans, too, the restructuring was completed under the auspices of the Survivors' Aid Development Committee. Mennonite Mutual Aid continued as the overarching corporate entity under its original 1945 nonprofit charter. The fraternal benefit subsidiary was Mennonite Mutual Aid Association (MMAA), which after 1965 included all the health and survivors' insurance programs. See "Merger of MMAA and Mennonite Aid Insurance, Inc." file, CF. Interview with Abe P. Hallman, June 28, 1995. See also Harold L. Swartzendruber, "The Development and Legal Implications of a Mennonite Fraternal Beneficiary Association," HF; "Problems Relating to Legal Status: Mennonite Aid, Inc., and Mennonite Aid Insurance, Inc.," HF; and the report of the first MMAA meeting, *Mennonite Weekly Review,* November 17, 1966:1-2.

47. Interview with Harold L. Swartzendruber, June 30, 1995. On (Old) Mennonite opposition to lodge membership, see Kauffman (1928:522-31). Lodges had always functioned, in a practical sense, primarily as a means of providing insurance (especially life insurance) to working-class families. See *Fraternal* (1938), Kauffman (1992), and Clawson (1989). MMA status as a fraternal organization remains a curious irony. Already in the 1960s, MMA officials received helpful advice as members of the National Fraternal Congress. Still, the legal definition provides some strange bedfellows. Schmidt (1980) gives a recent listing and description of all chartered fraternals in the United States that includes MMA—alongside the Ancient Free and Accepted Masons, United Order of Druids, Rosicrucian Order, Pythian Sisters, and the Ku Klux Klan. The family of fraternals

also includes dozens of ethnic, religious, and social bodies such as the Lithuanian Alliance of America, B'nai B'rith International, Benevolent and Protective Order of Elks, and the Loyal Moose Lodge.

48. Meeting of the Survivors' Aid Development Committee, January 26, 1963, p. 2., CF. Board minutes, April 25-26, 1963, minute 12 on lodge "terminology."

49. "Abstract of Background Items Concerning the Development of a Widows and Survivors Benefit Program Under Mennonite Church Structure," CF; Minutes, Consultation Concerning Widows and Survivors Benefit Program, item 1, CF.

50. Minutes, Consultation Concerning Widows and Survivors Benefit Program, September 28, 1970, items 10, 20, and others, CF. See also Eugene Headings, "Why Survivors' Aid," October 9, 1970, CF.

51. "Informant," 2 (February 1972): 1-2.

52. "The Pleasant Valley Story," 104-frame filmstrip, tape, script, and study guide, 1975. MMA media center materials. Script by Joel Kauffmann; narrator, Russel Kraybill.

53. Mennonite Mutual Aid Association, Life Agreements materials, March 1, 1975, HF.

54. Ron Litwiller to Mary Kerbs and Jean Smeltzer, May 14, 1980, regarding "Life Position Paper" (attached), CF.

55. Neff and Bender (1956). This was Harold S. Bender's addition to Christian Neff's originally-authored essay.

56. Another element playing into the demise of the congregational deacon during the period was the proliferation of home mission boards' planted and supported congregations. These congregations relied on financial backing from area conferences and were not self-supporting; indeed, in many cases home mission boards did not trust these young church plants with independent budgets. Local deacons were simply not needed since these churches had few funds to manage or distribute on their own. Over time, most of these congregations grew to independence, but they did so without the tradition of a local deacon.

57. Figures from historical tables in the *Mennonite Yearbook, 1995.* In 1994 there were only 248 deacons in 1,100 congregations. Moreover, their population was aging with few replacements recorded. Fifty-seven percent of these were age sixty or older; only six new persons were ordained to the office.

58. The Mennonite Foundation's first chair was a progressive-minded Iowa business man, Edwin E. Swartzendruber (1890-1976); he was also the father of MMA manager Harold L. Swartzendruber.

59. "Historical Sketch of the Development of Mennonite Mutual Aid and Its Subsidiaries," HF, p. 9.

60. Interview with John H. Rudy, August 11, 1995. See also Bowers (1990).

61. See "Mennonite Mutual Aid Reorganization" file, CF.

62. "The ABC's of Making a Will," n.d., but sometime after 1971, considering the given MMA office address. "Money: For Better or Worse" appeared in 1974.

63. "The Mennonite Foundation, Inc.," four-page text dated September 1976 and December 1977, HF. Also "Goals and Objectives Adopted by MMA Executive Committee," March 18, 1977, HF.

64. John H. Rudy, *"We Still Need Deacons,"* column in Mennonite Weekly Review, April 1983. Also Guy F. Hershberger, "The Congregation and Its Need for a Diaconate in a Changing Era," HF; "Wholeness of the Church's Ministry To-

day," November 1975, HF; Sears (1976); MMA *Memo,* September 12, 1980; John H. Rudy, "Financial Ministers in Mennonite Congregations," March 1982, HF.

65. Proceedings: Mennonite Church General Assembly, 1973, pp. 22 and 41.; *Proceedings: Mennonite Church General Assembly, 1975*, pp. 22-26. AMC.

66. Interview with John H. Rudy, August 11, 1995. The text of the "Call" appeared in a Mennonite Church General Board brochure, "To All Members of the Mennonite Church: A Call to Faithful Stewardship."

67. Kauffman (1981). Also "Prospectus: An Invitation to Participate in a Congregational and Conference Plan to Develop Some Models Which Will Help Congregations to Enter into Serious Dialogue About Money Matters and to Challenge Members to Greater Christian Faithfulness," HF. Daniel Kauffman (1990) later produced a work that summarized much of his teaching efforts in the area of stewardship.

68. John Rudy and Dwight Stoltzfus memo, June 24, 1981, HF.

69. Laban Peachey to Dwight Stoltzfus, November 15, 1984, HF; and "Progress Report: Stewardship Ministry," Board minutes, November 18, 1983.

70. "MMA Dateline," HF; Rudy (1984).

71. A number of these columns, along with others Rudy had prepared for the Mennonite Economic Development Associates publication, *The Market Place,* appear in Rudy (1989).

72. Such as Raber (1983) and Raber (1993). Also noted in Bowers (1990:13).

73. "Investment Guidelines: Ethical Criteria for Mennonite Mutual Aid Investment Programs," approved April 7, 1972: revised November 16, 1979, HF.

74. See Sommer (1994:257).

75. This story is told completely in Sommer (1994).

76. *Ibid.*, p. 274.

77. "Funds" is plural since Praxis includes two funds: one intermediate income and one growth fund. See press release in *Gospel Herald* 86 (May 25, 1993): 10.

78. "Two Christian Mutual Funds Enter the Field," *The Elkhart Truth* (January 30, 1994), section H, pp. 1-2.

79. See Comments of Reimer (1995). Relatively little has appeared on Mennonites and economics, but see the recent work of Redekop, et al. (1994), Redekop, et al. (1995), and Redekop and Redekop (1996).

80. Historically, of course, many of the older, local Mennonite fire and storm plans had included members of various branches of the Mennonite family. This background provided some inter-Mennonite precedent for midcentury mutual aid discussions. Of many examples, see Gross and Wedel (1983).

81. An interview with Guy F. Hershberger, 1986, transcript, p. 4, notes that in 1944 during discussion about a proposed MMA structure, there was "some considerable concern [in Virginia] that this should be for (Old) Mennonite Church only and not for other Mennonites."

82. Even this contact, however, was often less than enthusiastic. See *Mennonite General Conference Report, 1947*, pp. 31-33.

83. Board minutes February 15, 1946. The Lancaster Mennonite Conference also expressed interest in participating in MMA programs at this time, and the Board accepted their request. Although historically linked to the larger (Old) Mennonite church, the Lancaster Conference maintained organizational independence until 1971.

84. Board minutes, July 7, 1950.

85. Raid (1982); Swartzendruber (n.d.:16-17); Hernley (1970): v-vii; interview

with Harold L. Swartzendruber, June 30, 1995. The MMA board was on record as desiring a reinsurance corporation like Mennonite Indemnity as early as 1947, as reflected in Board minutes of July 11, 1947.

86. Board minutes, September 27, 1955.

87. Board minutes, September 12, 1956.

88. Interview with Harold L. Swartzendruber, June 30, 1995.

89. Paul Erb to Orie O. Miller, May 9, 1956, Board minute book, 1954-1956. Also Board minutes, September 12, 1956, where Harold L. Swartzendruber reported that the General Conference Mennonite Church triennial gathering in Winnipeg, Man., had recommended that its members join MMA plans. "[T]he problem," Swartzendruber reported, will be "with our own ['Old' Mennonite] General Conference in obtaining approval to offering our service to other Mennonites. . . ."

90. *Reports Submitted to Mennonite General Conference, 25-27 August 1957*, p. 45. According to the report, 6,274 enrollees were (Old) Mennonites; 4,713 were not.

91. Board minutes, September 12, 1955.

92. Interview with Abe P. Hallman, June 28, 1995. Hallman saw the reorganization as one of the most important events in MMA's history—not only because it streamlined the structure, but also because it altered the form and manner of representation.

93. "Listing of Board Members by Tenure," HF. The GC members were Harvey W. Taves (1926-1965) of Kitchener, Ont., and Leando M. "Al" Jungas (1903-1971) of Mountain Lake, Minn.; the MB member was Martin A. Kroeker (1900-1973) of Hillsboro, Kans. On MMA reorganization, including the integrations of all corporate boards into one seventeen-member board, see the summaries *in* Mennonite General Conference Proceedings, 1963, pp. 68-69; and *Reports Submitted to Mennonite General Conference*, 1965, pp. 89-90. Also, in 1965 the General Conference Mennonite Church Board of Business Administration established a regular working relationship with MMA's Mennonite Foundation and encouraged GC Mennonites to use MF services (brochure, "Services of Mennonite Foundation for Members of the General Conference Mennonite Church"). The Brethren in Christ, however, formed their own church trust department, the Jacob Engle Foundation.

94. Harold L. Swartzendruber to Paul M. Mininger, April 9, 1969, HF; Harold L. Swartzendruber to Paul M. Mininger, May 8, 1969, HF. *Reports Submitted to Mennonite General Conference*, 1969, p. 67.

95. "Report of Joint Conference on Church Organization, October 20-22, 1970, Yellow Creek Mennonite Church, Goshen, Ind.," HF.

96. Paul N. Kraybill to Harold L. Swartzendruber, January 1, 1971, HF.

97. Harold L. Swartzendruber to Paul N. Kraybill, January 14, 1971, HF.

98. "Today's MMA Membership," 1995, promotional materials from Fraternal Benefits office files.

99. Brenneman (1995:5).

100. V[yron] L. S[chmidt], "MMA Fraternal Denominations, March 31, 1995," Fraternal Benefits office files.

101. In one respect, MMA's circle has tightened rather than expanded over the years. After about 1950, several Canadians—notably businessman Milton R. Good, then of Waterloo, Ont.—served on the MMA board or subsidiary boards. Today, however, MMA functions solely in the U.S.

102. Mennonite Central Committee is often considered the holder of these

"titles," but in terms of participants, budget, and supporting constituent groups, MMA is clearly also a leader in inter-Mennonite cooperation.

103. Certainly the integration of the Mennonite Church and the General Conference Mennonite Church, approved in July 1995, will expand MMA's lines of direct organizational accountability.

104. "MMA Considers Expanded Life Insurance Program," *Gospel Herald, 88* (May 16, 1995); "Mennonite Mutual Aid Association 1994 Annual Report to Members."

105. Dean Preheim-Bartel to Steven Nolt, July 19, 1995.

## References

Albree, George
    1870    *The Evils of Life Insurance.* Pittsburgh: Boucle and Mashers.

Baird, John A., Jr.
    1982    *Horn of Plenty: The Story of the Presbyterian Ministers' Fund.* Wheaton, Ill.: Tyndale House Publishers.

Beard, Charles and Mary Beard
    1929    *The Rise of American Civilization.* New York: Macmillan.

Bender, Daniel H.
    1916    "Life Insurance." *Gospel Herald* 9 (September 28): 474-75. Reprinted in *Gospel Herald* 14 (March 30, 1922): 1010.

Bowers, Steve
    1990    "John Rudy: The Life of a Steward, or Getting the Honey is Worth the Sting." *Sharing* 24 (Winter): 10-13.

Bowman, Carl F., and Stephen L. Longenecker, eds.
    1995    *Anabaptist Currents: History in Conversation with the Present.* Camden, Maine.: Penobscot Press.

Brenneman, Howard L.
    1995    "A Solid Foundation for the Future." *Sharing* 29 (Summer): 3-6.

Burkholder, Rebecca
    1981    "Loans that Made a Difference." *Gospel Herald* 74 (October 27): 804-805.

Clawson, Mary Ann
    1989    *Constructing Brotherhood: Class, Gender, and Fraternalism.* Princeton, N.J.: Princeton University Press.

Diener, Harry A.
    1928    "Life Insurance." *Gospel Herald* 21 (November 8): 674-75.

*Fraternal Life Insurance*
    1938    Indianapolis: The Insurance Research and Review Service.

Fretz, J[oseph] Winfield
    1941    "Mennonite Mutual Aid, A Contribution to the Development of Christian Community." Ph.D. dissertation, University of Chicago.

    1957    "Mutual Aid." *The Mennonite Encyclopedia,* vol. 3. Scottdale, Pa.: Herald Press.

Graber, Christian L.
[1982] *Looking Back: An Autobiography by Chris L. Graber.* [Goshen, Ind.: L. Swartzendruber].

Gross, David P., and Eunice K. Wedel
1983 *One Hundred Years of Caring and Sharing: A History of the Mennonite Aid Plan of the U.S., 1882-1982.* North Newton, Kans.: Mennonite Press.

Henderson, Alexa Benson
1990 *Atlanta Life Insurance Company: Guardian of Black Economic Dignity.* Tuscaloosa, Ala.: University of Alabama Press.

Hernandez, José Amaro, ed.
1983 *Mutual Aid for Survival: The Case of the Mexican American.* Malabar, Fla.: Robert E. Krieger Publishers.

Hernley, H. Ralph, ed.
1970 *The Compassionate Community.* Scottdale, Pa.: Association of Mennonite Aid Societies.

Hershberger, Guy
1958 *The Way of the Cross in Human Relations.* Scottdale, Pa.: Herald Press.

Janzen, A. E., and Herbert Giesbrecht, comps.
1978 *We Recommend . . . Recommendations and Resolutions of the General Conference of the Mennonite Brethren Churches.* Fresno, Cal.: Board of Christian Literature, General Conference of Mennonite Brethren Churches.

Kauffman, Christopher J.
1992 *Faith and Fraternalism: The History of the Knights of Columbus,* rev. ed. New York: Simon and Schuster.

Kauffman, Daniel (1865-1944), ed.
1914 *Bible Doctrine.* Scottdale, Pa.: Mennonite Publishing House.

1928 *Doctrines of the Bible: A Brief Discussion of the Teachings of God's Word.* Scottdale, Pa.: Mennonite Publishing House.

Kauffman, Daniel (1922- )
1981 *Money and Economic Issues in Mennonite Congregations: A Report on a One-Year Special Project on Money.* Goshen, Ind.: Mennonite Mutual Aid.

1990 *Managers With God: Continuing the Work Christ Began.* Scottdale, Pa.: Herald Press.

*Mennonite Yearbook*
1995 Scottdale, Pa.: Mennonite Publishing House.

Neff, Christian and Harold S. Bender
1956 "Deacon." *The Mennonite Encyclopedia,* vol. 2. Scottdale, Pa.: Herald Press.

Nolt, Steven M.
    1995    "Reinterpreting Nonconformity: Mennonite and Brethren Thought and Practice." In *Anabaptist Currents: History in Conversation with the Present*, ed. Carl F. Bowman and Stephen L. Longenecker. Camden, Maine.: Penobscot Press. Pp. 183-97.

Raber, Ann
    1983    *Mennonite Mutual Aid Wellness Program: Toward More Abundant Living*. Goshen, Ind.: Mennonite Mutual Aid.

    1993    *A Life of Wholeness: Reflections on Abundant Living*, rev. ed. Scottdale, Pa.: Herald Press.

Raid, Howard D.
    [1982]    *Twenty-Five Years: A Brief History. Mennonite Indemnity, Inc.* Akron, Pa.: Mennonite Indemnity, Inc.

Redekop, Calvin W., Victor A. Krahn, and Samuel J. Steiner, eds.
    1994    *Anabaptist/Mennonite Faith and Economics*. Lanham, Md.: University Press of America.

Redekop, Calvin W., Stephen C. Ainley, and Robert Siemens
    1995    *Mennonite Entrepreneurs*. Baltimore: The Johns Hopkins University Press.

Redekop, Calvin W., and Benjamin Redekop
    1996    *Entrepreneurs in the Faith Community*. Scottdale, Pa.: Herald Press.

Reimer, Richard
    1995    "The Future of Mutual Aid and Stewardship." *Sharing 29* (Summer): 11.

"Report of the Committee on Fundamentals"
    1921    *Gospel Herald 14* (November 10): 627.

Ringenberg, William C.
    [1992]    *The Business of Mutual Aid: Seventy-Five Years of the Brotherhood Mutual Insurance Company*. Fort Wayne, Ind.: Brotherhood Mutual Insurance Company.

Rudy, John H.
    1984    *Christian Stewardship: Faith in Action Stewardship Kit*. Goshen, Ind.: Mennonite Mutual Aid.

    1989    *Moneywise Meditations: To be Found Faithful in God's Audit*. Scottdale, Pa.: Herald Press.

Schmidt, Alvin J., ed.
    1980    *Fraternal Organizations*. Westport, Conn.: Greenwood Press.

Sears, Earl
    1976    "Deaconing Today." *Gospel Herald 69* (November 16): 894-95.

Shreve, Susan H., and Rudolph J. Vecoli, eds.
    1981    *Records of Ethnic Fraternal Benefit Associations in the United States: Essays and Inventories*. St. Paul, Minn.: Immigration Research Center, University of Minnesota.

Sommer, Willis
  1994    "Mennonite Institutions and Mennonite Capital." In *Anabaptist/ Mennonite Faith and Economics*, ed. Calvin W. Redekop, Victor A. Krahn, and Samuel J. Steiner. Lanham, Md.: University Press of America. Pp. 255-78.

Swartley, Willard M., ed.
  1982    *The Bible and Law*. Elkhart, Ind.: Institute of Mennonite Studies.

Troyer, Herbert N.
  1932    *Life Insurance*. Scottdale, Pa.: Mennonite Publishing House.

Use of the Law: A Summary Statement, *The*
  1982    Scottdale, Pa.: Mennonite Publishing House.

Wenger, John C.
  1951    *Separated Unto God: A Plea for Christian Simplicity of Life and for a Scriptural Nonconformity to the World*. Scottdale, Pa.: Herald Press.

Weisser, Michael R.
  1985    A *Brotherhood of Memory: Jewish American "Landsmanshaftn" in the New World*. New York: Basic Books.

Zelizer, Vivian A. Rotman
  1979    *Morals and Markets: The Development of Life Insurance in the United States*. New York: Columbia University Press.

# Part Five

# Contemporary Issues and Practice

# 11

# Mutual Aid and the "New Voluntarism"

### Conrad L. Kanagy

Charting the shifting patterns of support for mutual aid, Conrad Kanagy argues that attitudinal changes in the broader society have affected Mennonite attitudes toward mutual care. Emphasis on voluntary choice has replaced some traditional reasons for participating in religious organizations. Kanagy suggests five ways the new voluntarism has changed Mennonite patterns of mutual aid. He concludes by summarizing changing Mennonite attitudes toward mutual aid as reported in the Church Member Profiles of 1972 and 1989.

## The Web of Community

In 1988 Delbert Wiens addressed a gathering of Mennonites in Laurelville, Pennsylvania, who were deeply concerned about cooperation, community, and mutual aid. For much of his discussion, Wiens was pessimistic about the ability of Mennonites to remain meaningfully connected to one another. He bemoaned the loss of the "godly concrete community" where geography and traditional cultural boundaries defined insiders and outsiders. This community had been, he recalled, a web where "everyone [was] connected" and "every life affect[ed] every other" (Wiens 1988:3). The norms or rules of the web were well-defined.

> Choices were simple—the community's way or the world's way. The religious or moral community was the primary community of interaction

247

(Wilson 1982). The secular aspects of life—such as work and everyday activities—in this setting take place in the bounds of the sacred canopy. There members of the community "live by the power of God, under God's care . . . and . . . reach out and help to create other such communities" (Wiens 1988:4).[1] Ministers—authorities both in and outside the church—were able "to affect the social and economic conditions that might diminish the goodness of the whole." (Wiens 1988:4)

The type of community described by Wiens is sometimes termed a *vil* by sociologists. This is a communal organization that is characterized by a traditional family structure, extensive cooperation, and a local setting or place (Hillery 1992). Without any one of these three traits, a vil disappears.

Since World War II, demographic trends in the larger American society—greater mobility, rising education, and expanding occupational opportunities—have eroded the extended Mennonite family structure and the importance of place.[2] Such trends threaten to destroy our motivation to mutually help one another. Wiens' community web—where mutual aid and cooperation were based on common needs and local responsibilities—has been replaced by the World Wide Web. There, choices are based on individual preferences and diverse opportunities.

The implications for Mennonites are that cooperation and mutual aid may be dependent on a kind of "new voluntarism." This concept is used by sociologists to interpret contemporary religiousness among Americans for whom religious participation and involvement have become voluntary (Roof and McKinney 1987).[3] Whereas in the past traditional community expectations motivated persons to attend church, many now do so for individual reasons. Whereas membership in a particular congregation or denomination was once largely determined by community, family, and cultural factors, membership today is typically based on individual tastes and preferences.

Likewise, I argue in this chapter that individuals engage in acts of mutual aid today because they *choose to* rather than out of duty to community norms and expectations. Wiens (1988:1) relates a story about MMA that reflects this new voluntarism.

> The Mennonite college where I teach . . . just voted to drop MMA health insurance for an HMO-like medical plan. I tried to tell my colleagues not to trust the figures, and I stuck with MMA; but the initial saving just looked too good. . . . Most of them cannot even imagine that a church community would look after them if they cannot work.

This chapter examines some of the transformations in Mennonite attitudes toward mutual aid in recent decades. I frame the discussion around sociological observations about the effects of a new voluntarism on American religious attitudes and behaviors. Since early advocates connected Mennonite mutual aid directly to *religious* motivations, it is likely that a new voluntarism—*if* it has affected Mennonite religious attitudes— has influenced attitudes about mutual aid.

In other words, I argue that the new voluntarism of American religion has affected Mennonite religiosity, including attitudes and values about mutual aid. To trace changes in the attitudes of Mennonites toward mutual aid, I will rely on three sources of data: a collection of lectures presented to gatherings of the Association of Mennonite Aid Societies from 1960-1970, findings of Mennonite scholars writing in the 1970s and 1980s, and survey data of Mennonites from 1972 and 1989 (Kauffman and Harder 1975; Kauffman and Driedger 1991).

## A "New Voluntarism"

How has the new voluntarism affected Mennonite aid?[4] First, *the social base of aid has changed.* Such characteristics as rural residence, low levels of education, agricultural occupation, and marital status may no longer reliably predict attitudes about cooperation and mutual aid.

Second, *the family plays a less important role in the transmission of mutual aid attitudes.* While still the primary agent of socialization, the family is forced to compete with other social agents. These include the educational system, peers with different values, community and after-school activities, and the mass media. Children are inundated with cultural messages that broaden their awareness of consumer choices and encourage them to satisfy their heightened wants. In this noisy cultural context, any message about the importance of mutual aid is likely to be reduced in volume or heard only amidst substantial static.

Third, with the deterioration of traditional Mennonite norms of one's responsibility to the community, *individual differences in beliefs about mutual aid are more important than in the past.* The church no longer has the authority it did. Like the family, it must compete with an increasing number of social organizations and agents. Expectations of church leaders are no longer sufficient to propel persons into activities aimed at collective well-being. Instead, individuals participate if *they* feel the activity is worthy of *their* time and resources. Thus, many local mutual aid efforts that depended on support of the entire congregation are replaced by activities sponsored by many denominational or other nonprofit organizations. Some of these are religious, some are not; some are Mennonite, some not. Even in the local church, the member is pulled in multiple directions.

Fourth, *mutual aid attitudes may be shaped along ideological rather than communal lines.* Individuals may choose to contribute to a need because they agree with the theological position or purpose of an organization or project, not because the church expects their involvement. Mennonite denominations are less likely to cultivate the same degree of commitment to denominational programs as they once did. Being a Mennonite program, activity, or agency is no longer enough. Mennonites may not give less than in the past, but the community of believers will have less influence on the direction of the giving.

Fifth, *differences about the meaning of mutual aid among Mennonites are intensifying*. Because the church has less authority and is competing with so many organizations and agents, individuals are freer to express their differences and less likely to conform. Even though overall support for Mennonite mutual aid may be increasing, its meaning is becoming broader. As a result, it is more difficult to arrive at a consensus about what mutual aid is and how it should be manifested in the local church and the denomination.

## What is Mutual Aid?

Early definitions of mutual aid by Mennonites emphasized its religious roots. Mutual aid was an "expression of Christian stewardship and mutuality."[5] Conducted under the "Lordship of Christ," mutual aid was to benefit the entire body of Mennonite believers and to promote "mutual accountability and responsibility in the body of Christ."[6] The Mennonite understanding of mutual aid is grounded in Old Testament concerns about the well-being of others and the command to "love your neighbor as yourself," a command reiterated by Christ and manifested in the daily life of the apostolic church (Fretz 1957).

J. Winfield Fretz, often noted for his architectural role in the development of Mennonite mutual aid, invoked four religious motivations in his 1958 lectures at the meeting of the Association of Mennonite Aid Societies. First, according to Fretz, *mutual aid is a universal principle of God's moral law* (Fretz 1958). Mutual aid is an ideal of all the world's major religions and a principle that humankind is given the capacity to carry out. Cooperation rather than competition is central to God's created order. Although even primitive cultures exhibit cooperation, Fretz argued for a "correlation between the growth of civilization and the growth of mutual aid" (Fretz 1958:7).

Second, Fretz contended that *mutual aid is an essential truth of the Christian religion*. In Jesus' teachings, the family is a model of "religious communism" characterized by " 'each according to his ability and each according to his need.' " (Fretz 1958:10). The "patriarchal father" is kind but firm. The mother cooks and sews. Hand-me-downs, daily duties, and emotional sentiments are all shared, for it is only a "poor family where either the father or the mother does everything for all the rest of the family members" (Fretz 1958:15). Religious communism was also the rule of the early church, partly because of the "family character [that] developed among them." The Scriptures, according to Fretz, are the foundation for "our later Mennonite Aid societies."

Third, *mutual aid is an essential quality of brotherhood.* Cooperation and mutual aid were part of the medieval structure of society out of which Anabaptism developed. Economic and social life necessitated such cooperation. Early Swiss Brethren were concerned for the economic and social welfare of their own and even sometimes for those outside their community of faith. Dutch Anabaptists did likewise. Menno Simons integrated religious, social, and economic aspects of life.

Early Mennonite mutual aid organizations included the "Private Fire Regulation of Tiegenhof" (West Prussia, 1623), the "General Committee for Foreign Needs" (Dutch Mennonites, 1710), the "Dutch Mennonite Committee" for emigrants (1930-32), the "Waisenamt" (orphan's office in Russia, Canada, Mexico, and Paraguay), and the "Land Fund" (Russia, Mexico).

Fourth, Fretz proposed that *mutual aid is religiously motivated.* The religious beliefs and values of Mennonites drive their aid. For them there is little distinction between sacred and secular. All is sacred. Mutual aid societies' constitutions are grounded in Scripture. Business meetings include prayer, hymns, preaching. They are often held in a church, advertised in church papers, and conducted as religious meetings. Mutual aid is rooted in divine plans and commands, and "[i]n all types of mutual aid among the Mennonites the religious factor or the God-consciousness is tremendously important" (Fretz 1958:15).

## Confronting Change

In 1963, only five years after Fretz's lectures, C. J. Dyck expressed concerns about the effects of dramatic societal transformations on Mennonites. At the annual meeting he presented a series of lectures entitled "Mutual Aid in a Changing Economy" (Dyck 1963:158-59).

> Great changes which may affect the program of Mutual Aid have also taken [place] in this country. America has shifted from an agricultural to an industrial economy. . . . People have moved to the city and the city has swallowed the farm. Wages and other incomes have increased and with it the standard of living. . . . Americans have never had it so good and, therefore, have never been so afraid of losing what they have as they are today.

Still, Dyck argues, Scripture provides an unchanging God to confront the problems presented by such changes. But shortly after this affirmation of faith, he acknowledges that Mennonites have blurred the boundaries between the sacred and the secular, the earthly and the heavenly. This blurring has occurred without sufficient thought as the "Mennonite church has moved from the historical strategy of withdrawal from the world to a rather free association with culture without having spelled out deliberately its theology of culture" (Dyck 1963:160).

Dyck calls Mennonites to be prophetic, to break through the increased affluence of the culture and the church, "pricking the conscience of a sensate culture and building the walls of Jerusalem besides" (Dyck 1963:175). In his own prophetic voice, Dyck (1963:175) again reflects on the challenges societal change is bringing to Mennonite notions of community, cooperation, and mutual aid.

> A major problem we face . . . is the great increase in total income among our people everywhere . . . fewer and fewer Mennonites are depending on farming for a livelihood. . . . Our young men are somewhat above the national average in level of education, and are being offered good positions, enabling them to begin married life in new homes, with a good car, furniture . . . and regular, paid vacations. Many of our lay ministers . . . have been completely unable to challenge these relatively *nouveau riche*. . . . Frugality and hard work have been among the highest virtues to which persons could aspire to gain status in the brotherhood, but these virtues have often become a serious liability.

But while Dyck appears concerned about Mennonites mixing with the world, he does not picture the past as idyllic. In fact, he believes that following the persecution of the early Anabaptists, mutual aid became little more than a justification for many Anabaptists to remove themselves from the world. A "gospel of wealth" replaced the "gospel of Christ."[7]

Yet if separation from the world leads to greed and integration with the world, which leads to contamination and complacency, what is the church to do? Simply, says Dyck (1963:196-97), trust and obey:

> Let us then pursue the high goal of simple obedience, seeking to serve rather than wait for social justice. In an awareness of the new configuration of the brotherhood through economic, political and social changes, let us be alert to new opportunities. . . . Let us serve humbly where no one else will serve, suffering, if need be dying, measuring our service by the standard of our Lord and Master, Jesus Christ. As long as the biblical understanding of the church as a brotherhood continues among us there will continue the feeling of responsibility for the brother. . . . The surest guarantee of remaining sensitive to the changing needs of brotherhood is to remain close to our elder brother, Jesus Christ, in whose steps we follow (Mark 3:35).

Fretz and Dyck provide us with different but equally important perspectives of Mennonite mutual aid. Fretz is important because he provides an *ideal* view of mutual aid, a backdrop against which mutual aid actions and attitudes can be assessed. Dyck, however, provides a view of mutual aid as actualized throughout Mennonite history and calls Mennonites to return to simplicity and the Lordship of Christ.[8] He is aware that both withdrawal from and embracing of the world present serious temptations and threaten to contaminate our message about and mission of mutual aid. The messages of Fretz and Dyck are similar, however, in that each would ground mutual aid in Scripture and the Lordship of Christ.

J. Winfield Fretz (1975), in his own analysis of community among Mennonites seventeen years after his somewhat idealistic comments in 1958, admits to significant changes in the world and among Mennonites. Any common meaning about what community is, Fretz (1975:5-6) says, has been lost.

> Mennonite churches today have increasingly less characteristics of community. They perform certain wanted functions: 1) they provide a place for regular corporate public worship; 2) they perform the function of religious education: 3) they provide an occasional opportunity for fellowship; and 4) they are the agency that performs the conventional religious ceremonies . . . the typical Mennonite church today does not perform many of the functions of a genuine community.

Fretz notes the rise of intentional communities among Mennonites, exemplified by Reba Place Fellowship of Chicago, Illinois, and sixteen other fellowships scattered across the United States and Canada. He observes that many individuals in these fellowships come from voluntary service groups or Mennonite colleges. The fellowships were "judgments" on conventional Mennonite congregations where persons are "passive participants." The latter had become superficial, too dependent on church leaders. They were individualistic, divided by class lines, and materialistic. Clearly the new voluntarism had come of age among Mennonites and was affecting attitudes and values about cooperation and mutual aid.

The intentional communities returned to many of the characteristics envisioned by the early leaders in the mutual aid movement. These included a foundation in discipleship, Scripture, and the lordship of Christ. In addition, members of the intentional communities described their new communities in vil-like terms, such as cooperation, family-like relationships, and a sense of place. Members saw the intentional community as a "refuge and a place to grow," a "place to discern the shape of discipleship in our world," a "primary relationship group in which we can help each other make decisions about vocation, about how to spend our money, discern gifts, and in short, explore the meaning of confessing that Jesus is Lord of every aspect of our lives," and a place that provides a "measure of security not experienced by living by ones and twos" (Fretz 1975:7).

Although the intentional community was not an alternative to what Fretz envisioned in 1958, by 1975 he understood that dramatic social change had left the Mennonite church in a very different condition. The church had lost many of its valuable qualities and was in dire need of reform. Thus Fretz affirmed the development of the intentional communities as an alternate model that would prod traditional Mennonites to change and be renewed.

In another analysis, Driedger (1986) observed that the effects of societal changes on Mennonites could be either negative or positive. Mennonites could lose traditional communal values through movement to urban areas or through separatism in rural ethnic communities.

Or Mennonite communities could be "saved" through appropriate openings and closings between the community and society. Good openness occurs when, despite integration with the larger society, self-identity of the community is preserved. Bad openness might be breakdown Mennonite families through divorce, damaging traditional kinship ties. A "saved" strategy cultivates strong ties to the community but weak ties to the outside. Strong social networks rather than ecological boundaries are important in a saved strategy. These networks are flexible and transportable. Appropriate brokers such as Harold Bender, E. G. Kaufman, and the Concerned Citizens Group of Saskatchewan are also necessary for a saved community, according to Driedger.

Both Driedger and Fretz appear to believe that a new voluntarism need not be entirely detrimental to the Mennonite sense of community and mutual aid. But mutual aid does increasingly depend on individual motivations and efforts and less on the local church and denomination. Still, given the tendency of traditional Mennonite communities to isolate themselves from the world, a new voluntarism might have the advantage of keeping Mennonite religious commitment sharp and vital. While fewer might choose to participate in mutual aid, those who do will be driven by a strong personal sense of its importance. And their commitment level will likely be higher than those motivated by communal norms and pressure.

# Behaviors and Attitudes Associated with Mutual Aid

In 1972 and 1989, Church Member Profile (CMP) surveys were conducted of five Anabaptist denominations: Mennonite (MC), General Conference, Mennonite Brethren, Brethren in Christ, and Evangelical Mennonite (see Kauffman and Driedger 1991). The 1972 study had 3,591 respondents and the 1989 study 3,083. The 1989 respondents were slightly more educated and older than 1972 respondents, but there were no gender disparities between the two samples.

Using the CMP data, it is possible to uncover beliefs and behaviors associated with mutual aid among Mennonites. Respondents were asked, "Given our affluent twentieth-century society and the availability of many commercial insurance companies, which statement best expresses your view of the need of mutual aid programs in the framework of the church such as those offered by Mennonite Mutual Aid (MMA)?"

Respondents could select one of four answers:

"Mutual aid is no longer needed,"

"Mutual aid is needed but it is not practical for the church to provide it,"

"Mutual aid is needed but can best be given only at the local congregation level," and

"Mutual aid is needed at the local level and in churchwide sharing programs."

**Table 1**. *Percent agreeing "mutual aid is needed at the local level and in churchwide sharing programs" by selected variables, 1989.*

| SELECTED VARIABLES | PERCENT SUPPORT FOR MUTUAL AID | | | | |
|---|---|---|---|---|---|
| Giving to church offering* (N=2,327) | Seldom 65[a] | Occasionally 71 | Fairly often 74 | Regularly 78 | |
| Satisfied with denominational stewardship*** (N=2,343) | Very S. 86 | Satisfied 79 | Somewhat 65 | S. Dissatisfied 47 | |
| Interest in serving congregation*** (N=2,338) | Little 70 | Lot 79 | | | |
| Poverty is due to lack of discipline (N=2,334) | S. Agree 67 | Agree 71 | Undecided 76 | Disagree 78 | S. Disagree 82 |
| Importance of self-reliance*** (N=2,331) | Not 57 | Not very 78 | Somewhat 80 | Important 78 | Very 71 |
| Importance of working hard to get ahead*** (N=2,330) | Not 83 | Not very 82 | Somewhat 78 | Important 71 | Very 66 |

*P=.05, **P=.01, ***P=.001

[a]Read "Sixty-five percent of those who seldom give to church offerings agree that mutual aid is needed at the local level and in churchwide sharing programs."

The following issues in the 1989 survey were all related to mutual aid: giving to church offerings, satisfaction with denominational stewardship, interest in serving the congregation, and attitudes about poverty, self-reliance, and work (see Table 1). Among those who regularly give to church offerings, 78 percent agree that mutual aid is needed at the local level and in churchwide sharing programs. Among those who give occasionally, 71 percent support mutual aid, and even among those who seldom give, 65 percent support mutual aid. The more satisfied one is with denominational stewardship, the more supportive one is of mutual aid. Eighty-six percent of those who are very satisfied with the denomination's stewardship support mutual aid. Sixty-five percent of those somewhat satisfied with denominational stewardship support mutual aid, and 47 percent of those dissatisfied with denominational stewardship support mutual aid.

Serving the local congregation is associated with support for mutual aid. Seventy-nine percent of those interested in such service support mutual aid, while 70 percent of those with little interest in serving the congregation support mutual aid. In general, as participation in the congregation increases, support for mutual aid also increases.

Personal attitudes about work and poverty also predict support for mutual aid. Individuals were asked whether poverty is due to a lack of discipline. Among those who strongly agreed, only 67 percent supported mutual aid. Of those who agreed, 71 percent supported mutual aid. Among those who strongly disagreed, nearly 82 percent supported it.

Respondents were also asked about the importance of self-reliance. Those most ambivalent about self-reliance were most likely to support mutual aid (80 percent), and those who viewed it as very important were least likely to support aid (the exception being the "Not" category).

Among those who saw hard work as very important to getting ahead, only 66 percent supported mutual aid. On the other hand, among those who agreed working hard is not very important to getting ahead, 82 percent supported mutual aid. As support for the notion that hard work allows one to get ahead declines, support for mutual aid rises.

## Who Supports Mutual Aid?

Besides behaviors and attitudes associated with Mennonite mutual aid, what demographic characteristics are found among supporters of mutual aid? Support for mutual aid among Mennonites differs by age, educational level, and occupation (see Table 2). In all age groups except those 13-19, 75 percent or more agreed that mutual aid is needed at the local level and in churchwide sharing programs. Among the very young (ages 13-19), support was lower, with barely 69 percent expressing agreement. Males and females were equally likely to support mutual aid.

Education also had an important effect on attitudes about mutual aid. The more education, the greater the support for mutual aid. Of those with elementary only, 72 percent supported mutual aid. This was not much different from those who attended high school (73 percent). College education, and particularly graduate education, affected mutual aid support. Among college graduates, 76 percent supported mutual aid while 85 percent of graduate students did so.

**Table 2.** Percent agreeing that *"mutual aid is needed at the local level and in churchwide sharing programs,"* 1989.[a]

| PERCENT SUPPORT FOR MUTUAL AID | | | | |
|---|---|---|---|---|
| Age* (N=2,349) | 13-19 | 20-29 | 30-49 | 50-69 | 70-94 |
| | 69[b] | 75 | 76 | 79 | 76 |
| Sex (N=2,350) | Male | Female | | |
| | 77 | 76 | | |
| Education*** (N=2,353) | Elementary | High School | College | Grad. school |
| | 72 | 73 | 76 | 85 |
| Occupation*** (N=2,328) | Professional | Business | Farmer | Blue collar | Housewife |
| | 81 | 78 | 72 | 79 | 71 |
| Income (N=2,220) | <15K | 15-29 | 30-49 | 50+ |
| | 77 | 78 | 77 | 73 |
| Attendance*** (N=2,357) | Low | High | | |
| | 71 | 79 | | |
| Prayer*** (N=2,354) | Little | Lot | | |
| | 70 | 78 | | |
| Region***(N=2,321) | US East | US West | Canada East | Canada West |
| | 83 | 76 | 67 | 62 |
| Residence (N=2,336) | Farm | Rural | Small city | Large city |
| | 76 | 77 | 79 | 74 |
| Ethnicity (N=2,203) | Swiss | Dutch | British | Other |
| | 82 | 72 | 68 | 74 |

*P=.05, **P=.01, ***P=.001

[a]Sixty-six percent agreed with the statement in 1972; in 1989 seventy-six percent agreed.
[b]Read "Sixty-nine percent of the 13-19 year olds agreed that mutual aid is needed at the local level and in churchwide sharing programs."

Why was education important? Sociologists have long argued that education helps raise awareness and break down prejudices. In the case of mutual aid, individuals with the most education may be more aware of other people and places where suffering is occurring and support is needed. Mennonites often mourn the loss of community life in this age of urbanization, education, and mobility. These findings, however, suggest that education positively affects concern for others, perhaps particularly those outside of one's immediate living situation. As a result of education, localism is minimized and a broader global view is encouraged.

Just as education affected CMP mutual aid support, so did occupation. In fact, it seemed to do so as much as education. Those in traditional roles associated with farming and rural communities were less likely to support mutual aid than those working away from home. The support among farmers was 72 percent; among housewives it was 71 percent. However, 79 percent of blue collar workers supported mutual aid, as did 78 percent of those in business and 81 percent of professionals.

These findings parallel those for education. Exposure to other individuals and circumstances may increase concern about others outside of one's locale. Income, however, made little difference. This finding is interesting, because sociologists typically discover that, for many issues, occupation, education, and income predict in similar patterns. However, in the case of mutual aid, increased wealth does not necessarily produce more concern for others. Awareness of needs may expand with greater education and mobility but not necessarily with more income. Ethnicity (Swiss, Dutch, British, and Other) did not seem to affect support for aid.

Besides the above demographic variables, two religious variables affect mutual aid support in ways that should please Mennonite church leaders. Among frequent church attendees, 79 percent expressed support for mutual aid while, among low attendees, 71 percent were supporters. Similarly, those who prayed a lot (78 percent) were more likely to value mutual aid than those who prayed less (70 percent).

Church attendance or prayer are not always predictors of broader social concerns or action. Thus this finding ought to be particularly gratifying. It suggests that among Mennonites, religion extends beyond one's self and one's situation to include a concern for others. Church attendance indicates more than social status, as is so often the case in the larger society. It also correlates with awareness of broader social issues. And prayer, while often individual, also extends to corporate concerns.

Rural sociologists have long argued that despite widespread changes in society—such as urbanization and industrialization—rural communities retain important characteristics that distinguish them from the larger society. Rural residents tend to be more religious, more orthodox, and more conservative with regard to social and political issues. In this analysis, however, farm residents, rural residents, those in small cities, and those in large cities held similar views toward mutual aid (see Table 2). This pattern is interesting, given the earlier finding that those in more traditional occupations were less supportive of mutual aid. Apparently, rural Mennonite congregations are able to articulate broad mutual aid concerns sufficiently.

Region of residence does influence support for mutual aid. Canadians were much less supportive (eastern Canada, 67 percent; western Canada, 62 percent) than U.S. residents. In the U.S. there were regional differences, with eastern residents being more supportive (83 percent) than westerners (76 percent). These regional and national differences may be partly explained by differences in national social welfare systems as well as in ethnic and immigrant backgrounds of Mennonites.

The CMP project also examines the relationship between attitudes toward mutual aid and participation in Mennonite Mutual Aid programs. As shown in Table 3, participation for auto insurance, health insurance, life insurance, long-term care insurance, and the retirement plan increased dramatically for U.S. respondents as churchwide support for mutual aid increased.[9] Those who felt there was no need for mutual aid at a local level as well as those who felt a need *only* at the local level were much less likely to participate in these five MMA programs. This lack of participation should come as no surprise, given that most churchwide mutual aid outreach occurs through denominational organizations.[10]

*Table 3. Percent of U.S. respondents participating in MMA programs by attitude toward need for Mennonite mutual aid, 1989.*

### NEED FOR MUTUAL AID

| MMA Participants | No need[a] | Local only | Churchwide |
|---|---|---|---|
| Auto insurance | 7[b] | 11 | 25 |
| Health insurance | 21 | 18 | 38 |
| Life insurance | 4 | 1 | 6 |
| Long term care insurance | 2 | 2 | 5 |
| Retirement plan | 2 | 2 | 11 |
| Mutual fund | 3 | 0 | 3 |

[a]The three response categories are: *no need*=mutual aid is no longer needed or mutual aid is needed but it is not practical for the church to provide it, *local only* =mutual aid is needed but can best be given only at the local congregation level, and *churchwide*=mutual aid is needed at the local level and in churchwide sharing programs.

[b]Read "Seven percent of those who think there is no need for mutual aid participate in MMA auto insurance programs."

## Tracing Changes in Mutual Aid Support

The Church Member Profile tracks change in Mennonite support for mutual aid from 1972 to 1989. In 1972, 66 percent of respondents agreed that mutual aid is needed at the local level and in churchwide sharing programs. In 1989, affirmation of this statement increased to 76 percent.[11]

Why the increase? Sociologists often attribute changes over time in attitudes and behaviors to three possible effects: period, cohort, and age.[12] Period effects are those events or conditions of a particular period or time in history. Relevant period effects in this analysis are events or conditions present in the early 1970s, because 1972 is the year of the first survey, and in the late 1980s, because 1989 was the year of the second survey.

Cohort effects result from characteristics common to those born during the same period in history. In this analysis there are five birth cohorts, composed of those born in 1878-1911, 1912-1928, 1929-1945, 1946-1962, and 1963-1979. Age effects occur as a result of the aging process. Table 4 indicates the extent to which period, cohort, and age have affected mutual aid attitudes.

**Table 4**. *Change in support for Mennonite mutual aid 1972-1989 by Period, Cohort, and Age.**

| Age | Period | |
|---|---|---|
| | 1972<br>Period 1 | 1989<br>Period 2 |
| 10-26 yrs. | 1946-62<br>Cohort 4<br>N=1,027<br>**1.53** | 1963-79<br>Cohort 5<br>N=290<br>**1.60** |
| 27-43 yrs. | 1929-45<br>Cohort 3<br>N=928<br>**1.52** | 1946-62<br>Cohort 4<br>N=833<br>**1.64** |
| 44-60 yrs. | 1912-28<br>Cohort 2<br>N=1,038<br>**1.52** | 1929-45<br>Cohort 3<br>N=650<br>**1.66** |
| 61-94 yrs. | 1878-1911<br>Cohort 1<br>N=299<br>**1.46** | 1912-28<br>Cohort 2<br>N=491<br>**1.66** |
| | | 1878-1911<br>Cohort 1<br>N=84<br>**1.71** |

*A value in bold is the mean support for Mennonite mutual aid, trichotomized so that 0=mutual aid is no longer needed or mutual aid is needed but is not practical for the church to provide it, 1=mutual aid is needed but can best be given only at the local congregation level, and 2=mutual aid is needed at the local level and in churchwide sharing programs.

In general, aging effects and period effects account for the increase in support for mutual aid among Mennonites. Cohort effects were unimportant. Period effects can be observed when comparing mean scores of 1972 and 1989 for each of the four age groups. In every case, support increased. Apparently, an event or condition existed in the 1970s and 1980s that caused Mennonites to become increasingly supportive of churchwide mutual aid. One could speculate about effects of national events, such as the 1970s energy crisis and the 1980s Reagan Revolution. Perhaps there were also churchwide events or conditions—such as an increase in the prominence of MMA's profile—that contributed to the increase in support.

Aging effects can be observed when comparing the same cohort over time. For example, Cohort 4 increased its mean support from 1.53 in 1972 to 1.64 in 1989. Similarly, each of the other three cohorts increased over time. As Mennonites aged over the past two decades, support for mutual aid increased. Why? Perhaps older Mennonites simply became more concerned about their own well-being in the face of potential health problems and their own need for mutual aid. Or perhaps aging itself contributes to a broadening of concern for others and their needs. Whatever the specific reasons for the period and aging effects, church leaders can take heart from the fact that Mennonites across the board became increasingly concerned about mutual aid from 1972 to 1989.

## A New "Vil"?

At the outset of this chapter, I suggested that Mennonite attitudes about mutual aid are being shaped by a "new voluntarism" affecting religious attitudes and behaviors among Americans at large. There are several consequences for Mennonite mutual aid. First, the social base of Mennonite mutual aid has changed. Second, the family plays a less important role in transmitting mutual aid attitudes. Third, with deterioration of Mennonite norms of responsibility to one's community, individual differences in mutual aid beliefs and values are more important than in the past. Fourth, mutual aid attitudes are shaped along ideological rather than communal lines. Finally, Mennonite views of the meaning of mutual aid are becoming increasingly different. Given the original definition of Mennonite mutual aid outlined by Fretz and others, it is relatively clear that a new voluntarism has increasingly shaped Mennonite attitudes toward mutual aid, community, and cooperation. Wiens (1988:11) concurs in part.

> It is true, on the surface, that MCC and MMA and MDS and MEDA and our other agencies and mission boards are organized like other parachurch agencies. It is true that our ministries are addressed to specialized aspects of what once took place concretely in the life of our communities. It is also true that they use the technologies that abstraction both makes possible and then demands. It is even true that they mostly function outside of and between our Mennonite denominational structures.

Although Wiens suggests that the development of Mennonite organizations like MMA may be an effort to create a tighter sacred canopy, he is not convinced that such efforts will be enough to keep us from the "spirits of this world."

He concludes by calling us back to primary communities in bounded places, communities of the family, tribe, and village—in other words, the "vil." Not a vil characterized by self-sufficiency and isolation. Rather, a vil where self-sacrifice and surrender are the norm.

> It is therefore . . . the task of all of us, to integrate our separated forms of mutual aid into the movement to integrate our churches to create levels of concreteness. Ultimately, the future of mutual aid among us will depend on our willingness to give up our attempts to be God or even to serve God, through our presumed mastery of our institutions by our communities. We are not God. We are not even sages. And that is why we must begin with repentance and with the admission that we have never known how to create our *halig* (mission).

The survey results of 1972 and 1989 offer an encouraging note. They indicate substantial increase in attitudinal support for churchwide mutual aid among Mennonites. The challenge for Mennonites entering the new millenium is to combine vil-like qualities with a concern for churchwide and global needs. Perhaps Mennonites should revise the popular slogan—think globally, act locally—to "think locally, act globally."

## Notes

1. For a sociological view of the "sacred canopy," see Peter Berger (1969).

2. See Conrad L. Kanagy and Leo Driedger (1996) for a more extensive discussion of such demographic changes and their impact upon Mennonite attitudes.

3. See Hart M. Nelsen and Conrad L. Kanagy (1993) for confirmation of a new voluntarism among American blacks, who, in many ways like Mennonites, were historically more oriented towards the vil.

4. This discussion of new voluntarism consequences draws heavily on the work of Roof and McKinney (1987).

5. See the Smithville, Oh., 1964 "Statement on Christian Mutual Aid" in Hernley (1970).

6. *Ibid.*

7. This is the same problem that Weber (1958) argued affected Calvinists, whose ascetic and frugal lifestyles led to wealth and in turn secularization.

8. Sociologists define *ideal culture* as expectations embodied in values and norms of a society and *real culture* as patterns of behavior typical of everyday life.

9. Canadians were excluded since MMA does not operate in Canada.

10. In findings not reported in Table 3, 56 percent of U.S. respondents in the survey indicated participation in at least one MMA program.

11. This difference is statistically significant, meaning that it is unlikely that the difference occurred by chance.

12. See Norval Glenn (1977) as well as Norman B. Ryder (1967).

## References

Berger, Peter
   1969    *The Sacred Canopy*. New York: Anchor.

Driedger, Leo
1986    "Mennonite Community Change: From Ethnic Enclaves to Social Networks." *Mennonite Quarterly Review* 60(3):374-86.

Dyck, C. J.
1963    "Mutual Aid in a Changing Economy." In *The Compassionate Community*, ed. H. Ralph Hernley.

Fretz, J. Winfield
1957    "Mutual Aid." *The Mennonite Encyclopedia*, vol. 3. Scottdale, Pa.: Herald Press.

1958    "Meditations on Christian Mutual Aid." In *The Compassionate Community*, ed. H. Ralph Hernley.

1975    "Mennonite Community: Traditional or Intentional." *Mennonite Life* 30(4):5-7.

Glenn, Norval
1977    *Cohort Analysis.* Beverly Hills, California: Sage.

Hernley, H. Ralph, ed.
1970    *The Compassionate Community.* Scottdale, Pa.: Association of Mennonite Aid Societies.

Hillery, George A., Jr.
1992    *The Monastery.* Connecticut: Praeger Publishers.

Kanagy, Conrad and Leo Driedger
1996    "Changing Mennonite Values: Attitudes about Women, Politics, and Peace, 1972-1989." *Review of Religious Research* 37(2):342-54.

Kauffman, J. Howard and Leland Harder
1975    *Anabaptism Four Centuries Later.* Scottdale, Pa.: Herald Press.

Kauffman, J. Howard and Leo Driedger
1991    *The Mennonite Mosaic.* Scottdale, Pa.: Herald Press.

Nelsen, Hart M., and Conrad L. Kanagy
1993    "Churched and Unchurched Black Americans." In *Church and Denominational Growth*, ed. David Roozen and Kirk Hadaway. Nashville: Abingdon.

Roof, Wade Clark and William McKinney
1987    *American Mainline Religion.* New Jersey: Rutgers.

Ryder, Norman B.
1967    "The Cohort as a Concept in the Study of Social Change." *American Sociological Review* 30:843-61.

Weber, Max
1958    *The Protestant Ethic and the Spirit of Capitalism.* New York: Scribners [orig. 1904-05].

Wiens, Delbert
1988    Untitled presentation at Laurelville Mennonite Church Center, unpublished paper.

Wilson, Bryan
1982    *Religion in Sociological Perspective.* New York: Oxford University Press.

## 12

# Mennonite Mutual Aid:
# A Margin of Difference?

### Keith Graber Miller[1]

*In this provocative essay Keith Graber Miller examines organizational struggles of Mennonite Mutual Aid as it seeks to care for church members in the contemporary world. He asks whether MMA is becoming isomorphic—similar to secular insurance agencies—or maintaining a real margin of difference. He explores organizational tensions in three areas: managed care, underwriting, and the role of profits.*

## The Margin of Difference

Near the close of a three-day conference on "Building Communities of Compassion," Donald B. Kraybill spoke passionately, almost evangelistically, about Mennonite Mutual Aid's "margin of difference," drawing on the language the church-related business often uses in promotional brochures. Kraybill cited MMA's continuing partnership with the church, its fraternal benefits program, its ecumenical constituency, its promotion of the core values of mutual aid and stewardship, and its sponsorship of a variety of educational and advocacy programs as evidence of the organization's distinctiveness from others in the industry who offer similar health, life, and financial products and services.[2]

In her response to Kraybill's affirmation, Beryl Hartzler Brubaker also reflected on the "margin," acknowledging honestly "the limitations imposed by the reality of staying in business." In her concluding remarks, the MMA board chair asked three perceptive questions: "How do we lead Mennonites to mutual aid when other sources are leading them down other paths?"; "How will we know when our institutional self-interest supersedes our mission?"; and "How do we avoid succumbing to the norms of the world?"[3]

Thanks be to God, this chapter does not attempt to answer those questions. Instead, it examines a few of the tensions Mennonite Mutual Aid experiences in remaining faithful to its half-century-old founding vision of assisting church members in "bearing one another's burdens."[4] Such a vision could easily erode in the midst of dramatic changes in health care costs and technology, constraints associated with necessary "partnering" with other investment and managed care providers, the realities of an increasingly urbanized and acculturated constituency, and the desire to rapidly expand product and service offerings.

Mennonite Mutual Aid is not what it used to be: a church agency which simply assisted Civilian Public Service (CPS) men as they moved back into civilian life, and which provided "burial expenses" for widows. In addition to what is now comfortably called health insurance and life insurance,[5] today MMA offers long-term care insurance, disability income protection, auto collision coverage, retirement investment programs, mutual funds, financial services, estate planning and management of planned charitable giving, Sharing Fund grants, annuity scholarships, congregational grants, educational resources, and advocacy programs. As it looks toward the twenty-first century, MMA comprises twelve corporate entities and manages over $900 million in assets, including Mennonite Foundation monies, Mennonite Retirement Trust funds, mutual funds, and other resources.[6]

Just before MMA was formally founded, its first board chair, Orie O. Miller, wrote, "In this changing situation, the church means (intends) to go along with its members and help them wherever in good conscience they need to go."[7] MMA president Howard Brenneman said Miller's statement was "as much a customer-driven statement as any quotation I have ever come across."[8] In recent years MMA planning documents have referred to it as a "customer needs driven" organization, providing "a range of products and services that fill current and emerging needs for the customer group that it serves."[9]

The more nuanced 1996 "MMA Corporate Strategic Plan" further breaks down this characterization into four categories of "forces pushing on the organization." The plan says customer needs drive the products and services MMA offers; government regulation both helps and hinders MMA's vision; "a competitive business environment drives MMA to deliver the best products, quality service, competitive prices, high visibility, and easy access;" and MMA's beliefs drive its "core values."[10]

Brenneman said some of the company's more recent strategic directions grew out of market research done for the company by the Life Insurance Marketing and Research Association (LIMRA) in 1991 and 1992, just as Brenneman was beginning as CEO.[11] LIMRA personnel interviewed Mennonite church leaders, pastors, boards of elders, conference leaders, and others who might be interested in MMA products. LIMRA asked them "what they expected of a church agency whose mandate was mutual aid and stewardship." Brenneman said MMA learned that its constituents tended to trust MMA, but that they also thought MMA products were high-priced and that "we didn't know how to run a business, to be competitive." According to Brenneman, potential clients also said they were ready to accept professional sales people more than MMA thought they might be.

> I think what they were really saying was, "Get in the modern age. You don't have to sacrifice principles to get in the modern age." I guess what they'd say is, "Don't try to make the product itself religious so that you think that is what makes the MMA product different." What makes the MMA difference is how you deliver it and how you treat people and how you look at the needy and how we're able to get the sharing part of it going. But don't try to make your life insurance or your health insurance or whatever the big margin of difference.[12]

"Listening to our customers" through LIMRA's research has had a significant impact on how MMA does its business today.[13]

## MMA and Institutional Isomorphism

As MMA has moved into new markets and reworked old ones in response to its perception of customer needs, stiff competition from others in its various industries, and government regulations, it has been served well by being reminded of the agency's founding purposes. Annual corporate plans consistently begin with an historically-based vision statement of MMA's foundations in the biblically-grounded concepts of mutual aid and stewardship and the early Anabaptist commitment to such principles. The reason such references are important is the extraordinary pull church-initiated institutions such as MMA experience toward functioning precisely like their commercial counterparts.

Institutionalization theorists John W. Meyer and Brian Rowan contend that "organizations are driven to incorporate the practices and procedures defined by the prevailing rationalized concepts of organizational work and institutionalized in society." When organizations do so, say Meyer and Rowan, they "increase their legitimacy and their survival prospects, independent of the acquired practices and procedures."[14]

In an article titled "The Iron Cage Revisited: Institutional Isomorphism and Collective Rationality in Organizational Fields," Paul J. DiMaggio and Walter W. Powell suggest that the engine of organizational rationalization is now "the structuration of organizational fields." An organizational field, for DiMaggio and Powell, means "those organizations that, in the aggregate, constitute a recognized area of institutional life: key suppliers, resource and product consumers, regulatory agencies, and other organizations that produce similar services or products." Isomorphism is

> a constraining process that forces one unit in a population to resemble other units that face the same set of environmental conditions. . . . [O]rganizational characteristics are modified in the direction of increasing compatibility with environmental characteristics; the number of organizations in a population is a function of environmental carrying capacity; and the diversity of organizational forms is isomorphic to environmental diversity.[15]

DiMaggio and Powell then note the homogeneity of organizational forms and practices within a given organizational field.

Similarly, sociologist Mark Chaves speaks about denominations' dual structures—the religious authority structure and the agency structure. He says that agencies that are increasingly autonomous from their denominational religious authority structures "are more apt to develop organizational forms and practices that adhere to the functional organizational fields in which they reside rather than to the religious traditions whose names they bear." In other words, relatively autonomous religious agencies' fundraising, service delivery, lobbying, and other practices—no matter what the denominational background—will be indistinguishable from comparable secular activities (Chaves 1993:165).

The tendency toward similitude has not gone unnoticed by those managing Mennonite Mutual Aid. "Some of MMA's products and services may not appear so different from their counterparts in the commercial insurance and financial services world," says one summary of the "current setting" for MMA. The statement goes on to suggest that, when taken together with other programs that assist needy persons, educational resources, and MMA's overall mission, "one can see that each product and program is a unique tool to give expression to the basic biblical concepts upon which MMA is built."[16]

Mennonite Mutual Aid also can forcefully argue—as it does in its promotional materials—that its authority structure remains deeply rooted in Mennonite denominations. MMA's board consists of seventeen officers, ten of whom are members of the Mennonite Church, the institution's founding denomination; five of whom are from the General Conference Mennonite Church; and two of whom are from the Mennonite Brethren Church. Nine of the officers are elected by their respective denominations, and the other eight are appointed by board members themselves. For many years the board has included several CPS men. They would have remembered well MMA's first assignment of providing loans to those who had provided church-related, nonmilitary services during World War II. However, in 1993 the remaining three CPSers retired from the board.[17]

In general, the board has moved toward greater professionalization in recent years.[18] The present board includes seven businesspersons, four members of college faculties or administrations, four persons involved in the health care field, one municipal employee, and one farmer. Since the 1980s MMA has in addition had a Board Development Committee,[19] which provides a board process "for making recommendations for and selecting new board members, for providing for board members' orientation and training, and for evaluating board members' performance."[20]

MMA also is dependent on members of the various constituent denominations it serves. With its fraternal benefit status, the particular pool from which it can draw is relatively limited. Recently MMA altered its mission statement to say that the institution offers "*all Anabaptists . . . the opportunity to help each other by sharing financial risks and resources.*"[21] That constituency now includes the Society of Friends (Quakers) as well as the Missionary Church and twenty-three other denominations "historically associated with the Anabaptist tradition."[22] Mennonite Mutual Aid's goal is to "touch every Anabaptist with an MMA product or service by the year 2000."[23] This is the goal, even though at present only about ten to twelve percent (81,555 persons) of its more than 650,000-member constituency has life, health, financial, or related products with MMA.[24]

While MMA has remained linked to Mennonite denominational structures, and while it is dependent on its Anabaptist-related customers,[25] it also lives with the realities of the business world. Those realities, combined with a changing and expanding Mennonite clientele, provide many of the forces that tug the agency toward the practices of other commercial businesses offering similar products and services. MMA believes it "uniquely blends church and business." However, "The church provides our core values, ultimate vision, and passion for action. Business provides the special discipline and tools necessary for sustained success."[26]

In the remainder of this chapter, I examine three places where MMA has sought to resist institutional isomorphism. I highlight both successes and complexities of such resistance. Two of the areas, managed care and underwriting, are related to health products, since the majority of MMA's membership still is in this arena. Finally I examine how a nonprofit organization deals with profits.

## Managing Care

Managed care, in the forms of precertification and large case management, has been a part of MMA's portfolio for many years. Such care first entered the institution's vocabulary in the 1980s. In the 1990s, managed care has become mainstream. Although it still includes traditional indemnity-type plans,[27] it also now includes *multiple* health care delivery systems which influence the cost and quality of services. Health Maintenance Organizations (HMOs) and Preferred Provider Organizations (PPOs) are two of the basic forms of managed care today.

In the "1996 MMA Corporate Strategic Plan," MMA's managers acknowledge that with rising competition

> MMA will not be successful just because it is part of the church. Rather, we must offer equal or better value, uniquely wrapped in our shared beliefs, than that available in the business market. . . . This may mean that MMA will need to find new structures, technologies, or arrangements with outside vendors in order to serve well.[28]

Managed care is an area in which it has been necessary to work with outside providers to compete.[29] HMOs contract with designated physicians, hospitals, and other providers of medical care. They then usually require members to seek care from a primary care physician functioning as gatekeeper. PPOs establish contracts with selected physicians, hospitals, and other providers of medical care, then offer better benefits for services received from these "preferred providers."

Both HMOs and PPOs are able to contain costs partly because, in exchange for a previously arranged, discounted fee, they will favor the providers who are a part of their network.[30] Seven years ago, before the Clinton administration's attempts at health care reform,[31] MMA was under little pressure to provide insurance coverage through HMOs and PPOs. Today, however, such arrangements are nearly unavoidable.

Daniel Grimes, director of provider relations for MMA, has said Mennonite clients will hear of managed care arrangements in their communities by reading about them on the front pages of their local newspapers or hearing about them from an area Mennonite doctor on a given HMO's advisory board. "This puts our counselors in a precarious situation," said Grimes, noting that both individuals and employers are interested in exploring other health care possibilities. "We're basically forced to come up with a managed care option."[32]

Because MMA is relatively small, it must by necessity "partner" with other providers for most of its formal managed care products. In such arrangements, MMA may design and market the health insurance product, set the premium, do the underwriting, and issue the certificate of coverage. It then essentially leases the services of a network, paying a fee to the managed care organization for its product. The managed care organization provides access to the network and may handle member services, claims processing, and adjudication and medical management.[33]

MMA has had a Preferred Provider Product in Kansas for just over five years and is developing or implementing similar arrangements in California, northern Indiana, Ohio, Pennsylvania, and Virginia.[34] What such arrangements mean is that MMA itself often has less direct control over the products it offers.

Grimes says MMA tries to evaluate how many of its clients would need to switch physicians or hospitals in a given HMO or PPO network. But he acknowledges that sometimes MMA can have minimal impact to shape the actual health care product offered. "The book of business that you can bring to the table" makes a difference, Grimes notes, and MMA's membership volume is quite small in some areas. He explains that when MMA's members are in a large metropolitan area, such as the Franconia Conference market in Philadelphia, MMA's influence becomes more insignificant. "Some people wouldn't even talk to us there," Grimes indicates. "The managed care firm isn't going to make all kinds of accommodations for us."[35]

The result is that Mennonite Mutual Aid's HMO and PPO health products become increasingly like those sold through other commercial companies. "I wouldn't say there's a major difference in product offering," acknowledges Grimes. However, Grimes—previously director of provider relations for Capital Blue Cross and Pennsylvania Blue Shield—believes the level of service and amount of concern for individual clients is a distinction between MMA and other insurance providers.[36]

Given that distinction, the PPO and HMO arrangements which remove from MMA the ability to process and adjudicate its own claims may be the most isomorphically threatening. In any event, the changing dynamics in the health care industry will likely continue to provide a constraining process forcing MMA to resemble others who face the same set of environmental conditions.

# The Pain of Underwriting

A decade ago, a second and more difficult transition for Mennonite Mutual Aid was reworking its underwriting policies for health insurance. As health care costs soared in the late 1980s, MMA found itself facing a crisis—losing as much as $3.9 million in one year on its total product offerings.[37] MMA managers and the board responded to increasing health care expenses by dramatically raising their premiums to cover their losses. Premiums jumped as much as thirty to forty percent with each renewal. As premiums rose, MMA saw a major exodus—as many as 400 to 500 per month—of healthy Mennonites, who could purchase policies with other companies at reduced costs.[38]

Shirley Yoder, then a board member and now vice president of operations at MMA, said that "it was a very painful realization" to see that "Mennonites were buying for price instead of concept." Yoder described herself and some of the other board members and administrators as "aging products of the 60s" who thought the concept of mutual aid and sharing one another's risks regardless of price were a part of Mennonite self-understandings. "We slowly began to realize that the ideal we had as a staff was not what people were willing to put their money behind," she said. "Mennonites are idealists, but also pragmatists."[39]

To stay price-competitive, MMA administrators began to alter the company's practices of underwriting. They carefully screened persons who fell into certain risk categories. Prior to the 1987-88 crisis, MMA had done only limited underwriting, requiring a small percentage of its members to undergo a short waiting period for particular pre-existing conditions before full insurance benefits became effective.[40] In "A Dream for an Alternative MMA Congressional Testimony (Witness) on Health Care Reform," then-board member Ted Koontz described the historical transition in underwriting this way:

> We began to offer health care coverage because we saw it as another concrete expression of our faith community's desire to follow Christ's command to "love one another as I have loved you." It was a part of mutual aid, helping each other with the financial difficulties we faced in relation to medical care. When we began we charged the same rate for all families enrolled, regardless of age, health, or geographical location. We wanted to make health care available without discrimination to all who

wanted and needed it and sought ways to include also those who could not afford to pay the regular premiums. . . . Over these forty years we have watched this vision erode, some might say we have watched it turn into a nightmare. As health care costs escalated and most of our people became more acculturated into mainstream American culture, some among us became more conscious of comparative costs of various insurance companies and turned to other companies for coverage. . . . Finally, in order to keep our company financially solvent, we have felt forced to actually exclude from coverage some of those who need it most—precisely those we had begun the business to serve—those with serious health problems. Nothing has been more distressing to us as a company which is also an arm of the church designed to show concretely our love for one another, than our need to exclude precisely those who need us most so that we can continue to serve some.[41]

Beginning in May 1987 and running through the next several years, underwriting policies were a major agenda item at MMA's regular board meetings. MMA's Mutual Aid Services Committee recommended to the board in May 1987 that "we implement improvements in our risk selection practices designed to assess individuals who join or change coverage their fair share of cost relative to the risk they bring to the sharing pool."[42] An April 15, 1987, MMA memo noted that the idea of "permanent exclusion" from MMA plans for prior illness is "counter to principles of love, caring and mutual aid." In the next sentence, the memo added that "congregations violate principles of fairness and equality . . . when they enroll a disproportionate number of high risk-high cost members in MMA plans."[43]

The memo also stated that, "In the past, we interpreted our mission being to help as many people as possible with medical problems. However, in the process we brought in a disproportionate share of people with medical problems at standard rates." Among the memo's concluding observations was recognition that permanent exclusions or denial of coverage for certain medical conditions is "very common in the insurance industry," and "competitors' rates are lower because of this practice." Nevertheless, "until we have a better way to work with local congregations through a true group arrangement, we do not believe it is feasible to adopt this practice."

For the next two years MMA sought to broaden its health insurance pool, working with local congregations to add healthier persons so the company could better cover higher-risk members.[44] In 1988 one of MMA's actuarial consultants told company officials, "MMA health plans are staring down the barrel of a loaded gun." The consultant said MMA had two choices: get broader membership from those at good risk or give up on poor risks and find a way to cut them out of the present pool.[45] According to MMA managers, at times healthy congregational members purchased MMA insurance for a short time so that unhealthy members could be allowed in the pool, but then soon dropped out and purchased less expensive insurance elsewhere.[46]

At the same time, MMA was phasing in new underwriting policies which included rate-ups (an increase in rates for the less healthy or older members), maximum waiting periods of thirty-six months for coverage of certain illnesses (up from the previous policy of two years), permanent exclusions of specific conditions, and even full declines of any health care coverage. But through the end of the 1980s, even a person with AIDS could get MMA health insurance with a rate-up and a waiting period of three years for AIDS-related coverage.[47]

In the midst of the underwriting debates, the MMA board and managers agreed to adopt "a widely used underwriting manual to translate specifics of the medical condition to an appropriate additional risk (premium)."[48] At the time, MMA was using quite loosely guidelines from Lincoln National Reinsurance Company of Fort Wayne, Indiana. Beginning January 1, 1988, MMA established a reinsurance agreement with Lincoln National.[49] This forced MMA to follow more strictly the company's underwriting policies or take full responsibility for extraordinary costs.

Since then, when MMA has chosen to accept members outside of Lincoln National's guidelines, MMA has taken on considerably greater risks since the reinsurer will not cover health-related expenses for such higher-risk persons.[50] Several times a week Shirley Yoder meets with an MMA underwriter to consider "hard cases" with unusual extenuating circumstances. But most of these also are turned down because of the additional risks.[51] According to Mennonite Mutual Aid's underwriting guidelines, MMA's policy is "to exercise full underwriting as described in our [Lincoln National] reinsurance manual."[52]

Another major underwriting issue MMA faces involves mental health care, a debate also heard in the halls of Congress as senators and representatives consider legislation requiring insurance companies to cover *mental* health care similarly to other health care expenses. According to MMA managers, Mennonites use mental health care services more frequently, on average, than the general U.S. population.[53] Moreover, according to a recent five-year retrospective study by MMA, those persons with mental health care needs cost the company 4.2 times as much per year in claims, including both physical and mental health care, as those without mental health needs.[54]

To manage the risks related to mental health care expenses, MMA now includes rate-ups, a waiting period, and a reduced lifetime maximum benefit for new members with pre-existing mental health conditions. For example, those applying for MMA's strictly underwritten Optima II plan may be offered instead the Team Care Health Plan. With Team Care Health Plan, the applicant could pay several times the standard premium, face a two-year waiting period for any mental, nervous, or emotional disease or disorder, then have a $10,000 lifetime maximum benefit for mental health care (one-quarter the usual maximum benefit for the plan).[55]

To counter, in part, such industry-like underwriting policies, MMA provides some assistance from its Sharing Fund and also encourages a potential member's congregation to assist with premium costs. With the rate-up mentioned above, for instance, MMA's Sharing Fund would pay up to one third of the premium if the applicant's congregation would pay one third. Through this arrangement, the applicant with mental health needs would be personally responsible for about the same amount of premium as a healthier person.

In the case of persons with AIDS, MMA understands its role as a church agency to include educating the church toward a "Christ-like understanding and response." Such a response includes being compassionate and helping relieve the fear of AIDS while preventing its spread. MMA also will work with other church organizations to solicit and disburse funds, relying on contributions for persons with AIDS.[56]

Nonetheless, recognizing that in terms of underwriting MMA now functions similarly to other commercial companies—partly because of requirements for reinsurance and the financial dangers of a high-risk pool—has been hard both for those at MMA and those in the Anabaptist constituency who desperately need health insurance. In her final report to the board of directors in 1991, then-chair Mary Swartley said she came to the end of her twelve years as a board member with one concern. "It seems to me," she said, "that the challenge for MMA in the 90s is to find some way to share the losses of the uninsured and uninsurable—is that not the vision behind the founding of this organization?" Swartley added

It seems like this is what we owe Mennonites. . . . [I]f we cannot do it, then either MMA has to go back to the drawing board and design a plan that shares the losses of these high risk people, or else the Mennonite Church needs to go back to the womb and give birth to a new organization that can.[57]

Given the apparent intractability of the underwriting problem and the necessity of resultant "uninsurables" during the reform debates of the early 1990s, some think MMA should have lobbied the federal government for a single-payer health care system and universal coverage. Such a system *may* have remedied some of the concerns about caring for "the least of these," though it also likely would have put MMA's health care divisions out of business.[58] In Ted Koontz's previously mentioned "Dream for an Alternative MMA Congressional Testimony," the former board member suggested that MMA say to legislators,

> We will not join the clamor of those insurers who seem more intent on saving insurance companies than on saving lives and saving money. For this reason we have severed our relationships with industry groups whose lobbying seems oriented primarily to defending their vested interests. . . . While we do not want to die as a health insurer, we care more about providing equal care to all, moving toward prevention, simplifying the system, orienting it toward cooperation in providing health rather than competition in shifting cost, and in reducing overall health care costs than we care about continuing as a health insurance company. . . . We hope that we will continue to have a role to play in a new health care system that will enable us to participate in achieving the dream for health care which we have held for more than 40 years. And we hope that the same dream can be achieved for all Americans.[59]

Koontz's letter was never sent to Congress. MMA eventually joined Mennonite Central Committee in calling on legislators to provide universal coverage. But MMA also continued its lobbying efforts focused on an amendment exempting it from other health care alliances and assuring it of an ongoing place in the health insurance field.[60] Ironically, given the current health care provider system and even proposals for reforms, MMA's survival seems inextricably linked to the reality that some persons will fall through the insurance cracks.

## Equity for Vitality

While raising premiums and tightening underwriting guidelines has created its own set of mission-related problems for MMA, it also has contributed toward a financial stability beyond what could have been anticipated—or dreamed of—during the 1987-89 crisis.[61] In contrast to MMA's situation in the late 1980s, in recent years the company has needed to determine what a nonprofit organization does with its surplus profits. "Should a church organization accumulate money, give it back to its members, or give it out to other endeavors?" MMA's chief financial officer Steve Garboden asked during his May 1996 presentation to my Goshen College Christian Ethics class during a field trip to MMA. "Can a church organization get too much money or power?"[62]

Any discussion of MMA's financial resources should note, of course, the company's fraternal programs. These give grants to congregations to make their facilities more handicap-accessible; to couples wanting to adopt a child; to survivors who can't cover funeral expenses of a family member; to individuals who can't pay premiums or basic living expenses during a time of crisis; to students attending Anabaptist-related colleges or seminaries; and for educational and advocacy programs.

In 1995 MMA distributed more than $1.6 million through fraternal grants and in 1996 provided over $2 million in fraternal grants.[63] The purpose of such programs, according to MMA policy, is "to provide a level of fraternal funding which will enable the Association to offer maximum benefits to its members, its participating denominations and institutions and not have an unfair advantage over taxable insurance companies." The intent is "to provide a basis or justification to maintain the tax-exempt status of the organization."[64] The bulk of the fraternal funding is garnered from calculating the "what if" state premium tax and the "what if" federal tax liability MMA would have needed to pay if it were a commercial insurance company.[65]

In essence, because of MMA's fraternal benefit status,[66] the government has allowed the organization to manage and disburse its own federal and premium "taxes" rather than to put them into the larger state and federal pools.[67] In the past, during years when there has been sufficient net income, MMA also has contributed some monies from its own nontax-like funds as well. In 1995 MMA regularized this additional giving to the fraternal funds by allotting a tithe of the company's net gains each year "to reflect the guiding principles of the organization."[68] Such a ten-percent formula allowed for a $624,151 fraternal tithe in 1995.

At this stage in MMA's history, such giving still leaves sufficient funding to support a viable business and provide ample room for rapid expansion. Even after the 1995 fraternal tithe, MMA recorded a $5.3 million profit.[69] But according to industry standards, an agency offering the financial and insurance products MMA does should set aside a certain amount of its prior gains to cover potential extraordinary losses. These could include a huge drop in the stock market, an epidemic, a widespread tragedy affecting many members, or a sudden increase in health care costs.

According to the calculations MMA uses, based on certain percentages of its various holdings and annualized premiums, in 1996 this "reserve" figure totaled about $37.1 million, including $2.8 million for growth and development and $1.8 million for health care inflation.[69]

That is the quantity MMA believes it should have to cover its bases in the event of some catastrophic events and to do ordinary expansion. The total amount of backup equity needed has risen dramatically in the last several years due to increasing assets and product offerings.

From 1986 to 1991, however, MMA was consistently below its targeted equity figure. At its lowest ebb, in 1988, the company had only fifty-five percent of its formula equity in reserve. Since 1992 the agency has reported equity considerably above its target. At the end of 1995, MMA had 153 percent of its formula equity available, meaning that in addition to the targeted amount it had an additional $19.4 million of surplus equity.[71]

The board's goal, said chief financial officer Steve Garboden, is to increase this "additional vitality equity" (the amount beyond that deemed necessary to cover all contingencies and provide for regular growth and development) to $26 million.[72] That amount would permit major expansion in health growth, health competitiveness and risk management, diversification, and distribution system development.

For example, $4 million is allotted for achieving 100,000 health members by the year 2000; $3 million is geared to holding down future rate increases; $7 million will cover life insurance risks, and another $1.5 million will assist with life insurance start-up costs; $3 million is designed for development in the senior market; and $1.6 million will provide incentives for counselors.[73]

In a November 1995 "Explanation of Additional Vitality Equity Entries," Garboden wrote, for example, that "life [insurance] offers great potential for net income margins," and that "through the use of commission overrides on new business of associate counselors, counselors are incented to expand the number of persons offering our products." He indicated that "the Medicare supplement product has served us well. New opportunities are emerging with the probable change in National Legislation for Medicare Plus and Long-Term Care."[74]

Mennonite Mutual Aid clearly is in a rapid-growth mode, prudently seizing the opportunities brought on by its recent financial success and legislative changes. But, as Garboden asked, "Can a church organization get too much money or power?" Or, as Beryl Hartzler Brubaker inquired, "How will we know when our institutional self-interest supersedes our mission?" At what point does a church-related agency such as MMA function too much like its commercial, for-profit counterparts?

The questions may arise both in regard to MMA's reserves as well as its "additional vitality equity." MMA uses industry standards to calculate its necessary reserves. Former MMA CEO Harold Swartzendruber recalled that, as he was working at the reorganization of MMA as a fraternal benefit organization in the mid-1960s, the chief actuary of the Indiana Department of Insurance warned him that the desire to require more reserves was "a failing of actuaries." The actuary's point, noted Swartzendruber, was that as a Mennonite Church agency, "we should resist the examiners and actuaries who were trained to reserve and reserve and then reserve some more just to be safe."[75]

One might also ask how much additional surplus a church-related company should accumulate for dramatic expansion. Is $26 million an appropriate amount—beyond $37.1 million in reserves—to develop other facets of the business? How much surplus, if any amount, is too much? MMA president Howard Brenneman says,

> My thought about this is, you'll have too much surplus the day you run out of new, creative ideas and vision about how to use that and when your members and church either do not see the necessity or quit buying your products or services or quit using them. . . . I'd say you have too much when you're building bigger barns, if you're not using it, not redeploying it, if you're not helping church members in the areas of stewardship and mutual aid. If you have to build bigger barns just to store it, you've got too much. We're not there.[76]

Brenneman reports that when he came to MMA, others in the organization believed that while there had to be some surplus to survive as a business, the margin must be small for the church to accept it. Brenneman recalls that when he began talking about major expansion with surplus profits, Steve Garboden told him, "Howard, you'll never sell this to the church."

But now, indicates Brenneman,

> This has all been very accepted. . . . That whole concept of surplus or profit or whatever, that worldly, terrible word, can suddenly be used for the Lord. . . .We probably have misread the church in that respect in their ability to accept some of these worldly things for the good of the whole. It's a big change of philosophy.[77]

Some, however, have asked whether more of MMA's excess profits could be routed directly through programs that care for the "uninsured or uninsurable," such as loosening up underwriting restrictions, or increasing fraternal funding. Steve Garboden notes that MMA managers have asked that question repeatedly, and

> The answer is. . . . We could take this amount of money and we could probably allow in . . . [maybe] 10 percent of the uninsurables in the Mennonite church, and probably be able to handle that. Now, in doing

that, we've put a Band-Aid™ on a very severe problem and we've utilized what we are starting to think of as the "seed corn" for something that's not going to yield further crop. The hope is that [the expansion plan] yields further crop that allows us to continue to do some of this other area, but it's long term, it's down the road. The Republican term is that it's "trickle down." It is trickle down.[78]

It is true that the more money is generated through MMA products and services, the more money there is available for fraternal benefit programs, since their funding is based on a percentage of profits and premiums. And some of the additional vitality equity goes toward helping hold down premium rates and subsidizing other programs which make MMA's current and future products more accessible.

It is also clear that many of Mennonite Mutual Aid's members or customers prefer to see the company financially strong. This may be particularly true for those who relate most closely with the Mennonite Foundation or who have Praxis Mutual Funds with MMA. In his presentation at the January 1996 "Building Communities of Compassion" conference out of which this book emerged, Brenneman said that some people are calling MMA to be at the water point.[79] "But when you're in business," he said, "people don't want you right at the water point, with your nose just above the water so you'll remain faithful. Our clients don't want us to be there."[80]

With $37.1 million already in reserves, and with "additional vitality equity" well on the way toward $26 million, MMA is not likely to be at the water point for some time. At the May 2-3, 1996, board of directors meeting, the board considered a policy outlining a "Rationale for Margin." The proposed policy said MMA intended "to generate as much financial margin (gains) as possible within the constraints of price competitiveness and moderate underwriting."[81]

The board, which had requested a policy, rejected this initial proposal as appearing "too blatantly, overtly greedy" and sent it back to MMA managers, reported Steve Garboden. "We're working on changing the wording," he added.[82] MMA no doubt will continue to face questions about how its handling of profit differentiates it from other commercial companies in its fields—or whether it should.

# A Real Margin of Difference

Multiple pressures have molded Mennonite Mutual Aid's present structure and function, forcing the agency to walk a rarely traveled road between successful business practices and church-agency status. However, Howard Brenneman and other MMA managers suggest that it is not as overwhelming to hold church and business together as once was thought. "Are these things compatible?" Brenneman asked recently. "I think we're working much more at recognizing how compatible they might be, then also trying to strengthen that compatibility."[83] The MMA CEO cited as examples businesses *and* churches' desires to use good stewardship principles, function effectively, and survive and thrive.

That is not to say, of course, that MMA has not changed in recent years. As MMA has needed to cooperate with other commercial companies to offer competitive values in its products, and as it has needed to respond to legislative changes in health care reform, it has moved closer to other companies in its organizational field. As it has needed to face the reality of staying in business, it has altered the ways in which it can help church members "bear each other's burdens."

As MMA has had to deal with substantial profits, it has been required to sort through appropriate use of such surplus. As it has added new denominations into its potential client pool, it has needed to recognize the distance some clients may have from the company's founding vision. And as it has recognized the acculturation of its original pool of Mennonite constituents, it has faced the perceived need for adjustments in its practices. "We're just not the same church that we were 30 or 40 years ago," said Karl Sommers, MMA's vice president of corporate planning.[84]

In his December 1992 president's report to the MMA board, Brenneman wrote with a defensiveness absent from his more recent reports. "The time has arrived for MMA to answer our critics," he wrote. Brenneman added,

> MMA is not just another insurance or financial services company as some people would suggest. Embodied in our products and services are many aspects of our biblical mandate. In addition to this, we are able to go beyond products and services with premium assistance, adoption allowances, catastrophe aid, community grants, educational resources, and matching contributions—both monetary and voluntary service. MMA's underwriting policies and practices are different. . . . MMA's investment guidelines and the method we use to charge costs to Mennonite Retirement participants and Mennonite Foundation clients reflect that we are more than business. . . . Yes, MMA must practice good business management principles. We must staff with excellent professionals. We must operate under prescribed regulations, but these in *no way* need to be a detriment to our mandate.[85]

MMA's internal reports repeatedly cite the agency's mission statement, which calls the company to lead Anabaptists "toward greater practice of the biblical principles of stewardship and mutual aid," offering "all Anabaptists the opportunity to help each other by sharing financial risks and resources." But great challenges lie ahead. MMA board chair Beryl Hartzler Brubaker's questions remain with us: "How do we lead Mennonites to mutual aid when other sources are leading them down other paths? How will we know when our institutional self-interest supersedes our mission? How do we avoid succumbing to the norms of the world?"

With this strong vision from MMA's board and managers and with close attention to Brubaker's questions, MMA should be in a position to resist some of the commercial insurance and financial services industries' isomorphic tugs toward homogeneity.[86] May Mennonite Mutual Aid's "margin of difference" continue to be a *real* margin and not simply a tool for marketing the same products and services offered commercially by others. May God grant the agency and its administrators sufficient wisdom and integrity to operate differently from others in its organizational fields, remaining deeply rooted in Mennonite understandings of mutual aid and stewardship.[87]

## Notes

1. A person should be honest about his or her biases in writing a paper such as this one. I have long had my health insurance and some retirement monies with Mennonite Mutual Aid. Soon I will probably transfer life insurance and mutual funds to the company because I trust MMA. Whatever criticisms I may have for MMA's isomorphic tendencies come out of a deep appreciation for the company and its stated mission. This paper was first presented at a conference on "Church-Related Institutions" at the Young Center, Elizabethtown College, June 1996.

2. From my notes of Kraybill's presentation, titled "Sharing Our Burdens: Contemporary Issues and Questions," at the "Building Communities of Compassion" conference at AMBS, January 28, 1996. The conference was sponsored by MMA and the Institute of Mennonite Studies. Kraybill added, "Formal institutions like MMA have preserved and perpetuated mutual aid. In this way we can bless bureaucracies: they are the way to achieve the goals of a collective group in an efficient fashion."

3. From my conference notes.

4. The phrase, from Galatians 6:2, is often used in MMA's promotional pieces.

5. In chapter ten, Steven M. Nolt traces the movement from the language of "burial aid" to "life insurance." In the "1996 MMA Corporate Strategic Plan," MMA managers write,

> In today's environment, life insurance has grown to become an essential tool for the family, businesses, and many non-profit institutions. A unique set of circumstances make this the ideal time for MMA to move aggressively into this arena. . . . Life insurance is perhaps the greatest mutual aid tool MMA has to offer, and it is the appropriate tool to lead the growth of MMA's distribution system and help secure a stable future.

From p. 109, 1996 MMA Board Policy Manual housed at MMA.

6. The total assets have risen dramatically in the last several years. This figure is from a May 1998 presentation to my Goshen College Christian Ethics class on a field trip to MMA.

7. This was the last of three points in Miller's summary of a April 10, 1943, meeting of the Committee on Industrial Relations, Chicago, Illinois, I-3-7, Committee on Economic and Social Relations, Archives of the Mennonite Church (hereafter AMC), Goshen, Indiana.

8. From "President's Report to the MMA Board of Directors," p. 5, MMA Board of Directors Meeting Board Book, December 4-5, 1992, not yet catalogued in AMC.

9. This particular quote is from the "1993 MMA Corporate Plan," MMA Board of Directors Meeting Board Book, December 4-5, 1992, not yet catalogued in AMC. Other plans have used similar language, though the description of the "driving force" has undergone some development since the late 1980s (see also the following in-text citation). The 1988 "Corporate Plan Summary" said MMA desired to be a "market needs-driven organization," and the following year's plan said "MMA desires to be a 'Concept-driven Products and Services organization.' " See Box XII-9, 4/7, MMA Board of Directors Minutes and Reports, August 21, 1987, "Corporate Plan Summary," p. 18, and Box XII-9, 4/12, MMA Board of Directors Board Book, "Corporate Plan Summary, " p. 8, AMC.

10. "1996 MMA Corporate Strategic Plan," p. 105, 1996 MMA Board Policy Manual housed at MMA.

11. The six-month study by the trade association cost MMA around $200,000, said Brenneman. Interview with Brenneman, May 28, 1996. Brenneman himself had served as a consultant to MMA in the late 1980s, when he was CEO of Hesston Corporation. He became president of MMA January 1, 1992.

12. Interview with Howard Brenneman, May 28, 1996.

13. It seems to me there may be an unacknowledged and unexplored tension between this "listening to our customers" and Beryl Hartzler Brubaker's suggestion that Mennonites are being led down paths other than that of mutual aid. On this question, see also Yoder (1992). Yoder writes about MMA's Organ Transplant Task Force, which had recommended limiting coverage on organ and tissue transplants in its new health insurance plans. The Task Force's recommendations were not adopted by the board. Yoder, then health systems development manager and educational resources analyst for MMA, wrote that

> My initial disappointment gave way to cynicism when I learned that the recommendation had been overturned by a market survey. The product design had incorporated a $100,000 cap on organ transplant coverage, until a telephone survey revealed that a majority of clients were unwilling to forgo this coverage to achieve a basic benefit plan. Bowing under the pressure of the market, MMA had decided to disregard the recommendation (p. 49).

Yoder said he recognized the various pressures on MMA, including its declining membership at the time, but added,

> I was disappointed that an organization accountable to the church, and one that prides itself on being "more than just insurance," would let market demand eclipse ethical principles. Were my hopes and expectations unreasonable? Should an insurer be expected to put ethics ahead of the market?

How or to what extent can health insurance companies put ethics into practice?

14. John W. Meyer and Brian Rowan, "Institutionalized Organizations: Formal Structure as Myth and Ceremony," in *The New Institutionalism in Organizational Analysis*, ed. by Walter W. Powell and Paul J. DiMaggio (Chicago: University of Chicago Press, 1991), p. 41. In an earlier study, I used DiMaggio and Powell's work to analyze Mennonite Central Committee's Washington lobbying office. See my *Wise as Serpents, Innocent as Doves: American Mennonites Engage Washington* (Knoxville: University of Tennessee Press, 1996), and my "Whirling toward Similitude: Mennonite Lobbyists in the U.S. Capital," *Conrad Grabel Review* 12.3 (Fall 1994): 283-297.

15. DiMaggio and Powell (1991:64-66). On isomorphism, see Jeavons (1994); and the firsthand comments of Bontrager (1996).

16. From "1993 MMA Corporate Plan," November 30, 1992, p. 2, MMA Board of Directors Meeting Board Book, December 4-5, 1992, not yet catalogued in AMC.

17. The three former CPS workers who retired that year were Arthur Jost, Wayne Kempf and Lester Kropf. Former board member and present MMA vice president of operations Shirley Yoder said CPSers brought a "wonderful quality, a compassionate quality" to the board over the years. Interview with Yoder, May 20, 1996.

18. In acknowledging this shift, MMA's Shirley Yoder added, "When you're managing up close to a billion dollars, you need that professionalization." Interview with Yoder, May 20, 1996. Harold L. Swartzendruber, CEO of MMA from 1953 until 1977, said the shift from board members comprised of those from "a variety of occupations chosen for their ability and interest in mutual aid" to professionals with experience in large operations resulted in a "somewhat different skew" in MMA's approach. The change, he said, was from "a creative form that learned from the world but adapted to our concerns" to that of "using professional management principles and forms from the commercial world." From "The Love/Hate Relationship between Mutual Aid and Mennonite Church Relationships," a five-page response Swartzendruber prepared for my interview with him April 5, 1996. Available in my files.

19. The policy is in the MMA Board of Directors' Minutes and Reports, Box XII-9, 4/6, May 8, 1987, and in the MMA Board Policy Manual housed at MMA.

20. Within the Mennonite Church, MMA takes a more active role in the selection process for board members than do the other four MC program boards. In its board election process, the Mennonite Church General Board invites the 21 district conferences to suggest names for the Nominating Committee. Miriam F. Book, interim general secretary, said she writes to the CEOs of each program board and asks what specific needs they have on the board, what types of people they need, with what characteristics and skills. "We welcome that response," said Book. With each of the other program boards, part of the boards are elected, while other members are appointed by the General Board. *MMA's* appointments come from the MMA board itself rather than from the General Board because of MMA's multi-denominational constituency. Most of the program boards reserve specific name suggestions for the *appointment* process rather than the *election* process, Book said. However, MMA is a "very specialized board," Book acknowledged, and sometimes the agency says, "Here is a person we hope you consider

[for the election process]." Book said she is impressed with the internal workings of the board, and its skills at board training and mentoring. Phone interview with Book, May 31, 1996.

21. Emphasis mine. Earlier statements had said, "Mennonites and related groups." The mission statement is found, among other places, in the "1996 MMA Corporate Plan," p. 104, 1996 MMA Board Policy Manual housed at MMA. A straightforward study of language alterations and professionalization of these corporate plans would make an instructive paper of its own.

22. In their debates about how broadly to extend their constituency,

> several board members stated that it is not necessarily the somewhat different theological positions of the denominational groups but rather the possibility of eventual representation on the board of directors that made them question the wisdom of moving ahead. . . . The board expressed agreement that Howard should be free to move ahead with those groups and relationships that are already under way, that no new overtures should be made to other groups at this point, and that no suggestions or insinuations should be made that any of these groups should expect representation on the board of directors as a result of the relationship.

From the minutes of the MMA Board of Directors Meeting, August 14, 1993, not yet catalogued in AMC.

23. The quote is from Howard Brenneman in "50 Years and Beyond," the 1995 MMA Annual Report, p. 5. To this end, a primary goal of MMA in the last several years has been to increase its field sales staff. In the earlier decades of MMA's health insurance products (until about 1984), its "counselors" were volunteers in local congregations. A new system was implemented in 1984, which, as for other products now offered by MMA, used professional counselors paid at least in part on a commission basis. MMA also provides special incentives to its counselors to encourage building agencies "in order to penetrate the area assigned to them." See "MMA Agency Builder Overrides," I.D. No. VI-A-21, 1996 MMA Board Policy Manual housed at MMA.

In a July 9, 1993 letter to the MMA Board of Directors, then-board member Ted Koontz asked,

> What do our incentive structures tell our representatives to tell people about buying insurance products, etc.? Do we, as an institution of the Mennonite church, provide them with incentives to sometimes sell less of our products if they are not "needed," on the one hand, or can't really be afforded on the other? Or do we assume, in the way we structure our incentives, that it is always good stewardship and good mutual aid to have our representatives encourage everyone to buy more of all of our products.

Koontz's questions seem valid in the face of rapid expansion plans. Letter from my files.

24. The member figure is taken from the 1995 MMA Annual Report. The total constituency is from Dean Preheim-Bartel's presentation to my Christian Ethics class, May 14, 1996. The 10 percent figure is from Howard Brenneman's presentation at the "Building Communities of Compassion" conference, January 28, 1996, and the twelve percent figure is derived from dividing the numbers in the text. The low percentage is partly because so many Mennonites have their insurance through their workplaces and for other reasons noted in the text below.

25. In a May 26, 1996 interview discussion with Steve Garboden, chief fi-

nancial officer at MMA, I had suggested that MMA was risking becoming so financially independent (see also below on "additional vitality equity") that it no longer needed the church. Garboden said I was probably thinking of the church in its institutional forms, whereas MMA tends to think more about the grassroots church—which the organization is *entirely* dependent on for its survival. This understanding of the church, while true, still gnaws at me a bit. This "church" is what MMA elsewhere refers to as "clients" or "customers," and such persons' needs and desires—at least in the contexts where MMA hears them—do not necessarily reflect the principles of the larger church. See also my footnote 13.

In personal correspondence, Scot D. Yoder wrote,

> I think that MMA makes the mistake of assuming that the purchasing decisions of their clients reflect religious convictions and are thus indicative of the church. In general people do not make such purchases or investments as church members or based primarily on religious conviction. I believe this is confirmed by marketing surveys which indicate that people will not pay extra for MMA's products.

See also below on this last point. E-mail correspondence from Scot D. Yoder to Keith Graber Miller, June 26, 1996.

26. From "1996 MMA Corporate Strategic Plan," 1996 MMA Board Policy Manual housed at MMA, p. 104.

27. Indemnity insurance, according to a handout prepared by MMA's Daniel Grimes, is a plan that pays

> specific dollar amounts to the insured individual for specified services and procedures without guaranteeing complete coverage for the full cost of healthcare services. These policies limit a subscriber's liability for claims incurred to a preset amount, usually with deductibles, copayments, and co-insurance up to a preset limit for out of pocket expenses, but with a maximum payment by the insurer. . . . The insured may use any physician or hospital.

28. From the 1996 MMA Board Policy Manual housed at MMA, p. 105.

29. This is also true for reinsurance, as noted in the text below, and MMA's new mutual funds, where MMA does the advisory work and sales but has another company do the regulatory work and record-keeping.

30. Shirley Yoder noted that this simply means providers participate in cost-shifting: they transfer higher costs onto those who have insurance with noncontracted companies. She also suggested that there is some discomfort with now being part of the larger pool of those receiving discounts, since that likely means costs are being shifted to someone else. Interview with Shirley Yoder, May 20, 1996.

Howard Brenneman also noted that some of the companies with whom MMA works—including such Mennonite-related ones as Oaklawn in Goshen—see this as good stewardship. "When we first went to Oaklawn [to negotiate prices for services], they said they were wondering when MMA was going to come and ask for a better price. . . . It was an expectation that good stewards would negotiate price." Interview with Brenneman, 28 May 1996.

31. At two points—during the 1987-89 premium rate-hike and underwriting period mentioned below, and also during the 1992-94 period of attempts at national health care reform—MMA considered getting entirely out of the health insurance industry, though this would have been less tempting in recent years

when the health plans have been making a considerable profit. See the minutes of the MMA Board of Directors Meeting, December 3, 1993, not yet catalogued in AMC.

32. Interview with Daniel Grimes, May 21, 1996.

33. This description is from the "Central Kansas Managed Care Organization Delivery System Model," July 19, 1995, Attachment X, Managed Care Report, MMA Board of Directors Meeting Board Book, September 8-9, 1995.

34. In northern Indiana and sometimes elsewhere, MMA has helped develop the managed care organization, owning a portion of it and then selling off its interest. For more on recent managed care network developments, see Daniel B. Grimes to J. Jerry Troyer, April 15, 1996, Attachment XIV to the Managed Care Report, MMA Board of Directors Board Book May 2-3, 1996, and J. Jerry Troyer's full Managed Care Report in the same location, not yet catalogued in AMC.

35. Interview with Daniel Grimes, May 21, 1996.

36. *Ibid.*

37. From "Mennonite Mutual Aid Association—Total," MMA Board of Directors Meeting Minutes and Reports, August 10-11, 1989, Box XII-9, 4/12 in AMC. The year of the $3,923,558 reported loss was 1988.

38. Steve Garboden reported that MMA experienced three consecutive years—1988, 1989, 1990—of fifteen percent declines in the number of its health plan memberships. Interview with Garboden, May 23, 1996.

39. Interview with Shirley Yoder, May 20, 1996. Steve Garboden said, "At one point we thought the power of mutual aid would make people willing to pay more. We no longer believe that." Interview with Garboden, May 23, 1996. Karl Sommers, vice president of corporate planning, said in 1992-93 MMA did a thorough study of what financial impact loosening up underwriting standards would have on MMA. Sommers said Sid Richard, MMA's health actuary, had calculated that premiums would need to rise in the range of 85 percent to 100 percent in order to remove underwriting standards. "I now recall that when we saw his initial estimates, and the actual additional dollars that would have been needed to subsidize this additional cost, we felt the cost of doing this would be far greater than what our existing members would be willing to pay," said Sommers.

Sommers also reported that in a 1987 MMA survey of 2,900 members and over 130 employers, MMA learned that if its prices were 10 percent higher than other insurers, two out of five individuals and one out of two employers would cancel their MMA policies and go to another competitor. If MMA's prices were 20 percent higher, one out of two individuals and seven out of 10 employers would cancel their policies with MMA. "There is a smaller minority who is willing to pay more to help others and will stay with MMA regardless of price," the 1987 research suggested. According to the survey, three out of seven individuals indicated this position, and three in 10 employers said the same. Faxed four-page message from Karl Sommers to Keith Graber Miller, June 11, 1996.

40. Until 1987 the policy was "underwrite as few people as possible, and only assign waiting periods in the underwriting process." From a memo from Karl Sommers, Jerry Troyer, and Laban Peachey to Division Management, April 15, 1987, available in MMA Board of Directors Meeting Minutes and Reports, May 8, 1987, Box XII-9, 4/6 in AMC. On the issue of MMA's underwriting, see also Yoder (1992).

41. From "A Dream for an Alternative MMA Congressional Testimony

(Witness) on Health Care Reform," May 6, 1994. The letter by Ted Koontz, who later resigned from the board, was a response to MMA's lobbying posture. Koontz was arguing for a very different approach than that which MMA was taking, and his letter was suggesting what MMA "ought to say on health care if we would put first things first." Although the larger context of Koontz's letter was in basic disagreement with the direction of MMA in its lobbying efforts, the paragraph cited here likely would speak for a number of board members at the time. The letter was never sent to members of Congress. Letter from my files.

42. From "Recommendation No. 7," Mutual Aid Services Committee, April 22, 1987, in MMA Board of Directors Meeting Minutes and Reports, May 8, 1987, Box XII-9, 4/6 in AMC.

43. This and the following quotes in this paragraph are from a memo from Karl Sommers, Jerry Troyer, and Laban Peachey to Division Management, April 15, 1987, in MMA Board of Directors Meeting Minutes and Reports, May 8, 1987, Box XII-9, 4/6 in AMC.

44. Today a total of about 57,320 persons are enrolled in MMA health plans, up about 15,000 from three years ago. From "All Plans Growth," Attachment F in the Managed Care Report, MMA Board of Directors Meeting Board Book, May 2-3, 1996, not yet catalogued in AMC. Steve Garboden noted that during the health cost crisis of the late 1980s MMA tested with congregations some noninsurance-type models of mutual aid, but these were not attractive to pastors and congregational leaders without the insurance mechanism, since congregations would take on additional risks. Interview with Garboden, May 23, 1996.

45. From the quite thorough "Report and Recommendation of the Health Strategy Task Force," September 21-23, 1988, p. 18, MMA Board of Directors Meeting Board Book, December 2, 1988, Box XII-9, 4/11 in AMC. The report said giving up on poor risks and instituting strict underwriting "is contrary to MMA's mission," and "should not be our first choice." Earlier, on p. 13, the report said, "We are caught between these conflicting needs of serving the church and being a sound business. We cannot fulfill both needs in our current environment without broad support from the church." In regard to underwriting and other tough decisions, CEO Howard Brenneman said, "There's trade-offs. . . . You have to look at the institution and its survival and its ability to carry out the mandate the church has given it rather than to look at each case. So it's that area of ambiguity." Interview with Brenneman, May 28, 1996. Brenneman said he's heard Mennonite ethicist J. Lawrence Burkholder talk about ambiguity, and "When I really get to stumbling around, I visit with him at breakfast."

46. Both Steve Garboden and Shirley Yoder mentioned this in my interviews with them, as did other MMA staff members in presentations to my Christian Ethics class.

47. From "Minutes of the Mutual Aid Services Committee," April 27, 1988, p. 4, MMA Board of Directors Meeting Minutes and Reports, August 11-12, 1988, Box XII-9, 4/10 in AMC. Still today, of course, a person who becomes infected after joining an MMA life or health plan will be covered for AIDS and AIDS related illnesses according to "AIDS: MMA's Responsibilities as a Mutual Aid Organization," I.D. No. V-I-12, 1996 MMA Board Policy Manual housed at MMA.

48. From "Minutes of the Mutual Aid Services Committee," April 27, 1988, p. 3, MMA Board of Directors Meeting Minutes and Reports, August 11-12, 1988, Box XII-9, 4/10 in AMC.

49. *Ibid.*

50. Shirley Yoder said, for instance, that Lincoln National will cover health expenses over $300,000, up to $1,000,000. If MMA accepts a person against the Lincoln National underwriting guidelines, it takes on an additional $700,000 in risk. Interview with Yoder, May 20, 1996. In his March 28, 1996 presentation to my Christian Ethics class, Steve Garboden said, "We adopt industry practices in this regard [underwriting]. We don't have the time to develop all of our own screens."

51. Interview with Shirley Yoder, May 20, 1996.

52. From "Underwriting Guidelines," I.D. No. IV-D-3-1, 1996 MMA Board Policy Manual housed at MMA.

53. From a presentation by Steve Garboden to my Christian Ethics class, March 28, 1996. Garboden suggested that among the reasons Mennonites may more frequently use mental health care services are that CPS workers were on the forefront of mental health reform in the U.S. and many Mennonites now enter mental health care professions. Mennonites therefore have less of a stigma about using mental health services.

54. From "Average Submitted Claims Per Member Per Year," an overhead used by Steve Garboden for my Christian Ethics class, March 28, 1996.

55. From "Highlights of Mental Health Plan," an overhead used by Steve Garboden for my Christian Ethics class, March 28, 1996, and Garboden's explanation. One of the most poignant and difficult moments in my field trips to MMA came on this visit when a Mennonite student who has struggled with clinical depression discovered, in the midst of asking questions during Garboden's presentation, that she would not be able to get full insurance coverage through MMA when she was married that summer. Shirley Yoder said she recently asked an underwriters' association official for the name of a mental health underwriting expert. The official said he wasn't aware of any such expert, since mental health is not a major part of most insurers' plans. Interview with Yoder, May 20, 1996.

56. From "AIDS: MMA's Responsibilities as a Church Agency," I.D. No. V-I-11, 1996 MMA Board Policy Manual housed at MMA.

57. Mary Swartley, "Report of the Board Chair to the Mennonite Mutual Aid Board of Directors," December 7, 1991, MMA Board of Directors Meeting Board Book, December 7, 1991, Box XII-9, 4/24 in AMC. She notes that the executive committee and staff did some brainstorming about alternatives in 1990, but that the problem was not yet resolved. "It still seems there must be a way in which we can design a plan in which each congregation pays a per member fee to be a part of a churchwide health insurance plan that is unregulated and spreads the risks and the losses for all members."

58. Howard Brenneman reported that "without a level playing field requiring all companies to provide universal access, for MMA to try to be on the leading edge with this concept would result in MMA becoming insolvent in approximately three years." See the health care reform report in the minutes of the December 3, 1993 MMA Board Meeting, not yet catalogued in AMC.

59. From "A Dream for an Alternative MMA Congressional Testimony (Witness) on Health Care Reform," May 6, 1994.

60. See Koontz's 1994 "Dream" and minutes of MMA's subsequent board meetings. For MCC's perspective, see, e.g., Karl Shelly's "Health Care Questions & Answers: Mennonite Call for Universal Coverage Needed," *Washington Memo* (May-June 1994), p. 4.

61. The Board of Directors' meeting minutes and staff reports from the late 1980s were terribly heavy—even depressing—to read. Those from the last five years are consistently and increasingly upbeat, light, and hopeful. This may be partly because of a change in top administrative personnel but also reflects the reversed financial status of the company.

62. From my notes of Garboden's presentation at his May 14, 1996 presentation to my Christian Ethics class.

63. The $1.6 million figure is from "50 Years and Beyond," the 1995 MMA Annual Report, p. 13. The estimate for 1996 fraternal giving is from Dean Preheim-Bartel's presentation to my Christian Ethics class, May 14, 1996.

64. From "Fraternal Funding Formula," I.D. No. V-E-4, 1996 MMA Board Policy Manual housed at MMA.

65. *Ibid.* The policy says, "The detailed formula used to generate fraternal funds will not generally be communicated to our constituency. . . . The focus of our communications efforts will be on the sharing that occurs among members." My sense is that these factors make it difficult for MMA with integrity to draw too much on its fraternal benefit funding as providing a significant "margin of difference" from commercial companies. On the other hand, one must recognize that feeding $1.5 to $2 million back into the church is a good thing, particularly since some of the money is used as matching grants, which generate additional "mutual aid" from congregations and their members. It also allows MMA a certain amount of control over what projects, programs, and new directives will be funded in the church, since MMA has more of such discretionary money than do other church agencies.

66. MMA has been a fraternal benefit organization since 1965. This status allows its nonprofit corporate entities to be tax-exempt as long as what would have been tax liability is used for charitable purposes. The development of MMA's fraternal benefit status is described by Nolt in chapter ten of this book.

67. MMA *does* pay taxes on the earnings of its corporate entities which are not tax-exempt.

68. From "Tithing Gain," I.D. No. V-I-19, 1996 MMA Board Policy Manual housed at MMA. MMA should be affirmed for its decision to begin tithing from its net profits. Of course, some other profitable, Mennonite-owned, commercial companies also contribute generously to church causes from their surplus.

69. The exact figure is $5,349,332. From "Mennonite Mutual Aid Entities Combined Income, Expense, Equity and Assets for the Year Ended December 31, 1995," MMA Board of Directors Meeting Board Book, May 2-3, 1996, not yet catalogued in AMC. In the span of only a few years, MMA has managed to turn around a loss of about $4 million in its worst year to a profit of between $6 million and $8 million per year. See MMA's annual reports since 1991.

70. The figures are from "Exhibit 2: Mennonite Mutual Aid Association Comparison of Actual to Formula Equity," March 31, 1996, a one-page description of the way MMA figures its formula equity. Available from Steve Garboden.

71. From "MMA As of 12/31/95," an overhead used by Steve Garboden in his presentation to my Christian Ethics class, May 14, 1996, and "Exhibit 2, Administrative Services Report," MMA Board of Directors Meeting Board Book, May 2-3, 1996, not yet catalogued in AMC.

72. From Garboden's May 14, 1996, presentation to my Christian Ethics class.

73. From "Exhibit 2, Administrative Services Report," MMA Board of Directors Meeting Board Book, May 2-3, 1996, not yet catalogued in AMC.

74. "Explanation of Additional Vitality Equity Entries, Administrative Services Report," MMA Board of Directors Meeting Board Book, May 2-3, 1996, not yet catalogued in AMC. "Today we do better at responding to what people want in a way that provides good value for them than we had in the past," said Karl Sommers, MMA's vice president of corporate planning. Interview with Sommers, April 3, 1996.

75. From "The Love/Hate Relationship Between Mutual Aid and Mennonite Church Relationships," a five-page response Swartzendruber prepared for my interview with him April 5, 1996. Available in my files. Much has changed in health care, business, and the church since the 1960s, of course.

76. Interview with Brenneman, May 28, 1996.

77. Interview with Brenneman. The CEO added, "Our fraternal status is only good if you need to pay taxes. If you don't need to pay taxes, it doesn't make any difference." In other words, the more profit MMA makes, the more it sets aside for fraternal funds.

78. Interview with Steve Garboden, May 23, 1996. The 10 percent figure was simply a rough estimate, not a precise figure.

79. Brenneman may have been responding, in part, to my response to Joe Kotva's paper, "Mutual Aid as 'Practice'," at the "Building Communities of Compassion Conference." There I said,

> We should at least note the irony that the church agency responsible for leading in the areas of mutual aid and stewardship is enormously secure financially while nearly all of its sibling church institutions cut corners, right-size and otherwise reduce in the face of repeated shortfalls. What does it mean to be the "mutual aid" institution in the face of such great disparity?

This may say as much about the other church institutions as about MMA, and certainly institutions ought not be kept alive if they no longer serve a purpose in the church. On the question of aiding other institutions, Steve Garboden said, noting the areas MMA has marked for growth, "You have to look at these categories and say, is it clear that sister agencies have a better use for these resources than these identify? I'd imagine that we'd come out all over the board on that question." Interview with Garboden, May 23, 1996.

80. From my January 28, 1996 conference notes. In my response to Joe Kotva's paper, I also asked whether it was possible that some of MMA's programs and promotions negatively impact the practice of mutual aid. I might ask a similar question about MMA's *institutional* modeling of the need for mutual aid at a time when it has sufficient reserves and millions in "additional vitality equity."

> In regard to MMA's various programs, I said at the January conference,

> When we buy insurance of various types, and when we plan so carefully for our futures, do we protect ourselves from the vulnerability necessary to be sensitive to those around us with needs? In other words, if the reciprocal nature of mutual aid requires mutual dependence, helping others and receiving assistance, *needing* other people, do we find *too much* security in protecting ourselves through MMA's multiple programs? With MMA, do we still *need* each other in our face-to-face interactions or in our congregations? Is the unintentional goal of some programs to eliminate our *need* for mutual aid? And do we criticize those who haven't planned as wisely as

we have? This point may be the sense in which mutual aid practices are most threatened.

The language here draws somewhat on Ted Koontz's July 9, 1993 letter to MMA board members and his August 1994 presentation to the board. All materials from my files.

81. "Rationale for Margin," no I.D. number because of nonacceptance by the board, from an overhead used in Steve Garboden's May 14, 1996 presentation to my Christian Ethics class. In the proposed policy, "moderate underwriting is defined as health screening that is slightly more generous than most companies. It describes our practices during the mid-1990s."

82. From Steve Garboden's May 14, 1996 presentation to my Christian Ethics class.

83. Interview with Howard Brenneman, May 28, 1996.

84. Interview with Karl Sommers, April 3, 1996.

85. "President's Report to the MMA Board of Directors," December 1992, MMA Board of Directors Meeting Board Book, December 4-5, 1992, not yet catalogued in AMC. Emphasis in original. Later in the report, Brenneman said,

> Building our distribution network has been identified as one of our major strategies for 1993 and beyond. We want to do this in an umbrella fashion and will be concentrating on leading with our margin of difference. This will require a much higher level of synergy between our sales and fraternal arms than has occurred in the past.

In my interview with Brenneman May 28, 1996, he said,

> I really believed in the margin of difference of our product and that the church could be highly competitive with the product we sell and still go beyond the product with the whole fraternal thing and all that, and if you've done that well and packaged that well, people would buy into that and it would be a way of serving out the mandate the church had given us. And some of the thought here was that that was just slick marketing. To me it was very much a part of who we were.

86. For some specific recommendations about what health insurers such as MMA might do to work at health care reform and justice issues, see also the closing pages of Yoder (1992).

87. An assumption of this paper has been that church-related institutions *should* function differently than similar commercial businesses. Based on its mission statement and repeated references in presidents' and board chairs' reports, MMA also believes this. In a paper titled "Church-Related Institutions: Signs of God's Reign?" Ted Koontz (1996) provided a theological/ethical backdrop for such an understanding. Koontz's AMBS syllabus for his "Ethics for Church Institutions" course says,

> If we believe that Christian ethics make a difference, then it seems reasonable to assume that a church organization should operate in some ways differently from those other organizations which have no connection to Christian faith . . . and perhaps that Mennonite church institutions should operate differently from other church institutions operating out of different theological/ethical frameworks.

The tension is in sorting out what those differences should be, and to what extent the differences should be evident in a business which wants to be viable.

## References

Bontrager, Herman
   1996   "Mission, Image and Promotion." Unpublished paper presented at the Church-Related Institutions Conference at Elizabethtown College, June.

Chaves, Mark
   1993   "Denominations as Dual Structures: An Organizational Analysis." *Sociology of Religion* 54 (Summer): 147-169.

DiMaggio, Paul J., and Walter W. Powell
   1991   "The Iron Cage Revisited: Institutional Isomorphism and Collective Rationality." In *The New Institutionalism in Organizational Analysis*, Chicago: University of Chicago Press. Pp. 63-82.

Graber Miller, Keith
   1996   *Wise as Serpents, Innocent as Doves: American Mennonites Engage Washington.* Knoxville: University of Tennessee Press.

Jeavons, Thomas H.
   1994   *When the Bottom Line is Faithfulness: Management of Christian Service Organizations.* Bloomington, Ind.: Indiana University Press.

Koontz, Ted
   1996   "Church-Related Institutions: Signs of God's Reign?" Paper presented at the Church-Related Institutions Conference at Elizabethtown College, June.

Meyer, John W., and Brian Rowan
   1991   "Institutionalized Organizations: Formal Structure as Myth and Ceremony. In *The New Institutionalism in Organizational Analysis*, ed. Walter W. Powell and Paul J. DiMaggio. Chicago: University of Chicago Press. Pp. 41-62.

Yoder, Scot D.
   1992   "Transplants, Justice, and Health Care Reform." *Second Opinion* 18.1 (July): 49-67.

## 13

# The Changing Face of Corporate Care

## Donald B. Kraybill

In this concluding and summarizing essay, Donald B. Kraybill traces major ways in which the nature of mutual aid has evolved and changed in the twentieth-century Mennonite church. After identifying the social and cultural shifts in the larger society that have prodded the changes, Kraybill sketches a profile of the differences between informal and formal modes of corporate care. He suggests that formal programs like Mennonite Mutual Aid embody a Mennonite margin of difference in comparison to other commercial insurance companies.

As preceding chapters of this book have shown, Mennonite life is rife with examples of mutual aid that stretch from its early European beginnings to present day. Most expressions of aid in the first four centuries of Mennonite history (1525-1925) were spontaneous responses to material need on the local level that involved informal sharing of food, clothing, and shelter. These expressions of corporate care included work frolics to help the sick and injured, communal efforts to clean up after storm and fire, and alms offerings to aid the poor or widows within local congregations.

A few of these early efforts to aid brothers and sisters within the church were formally organized. For instance, Mennonites living in villages in Russia in the nineteenth century created several forms of organized mutual aid. These included mutual credit banks, aid to widows, orphanages, fire and storm assistance plans, as well as other forms of economic support. The first formally organized fire aid plan was established in West Prussia (Germany) in 1623. Although some of the early ventures in mutual aid were officially organized, many of them were spontaneous and informal responses to needs that arose within local congregations.

The most striking feature of Mennonite mutual aid in twentieth-century North America is the extent of its formal organization. Like other North Americans, Mennonites discovered that the brand of social organization which the German sociologist Max Weber tagged bureaucracy provided the most efficient and predictable means of delivering mutual aid. At the century's turn, Mennonite institution-building impulses which first organized mission boards, publishing houses, and colleges were also applied to the need for mutual care. The formally organized vehicles for providing mutual aid were more reliable and dependable in meeting large-scale need than unpredictable and informal efforts on the local level. Moreover, larger-scale aid plans were able to spread risk across a much broader population.

**Table 1.** *Mennonite mutual aid organizations established 1850-1954 in North America*

|  | 1850-1899 | 1900-1956 | Total |
|---|---|---|---|
| Property Insurance | 12 | 24 | 36 |
| Automobile Insurance |  | 7 | 7 |
| Burial Aid Societies | 1 | 13 | 14 |
| Medical/Hospital |  | 6 | 6 |
| Loan Aid Plans |  | 6 | 6 |
| Homes for the Aged |  | 38 | 38 |
| Children's Homes |  | 7 | 7 |
| Hospitals |  | 14 | 14 |
| **TOTAL** | **13** | **115** | **128** |

Source: extrapolated from *The Mennonite Encyclopedia*, Vol III: 799-800.

As shown in Table 1, about 115 mutual aid organizations were established in North American Mennonite communities between 1900 and 1956. Property insurance plans, especially those designed to provide protection from fire and storm, were taking root in the last half of the nineteenth century. The changing structure of an industrializing society brought the need for automobile insurance, burial aid, homes for the elderly, and medical assistance. The rapid rise of formal mutual aid organizations in the twentieth century reflected the major structural shifts underway in the larger society.

## The Shifting Social Context

The twentieth century brought a variety of changes to the church and the larger society which have altered some of the historic practices of mutual aid. Several structural and ideological shifts had pertinent ramifications which changed the face of corporate care across the Mennonite church. Growing *urbanization* brought greater interdependence with the larger society and weakened the significance of social ties in the local community. Individuals, families, and congregations, for a variety of reasons, became less anchored and focused on the local community and more oriented to the broader national and international culture. A sense of rootedness in a local community where congregation, family, friendship, and social life overlapped had provided a rich soil for informal expressions of mutual aid. In the course of the century, this soil eroded somewhat with the currents of industrialization and urbanization.

Greater geographic and social *mobility* in the twentieth century has unraveled the ties of individuals to stable and enduring communities. We are often strangers in transit—on the move between jobs, homes, marriages, communities, and congregations. Few persons live from birth to death in the same community or congregation. The stable structures and networks of care, which characterized many local congregations and extended families of the past, have been disrupted by the transitory nature of modern life. The rise of small and mobile nuclear families means few individuals have the support of extended families in the local community as was often the case in the past and which continues today in many Old Order Anabaptist communities. Stable and enduring communities as well as thick family networks provided a safety net of care that was mobilized as needs arose.

Urbanization and mobility are coupled with *occupational specialization*. As many Mennonites abandoned their plows in the early and mid-twentieth century, they entered a variety of professional and nonprofessional jobs in the larger society. The occupational shift carried implications for the practice of mutual aid. The daily life of church members was less visible because they were working away from home often outside the confines of the local neighborhood. Friendship networks were expanding, diversifying and separating from one another. The income from professional jobs enabled some people to become financially self-sufficient and less dependent on the church for aid.

Most important, in the last half of the twentieth century, many jobs carried significant fringe benefits. These economic perks provided various forms of health and disability insurance as well as pension plans which also weakened economic ties to the church. Moreover, as men and women entered the professional workforce in recent years, fewer families had spare hours to share as volunteers in aid-related activities. These occupation-driven changes helped to revise the complexion of corporate care in the church.

At the ideological level, there was a growing *rationalization* in the larger culture as both individual and corporate levels emphasized having plans, goals, and strategies. Indifference to planning is surely considered one of the cardinal sins of modern culture. Individuals and groups alike are expected to plan for the future. Such planning typically includes preparations for unforeseen hardship, accident, or calamity. Increasingly, Mennonites who did not plan appropriately, by enrolling in insurance plans or buying life insurance, were seen as irresponsible people. They were deemed callous and careless about the needs of their loved ones.

In tandem with the emphasis on rational control was a growing spirit of *individualism* at the very core of North American culture. This pervasive value accented the importance of individual responsibility and accountability. With the decline of local communities and shrinking extended families, individuals were increasingly expected to take responsibility for their own affairs and those of their families and not to shuck them off on the church by default. In the case of fire, some Mennonites would grumble and only grudgingly give to an offering lifted for a fellow member who had neglected to buy adequate fire insurance.

Other changes afoot in North American society also prodded revisions in the delivery of mutual aid because they built on the cultural values of rationalization and individualization. The development of *commercial insurance* programs, proliferating in the twentieth century, offered church members a variety of commercial products to protect them from loss. Third party insurance carriers became the standard way of protecting individuals against all sorts of risks. The availability and attractiveness of commercial programs made them appear superior, at least on the surface, to the homegrown aid programs of the church.

Forward-looking church members who wanted dependable insurance often opted for the commercial programs.

Moreover, *social welfare* services provided by the state also proliferated in the course of the twentieth century. Social security payments and medical subsidies became available to help the elderly. Other social support programs aided the disabled and the destitute. Unemployment and disability insurance helped the unemployed and those injured on the job. Federal programs for disaster assistance also offered subsidy for the victims of flood and storm. Greater access to legal help enabled the injured and insulted to use litigation to redress their grievances. In Canada national health insurance provided Mennonites public access to health care. Corporate care distributed by the hand of government became a growing reality in the aftermath of the Great Depression.

All of these changes had a profound impact on the nature and need for mutual aid in Mennonite communities. The availability of commercial insurance, the benefits attached to many jobs, and the safety net provided by government programs eroded the dependence of many people on the church for mutual aid. The growing emphasis on individual responsibility and planning led many Mennonites to buy commercial insurance policies to protect and provide for their families rather than to worry about how the church might respond in the face of disaster. Not all members were covered by commercial programs, and many preferred to be insured through the less professionalized church programs, but the move to commercial insurance certainly accelerated throughout the decades of the twentieth century.

The mobility of members and the geographical expansion of the church, as well as the need for a larger base of customers to share risk, made it increasingly difficult for local congregations to provide adequate spontaneous coverage for their members. The development of regional and national Mennonite aid societies by mid century enabled the church to spread risk across a larger base and to provide nearly the equivalent of commercial insurance under the umbrella of the church.

As noted earlier, bureaucratic forms of social organization in the church as well as in the broader culture became the optimal vehicles for achieving collective goals with the least use of resources. Formal organizations, built on the bureaucratic principles identified by Max Weber, were deemed the most efficient means of organizing human and economic resources to meet strategic objectives. This tendency toward formal organization in the broader society would, in time, change the face of corporate care in the Mennonite church as well.

In summary, the structural and ideological changes in American society in the twentieth century have produced three significant and enduring changes: (1) the rise of commercial and government aid, (2) the emergence of formal agencies in the church that provide insurance and other forms of aid, and (3) the decline of many traditional patterns of aid which were often typical in rural Mennonite communities. All of these transitions have altered the complexion of Mennonite aid in the twentieth century.

# Multiple Modes of Mutual Aid

The rise of mutual aid organizations has created a dual system of aid in Mennonite circles which provides formal *and* informal care. The *formal* modes of care are organized according to standard bureaucratic principles. Examples include church-owned insurance plans for motor vehicles, property, and medical expenses. The *informal* patterns of aid are typically spontaneous responses to a particular need on the local level. On occasion an urgent need—a drought or flood—may trigger a spontaneous response of regional or national scope, but, typically, informal responses to need occur quietly at the local level. In recent years, the term *mutual aid* has been an overarching label stretching across traditional forms of spontaneous aid as well as the evolving programs of formal aid.

Significant differences underlie these different forms of aid. At first glance spontaneous aid seems more genuine—a simple heartfelt care for the plight of a sister or brother. But despite its warm spontaneous character, informal aid is always unpredictable and uncertain. The routinized character of formal plans assures predictability and spreads risk across larger numbers of people. Some of the differences that distinguish informal from formal patterns are profiled in Table 2.

*Table 2. Differences between informal and formal patterns of mutual aid*

**INFORMAL <** ——————————————— **> FORMAL**

| INFORMAL | | FORMAL |
|---|---|---|
| Relational | AUTHORITY | Contractual |
| Communal | ORGANIZATION | Bureaucratic |
| Local | SCOPE | Regional/National |
| Spontaneous | RESPONSE | Standardized |
| Generalist | PERSONNEL | Specialist |
| Voluntary | LABOR | Compensated |
| Contributions | RESOURCES | Premiums |
| Generosity | MOTIVATION | Self/family interest |
| Collective | MODE | Individualistic |

The *formal aid* programs are typically organized as an insurance company, where clients pay a premium in return for the promise of coverage in the event of accident, storm, or injury. The risk is shared among all the client subscribers. Formal policies set the premiums and specify the acceptable amounts and limits of compensation for loss. Formal aid programs are *predictable*. Clients know what to expect in the event of injury or loss. Premiums, from the client's perspective, are viewed as prepayment for possible future losses. The formal plans are *rationalized* in explicit policies and procedures which specify expectations, guidelines, and regulations. And while many cases require decision making and judgment calls, the bulk of the decisions have been decided in advance by policy stipulations.

Formal plans of mutual aid are typically *institutionalized*. Bureaucratic organizations are the most efficient means of delivering the maximum care with the fewest resources in a predictable fashion. Formal organizations are *specialized*. Specialists employed by mutual aid agencies are responsible for administering the programs of aid. The specialists are *compensated* for their work. As in other formal organizations, employees expect to be paid for their work. Managers of formal plans must balance premiums against risks to insure that the program is *profitable* and operates with adequate reserves to meet any avalanche of possible claims in the face of disaster.

Systematic *premiums* provide the primary source of income. *Self-interest* is relatively high. Customers pay the premiums out of self interest to protect themselves and/or their family against possible and unforeseen losses. The transactions are primarily *individualistic* and *contractual*. They are enacted between clients and agents without the communal involvement or social activities of the traditional work frolics which promote collective solidarity or communal self actualization. Whereas a barn raising might energize a local community in work, food, and fellowship for several days, the insurance check to cover the loss of a fire is handled privately through a small number of individual transactions.

In sharp contrast, *informal means* of providing aid are *spontaneous* and often *unpredictable*. In many Mennonite communities over the centuries, individuals in need could expect help if they were caught in material distress. Often the aid was quietly ritualized through traditional practices. These might include an alms fund, the duties of the deacon, a harvest bee, and other work-related frolics. Guided by established norms, the aid was a spontaneous response to a particular need.

Such informal communal efforts targeted on a particular need were not rationalized by written policies or guidelines. They were directed by the authority of *traditional* norms designed to care for the needy in the community of faith. Although established traditions guided the provision of aid, it was not administered through formal organizations. Apart from the leadership role of a deacon, an ordained leader, a foreman at a barn raising, and others who led mutual aid efforts, there were no specialists. No one was compensated for time. Indeed, a key factor in the matrix of traditional mutual aid is the *voluntary* contribution of labor and supplies to the party in need.

*Sacrifice* rather than self-interest motivated members of the community. Members sacrificially contributed their energy, labor, and goods to aid a sister or brother. The only self-interest was the expectation of reciprocal care in the event of their own need some day. The motivating force in the minds of individual members was a compassionate and heartfelt response to the needs of fellow members as guided by established norms of aid.

The informal patterns were collective responses which usually involved several persons, if not an entire congregation, in ritual events, sometimes called frolics, which blended work and play in the mission of mutual aid. These collective events enhanced communal solidarity and fellowship. They were ritual reminders that underscored the theological values of mutual care. Such moments also contributed to communal self-actualization. In responding to need, the community defined itself as a compassionate community that cared for the unfortunate in its midst.

Although formal and informal patterns are polar ends of a spectrum of care, many types of aid combine both types together. One form is not inherently better or worse; they are simply two different ways of organizing social behavior to address material need. Individual need is addressed and cared for in both modes of delivery. However, the social consequences for the larger community are quite different. Without the spontaneous element of grassroots response, formal delivery systems minimize the communal benefits of fellowship and solidarity on the local level. In the formal system, specialists or company agents interact with recipients to meet needs with little social fanfare.

The communal benefits, at least on the local level, arise when mutual aid is the spontaneous and shared response of a larger community. For the individual in need, however, the informal system is often unpredictable, sporadic, and at times inadequate to meet the need. The dual system of care available today seems to offer Mennonites the best of both worlds. Predictable care is available for major needs through church-operated insurance companies, and most congregations continue to spring into action when needs arise not covered by the formal programs.

# The Mennonite Margin of Difference

Is there a Mennonite margin of difference? As North American Mennonites approach the dusk of the twentieth century, four broad sources of aid are available to church members in need: spontaneous forms of aid, denominational insurance programs, commercial insurance vendors, and government programs.

Spontaneous outbreaks of sharing continue to surface in many congregations when members face need prompted by childbirth, child care, illness, death, divorce, distress, and relocation—to name a few. Two recent books, *Shared Burdens* (Schlabach and Roth, 1993) and *An Instrument of God's Grace* (Roth and Lehman, 1995), as well as many anecdotal stories, document the vitality of the spirit of corporate care in hundreds of congregations across the church.

These informal expressions of care are not unique to Anabaptist congregations; many believers from a variety of Christian tribes respond with a helping hand in the face of distress. Is the rate and frequency of care in Anabaptist congregations higher than that in other denominations? We really do not know. Despite a multitude of anecdotal data suggesting that mutual aid is a widespread habit in Mennonite circles, we do not have comparative studies to confirm whether or not Mennonites score higher in helping each other in informal ways.

What is certain, however, is that the number of formal agencies and programs of aid in Mennonite communities is substantially higher than in many other churches. Mennonites have created a remarkable number of mutual aid societies and agencies. Denominational insurance programs, at first blush, are in many ways comparable to commercial insurance programs. Mennonite Mutual Aid, of course, is the largest Mennonite aid agency in its size and scope. Although it follows many of the standard principles of the insurance industry, Mennonite Mutual Aid stands apart from commercial vendors in at least five significant ways: in its purpose, partnership with the church, distinctive values, social enhancements, and fraternal benefits. These distinctives create a Mennonite margin of difference in the practice of corporate care.

(1) *Purpose.* As a denominationally-based program, Mennonite Mutual Aid strives to serve the members of the parent denomination as well as those affiliated with other Anabaptist-related groups. Such a mission stands apart from the purposes of commercial enterprises which seek to develop and sell products to earn profits for stockholders.

Mennonite Mutual Aid, by contrast, is rooted in a particular theological tradition and strives to serve a specific and limited constituency. A denomination-based program develops products and programs designed to serve a particular community in ways that reflect Anabaptist values and beliefs. In addition to providing direct services, Mennonite Mutual Aid also serves the church with a variety of educational programs that inform members about the importance of mutual care and in so doing help to transmit its legacy across the generations. In all of these ways, the purpose of Mennonite Mutual Aid stands apart from commercial enterprises.

(2) *Partnership with the church.* As a natural consequence of its special purpose and mission, Mennonite Mutual Aid has developed a unique partnership with the church. The partnership is expressed in several ways. Members of the board of directors are appointed by the church and are held accountable to the church. As one of several churchwide program boards, Mennonite Mutual Aid coordinates its work with the larger mission of the Mennonite Church. This governance structure couples the work and long-term efforts of the agency with the ongoing life of the church. Many of the employees and agents of Mennonite Mutual Aid are members of the Mennonite church, which provides a natural interface with the life of the church.

Another form of partnership with the church comes in consultation and dialogue with regional conferences and local congregations. As particular issues emerge, representatives of Mennonite Mutual Aid initiate conversations with conference and congregational representatives. Moreover, in local congregations an officially appointed Mutual Aid Advocate serves as a bridge between churchwide and local concerns. Over 1500 advocates serve the important role of advocacy and feedback in local congregations.

Finally, the 70,000 policyholders of Mennonite Mutual Aid are people who hold membership in one of some twenty-five Anabaptist-related denominations. Although a significant number of these policyholders are members of the Mennonite Church, a substantial number are members of a variety of other Anabaptist-related groups, including General Conference Mennonite, Mennonite Brethren, Brethren in Christ, and the Missionary Church. From membership to governance, Mennonite Mutual Aid has developed a substantial partnership with the church.

(3) *Distinctive values.* The organizational arrangements of MMA rest on a bedrock of distinctive values which also contribute to its margin of difference. Mutual aid and stewardship are the dual values that undergird and guide MMA. These biblical principles provide a different ethos than the profit impulse so common in commercial insurance. Guidelines reflecting concerns for peace, justice, and the sanctity of life regulate the investment of the financial resources held by MMA.

Moreover, MMA's eligibility guidelines for prospective clients are typically more inclusive and flexible than those of some other insurance carriers. Based on long-standing Mennonite commitments to nonresistance and mediation, fewer resources are devoted to litigation and other legal maneuvers. Finally, MMA, as part of its corporate mission, seeks to promote biblical values of compassion and care among the constituencies that it serves.

(4) *Social Enhancements.* Beyond the tangible benefits provided by a denominational program like MMA, numerous social benefits, flowing from its activities, help to strengthen the identity and solidarity of the denomination as a whole. A denominational insurance program not only provides a service to members, it also helps to keep economic resources circulating in the conduits of the church. Without an agency like MMA, more Anabaptist dollars would flow into commercial insurance programs and thereby generate profits for corporate interests outside the church.

MMA also enhances denominational identity by adding to the institutional completeness of the church. The greater the number of social functions provided through its own denominational agencies, the greater the institutional completeness of a group. A denomination which creates institutions to meet many of the socioeconomic needs of its members—work, leisure, retirement, health, and insurance, to name a few—approaches what sociologists sometimes call institutional completeness. By providing insurance programs for its members under a Mennonite umbrella, the church bolsters Mennonite identity and strengthens social ties across the church.

Thus, apart from its manifest functions, an organization like MMA enhances denominational loyalty, identity, and solidarity. These are "added values," so to speak, fringe benefits that enhance the otherwise commercial nature of denominational insurance programs. In other words, even apart from its insurance functions, the church would be weaker and leaner without an agency like MMA.

(5) *Fraternal benefits.* Because it is a fraternal program enjoying certain tax advantages, MMA can channel resources, through its fraternal funds, back to local congregations for the benefit of members. A special feature of MMA is its fraternal status as a legal entity. This exempts it from certain taxes, including state premium tax and federal income tax on profits.

In addition, MMA has created its own internal discipline by placing a ten percent tithe on profits generated by its various units. These financial structures funnel funds into the fraternal benefits programs which are then used to serve MMA's constituent members. Fraternal funds are given back to members through a variety of programs and grants. Some are disbursed as matching grants to congregations to stimulate local initiatives. Other fraternal funds are used to promote the basic concepts of mutual aid and stewardship. In any event, the fraternal benefit program is a badge of distinction for MMA that has helped the church in significant ways.

# Seeds of Goodwill

As noted elsewhere, particularly in chapter 12, MMA's legal status as a fraternal organization is an important distinctive and thus deserves additional comment here. In many ways fraternal funds function as a form of profit sharing that enables "instead-of-tax" resources to circulate back into the church.

In the late 1990s, MMA was able to distribute over $3 million a year through its fraternal programs. These seeds of goodwill helped alleviate urgent material needs as well as promote the cause of mutual aid across the church. Over half of these funds are used to match mutual aid efforts in local congregations. The matching fund program not only meets real needs; it also provides incentives for local congregations to practice mutual aid and in so doing multiples the cumulative effect of goodwill.

The remainder of the fraternal funds are funneled through a variety of programs administered by MMA. These programs include stewardship education, health education and advocacy for persons with disabilities and mental illness, the Sharing Fund, the Urban Initiative Fund, and the Global Church Sharing Fund. These goodwill programs lean on fraternal funds for their support and would wither without them.

The Giving Project, an educational initiative, promotes the importance and value of Christian stewardship across the church. The Sharing Fund provides special grants that address a variety of unusual and special needs: living expenses in times of crisis, medical expenses for the underinsured, adoption expenses, insurance premium help for families on low incomes, and burial expenses for needy families.

In a recent year MMA made some 4,900 grants through the Sharing Fund program, totaling $2.35 million. These seeds of goodwill touched some 2,500 households and nearly 1,070 congregations. Community Service Grants support projects in which local congregations target special needs in their community, including food pantries, preschool programs, and aid to the homeless. The Annuity Scholarship Program provides some modest scholarship grants to students of families that hold an annuity with MMA.

Several inner city projects have received support from the Urban Initiative Fund in recent years. The Global Church Sharing Fund helped make it possible for members of national churches in developing countries to finance self-help projects.

The Pastoral Leadership Program provides scholarship help for some seminary students in conjunction with matching grants from their congregations. This fund also supports continuing education programs for pastors. MMA also supports a variety of educational activities designed to promote wellness and stewardship education. All of these seeds of goodwill have blessed the church in many ways and have helped meet the material needs of thousands of persons both in and beyond the Anabaptist family of faith.

The face of mutual aid has indeed changed—sometimes in dramatic ways—in the twentieth century. The complexity of corporate care has increased amid rapid social and technological change. Despite our social context, the nature of need or the exact form of aid, the reality of human need remains a constant. Technology, prediction, planning, and the best of insurance sometimes fail to meet the needs that arise from misfortune, accident, carelessness, or genetic inheritance.

One last time it bears saying that commitments to mutual aid are rooted in the biblical injunction to "bear one another's burdens." With changing social settings, the nature of our burdens do change as well as the manner in which we shoulder them together. Nevertheless, we do need each other, for the burdens are sometimes heavy and often come by surprise. As we share our burdens together, we not only actualize the deepest meanings of Christian community and acknowledge that we are "members one of another," we also signal our faithfulness to the caring way of Jesus. In so doing we contribute our share to building communities of compassion.

# Epilogue: A Vision
# for the Future

In the winter of 1996, MMA sponsored a conference on the biblical and theological foundations of mutual aid. I believe this gathering surprised us all when it ended with a high-energy grand finale—a new communal understanding of mutual aid. Donald Kraybill describes this understanding well in this book's introduction.

The energy did not end when the meeting did. In fact, the conference spawned a string of invigorating discussions among MMA leaders on how our organization works at stewardship and mutual aid. We have sharpened our own vision for the future of MMA as a stewardship organization. Mutual aid is a key way we practice Christian stewardship.

We were inspired by the words and deeds of our ancestors. I believe many of us walked away from the conference with renewed appreciation, even awe, for the genius that has been part of our faith community from the beginning. Our ancestors were people of vision. But more than that, they were able to translate their vision of faith into practical action in unique and wonderful ways:

- They were not afraid to step into the unknown.
- They were not afraid to embrace and adapt new tools.
- They were not content simply to identify a problem.
- They were people who sought a solution.
- Then they went about finding ways of doing it.

I suspect the book of James has inspired many Anabaptists. This letter, traditionally believed written by the brother of Jesus, reminds us that if our faith is real, it leads to faithful living. The heart of the matter, for me, is in James 2:14-17.

> What good is it, my brothers and sisters, if you say you have faith but do not have works? Can faith save you? If a brother or sister is naked and lacks daily food, and one of you says to them, "Go in peace; keep warm and eat your fill," and yet you do not supply their bodily needs, what is the good of that? So faith by itself, if it has no works, is dead.

This idea of moving from a vision of faith to practical action has great appeal to me. I want to know how we are practicing our faith today. Faith in action is what drives MMA as we help people in our Anabaptist community apply their faith in their daily lives.

Applying stewardship and mutual aid at MMA has resulted in a number of unique programs, such as insurance plans, financial services, charitable programs, and educational resources. Consider life insurance as an example. It's a modern alternative to barn-raising.

A few months before the mutual aid conference, this modern method financially saved one farm family. It happened after an early winter storm blew across a farm owned by a Mennonite couple in their early forties. The storm dumped lots of snow, and its high winds tore a hole in the roof of this couple's barn. After the storm, the father climbed on the barn roof to make repairs. Tragically, the roof was structurally defective, and the farmer fell to his death, leaving a wife and several children.

Amid this calamity there was also good fortune. When the couple purchased the farm a few years earlier, they recognized a need. They contacted an MMA counselor who helped them purchase a life insurance plan to protect them in case of just such a tragedy. Because the larger church banded together in community, this family can remain together on the farm they love.

In addition, the family's church received a check because the family had chosen their congregation as the beneficiary of a charitable life benefit that came as part of the plan. This demonstrates the transforming power of modern mutual aid.

Today, since we are geographically dispersed, life insurance is a way to provide aid among our families who face economic hardship when a breadwinner dies. As Anabaptists move away from a close geographic community, there will be more implications for the practice of stewardship and mutual aid in the future. But other trends occurring today will likely shift our methods. Such trends include—

• increased urbanization of Anabaptists;

• the aging of the baby boomers, a large segment of our population;

- globalization of our church family while resources are being focused locally;
- rapidly changing technology;
- racial and ethnic diversity in the church and in society; and
- consumerism and bulging consumer debt.

I don't have specific new methods to respond to these patterns but do believe we can find them. The first place to look for new ways is in our churches and among our members. At MMA we rely heavily on our members, their experiences, and the answers they have found in their personal lives. Virtually all our programs come from talking to church members.

Church institutions are called to be servant leaders. We are called to listen to the collective voice of our church members and to learn from their life journeys. The church can foster new forms of stewardship and mutual aid if it pays attention to its members. The church then turns what it learns in the pews into practical kingdom building.

The beginnings of new forms of stewardship and mutual aid are here now among us. We just need to discover them, then work at transforming our old methods into new ones. Like our Anabaptist ancestors, we can turn our belief into action. This is the key to keeping our faith living, breathing, and relevant rather than an empty, dead husk with no works.

—*Howard L. Brenneman*
*President and CEO*
*Mennonite Mutual Aid, Inc.*
*January 30, 1998*

# Select Bibliography
# on Mennonite Mutual Aid

"Aid for Immigrants"
   1974   *Mennonite Historical Bulletin* 35(4): 4.

Augsburger, Myron
   1968   "Mutual Aid in the Congregation." In *The Compassionate Community,*
          ed. H. Ralph Hernley. Pp. 407-440.

Bare, Lois K.
   1980   "Strong Roots: The Beginnings of Mennonite Mutual Aid." *Sharing* 14
          (Summer): 2-5.

Bender, Daniel H.
   *1916*   "Life Insurance." *Gospel Herald* 9 (September 28): 474-75. Reprinted in
          *Gospel Herald* 14 (30 March 1922): 1010.

Bowers, Steve
   1990   "John Rudy: The Life of a Steward, or Getting the Honey is Worth the
          Sting." *Sharing* 24 (Winter): 10-13.

Brenneman, Howard L.
   1995   "A Solid Foundation for the Future." *Sharing* 29 (Summer): 3-6.

Burkholder, J. L.
   1960   "Love and Justice in Mennonite Mutual Aid." In *The Compassionate
          Community,* ed. H. Ralph Hernley. Pp. 51-78.

Burkholder, Rebecca
   1981   "Loans that Made a Difference." *Gospel Herald* 74 (October 27): 804-805.

Clasen, Claus-Peter
    1972    *Anabaptism: A Social History, 1525-1618.* Ithaca: Cornell University Press.

*Confession of Faith in a Mennonite Perspective.*
    1995    Scottdale, Pa.: Herald Press.

Diener, Harry A.
    1928    "Life Insurance." *Gospel Herald* 21 (8 November): 674-75.

Durnbaugh, Donald F.
    1968    *The Believers' Church.* New York: The MacMillan Co. Pp. 264-282.

    1974    *Every Need Supplied: Mutual Aid and Christian Community in the Free Churches, 1525-1675.* Philadelphia: Temple University Press.

    1988    "Mutual Aid in Ministry to God's World." *Brethren Life and Thought* 33 (Spring): 87-97.

Dyck, Cornelius J.
    1963    "Mutual Aid in a Changing Economy." In *The Compassionate Community,* ed. H. Ralph Hernley. Pp. 155-198.

    1964    *They Gave Themselves: Lessons in Christian Stewardship.* Newton, Kan.: Faith and Life Press.

    1983    "People of the Open Heart." *Sharing* (Summer): 7-8.

Erb, Allen, et al.
    1978    "Mennonite Mutual Aid: A Plan for the Organization of a New Board to Carry on an Effective Program of Mutual Aid within the Mennonite Church." *Mennonite Historical Bulletin* 39(3): 5-6.

Fretz, J. Winfield
    1938    "Christian Mutual Aid Societies Among the Mennonites." M.A. thesis, University of Chicago.

    1939a    "Mutual Aid among the Mennonites, I." *Mennonite Quarterly Review* 13:28-58.

    1939b    "Mutual Aid among the Mennonites, II." *Mennonite Quarterly Review* 13:187-209.

    1940    "Mennonites and Their Economic Problems." *Mennonite Quarterly Review* 14:195-213.

    1941    "Mennonite Mutual Aid, A Contribution to the Development of Christian Community." Ph.D. dissertation, University of Chicago.

    1942    "Rural Life Problems And The Mennonites." *Mennonite Quarterly Review* 16:167-173.

    1945a    "Mutual Aid Strengthens The Local Congregation." *Gospel Herald* (October 5): 506.

    1945b    "Principles Of Mutual Aid In The Local Congregation." *Gospel Herald* (October 12): 532.

1947 *Christian Mutual Aid: A Handbook of Brotherhood Economics.* Akron, Pa.: Mennonite Central Committee.

1951 "What Mutual Aid Can Mean to a Church." *Mennonite Community* 5, (May): 22-23, 29.

1953 *Pilgrims in Paraguay.* Scottdale, Pa.: Herald Press.

1957a "Mutual Aid." *The Mennonite Encyclopedia,* vol. 3. Scottdale, Pa.: Herald Press.

1957b "Brotherhood and the Economic Ethic of the Anabaptists." In *The Recovery of the Anabaptist Vision,* ed. Guy F. Hershberger. Scottdale, Pa.: Herald Press.

1958 "Meditations on Christian Mutual Aid." In *The Compassionate Community,* ed. H. Ralph Hernley. Pp. 1-36.

Fretz, J. Winfield and Harold S. Bender
 1957 "Mutual Aid." In *The Mennonite Encyclopedia,* vol. 3. Scottdale, Pa.: Herald Press.

Gish, Arthur G.
 1983 "Mutual Aid." In *The Brethren Encyclopedia,* Elgin, Ill.: The Brethren Encyclopedia, Inc.

Good, E. Reginald
 1984 "War as a Factor in Mennonite Economic Policy: A Case Study of Insurance Institutions Sponsored by the Ontario Conference, 1864-1954." M.A. Thesis, University of Waterloo.

Graber, Christian L.
 [1982] *Looking Back: An Autobiography by Chris L. Graber.* [Goshen, Ind.: L. Swartzendruber].

Graber, J. D.
 1957 "Anabaptism Expressed in Missions and Social Service." In *The Recovery of the Anabaptist Vision,* ed. Guy F. Hershberger. Scottdale, Pa.: Herald Press.

Graber, O'Ray C.
 1964 "Why Christians Help One Another." In *The Compassionate Community,* ed. H. Ralph Hernley. Pp. 199-226.

Gross, David P., and Eunice K. Wedel
 1983 *One Hundred Years of Caring and Sharing: A History of the Mennonite Aid Plan of the U.S., 1882-1982.* North Newton, Kans.: Mennonite Press.

Hernley, H. Ralph, ed.
 1970 *The Compassionate Community.* Scottdale, Pa.: Association of Mennonite Aid Societies.

Hershberger, Guy F.
 1944 *War, Peace and Nonresistance.* Scottdale, Pa.: Herald Press.

 1944a "What is Meant By Mutual Aid?" *Gospel Herald* (March 16): 1075.

1944b "On What Problem Has the Stewardship Committee Been Working?" *Gospel Herald* (March 23): 1091

1944c "What Are Some Changes Taking Place in Mennonite Community Life?" *Gospel Herald* (March 30): 1107.

1944d "What Is the Relation of Nonresistance To The Mennonite Community?" *Gospel Herald* (April 7): 4.

1944e "What Is The Proposed New Organization: Mennonite Mutual Aid?" *Gospel Herald* (April 14): 36.

1944f "How Is The Proposed Mennonite Mutual Aid Expected To Function?" *Gospel Herald* (April 21): 52.

1944g "What Are To Be The Policies Of The Proposed Mennonite Mutual Aid?" *Gospel Herald* (April 28): 68.

1945a "Mennonite Mutual Aid Is Now Organized." *Gospel Herald* (September 21): 474.

1945b "How Will Mennonite Mutual Aid Obtain Its Working Capital?" *Gospel Herald* (September 28): 492.

1945c "How Will Mutual Aid Assist the Person Who Needs Help?" *Gospel Herald* (October 5): 508.

1945d Mennonite Community Life Number, *Mennonite Quarterly Review 19:* Entire Issue.

Hildebrand, Hilda Anne
1989 "Mennonite Mutual Aid and the Concept of Social Welfare: A Case Study of the Bergthaler Waisenamt and the Co-operative Movement in the Rhineland Municipality." Master of Social Work thesis, University of Manitoba.

Johns, Lois
1945 "Mutual Aid In Panorama." *Gospel Herald* (September 21): 474.

Kauffman, Daniel
1966 "New Frontiers: Stewardship and Mutual Aid." In *The Compassionate Community*, ed. H. Ralph Hernley. Pp. 297-362.

1981 *Money and Economic Issues in Mennonite Congregations: A Report on a One-Year Special Project on Money.* Goshen, Ind.: Mennonite Mutual Aid.

1990 *Managers With God: Continuing the Work Christ Began.* Scottdale, Pa.: Herald Press.

Klassen, Mary
1985 "MMA History." Unpublished paper in archives of Mennonite Mutual Aid, Goshen, Ind.

Klassen, Peter James
1963 "'Mutual Aid among the Anabaptists: Doctrine and Practice." *Mennonite Quarterly Review* 37:78-95.

1964    *The Economics of Anabaptism: 1525-1560.* London: Mouton & Co.

1967    "The Anabaptist-Mennonite Witness Through Mutual Aid." In *The Church in Mission: A Sixtieth Anniversary Tribute to J. B. Toews,* ed. A. J. Klassen. Fresno, California: Mennonite Brethren Church, Board of Christian Literature.

1970    "Mutual Aid Among the Anabaptists: Doctrine and Practice." In *The Compassionate Community,* ed. H. Ralph Hernley. Pp. 549-568.

Klassen, William
1961    "Christian Realities in Mutual Aid." In *The Compassionate Community,* ed. H. Ralph Hernley. Pp. 79-112.

Kulp, Isaac Clarence
1975    "Love Stories from Old Alms Books." *Sharing* (Summer): 5-7.

Kurowski, Lois Landis
1987    "Guy and Clara Hershberger: They Help Things Happen." *Sharing* (Winter) 1987:6-11.

Lapp, John E.
1944    "The Biblical Basis for the Christian Practice of Mutual Aid." *Gospel Herald* 37 (June 30): 241-242.

Lehman, J. Irvin.
1950    "An Appreciation." *Gospel Herald* (May 9): 439-440.

Menno Simons
1956    *The Complete Writings of Menno Simons.* Translated by Leonard Verduin, ed. J. C. Wenger. Scottdale, Pa.: Herald Press.

Mennonite Central Committee
1947    "What is Mutual Aid?" Akron, Pa.: Mennonite Central Committee.

Miller, Lynn
1991    *Firstfruits Living.* Scottdale, Pa.: Herald Press.

Miller, Orie O.
1961    "Operation Brotherhood." *Mennonite Observer* 7, 12 (March 1954): 8, 11.

"A Mutual Aid Plan from the Civil War Era"
1973    *Mennonite Historical Bulletin.* Vol. 34( 4): 4.

Neff, Christian and Harold S. Bender
1956    "Deacon." *The Mennonite Encyclopedia,* vol. 2. Scottdale, Pa.: Herald Press.

Nolt, Steven M.
1995    "Reinterpreting Nonconformity: Mennonite and Brethren Thought and Practice." In *Anabaptist Currents: History in Conversation with the Present,* ed. Carl F. Bowman and Stephen L. Longenecker. Camden, Maine: Penobscot Press. Pp. 183-97.

1998    "Formal Mutual Aid Structures Among American Mennonites and Brethren: Assimilation and Reconstructed Ethnicity." *Journal of American Ethnic History* 17 (spring): 71-86.

Peachey, Laban
　1990 "Mutual Aid." *The Mennonite Encyclopedia*, vol. 5. Scottdale, Pa.: Herald Press.

Raber, Ann
　1983 *Mennonite Mutual Aid Wellness Program: Toward More Abundant Living.* Goshen, Ind.: Mennonite Mutual Aid.

　1993 *A Life of Wholeness: Reflections on Abundant Living*, rev. ed. Scottdale, Pa.: Herald Press.

Raid, Howard D.
　1967 "Men, Materials and Mennonites in Mutual Aid." In *The Compassionate Community*, ed. H. Ralph Hernley. Pp. 363-406.

　1982 *Twenty-Five Years: A Brief History of Mennonite Indemnity, Inc.* Akron, Pa.: Mennonite Indemnity, Inc.

　1985 "Living the Mutual Aid Way." *Sharing* (Fall): 4-7.

　1989 "The GCs Come In: The Politics of Partnership." *Sharing* (Spring): 6-11.

Raid, Pauline and Howard D.
　1990 *A Report of Meetings with Mennonite-Amish Mutual Aid Plans.* Bluffton, Ohio, privately printed, 1990.

Redekop, Calvin
　1989 "Mutual Aid: Unlimited Obligation." *Gospel Herald* (June 13):436-38.

Redekop, Calvin, Victor A. Krahn, and Samuel J. Steiner, eds.
　1994 *Anabaptist/Mennonite Faith and Economics.* Lanham: University Press of America.

Redekop, Calvin W., Stephen C. Ainley, and Robert Siemens
　1995 *Mennonite Entrepreneurs.* Baltimore: The Johns Hopkins University Press.

Reimer, Richard
　1995 "The Future of Mutual Aid and Stewardship," *Sharing* 29 (Summer): 11.

Roth, Glen A., and Susan V. Schlabach
　1994 *Shared Burdens.* Intercourse, Pa.: Good Books.

Roth, Glen A., and Glenn M. Lehman
　1995 *An Instrument of God's Grace.* Lancaster, Pa.: Sharing Programs Inc.

Rudy, John H.
　1984 *Christian Stewardship: Faith in Action Stewardship Kit.* Goshen, Ind.: Mennonite Mutual Aid.

　1989 *Moneywise Meditations: To be Found Faithful in God's Audit.* Scottdale, Pa.: Herald Press.

Rupp, George
　1991 "Communities of Collaboration: Shared Commitments/Common Tasks." In *Theology at the End of Modernity: Essays in Honor of Gordon D. Kaufman*, ed. Sheila Greeve Davaney. Philadelphia: Trinity Press International. Pp. 210-218.

Sears, Earl
  1976    "Deaconing Today." *Gospel Herald* 69 (November 16): 894-95.

Shank, J.R.
  1950    "God's Plan for Caring for the Needy." *Gospel Herald* (March 14): 244-45.

Snyder, John M.
  1944    *"Is Mutual Aid Scriptural?" Gospel Herald* 37 (September 15): 477.

  1944a   "Some Thoughts on New Testament Mutual Aid." *Gospel Herald* 37 (December 22): 764-765, 772-773.

Sommer, Donald
  1954    "Peter Rideman and Menno Simons on Economics." *Mennonite Quarterly Review* 28:205-223.

Sommer, Willis
  1994    "Mennonite Institutions and Mennonite Capital." In *Anabaptist/ Mennonite Faith and Economics*, ed. Calvin W. Redekop, Victor A. Krahn, and Samuel J. Steiner. Lanham, Md.: University Press of America. Pp. 255-78.

Sprunger, Mary S.
  1993    "Rich Mennonites, Poor Mennonites: Economics and Theology in the Amsterdam Waterlander Congregation during the Golden Age." Ph.D. dissertation, University of Illinois, Champaign-Urbana.

  1994    "Waterlanders and the Dutch Golden Age: A Case Study on Mennonite Involvement in Seventeenth-Century Dutch Trade and Industry as One of the Earliest Examples of Socio-Economic Assimilation." In *From Martyr to Muppy. A Historical Introduction to Cultural Assimilation Processes of a Religious Minority in the Netherlands: The Mennonites*, ed. Alastair Hamilton et al. Amsterdam: Amsterdam University Press.

"Statement On Christian Mutual Aid"
  1964    Smithville, Ohio, June 4-6. In *The Compassionate Community*, ed. H. Ralph Hernley. Pp. 569-573.

Stayer, James M.
  1990    *The German Peasants' War and Anabaptist Community of Goods.* Montreal: McGill-Queen's University Press.

Stoesz, Edgar
  1962    "A New Frontier in Mutual Aid." *Mennonite Life* 17:182-84.

*Strength through Sharing*
  1995    Directory. Lancaster, Pa.: Association of Mennonite Aid Societies.

Stoltzfus, Grant M.
  "Toward New Horizons in Mennonite Mutual Aid." In *The Compassionate Community*, ed. H. Ralph Hernley. Pp. 37-50.

Studer, Gerald C.
  1965    "Toward a Theology of Servanthood." In *The Compassionate Community*, ed. H. Ralph Hernley. Pp. 227-296.

Swartley, Willard M.
    *1978*   *"Biblical Sources of Stewardship."* In *The Earth Is The Lord's: Essays on Stewardship,* ed. Mary Evelyn Jegen and Bruno V. Manno. New York: Paulist.

Swartzendruber, H. L.
    1959   "Mennonite Mutual Aid." *Gospel Herald* 52(48): 1058, 1069.

Toews, Paul
    1996   *Modernity And The Persistence Of Community.* Scottdale, Pa.: Herald Press.

Troyer, Herbert N.
    1932   *Life Insurance.* Scottdale, Pa.: Mennonite Publishing House.

Umble, Jeni Hiett
    1995   "Meeting Around the Distaff: Anabaptist Women and Social-Economic Status in Augsburg, 1527-1528." Unpublished paper.

"The Use of Affliction"
    1865   *Herald of Truth* 2:57.

*The Use of the Law: A Summary Statement*
    1982   Scottdale, Pa.: Mennonite Publishing House.

Wenger, A. Grace
    1964   *Stewardship of the Gospel: A Resource Book for the Study of Christian Stewardship.* Scottdale, Pa.: Herald Press.

Wiebe, Bernie
    1977   *Biblical Mutual Aid: A Model for the 1980s.* Baden, Ont.: Association of Mennonite Aid Societies.

Wiens, Delbert
    1988   "Mutual Aid in the Twenty-First Century." Unpublished paper presented to gathering of the Association of Mennonite Aid Societies in Laurelville, Pa.

    1969   "Mutual Aid in a Culture of Abundance." *Missionary Messenger* 46 (October): 4-5, 10.

Yordy, Richard
    1962   "Mutual Aid an Expression of Basic Christian Experience." In *The Compassionate Community,* ed. H. Ralph Hernley. Pp. 113-154.

# CONTRIBUTORS

**Wilma Ann Bailey** received her Ph.D. in Hebrew Bible from Vanderbilt University. She is author of numerous publications dealing with biblical studies. Bailey is associate professor of Biblical Studies and Religion at Messiah College (Pa.).

**Cornelius A. Buller** received his Ph.D. in theology from McMaster University. He has taught courses in religious studies at several universities and is author of *The Unity of Nature and History in Pannenberg's Theology*.

**E. Reginald Good** is a consultant in historical research and writing and archival management. He received his Ph.D. in Canadian History from the University of Saskatchewan. Good has written many articles on Mennonite History and is president of the Mennonite Historical Society of Ontario.

**Keith Graber Miller** received his Ph.D. in Ethics and Society from Emory University. He currently serves as associate professor of Bible Religion and Philosophy at Goshen (Ind.) College. He has authored numerous publications, including *Wise as Serpents, Innocent as Doves: American Mennonites Engage Washington*.

**Conrad L. Kanagy** is assistant professor of sociology at Elizabethtown (Pa.) College. He received his Ph.D. in sociology from the Pennsylvania State University. His publications reflect his research interests in the sociology of religion.

**Albert N. Keim** is professor of history at Eastern Mennonite University (Va.). He is author of numerous articles dealing with Amish and Mennonite history and several books, including *The Politics of Conscience: The Historic Peace Churches and America at War, 1917-1955*.

**Joseph J. Kotva, Jr.** received his Ph.D. from Fordham University in theology and ethics. He has written *The Christian Case for Virtue Ethics* as well as numerous articles on ethics. He currently serves as the pastor of the First Mennonite Church in Allentown, Pennsylvania.

**Donald B. Kraybill** serves as provost and professor of sociology and Anabaptist studies at Messiah College (Pa.). Trained in sociology, he has authored many books on Anabaptist groups, including *The Riddle of Amish Culture* and *Mennonite Peacemaking*.

**Steven M. Nolt** has written *A History of the Amish* and co-authored other books as well as scholarly articles related to Mennonite history. His Ph.D. in history is from the University of Notre Dame.

**John D. Roth** is editor of *Mennonite Quarterly Review* and professor of history, Goshen (Ind.) College, where he also directs the Mennonite Historical Library. Roth is author and editor of numerous publications, including *The Letters of the Amish Division*.

**Mary S. Sprunger** received her Ph.D. in history from the University of Illinois. Her research and publications focus on the history of the Dutch Mennonites. She has co-authored, with Piet Visser, *Menno Simons: Places, Portraits and Progeny* and is associate professor of history at Eastern Mennonite University (Va.).

**Willard M. Swartley** is dean and professor of New Testament at the Associated Mennonite Biblical Seminary in Elkhart, Indiana, where he has also directed the Institute of Mennonite Studies. Swartley is author of many scholarly articles and books, including *Slavery, Sabbath, War, and Women* and "War and Peace in the New Testament" in *AWRW* II.26.3.

**Jeni Hiett Umble**'s research and publications have explored the roles of sixteenth-century Anabaptist women, especially their involvement in suffering and martyrdom. She received her M.A. in Modern European History from Southern Methodist University and her M.Div. from Associated Mennonite Biblical Seminary (1998). She is pastor of Southside Fellowship, Elkhart, Indiana.

# About Herald Press, Pandora Press, and Pandora Press U.S.

Responding to challenges and opportunities of a changing publishing environment amid recognition of shared visions, three presses have developed innovative relationships. Herald Press can efficiently produce, distribute, and market books which sell in the thousands. Pandora Press and Pandora Press U.S. are pioneering ways economically to publish shorter runs.

By coordinating their programs, the presses can match their respective strengths with what best suits a given book, share in Herald's ability to provide marketing support, and experience rewarding synergies as the Pandoras enable Herald to support publication of an even wider variety of books that fit the Herald Press mission.

The story begins with **Herald Press**, Scottdale, Pennsylvania. Largest of the presses and long the denominational publisher of the Mennonite Church, Herald publishes books from an Anabaptist-Mennonite perspective that address honestly and creatively such issues as peace and social concerns, a biblical understanding of Christian faith, the mission of the church, and the importance of marriage and family. Herald Press aims to offer church and world the best in thinking and spiritual leadership.

**Herald Press**

**Pandora Press**, Kitchener, Ontario, was founded in 1995 to make available, at reasonable cost to publisher and public, short runs of books dealing with Anabaptist, Mennonite, and Believers Church topics, both historical and theological. Pandora Kitchener provided models and inspiration for Pandora U.S.

**Pandora Press U.S.**, Telford, Pennsylvania, was then founded in 1997 by a former Herald Press editor after Herald, though still committed to scholarly books, moved toward publishing fewer. Bringing together the light of the gospel and a Pandora's box of challenges, complexities, questions, Pandora U.S. publishes thought-provoking theological and scholarly as well as popular books of interest to Anabaptist, Mennonite, Christian, and general readers.

Though independent, the two Pandoras support each other's programs by consulting on books each press publishes, contracting for each other's services, and coordinating distribution, promotion, and marketing operations to develop distinct but related public images for their similarly-named ventures.

*Building Communities of Compassion*, produced through prepress by Pandora U.S., then printed, marketed, and distributed by Herald Press with joint Pandora U.S. imprint, exemplifies coordinated publishing.